TABLE OF RAILROADS BY SYSTEMS.

LEON ABBETT'S NEW JERSEY

The Emergence of the Modern Governor

Eng. by E.G. Williams & Bro. N.Y.

Leon Abbett, 1836–1894.
Engraving by
E.G. Williams & Bro.
New York

LEON ABBETT'S NEW JERSEY

The Emergence of the Modern Governor

Richard A. Hogarty

Professor Emeritus of Political Science
University of Massachusetts, Boston

American Philosophical Society
Independence Square • Philadelphia
2001

Memoirs
of the
American Philosophical Society
Held at Philadelphia
For Promoting Useful Knowledge
Volume 243

ISBN: 0-87169-243-0
US ISSN: 0065-9738

Hogarty, Richard A.
Leon Abbett's New Jersey: the emergence of the modern governor / Richard A. Hogarty.
    p. cm.— (Memoirs of the American Philosophical Society held at Philadelphia for
promoting useful knowledge, ISSN 0065-9738 ; v. 243)
includes bibliographical references (p.) and index.
ISBN 0-87169-243-0 (cloth)
1. Abbett, Leon, 1836–1894. 2. Governors—New Jersey—Biography. 3. New Jersey—Politics and
government—1865–1950. I. American Philosophical Society. II. Title. III. Memoirs of the American
Philosophical Society ; v. 243.

Qll .P612 vol. 243 [F139]
974.9 041 092—dc21
[B]   2001022079

Design and Composition
Book Design Studio

For Ann,
who in her own gentle and gracious manner,
contributed more than anyone will ever know

CONTENTS

LIST OF ILLUSTRATIONS

PREFACE

> *It is never easy to explain to a later generation the achievements of an earlier one in shattering an unacceptable status quo, because these achievements in turn have become a status quo beyond which it wishes to advance.*
>
> Historian Frank Freidel

This book is a political and cultural biography of Leon Abbett, an accomplished political leader, who twice served as governor of New Jersey during the late nineteenth century. An ardent Democrat, he had the flexibility and manipulative skills of a person who maximized his power. He was clearly the dominating figure on the political scene. A man of multiple talents, Abbett was a master of persuasion. In a sharply divided political climate, he convinced skeptical Democrats to support his programs. Adept in the political arts, he became the most charismatic, controversial, and passionate politician in the Garden State. In fact, he was a power in the state party for the better part of two generations. Yet, ironically, he was twice defeated for the United States Senate by the state legislature, not by the will of the voters. Indeed, he paid a heavy personal price for power.

The son of a journeyman hatter, Abbett was born and raised in antebellum Philadelphia, where he became a lawyer and moved to New Jersey. As governor of his adopted state, he did not embrace the social aristocracy or those who had inherited wealth and social position. On the contrary, he built a remarkable political career on the plainest of foundations, appealing mainly to the impoverished urban lower classes and the hardscrabble farmers earning a bare subsistence. Early in his career as a state legislator, he saw the importance of connecting with the masses. Abbett was man of the people, whose roots in the working class ran deep. His compassion for the working poor was genuine. Staunchly pro-labor and pro-immigrant, he cared passionately about the plight of the wage-earning class and the thousands of foreign immigrants who flocked to New Jersey struggling to gain a foothold in America.

Reared as a commoner, Abbett was imbued with the ideological elixir of Jacksonian democracy, and he presented himself to the electorate as a candidate who would fight to defend "the little people" against "the powerful." Conflict in

his view was the key to great leadership. In shattering an unacceptable status quo, he provided the kind of leadership that attracted emotional identification among the working class and the poor. The little people repaid him in kind with their votes and gratitude. Abbett's public career provides a classic illustration of the little guy versus the big guy. Certainly all the makings for high drama are in place here. It is an irresistible story; one that reveals a dramatically contested past and conveys the spirit and vitality of the Gilded Age. In all, this book covers that period of American political and social history beginning in the immediate aftermath of the Jacksonian era (the early 1840s) and extending through the origins of the Progressive movement (the early 1890s).

Amid a rising tide of cultural conservatism and an industrializing economy, these were dramatically changing times. New Jersey underwent tremendous social, economic, and cultural change that had profound consequences on its society during the second half of the nineteenth century. Many things were happening simultaneously in the state. Among the more pronounced changes were massive immigration, the explosive growth of cities, great railroad expansion, rapid industrialization, and the emergence of political machines. The convergence of these forces, coupled with startling new inventions and advances in technology, brought about a much different world. The state was being transformed. It was a postagrarian society engulfed in social turmoil, on the brink of modernity.

A powerful symbol of machine politics, Governor Abbett was viewed with deep suspicion and contempt by his critics and the partisan news media. They saw him as a rabble-rouser, a power-hungry politician, an unscrupulous demagogue, and a political charlatan of the worse stripe. A veteran of the political wars and a tough political infighter, Abbett challenged the established order and did not conform to the political correctness of his time. People everywhere in New Jersey had reason to feel worried about the distorted picture of the governor that emerged in the print media. Undoubtedly, Abbett made waves and loomed as a maverick in his own party, standing against the wind. Even those who deplored his actions and objectives recognized him as a man of unusual talents. His actions and policies were a harbinger of things to come. In fact, he became the first modern governor in New Jersey and one of the first in the nation. He invented a new style of executive politics that subsequent governors emulated decades later. It is also the main reason why his rediscovery is worthy of scholarly attention.

Leon Abbett was an enormously engaging political actor, who presided over transformations in state politics and public policy. He displayed the fluidity of a natural campaigner. Elected governor in 1883 and again in 1889 for three-year terms, he had a firm grasp of the salient issues and laid out a vision for the future. He is an important public figure historically, even if his name is barely recognized today. Reviled and discredited by the greedy corporations and powerful special interests that he fought so vigorously, Abbett was denied the recognition that he properly deserved during his lifetime. Many of his reforms and policy actions were undone after he left office. Anyone who embraced "populism" could be made to seem like a pandering demagogue and a cheap political opportunist. But pejorative words like populism, demagogue, and rabble-rouser were used more to distort and discredit rather than to explain and clarify. Similar to the fate that

befell his fellow Democrat, Governor John P. Altgeld of Illinois, Abbett remains to this day a "forgotten eagle."

Abbett specialized in the politics of spoils, patronage, and class protest like many Gilded Age politicians. He was closely identified with the downtrodden Irish of Hudson County, who were a despised ethnic group. Worse, he was closely tied to the liquor interests and with a corrupt Democratic political machine. In the eyes of many, the Irish were disreputable people and considered the lowlife of New Jersey politics. Everyone heaped scorn on them. Blaming the urban poor for lawlessness and the various ills of society was a common phenomenon. All of which explains why Abbett was so reviled and denigrated by the upper classes. His idea of greatness was to foster strong executive leadership within the strictures of the state constitution. He did a job that essentially reflected his own personal beliefs.

A solidly built man of medium height, Abbett radiated executive energy and drive and had a work ethic second to none. An urban populist well before the term became fashionable, he battled concentrated economic wealth and power in a political system in which class hatreds, religious antagonisms, racial conflict, and ethnic resentments abounded. The governor exploited these divisions and conflicts and had no qualms about playing off the poor against the rich. He was a populist fighter for New Jersey's farmers and factory workers and frequently showed his combativeness. Populism to him was nothing more than the expansion of political democracy. No wonder the elites feared him as a dangerous demagogue. Some of the political battles that Abbett fought were far more noble and far more courageous than conventional wisdom acknowledged. This is especially true of the way he navigated the often fractured terrain where religion and politics collided. The political assault against Abbett was constant from the moment he took office. Subjected to abusive criticism and editorial invective, he was much maligned in the partisan press and defamed by his political enemies.

Abbett governed at a time when big business was colliding with American democracy. Corporations were extremely powerful as they conspired to form new combinations and to fix prices. Megamergers and monopolies were reshaping just about every major industry. By sharp contrast, labor unions remained relatively weak because of the legal constraints imposed by criminal conspiracy laws. The day of corporate combinations was here to stay, while individualism declined. It was the time of the robber barons, when business moguls exercised excessive power and ran roughshod over the people they oppressed or excluded. Taking on the mighty railroads in an epic battle over state and local taxation, Abbett fought and beat them at their own political game. It was a supreme test of his political skills and the defining moment of his governorship. At the time, he was at the top of his career and in the fight of his life.

No man had as much influence in New Jersey for so long a period as Abbett did, an influence derived mainly from his vibrant personality, his indomitable spirit, the patronage he dispensed, and the powerful Democratic party machine he controlled. No governor in his day attained such incredible reach. Ruthless and defiant of the establishment, he displayed an unusual capacity for personal growth and maturity. His story shows that a public figure can learn and mature, even under the most stressful circumstances. He had a unique ability to connect

with people across ethnic, racial, religious, and class lines. That is what made him such a remarkable politician. He had all the intangibles.

An astute and accomplished party leader, Abbett was an extraordinary mixture of old-style machine politician, class warrior, and reformer. Although caught in the eye of many political storms, he managed to broaden his appeal beyond Hudson County and rose to power at a time when machine politics and political bossism flourished. Abbett was an activist governor intent on innovation and change and did things that most other governors shied away from doing and tackled public issues they thought were politically impossible to resolve. Over time, he accumulated various sources of power and used them fully. In uncharted waters, he emerged as a precursor of the modern governor. Abbett broke out of the party machine mold and overcame the sizable barriers that heretofore had impeded executive leadership; he recast and redefined the governorship and thereby carved a distinct niche for himself in the annals of New Jersey political history. The result was an unusual moment in American politics. Abbett's public career had considerable importance for an America in search of new models of political leadership; we can learn as much from his flaws and failures as from his astounding successes.

A biographical portrait is at best an approximation. Definitive biographies are a rare commodity because there are always opposing perspectives on a subject. The political biographer's primary challenge is to capture the spirit of the person and to locate the moment in which an entire age seems to seek its meaning through the moral drama of a particular life. The ultimate challenge is to make the subject come alive by inhabiting the world in which that person lived. In trying to imagine how Abbett lived and thought and felt, I found it necessary to walk the old neighborhoods where he grew up in Philadelphia and where he subsequently lived in Hoboken and Jersey City. For me, this experience was like reentering the Gilded Age and living mentally in a different era.

My views, of course, are those of a political scientist, not a historian. I constantly found myself trying to visualize Abbett's state of mind, but that in itself presented a special problem. This study therefore focuses primarily on Abbett's performance as governor, his uses of political power, and the ways in which he influenced public policy and reshaped the governorship as a political institution. My interpretation follows closely, yet departs significantly from, the path first marked by Duane Lockard in his superb book *The New Jersey Governor*. As a former student of Lockard, I was hardly surprised when my own research took me in similar directions.

My first encounter with Leon Abbett began many years ago in 1964, when as a graduate student at Princeton, I finished a respectable, if not distinguished, dissertation on Abbett. Although my initial take on the governor was accurate, it lacked depth of interpretation and was not a fully rounded portrait. Abbett seems to have kept much of his private life secretive or at least mysterious. The period we know least about is his early life, because it is so vaguely documented. Naturally, it would better if we knew more about it, because the personal element was significant in his public life.

The major limitation in conducting this current study has been the lack of Abbett's personal papers. Regrettably, they are not available. At the end of his

second term as governor, the press reported that Abbett had shipped these papers to his law firm. On March 19, 1895, a reporter for the Trenton *State Gazette* wrote, "When Governor Abbett retired from office, all his papers—both official and private—were sent to his law office at Jersey City by express by his order. Something no other Governor had done before." This is the only clue to their whereabouts that I uncovered during my research. A careful reading of Abbett's last will and testament makes no mention of them. After conducting an exhaustive search, which entailed contacting family relatives and probing various manuscript collections, I am convinced that his personal papers are, in effect, buried with him.

Whether by chance or design, these papers have vanished. The teller of Abbett's life therefore must reconstruct the whole of him from the parts that remain on the public record. Fortunately, Abbett left an extensive public record. His public papers are available and they include his formal gubernatorial addresses and his special messages to the state legislature. These documents become our best evidence about the man. They also provide a window to his political thinking.

Over and beyond that, Abbett is more than adequately explained by his own actions and political behavior, by his personal history, and by the events surrounding his public career. By highlighting these events and illuminating the personalities involved, we get a much clearer picture of the governor and his political style and manner. In real life, Abbett was a complicated man, who was never easy about revealing himself to others. As he grew older, his reticence increased so that he did not put much in writing, or at least not in private notes, diaries, and personal correspondence.

ACKNOWLEDGMENTS

In the preparation of this book, I have accumulated substantial debts. My former professors at Princeton University have helped in many ways too numerous to detail. Especially helpful have been Duane Lockard, Walter Murphy, Jameson W. Doig, William M. Beaney, John F. Sly, Herman M. Somers, and Paul Ylvisaker. As someone trained in American state and local politics, I was emboldened by Lockard's example to tackle the complex realities of New Jersey politics during the late nineteenth century. His constant availability and thoughtful guidance stand out.

Several other colleagues read all or part of the manuscript. None bears any responsibility for its flaws, but all helped to reduce them. They made the story better. These include John Bebout, Herbert Ershkowitz, Henry Frank, Sanford B. Gabin, James Green, Kathryn Grover, Nigel Hamilton, Morton Keller, Bruce Laurie, Maxine N. Lurie, Richard P. McCormick, Douglas V. Shaw, and Robert C. Wood. They offered welcome advice and encouragement at crucial moments in writing this book. I owe a special intellectual debt to two of my faculty colleagues at the University of Massachusetts, namely, Thomas N. Brown, a splendid historian, who broadened my understanding of the Irish and the impact of Irish-American nationalism on urban politics; and Julie Winch, another historian, who helped me to comprehend what life was like in antebellum Philadelphia, especially with regard to its black elite.

Outside the academy, I have incurred similar debts. I especially want to express my gratitude to the following people who kindly gave me much of their time to talk about the politics of Hudson County, some of whom have since passed on. These include former U.S. Senator John Milton, Raymond Coleman, John Dryden, and Joseph Davis. Much credit goes to Helen Fairbanks, librarian at Princeton University, and J. Owen Grundy, former secretary of the Hudson County Historical Society, both of whom assisted me in finding relevant data and made research a pleasant experience. Although none had any obligation to assist me, all were more than helpful. I was given many leads and explored each to its end.

I also received valuable assistance from the staffs of several libraries, particularly those of the American Philosophical Society Library, the Firestone Library at Princeton, the Jersey City Public Library, the New Jersey Historical Society Library, the New Jersey State Library, the New York Public Library, the Philadelphia Historical Society Library, and the Rutgers University Library. Collectively, these librarians helped me retrieve countless documents and records that made this book possible. Without their generous help, I would never have been able to rediscover Leon Abbett.

Grateful acknowledgment is made to the late Leon Abbett Post, the governor's grandson, who corresponded with me about his grandfather and his family

history. Nina Howell Starr of Marlboro, New Hampshire, allowed me to examine the papers of her grandfather, Robert Gilchrist, who served as attorney general of New Jersey and was a political ally of Governor Abbett. Ruth Dallas of Central High School of Philadelphia and Joseph Hepburn of the Franklin Institute provided information about the education of Leon Abbett. Zara Cohan of Newark State College informed me about the fire that partially destroyed the state capitol building in Trenton in 1885. Substantial portions of the two chapters on Abbett's political apprenticeship and his battle to tax the railroads originally appeared in *New Jersey History*. A very special thanks goes to the New Jersey Historical Society for granting me permission to use this material.

After the book was in manuscript, I had the editorial assistance of Carole LeFaivre-Rochester of the American Philosophical Society in Philadelphia. She gave more than skillful editorial help. For her unfailing sympathy, suggestion, and inspiration, I owe her a large debt and am heavily obligated to her for revisions, corrections, and uncanny detection of discrepancies.

My greatest debt is to my family. My wife Ann and six children, all of whom are now grown adults, reminded me daily about the most important things in life. Without their unstinting support, I would never have finished writing this book. My wife has been a steady influence during the inevitable highs and lows that I experienced in my struggle to understand and portray Abbett. I thank her for her patience, her kindness, her love, and her unflagging support.

Richard A. Hogarty

Marblehead, Massachusetts
November 15, 2000

October 8, 1836	Born in Philadelphia
1853	Graduated Central High School, A.B.
1853–1857	Clerked in law office of U.S. District Attorney
February 5, 1857	Admitted to Philadelphia Bar
1858–1860	Practiced law in Philadelphia
1860–1893	Practiced law in New York City
October 8, 1862	Married Mary Briggs
1863–1866	Corporation Attorney for Hoboken
1865–1866	Served as Assemblyman from Hoboken
September 7, 1865	Appointed to Democratic State Committee
1869–1870	Served as Assemblyman from Jersey City
1869	President, Jersey City Board of Education
1869–1870	Speaker of New Jersey General Assembly
1875–1877	Served as state senator from Hudson County
1877	President of New Jersey Senate
1876–1883	Corporation Counsel for Jersey City
1878	Appointed member Local Government Commission
1881	Appointed member Constitutional Commission
November 6, 1883	Elected Governor of New Jersey
June 18, 1884	Awarded honorary L.L.D. at Princeton
March 4, 1887	Defeated for U.S. Senate
1887–1889	Legal Counsel for State Liquor Dealers Association
November 5, 1889	Reelected Governor of New Jersey
March 4, 1893	Defeated for U.S. Senate
March 7, 1893	Appointed Justice on New Jersey Supreme Court
December 4, 1894	Died in Jersey City

PRINCIPAL CHARACTERS

LEON ABBETT,	Democratic Governor, 1884–1887; 1890–1893
CULVER BARCALOW,	Lobbyist for powerful Pennsylvania Railroad
MERCER BEASLEY,	Chief Justice of the New Jersey Supreme Court, 1864–1897
JOSEPH D. BEDLE,	Democratic Governor, 1875–1878
RUFUS BLODGETT,	Democratic U.S. Senator, 1887–1893, and railroad manager
WILLIAM BRINKERHOFF,	Hudson County Democratic state senator, 1884–1886
ORESTES CLEVELAND,	Democratic Congressman and Mayor of Jersey City
CHARLES L. CORBIN,	Prominent attorney and expert on railroad taxation
ROBERT DAVIS,	Sheriff of Hudson County and local Democratic boss
JONATHAN DIXON,	Republican candidate for governor, 1883
JOHN P. FEENEY,	Jersey City Assemblyman and head of New Jersey State Police
FREDERICK T. FRELINGHUYSEN,	Republican U.S. Senator, 1866–1869 and 1871–1877
WILLIAM J. A. FULLER,	Law partner of Leon Abbett
ROBERT GILCHRIST,	Attorney General of New Jersey, 1875
ROBERT S. GREEN,	Democratic Congressman and Governor, 1887–1890
JOHN W. GRIGGS,	Passaic County Republican state senator 1883–1888; Governor, 1896–1898
EDWARD B. GRUBB,	Republican candidate for governor, 1889
GEORGE A. HALSEY,	Newark leather manufacturer and Republican Congressman, 1866–1868
WILLIAM HEPPENHEIMER,	Jersey City Assemblyman, and State Comptroller, 1891–1894
SIMON KELLY,	Local Democratic boss and Mayor of Weehawken
HENRY C. KELSEY,	Secretary of State, 1871–1892
PATRICK H. LAVERTY,	State Prison Keeper, 1881–1886
BENJAMIN F. LEE,	Clerk of the New Jersey Supreme Court
HENRY S. LITTLE,	Monmouth County state senator and Clerk in Chancery
GEORGE C. LUDLOW,	Democratic Governor, 1881–1884
WILLIAM McADOO,	Hudson County Democratic boss and Congressman, 1883–1891

GEORGE B. McCLELLAN, Democratic Governor, 1878–188

ALLAN L. McDERMOTT, Jersey City Assemblyman, and chairman of the state Democratic party

JOSEPH P. McDONNELL, socialist editor of *Labor Standard* and New Jersey labor leader

ALEXANDER T. McGILL, Jersey City Assemblyman, and Chancellor of Court of Chancery

DENNIS McLAUGHLIN, Jersey City Assemblyman and Democratic ward boss

ARCHIBALD McLEOD, President of the Philadelphia and Reading Railroad

JOHN R. McPHERSON, Hudson County Democratic state senator and U.S. Senator, 1877–1895

PATRICK H. O'NEILL, Jersey City Assemblyman and local Democratic ward boss

CORTLANDT PARKER, Railroad attorney and president of the American Bar Association

JOEL PARKER, Democratic Governor, 1863–1866, and 1872–1875

WILLIAM W. PHELPS, Railroad magnate and Republican Congressman

JAMES N. PIDCOCK, Hunterdon County Democratic state senator; Congressman, 1885–1889

FREDERICK A. POTTS, Somerset County Republican state senator and candidate for governor

WILLIAM PRALL, Democratic Assemblyman from Passaic County

THEODORE F. RANDOLPH, Democratic Governor, 1869–1872, and U.S. Senator, 1875–1881

MILES ROSS, Middlesex County Democratic boss and Congressman, 1875–1883

THEODORE RUNYON, Chancellor of the New Jersey Court of Chancery, 1873–1880

WILLIAM J. SEWELL, Camden County Republican boss, and U.S. Senator, 1881–1887

JAMES SMITH, Essex County Democratic boss, and U.S. Senator, 1893–1899

JOHN P. STOCKTON, U.S. Senator, 1865–1866 and 1869–1875; Attorney General, 1877–1897

NOAH D. TAYLOR, Hudson County Democratic state senator, 1869–1871

GEORGE T. WERTS, Morris County Democratic state senator and Governor, 1893–1896

JAMES S. YARD, Railroad tax commissioner

EDWARD F. C. YOUNG, Hudson County banker and businessman

JAMES C. YOUNGBLOOD, Morris County Republican state senator, 1881–1886

Political Change in Abbett's New Jersey

Few people recognize the name of Leon Abbett today. Fewer still under-stand the crucial role that he played in governing New Jersey during the late nineteenth century. With the passage of time, the once luminous polit-ical star from the Victorian past has faded into undeserved obscurity and is now all but forgotten. He was very much a man of his time—the Gilded Age. He believed in competition and laissez-faire, but he did not let the business community control him. Since Abbett did not win fame or glory in his time, he has been long-neglected but richly deserves reconsidera-tion. He is now more a figure from history than from politics.

At the height of his power and popularity, Abbett was New Jersey's foremost Democrat and undisputed party leader. He was the preeminent power at the State House in Trenton. Tough-minded and politically astute, he was an ambitious man with a quick mind and seemingly limitless ener-gy. He had an impressive technical command of the issues. Astonishingly, he was a capsule blend of a traditional Democratic populist with an antag-onism toward entrenched interests; a fighter with a taste for battle; and a reformer with an impatience for the way things were. Articulate and dis-ciplined in thought and action, Abbett was the most resourceful, eloquent, energetic, and durable political personality of his time and place. Few men could match his talents or his power. According to William E. Sackett, an able columnist and reporter for the New York Times, who actually watched him in action, "Abbett was a law unto himself."[1] In short, he excelled in projecting an image and provoking a reaction.

In his prime, Abbett was a dynamic and visionary party leader and twice served as governor of New Jersey; from 1884 to 1887; and again from 1890 to 1893. His grassroots appeal, combined with his strong executive leadership, inspired loyalty and cooperation among thousands of supporters. At the time, railroad taxation was the hot political issue in

New Jersey. This was an audacious venture fraught with political risk. Fighting the railroads on the highly charged tax issue was tantamount to taking on a political juggernaut. Most previous governors, except for George Ludlow, had ducked the issue. Staying on message, which was couched in classic Jacksonian rhetoric, Abbett fought a protracted battle with the mighty rairlroads and won a decisive victory over them. He accomplished this amazing feat while facing almost insurmountable odds. But the fact is that, whatever else the man's flaws and failings, during this ultimate test of wisdom and character, he behaved more heroically than the standard history books have revealed. All of which made him an impressive and compelling public figure. More than that, Abbett's epic battle with the railroads made him a popular hero in the public mind as an "antimonopoly" defender of the small man. The governor obeyed a pragmatic political ethic, but many believed him to be a man of courage. He could be trusted to confront the power and arrogance of the privileged class. By shattering an unacceptable status quo, he changed the culture of politics in New Jersey, which in turn sent shock waves throughout its political system.

In governing New Jersey, Leon Abbett was beset by all kinds of anomalies and difficulties. For openers, New Jersey had a weak governorship. Most obvious was the fact that the state constitution prohibited governors from serving consecutive terms. Barred from succeeding himself, Abbett was forced to sit out a full three-year term before he could seek reelection as governor. In the meantime, he sought to get elected to the U. S. Senate, but the railroad power, which he had fought so tenaciously, conspired to defeat him in the state legislature (U.S. senators were not popularly elected in those days). Recovering from this humiliating defeat, Abbett was then reelected governor in 1889 by more votes than he previously had received in 1883. It was not only his biggest victory margin, but it was also the largest numerical vote that any gubernatorial candidate had ever received. By the time he had finished his second term as chief executive in 1893, the fifty-seven-year-old Abbett emerged as one of the ablest and most intriguing men ever to be governor. His personal charisma and his ability to persuade, compromise, and lead helped him to become a reformer with results. More than was appreciated at the time, he reshaped, redefined, and remade the New Jersey governorship. He accomplished this through a combination of brilliant leadership and party machine power, which he used to further his broader political ends. In 1893, he again sought election to the U.S. Senate but was defeated. The railroad power had exacted its last full measure of revenge in thwarting his ambition.

As a groundbreaker and change agent, Abbett upset the established order and shook things up in New Jersey, disrupting the status quo that prevailed in an overly rigid society. On balance, it was his daring nature and the brazenness of his tactics that distinguished him from other governors. Over the years, Abbett had become a controversial and polarizing public figure. At the outset of his political career, he had been subject to scrutiny. The daily political assault against him began from the moment he took office. A Democratic party wheelhorse, Abbett enjoyed a long and productive public career. In fact, he remained a fixture in New Jersey politics for nearly three decades. His public career covered a period that extended from 1864 to 1894. He became governor twenty years after he had first entered politics in Hoboken, where he initially made a name for himself. From there he moved his residence to Jersey City, the county seat of Hudson, where he built his political base mainly among immigrants and the children of immigrants, and where he advanced politically with the help of a notoriously corrupt Hudson County Democratic machine. Operating in an era disdainful of spoils politics and machine power, he soon came to grips with mastering the complex role of politician in all its intricate and multifaceted details.

During these turbulent and event-filled years, Abbett braved the passions and divisions spawned by the Civil War and Reconstruction. He led the people of New Jersey into the dawn of a new urban industrial age that brought with it a prosperous economy and myriad unforeseen social and political problems. Confronted with massive immigration, rapid industrialization, and expansive urban growth, the state was being transformed both demographically and economically. The expansion of the railroads had a great deal to do with this dramatic transformation. Industry replaced agriculture; cities replaced farms. New communities sprang up along the railroad routes. New fortunes were made; old fortunes were lost. New tensions were created; old tensions were muted. It was a permanent change, wrought by a labor force that had no equal.

With the advance of industrialization, New Jersey experienced the end of an agrarian society and the beginning of an urban industrial order that was characterized by a great disparity of wealth and power. Government and business high-handedness ruled the day. Based on his stunning performance, Abbett was a colorful and flamboyant chief executive, maybe the most inventive, surely the most vigorous. This is his remarkable life story, drawn primarily from the public record and told in all its rich and poignant detail. It is ultimately a story about the crucial role that Abbett played in governing New Jersey during the Gilded Age. Over and beyond that, it is a story that casts into sharp relief a clash between two competing political cultures: one urban and progressive, the other rural and reactionary.

Contemporary commentators and observers painted Abbett in the dark hues of an arrant public knave who was hungry for power. He had great ambition for himself, and more important for his adopted state. A hero to some, a villain to others, he was a spoils politician, a party machine boss, an urban populist, a class warrior, and a dispenser of

political patronage all wrapped into one. His name was synonymous with machine politics. Nevertheless, he was a man of far greater complexity and mixed motives than these negative stereotypes suggest. Most politicians have mixed motives, and Abbett was certainly no exception, but to see him solely as an autocratic party boss would be a mistake. He was much more than that. Altruistic and avaricious, dedicated and domineering, talented and tough-minded, sensitive and cynical, principled and preemptory, Abbett was far too complex to be reduced to such simplistic characterization. Among other things, he was a first-rate lawyer, a superb party organizer, a masterful strategist, a manipulator of men, a savvy wheeler-dealer, and a public entrepreneur extraordinary. Most of all, he was an active, reform-minded governor of considerable importance. In later life, Abbett retired from politics and was appointed a state supreme court judge. There was in him much of the intensity and drive of the self-made man. By all accounts, he was a bold, talented, and resourceful individual, who used his political assets to advance his policy agenda. A relatively progressive Democrat in a state with a highly competitive two-party system, he grappled with the new realities of changing life in America and dealt in practical fashion with the pressing public issues of his day. He reached out for contact and indeed for confrontation. More than anything else, he was a smart politician who was shrewdly attuned to the temper of the times.

FIG. 1
The ferry landing, the terminus of the New Jersey R.R., the Taylor House, and the Cunard steamers, the Morris Canal and the cars of the N.J. Central R.R.

A DEMOCRATIC PARTY WHEELHORSE

A formidable adversary, whose grudges were held as fiercely as his loyalties, Abbett had the political wherewithal to defeat two impressive Republican candidates for governor. Drawing on his popularity and political machine, he defeated Jonathan Dixon in 1883 and Edward Burd Grubb in 1889. For Abbett, political power was meant to be used, and he used it adroitly. He was a supremely successful politician and leader because he allowed himself plenty of room to maneuver. Coming to power as he did during the heyday of machine politics and political bossism, the Hudson County Democrat understood the political world in which he lived, accepted it for what it was, and moved through it with a dash and verve rarely seen in American politics in those days. He was a man on a mission trying to win elections, but also trying to build a party. For as long as he was in office, Abbett made the most of his political opportunities. A dyed-in-the-wool Democrat, he had the requisite fire and desire to succeed in politics. Early in his career, he adopted the Jacksonian credo of "to the victor belong the spoils." He was a genius at brokering political differences and in knowing what worked politically. Much of it had to do with his extraordinary personality—brilliant, incisive, charming, analytic, confident, experienced, and at times utterly ruthless. Abbett was a pragmatist of large dimension; he would do whatever it took to win. More was involved: his message, his reputation for getting things done, and the appeal of his magnetic personality in an age of extremes, of poverty and plenty, of squalor and opulence.

The interplay of personality and politics accounted for much of Abbett's success both in governing and in accumulating unprecedented political power. A dedicated and unrelenting professional politician, Abbett enjoyed the public limelight and the excitement of politics, but he also knew its dark side. He understood the allure and treachery of politics and experienced the perils and travails that went with public life. He came across as a complicated and compassionate human being, not easily deciphered. It is therefore difficult to take the full measure of the man. To this day, he remains an almost impenetrable political enigma.

Bucking a strong tide of cultural and political conservatism, Abbett led the politically active masses in a grassroots movement that fundamentally challenged New Jersey's old guard that was largely Yankee and largely elite. This dominant ruling class held power in the state that was disproportionate to their numbers. Some of these aristocrats used their political influence to enhance their own economic well-being. As boosters of American capitalism, they extolled the virtues of free enterprise and advocated a minimalist approach to government. From the very outset, Abbett became a thorn in the side of these native Protestant politicians, both Democrats and Republicans alike. He angered members in his own

party; they disliked his combative style of politics and what they perceived as his rude behavior. He in turn lacked the protection that birth and class and breeding still conferred on aristocrats. Viewed as a brazen upstart in their eyes, he was not their kind of Democrat. They were openly contemptuous of him, and they especially resented the way he pandered to the interests of the Irish and shrewdly cultivated the immigrant vote. Since the Jacksonian era, Democratic politics in New Jersey depended on catering to group interests and prejudices. This pandering was necessary to build a majority coalition out of mutually hostile constituent groups of Protestants, Catholics, and Jews. The overall result of such coalition politics was good for the party and good for the state.

Strangers in a new land, mired in abject poverty, and devout in their Catholicism, the Irish encountered a hostile environment of religious intolerance and bigotry. As a despised subculture, they had reason enough to resent the Protestant elite who possessed wealth and status and seemed disposed to social snobbery. Relations between these two groups had many abrasive edges. Even when exploitative economic relationships and class differences did not exacerbate tensions and resentments, religion and culture would cause hostility. The Irish shared a common language with these people, but little else. Ireland, of course, had been subjugated by the British. To keep the Irish docile, their British rulers had enforced illiteracy through the Penal Laws, which denied Catholics the right to attend school. Some of them had been taught clandestinely behind the hedge-row schools, but most were illiterate.

The Irish politicians came to City Hall as outcasts, and as people scorned, they had no great respect for the scorners or their vaunted principles of government. Scarred emotionally by the devastating impact of the great famine (1845-1849) and by the cruel oppression they suffered from the British, the Irish brought with them clannishness, a talent for extralegal politics, and a tradition of personal loyalty to their leaders. Somewhat in the manner of ex-colonials who have grown used to bribery and other means of cheating the prevailing powers, the Irish newcomers set some unsavory records for public plundering. But they were no more dishonest than the robber barons or business moguls who dominated politics and exploited their people. These ethical lapses were endemic in the big cities.

Many Irish immigrants flocked to Abbett's Democratic party machine, which they found friendly in a hostile, Protestant America. They admired the governor for the gutsy way he took on entrenched power. He was a friend to the Irish in Hudson County, and a friend to the Irish cause of nationalism. At the time, the Irish were the fastest growing ethnic group in the state. With typical daring, Abbett won their favor by battling for home rule in Jersey City, which had been repealed by a Republican-controlled state legislature. The governor was an unconventional

politician who was not afraid to support unpopular causes, especially if it meant cultivating a core constituency that would remain loyal to him. He valued the concept of cultural diversity and had a special feel for what was going on. His independent actions did not always endear him to other party leaders. A tireless activist, he drove himself relentlessly and thereby captured the public's imagination. He worked hard at knowing his constituents and their concerns, but he did not always provide them with easy answers. Several new ideas were transformed into policy during his tenure. Some of these adjustments required trial and error, as well as the courage to face and learn from mistakes.

Medium in height, trim, handsome, and well educated, Leon Abbett cut a neat, compact figure at 5 feet 8 inches and 170 pounds.[2] Gracious and invariably well dressed, he was also endowed with the bonhomie of the successful politician and with that gift for gesture so beloved in the Irish community. It was a harsh world in which rugged individualism, opportunism, and survival of the fittest all had equal play. Abbett's outgoing personality radiated warmth and charm. But it was his personal demeanor that awed people. The governor carried himself in a courtly manner and walked that narrow line between overbearing arrogance and supreme self-confidence, which was slightly disguised by an old-fashioned courtesy. He had a wry sense of humor and a talent for spotting the absurd.

From available period photographs and from the oil portrait painted by Charles H. Sherman in 1896, Abbett looked like a Gilded Age

FIG. 2
Hudson River Front, looking toward Jersey City, 1853. From the Free Library of New Jersey.

politician. His features complimented his strong personality. He had a handsome face with a prominent forehead, high cheekbones, and a jutting jaw that were accentuated by a medium-shaped nose and large bushy eyebrows. Early in his career, he grew a beard and moustache that he kept neatly trimmed. His bright blue eyes and wavy brown hair, which had begun to recede and turn gray, lent an aura of distinction to his mature features. He was meticulously groomed and dressed in a style that befitted his professional status. He usually wore a black double-breasted suit along with a vest and bow tie. In cold weather, he donned a fashionable Prince Albert overcoat and brown derby hat. He wore a high silk hat and tails whenever a formal occasion warranted it. Abbett made an image for himself and stuck with it. He understood the new media of the time, namely the photograph, and he knew it would allow his image to become better known.

Affectionately known as the "Great Commoner," Abbett appealed primarily to the deprived urban lower classes and the marginally deprived agricultural yeomanry. He capitalized on labor unrest, ethnic conflict, and a generation of agrarian discontent and demonstrated a capacity to arouse enthusiasm among constituencies demoralized by the domination of big business and concentrated wealth. The industrial workers in the cities and the farmers in the small rural towns formed his natural constituency. He understood their problems and did his best to improve their living standards. An urban populist reared in the Jacksonian spoils tradition, Abbett expressed the sentiments of the common man beset by the intransigent forces of unrestrained capitalism and special privilege. He stood up for little people who were weak and vulnerable as well as those who felt powerless and excluded from the political process. Abbett had always been a city person, and he knew firsthand the problems New Jersey citizens faced and prided himself on being in the forefront on many social issues. In New Jersey's highly competitive two-party system, he was a fierce competitor as well as a fierce partisan. Adept at reading people and sorting out power relationships, he was astute at gauging public opinion and calculating electoral interests. He carefully weighed how the prospective benefits and risks stacked up. As might be expected of a populist, Abbett advocated policies calculated to offend entrenched interests, especially the railroads. Given his home base of Hudson County, his policy expertise on the railroad tax issue was his forte.

To do battle with the railroads over the issue of "equal taxation" was Abbett's calling; and that calling, which struck at the heart of free enterprise, put him on a collision course with the dominant economic elite in New Jersey that looked on railroading as the lifeblood of its political economy. It was the biggest moment in Abbett's career. No issue, in his view, was more urgent. His sparkling oratory in his inaugural message in January 1884 created a sensation. This audacious venture was extremely

Eng'd by A.H.Ritchie

Edw. B. Grubb

FIG. 3
*Edward B. Grubb,
Republican candidate for
governor, 1889. Engraving
by A.H. Ritchie.*

risky. From the early 1830s on, the railroads had stimulated economic growth and development in New Jersey. Over the years, they had amassed an enormous amount of economic and political power. Railroad lobbyists used the ample funds at their disposal to curry favor with politicians and to contribute to their campaign coffers. They extended free railroad passes to public officials and persuaded governors to appoint judges who were friendly toward their interests. By the time Abbett became governor, the railroad industry was by far the single most powerful special interest group in the state. Collectively, the railroads constituted a power elite in the fullest sense of the term.

Outsiders mockingly referred to New Jersey as the "State of Camden and Amboy" that referred to the name of its famous railroad monopoly. These powerful railroad corporations feared leaving their protective cocoon, a cocoon that guaranteed them a certain degree of tax immunity. This tax immunity issue was ensnarled in a series of court cases and a web of legalistic complexities. Most New Jerseyans found the language of the court decisions limiting taxation convoluted and almost incomprehensible.

Sensing that the present was alive with change, Abbett appeared to stand astride a fault line of ethnicity, race, class, and religion. He exploited the various resentments and hatreds that prevailed. Some of them were embedded in an American suspicion of aristocrats and their superior rank in society. There was a huge class divide between the haves and the have-nots. There was also a general sense of alienation among farmers and urban industrial wage earners, who worked hard without much to show for their arduous labor. To right the wrongs of oppressed labor was Abbett's passion and overriding commitment. He loved to cast himself as the champion of New Jersey's working people, many of whom lived lives of quiet desperation. They viewed him as their hero because he not only represented their genuine interests, but he also gave them a sense of identity and hope. A product of Philadelphia's working class, he brought a philosophy of "free labor " to the governor's office.

A NEW KIND OF GOVERNOR

Abbett was the twenty-sixth governor of New Jersey, and both in style and in strategy, he represented a sharp break from those who preceded him. Viewing the governorship as a unique position of responsibility, he saw himself as the chief problem solver. Politics for him was a game of risk. Like most elected officials, he kept his advocacy general, positioning himself to take credit for successes and to join the critics in the event of failure. Even this approach entailed a modicum of risk that he would be blamed if things went wrong, but he realized that it need not be fatal. His

FIG. 4
Jonathan Dixon, Associate
Justice of the New Jersey
Supreme Court and
Republican nominee for
governor of New Jersey.

politics were hardly cautious. He was a daring man who believed that the bolder the political risk the greater the potential gains. A nonconformist in his political behavior, Abbett defied conventional standards and did things other politicians were reluctant to do. He differed most from his predecessors in his willingness to lead and mobilize the body politic rather than simply follow the dictates of a legislature that had long been the prime focus of state government.

Abbett readily performed the ceremonial functions as head of state, but he refused to be relegated to a mere ceremonial figurehead. Over time, he broke new ground and became both a party leader and a policy leader. That was a formidable combination for his time.[3] While he frequently "went along to get along," he was no purist and had little difficulty in cutting deals. He had the ability to bargain and compromise which is necessary to succeed in politics. Although his temperament disposed him toward making bargains, he was determined to lean hard in directions that he believed to be right. Because he was such a polarizing figure, he made more than his share of political enemies, but few dared to take him on publicly. Those who did soon learned to regret it. Yet, he understood the subtle difference between enemies and adversaries.

Operating behind the façade of a powerful party machine that was corrupt and boss-ridden, Abbett was emblematic of that machine in all its varied manifestations, the good, the bad, and the indifferent. Hence, he became a lighting rod for criticism. He had built his political base among the impoverished Irish immigrants in Hudson County, a Democratic stronghold that sustained his power. Stealth, guile, nuance, and deception were all part of his political repertoire. Gifted with persuasive powers, he knew how to motivate people and to bring them together to work as a cohesive force. In terms of public perceptions, he projected multiple personae, not all of which were favorable. Some people saw him as a greedy-spoils politician, who seemed overly ambitious and desirous of too much power. Others looked on him as a counterforce to the greedy corporate interests of American capitalism. Still others found him to be a staunch supporter of organized labor and the wage-earning class.

In sum, he was an implausible blend of reformer and spoils politician. That unusual combination is what baffled most people. The discrepancies between these perceptions made him inscrutable and difficult to fathom. He was defined to a large extent by his contradictions and ambiguities. At rock bottom, Abbett was a popular leader who could adjust and rearrange his positions to suit his political needs. Part of this facility was attributable to his political growth and maturity, and part of it was due to political expediency.

No stranger to controversy, Abbett fought hard for what he truly believed in, but social conservatives and hard-shell Republicans were scared to death of him. They saw him as a dangerous demagogue pandering to the hatreds, fears, and insecurity of the Irish. Few New Jerseyans felt neutral about Abbett. Those who knew him best admired him the most. To his supporters, he was invigorating proof of a politician willing to fight for the small man and the working poor. To his detractors, he was vilified as a cheap politician who degraded the political system. There were legions on both sides; each engulfed in its own militant brand of partisanship. In an age when the label "spoils politician" was becoming increasingly associated with greed, corruption, and venality, Abbett was much maligned by a partisan press that cut him little or no slack. News stories were often written to conform to conservative and reactionary editorials. Stung by the ferocity of these attacks, Abbett endured all kinds of barbs and insults, some of which were wildly exaggerated. But it was his ability to survive repeated attacks on his character and bruised reputation that set him apart. The governor had developed a tough skin and managed to shed these barbs without too much trouble. A master at deflecting criticism and putting his own spin on events, he blithely dismissed scandals within his administration. Whatever the inspiration, he had the ability to educate and to appear concerned with everyone's problems while remaining calm and collected in the midst of a political whirlwind.

Loved and hated with equal passion, seeking improvement for the downtrodden, and using his charm and wit with a flourish, Abbett was a consummate politician. Paradoxically, he represented the best and the worst in American politics; the ambiguities and contradictions were endless. To the dismay and consternation of his critics, he often combined the admirable with the obnoxious. That is what made him so controversial. By instinct and disposition, Abbett was a shrewd, cunning, and devious party boss, who had a flair for the dramatic and the unexpected. He never lost his capacity for the element of surprise, for saying and doing the unexpected. His capacity to perplex, confuse, and contradict the prophesies of his enemies was legendary. No one knew for sure what he was going to do or say from one moment to the next. His unpredictability simply added to the legend. However much and in what measure these factors figured in his drives for political equality, the net result was an empowerment of urban ethnic minorities. To anyone who knew anything about Abbett, these personal qualities would have come as no surprise. At least that is what a close examination of his public life reveals. Nothing written about him disputes this interpretation.

To be sure, Leon Abbett energized his party base in New Jersey. Under his leadership, the party sought to represent the major interests of business, labor, and agriculture. His career provides a vivid illustration of the kind of power the party had and how it was used. Toward the end of the Civil War, the Hoboken Democrat had been a minor party figure with minor patronage appointments before his emergence as party mogul in the last quarter of the nineteenth century. He had an alliance with powerful U.S.

Senator John R. McPherson, but in matters pertaining to internal politics, he was the man in charge. He shaped the action and called the shots.

Abbett's control over the party apparatus was reinforced in two ways. One, the party was financed by assessments made on the salaries of those holding patronage appointments and on candidates who ran for office on the party ticket. Money was also obtained from special interest groups wanting favors from the state. Two, Abbett had a faithful organization with which to discipline the recalcitrant. If his orders were disobeyed, the word would be passed down and only rarely would the offender be able to withstand the disciplinary action. Such a person might be denied advancement, patronage, or other favors that the party granted to the faithful. There is evidence that many jobs were delivered to them, but the more lucrative rewards were dangled before other ambitious politicians. Serving as legal counsel to the New Jersey Liquor Dealers Association during his gubernatorial interregnum (1887–1889), Abbett had ample money with which to work. Cash was used in elections in a most undignified manner: it bought votes.

The buying and selling of votes were fairly common. Voters in New Jersey were often paid anywhere from $1 to $3 for turning out, with as many as one-fifth to one-third of the electorate anticipating payment on election day. Party workers were employed as canvassers, identifying voters sympathetic to the party before election day. Parties also hired heelers to coax voters to the polls, and ticket peddlers were stationed near polling places to distribute preprinted party tickets that voters could simply deposit, without having to mark them in any way, in the ballot box. The ticket peddlers did the actual vote buying and rounded up whomever they could find, however disreputable. Among these voters were the so-called floaters, repeaters, winos, drifters, and derelicts. Frequently, it involved haggling over price. Party agents in Newark in 1888 bargained with voters outside the polls, agreed on a price, and paid voters in brass tokens redeemable at the backroom of a nearby saloon.[4] Reformers saw this vote buying as political corruption, but to seasoned practitioners it was merely a routine extension of the spoils system. "The pecuniary nature of the nineteenth-century's electoral system," historian John Reynolds observes, "made it difficult to draw sharp distinctions as to where payment for services rendered ended and bribery began. If the parties paid for carriages to round up citizens on election day, why should a farmer carting his laborers or neighbors not expect payment? If the ticket peddlers and heelers were rewarded for their efforts, why not the voters?"[5]

For the six years that he occupied the governor's office, Abbett was no ordinary, run-of-the-mill chief executive. Initially at odds with his own party's leadership, he led a popular grassroots movement that not only challenged the established order, but also challenged corporate power and the rapacious titans of American industry. New voices of unrest and

change were abroad in the land, and Abbett's voice was certainly one of them. A new breed of politicians had appeared on the scene. Governors like John P. Altgeld of Illinois, Benjamim F. Butler of Massachusetts, and David B. Hill of New York believed that the new social realities in American life required fresh ideas and new approaches to governance, but they were minority voices. They found satisfaction and some degree of fulfillment in providing a voice for the voiceless. For his part, Abbett articulated a "free labor" ideology of equal opportunity and upward mobility.

A citydweller throughout his life, Abbett was the first governor in New Jersey to come to office with a pronounced urban mission. Aware of the discontent found in the industrial cities, he focused on their needs, whereas his predecessors catered mostly to the needs of an agrarian society. Cities were beset with seemingly intractable problems that resulted from rapid industrialization, huge immigration, and dramatic urbanization. The state was both blessed and cursed by the convergence of these forces that served as a catalyst for social change. The Gilded Age, as humorist Mark Twain dubbed it, was the best of times and the worst of times. Slums, poverty, street crime, gang wars, illiteracy, and contagious diseases like tuberculosis menaced the quality of urban life. With limited tax revenues and unprecedented urban growth, the cities were hard-pressed financially to build the infrastructure and provide the municipal services (mainly police and fire protection) that were necessary to sustain such growth.

Fires were a dreaded scourge of nineteenth-century cities. Wooden structures were often built in close proximity to each other. With no zoning ordinances to separate industrial from residential areas, these buildings presented a constant fire hazard. Fire fighting was handled by volunteer fire companies that proved inefficient and expensive to maintain. They were soon replaced by paid fire departments in which employment became a bountiful source of local patronage. The horse-drawn, steam-powered pumper made the volunteer bucket brigades obsolete.

While much of urban society was preoccupied with industrialization, the Panic of 1873 caused the public debt of cities to skyrocket. Teetering on the brink of insolvency, a few cities in New Jersey actually went bankrupt; Elizabeth and Rahway among them. The state government also incurred large indebtedness. By taxing the railroads, Governor Abbett sought to remedy these fiscal problems with an infusion of new revenue and without imposing a direct tax on the people. It was a populist message that resonated with New Jersey voters. He played to the party base.

In tracing his family history, one discovers that Leon Abbett came from humble Quaker origins. His antecedents had been Pennsylvania farmers and millers. Born in antebellum Philadelphia in 1836, Abbett was the son of Ezekiel and Sarah Abbett. His father was a journeyman hatter by trade, while his mother, who came from southern New Jersey, was a successful milliner who sold women's bonnets. His parents scrimped and saved every spare nickel to raise their five children, one of whom died of cholera in infancy. Deeply affected by the economic depression of 1837, they instilled in their children a positive work ethic and a sense of civic duty. Raised in Philadelphia during the age of Andrew Jackson, young Abbett was a poor boy who lived at 109 North Fifth Street. It was a rough, working-class neighborhood, where he was exposed to the seamy side of urban life that nurtured his egalitarian roots. Many of his political beliefs were shaped during these formative years by his family's Jacksonian values and loyalties. A graduate of Central High, an elite exam school in Philadelphia, Abbett came of age when the national debate over slavery had reached its zenith. Before his admission to the bar in 1857, he had spent three years clerking in the law office of John Wayne Ashmead, the U.S. Attorney for eastern Pennsylvania. His city upbringing, suffused in an artisan culture, formed his world view.[6] Later on, as governor, he drew deeply on the painful events of his early life.

The simplicity of Abbett's boyhood world, however, was long gone by the late nineteenth century. He followed the Horatio Alger model of "poor boy made good." With none of the advantages of family fortune, the hatter's son made his mark through ability rather than inherited wealth and social position. Most New Jersey governors came from wealthy patrician families and were usually educated at either Princeton or Rutgers, the state's two colonial colleges. Although Abbett's parents could not afford to send him to college, he was a voracious reader and largely a self-educated lawyer. His elevation to the governorship was an indication of his native intellectual ability and of his political skills.

Intelligent, energetic, and ambitious, Abbett possessed the mental toughness and the combativeness necessary to survive in the internecine warfare and the rancorous partisan atmosphere that prevailed at the State House in Trenton. He began his legal career in Philadelphia, then moved to New York City on the eve of the Civil War in 1860. Before long, he formed a legal partnership with William J. Fuller. Two years later, Abbett married well and certainly above his station in life. His glamorous bride, Mary Ann Briggs, was a beauty of impeccable Philadelphia lineage and the daughter of a municipal court judge. Charming, intelligent, and well spoken, she was considered a prize catch. The young couple took up residence in Hoboken, where Abbett devoted himself to his career and to raising a family. In due course, Mary gave birth to two sons and a daughter. Abbett got his political start in Hoboken in 1864 by winning a seat in the state General Assembly. He used state office-holding and Democratic party politics as available stepping stones.

Considered a rising political figure from his earliest days in the legislature, Abbett was perceived as a real comer with potential star quality. He learned how to survive in the divisive politics of the Civil

War and Reconstruction era. Relying on his traditional base of Democratic support in Hudson County, he steadily moved up the ranks in his party until he eventually became governor in 1884. He had previously served as speaker of the assembly from 1869 to 1870 and then as president of the state senate in 1877. Nor did his hunger for public office stop there. He wanted very much to become a U. S. Senator. It was a logical progression to a career that had long defied the politics of deference. He had developed a public image of a courageous figure who often stood alone in defending the progressive agenda of the Democratic party.

A master politician, Abbett enjoyed marching in parades, shaking hands, kissing babies, and courting Irish and German ward heelers who turned out the vote on election day. His memory for names was incredible. These leadership skills helped to get him elected governor. He won people over by his extroverted personality and his compassion, a quality that enabled him to identify with the condition of others. Of such endearing habits lasting friendships were made, and personal politics mattered in those days. New Jersey was a state in which a candidate was expected to campaign in person and to talk directly with the voters. An attentive listener, Abbett was as much at ease in talking with urban industrial workers as he was in trading yarns with hardscrabble farmers whom he met on the campaign trail while electioneering at county and state agricultural fairs. His folksy, down-home style went over well with them. The common people, who hoped for a better life, not only admired him, but also embraced him as one of their own. Abbett's continuing popularity owed as much to his personal charm and charisma as it did to his ability to deliver for his constituents.

Abbett was a man in a hurry and not especially given to patience. He did not suffer fools gladly, nor did he forget a personal slight. He played what is known today as hardball politics. As a hard-nosed lawyer, he did not shy away from conflict. If he could be hard on himself, he could be even harder on those who did not play ball with him. His gentle demeanor and courtesy masked a disciplined and demanding political style. In an age when rugged individualism was greatly admired in America, Abbett established himself as a combative politician. He relished a good political fight and earned the grudging respect of his adversaries. Winning for Abbett was all-important, whatever the issue or whatever the cost. The will to conquer and to make a difference also came into play. He thrived on the competition for attention and approval that normally exists in state government. The reputation he acquired along these lines invited other politicians either to go along with him or to risk defying him. Discipline came not only from clearly stipulated orders, but also with beliefs about what those with authority had up their powerful sleeves. When politicians got the impression that Abbett was popular, he was

FIG. 5

View of Montgomery Street, Jersey City. From Historical Society of Hudson County.

thereby empowered, for reputations became a form of currency in the transactions of politics.

When Abbett first became governor in 1884 at the age of forty-eight, he had spent twenty years trying to achieve this elusive goal. Tired of waiting his turn, he first seized the opportunity in 1877, when he was considered the presumptive favorite, but this effort failed. In an episode filled with palace intrigue and surreptitious maneuvering, a small group of aristocratic Democrats, known as the "State House Ring," plotted against him and derailed his drive for the gubernatorial nomination. As part of their scheme, they persuaded George B. McClellan, a military hero, businessman, and Democrat, to jump into the fray. The popular ex-Civil War general not only won the party's nomination, but also the governorship. Despite his intense disappointment, Abbett sublimated his ego and showed his party loyalty by actively campaigning for McClellan. Yet, it was a bitter pill for him to swallow. He felt that he had earned his party's nomination.

To add to his personal troubles, Abbett lost his wife in June 1879. Mary died after battling an incurable cancer for the better part of two years. Consumed in grief, Abbett was overwhelmed and inconsolable. He would never fully recover from her death, and like most people who experience a sudden loss, he felt isolated and alone. His grief and internal turmoil were exacerbated by a period of dark depression and indifference. He had to work his way through the grieving process before he could put his life back together again. Once he resumed his political career, he then ran for governor and won the office twice. Tragedy struck again in 1893, when his oldest son, William F. Abbett, suddenly died of a brain aneurysm. Described by many as strikingly like his father in personality, William had graduated from Columbia Law School and became judge advocate general in his father's second administration. Even though life had dealt Abbett his share of blows, his resilience and real inner strength enabled him to bounce back from the cruel caprices of life.

FIG. 6
Rearview of Leon Abbett's residence in Jersey City.

Impatient waiting and striving had simply whetted Abbett's appetite for the leadership opportunities that he saw in the governorship. Twice elected to the position, first in 1883 and again in 1889, he brought vigor and imagination to the office. Probably no governor in the Gilded Age had come to the state capital in Trenton with as full a comprehension of the power and limitations of the office. Abbett's intention from the outset was to make himself a highly visible chief executive, a symbol of energy and motion, who accepted responsibility for a wide range of public issues and sought to be omnipresent and invincible rather than simply dignified. Sometimes he used his position as a bully pulpit, but he rarely preached to people. He fully exploited the public relations potential of the office. His messages to the legislature were consciously addressed to a wider public. He saw policy leadership as a necessary element of the governor's task and did his best to persuade legislators to accept what he thought necessary. In all, he created a public image that was aptly suited to the times, to his own personality, and to the lessons of his own embattled career.

Abbett's brilliance lay in fashioning political strategy and tactics, his intuitive grasp of personalities, and his manipulation of people to do what they otherwise would not have done. He was a thoroughly political man whose leadership skills had been honed by his legislative experience. A lifetime in politics had made him wise and ruthless when it came to dealing with the key players in the political process, whether they were hostile Republicans or defiant Democrats from rival factions within his own party. This knowledge and experience, coupled with his determination to lead rather than follow, made him a master of institutional politics as practiced in Trenton. He saw the governorship as a resource for someone to come in with new ideas, a new approach, and a different way of doing things.

Abbett came to office determined to be the titular party leader as well as the chief initiator of public policy. The tempo of gubernatorial initiative varies with the disposition of the incumbent, whether he be passive or active, positive or negative. Abbett was inclined to be active and positive, and the pace of the policy process increased accordingly. He understood the problems underlying the issues on the public agenda and was now the central figure for translating campaign promises into policy initiatives. As he struggled to take the initiative, he made something astoundingly different out of the governor's office; he turned it into an instrument of vigorous leadership. For the first time in the history of the state, the governorship appeared to be an important and influential office in American politics.

That transformation of the office did in fact occur. In the twentieth century, New Jersey has had a number of notable governors: Woodrow Wilson, Walter Edge, Alfred Driscoll, Robert Meyner, Richard Hughes, Brendan Byrne, Thomas Kean, and Christine Todd Whitman come readily

to mind. They all made their presence felt in the governor's office. Long before they arrived on the scene, however, Abbett had pioneered in the uses of executive power and blazed a trail that prepared the way for them. By 1893, he cast himself in a precursor role as an archetype of the activist governor intent on innovation and change.

Abbett displayed all the requisite instincts and characteristics of the so-called "modern governor." Duane Lockard, author of the leading study entitled *The New Jersey Governor*, distilled the type in his book. According to Lockard's definition, a "modern governor shows a certain independence of party organizations, makes the most of his having been popularly elected by appealing for public support, and seeks to maximize his power to govern by increasing his control over governmental organization, and by frankly cultivating a public image."[7] Abbett did all these things and did them well.

THE DEVELOPMENT OF THE OFFICE

Such a phenomenon was something entirely new in state politics. Before Abbett became governor, New Jerseyans had been accustomed to a succession of patrician governors who came from established first-families. Some were men of ability and personal distinction, but they tended to be passive observers in the policy process. They typically followed a path of least political resistance or inaction. As a result, the public agenda was usually light and the governorship was largely a ceremonial position. As a vestige of colonial government, the institution suffered from a tradition of a weak governor and one who was lacking in power, prestige, and importance. The historical roots of the problem can be traced to the colonial governors, whose tyrannical rule and abuse of authority had instilled fear and distrust among the colonists from the eighteenth century on.

At the request of the Continental Congress, New Jersey was among the first states to adopt a constitution in 1776, and the provisions of that document illustrate how the mood of the times affected those who drafted it. Angry at the King and at his royal governors who attempted to carry out imperial policy, the revolutionists distrusted the executive. As a consequence, the framers of the first constitution provided for legislative supremacy and denied the governor any significant executive power. Prime authority rested with the legislature. The governor lacked the veto power to curtail legislative actions. In fact, he had more judicial than executive authority since he served as chancellor and surrogate general. Lacking powers of appointment, subject to annual election by the legislature, and performing most of his formal duties in conjunction with the upper house of the legislature, the governor derived most of his power from other than constitutional sources. None of the fourteen governors who served under the 1776 constitution exercised strong leadership.[8] The legislature was for all practical purposes the state government, and it remained so until the second half of the nineteenth century. Neither the executive, the bureaucracy, or the courts could match the unique, broad rule-making authority that the legislature possessed.

Fear of an overpowerful executive waned slowly. The Jacksonian movement, which witnessed the emergence of mass-based political parties, did much to lessen such fear. While efforts to separate and distribute governing powers more evenly continued in this era, they were initiated less by those seeking to establish strong executive power than by those whose primary goal was greater control of the political process. From the 1820s on, constitutional conventions were held in many states. New Jersey adopted its second constitution in 1844. At that time, its framers added a separate Bill of Rights and eliminated property requirements for voting, but restricted the franchise to white males. The state constitution made the governor directly elected by the people, gave him a veto power, and lengthened his term of office from one to three years, but they denied him the opportunity to succeed himself.[9] Despite these favorable changes, the executive still faced sizable barriers to effective participation in the political process. As Robert Wood explains, "The residue of by-gone tradition, rooted firmly in the preceding constitutions of 1776 and 1844 had engulfed the governor in a maze of legal details and duties. The men whom it was important to appoint were usually beyond his reach; the insignificant were continually his responsibility. The executive had no power to check hasty legislation, to prevent log rolling, and effective minority pressure."[10]

Throughout the Gilded Age, the governor's formal role in policy-making remained relatively small and his informal authority depended on his personality and his party strength. A few post-Civil War governors attained considerable power, but none dominated the institution the way Abbett did during his six years in office. Overshadowed by a dominant legislature and subservient to the business community, most Gilded Age governors were men of timidity and limited vision. They were passive, complacent, or even worse, captured by powerful special interests. The political debts they owed kept them on a course that was more status quo than reformist. They did not seem to grasp the opportunity that the governorship offered to those who could surmount these barriers.

With the exception of Joel Parker, these governors were simply not up to the task. Parker, a Princeton graduate, had been a strong party leader during the Civil War and was quite popular. Like Leon Abbett, he served two nonconsecutive terms as governor: from 1863 to 1866, and again from 1872 to 1875. The other governors seldom reached out for the views of others and pursued policies that were mundane and far removed from political reality. They conformed to the comfortable conservatism of the industrial age and were co-opted by the business community. Put another way, they seemed

perfectly content to allow the legislature to do most of the governing. Not only that, they ignored the issue of equal taxation and allowed the railroads to acquire the Hoboken and Jersey City waterfronts for a mere pittance.

By his own admission, William A. Newell, governor from 1857 to 1860, believed that he should follow rather than lead the legislature. He felt that he should use his veto power sparingly, which says something about the relative importance of the governor to the legislature in those days.[11] Measured against his peers, governors like Charles S. Olden, Marcus L. Ward, Theodore F. Randolph, Joseph D. Bedle, George B. McClellan, George C. Ludlow, Robert S. Green, and George T. Werts, Abbett towered above them. On the intellectual plane only the scholarly Robert Green came close to matching him. He was an even-tempered man with a judicial mind and fine judgment. Indeed, Green proved to be a much better judge than a governor because he lacked the passion for politics.

Skeptical of labor unions and decidedly pro-business, these governors had cozy working relationships with the business community. They were either involved in business themselves or else they catered to business interests, especially the powerful railroads. As Lockard explains: "It would not be accurate to say that they were 'controlled' by businessmen, for they had party and other connections that also influenced their behavior, but of all the significant sources of influence on their official behavior the world of business was certainly predominant."[12] More often than not, they capitulated to the incessant pressure of the business world. To a nation traumatized by civil war and transformed by industrialization, the country seemed hell-bent for a glorious new age. Industry was rapidly expanding in America in general and in New Jersey in particular. However disposed, these governors were reluctant to take risks and even more reluctant to challenge the prevailing status quo.

THE POLITICAL ENVIRONMENT

Abbett's style was the opposite. A shrewd political operator, he responded effectively to the issues that arose largely from the excesses of corporate capitalism. After the Civil War, business entrepreneurs formed large national corporations and combinations that cornered the market on their products and stifled competition. Some corporate giants actually became more powerful than the state and thereby undermined American democracy.

Farmers and industrial workers began to organize to protect their interests and to counteract what they perceived as irresponsible corporate power. Farmers organized the Grange in 1867 and the Farmer's Alliance in 1874. Labor founded the Knights of Labor in 1869 and the American Federation of Labor in 1886. The Knights of Labor played a vital role in democratizing American society. Originated among the needle trades in

Philadelphia, the Knights advocated a broad reform movement that envisioned a community-controlled, producer-oriented economy. They opened their ranks to all workers equally. They accepted women as well as men, blacks alongside whites, inexperienced immigrants and skilled natives, professional people, craftsmen, laborers, small businessmen, and farmers. The Knights believed in temperance, popular education, and democracy; they were apprehensive about the power of capital and the evils of monopoly. They opposed strikes and violence, advocating conciliation and arbitration of labor-management disputes.

PARTY BUILDER AND PARTY LEADER

Seen against this background, Abbett and his Democratic followers built a disciplined and cohesive party organization that they used to win elections and to achieve their political goals and objectives. In an era noted for its intense partisanship, the governor was an avowed partisan who steadfastly maintained his Democratic loyalty. Much of his success as a party leader can be attributed to his proclivity for organizational politics. Men could be found in both major parties who could organize, but few could match his organizational talents. He insisted on strict party discipline and regarded party loyalty as a supreme virtue.

As a party machine governor, Abbett ran things in New Jersey in the heavy-handed and oligarchical fashion of the classic party boss. If he helped to enlarge the state Democratic party, he also ruled it with an iron hand. He rode roughshod over party conventions and quashed insurgents by using preemptive tactics. This was no accidental phenomenon. "The most distinctive feature of late nineteenth century American politics," writes historian Morton Keller, "was its domination by highly organized parties and highly professional politicians. Machines and bosses ran a pervasive, tenacious political system, as third parties and independent reformers repeatedly learned to their sorrow."[13]

American politics was entering an era of maximum popular participation. In his magisterial work *The Good Citizen*, Michael Schudson observes, "These were the years of the highest voter turnout in our entire history. Americans of that era enjoyed politics. They found it simultaneously serious and entertaining, both intellectually and emotionally satisfying."[14] In the northern states, eighty percent or more of those eligible to vote usually voted in presidential elections. This high turnout was partly a tribute to the efficiency of political machines that specialized in turning out voters. The Gilded Age was the golden age of American political parties. The parties owned politics, defined political life, and decided who contested for power. Voters perceived their interests through the parties. As Arthur Schlesinger says, "Party regularity was higher, party loyalty

deeper and party stability greater than at any other time in American history."[15] It was an era when party bosses retired to the smoke-filled rooms and came out with strong candidates and a balanced ticket. These bosses rarely picked candidates they could not control. The smoke-filled rooms were places for cutting deals, making threats, and trading bribes. Simon Cameron, the crusty old Republican boss of Pennsylvania, defined an honest politician as one "who when he is bought stays bought."

The intensity of party competition made it imperative for party managers to turn out as many favorable voters as possible. In addition to buying votes and herding immigrants to the polls, party managers appealed to emotion, ideology, and the self-interest of various social groups. Politics was labor-intensive and this put a premium on organization, especially in states in which the two major parties were evenly matched and the competition was keen. Connecticut, Indiana, New York, and New Jersey were among the most evenly divided and the most competitive states in America. Political campaigns included a wide variety of preliminary meetings. There were numerous assemblies, caucuses, and primary elections that were held to select a ticket of party nominees. A thousand delegates attended the 1877 New Jersey Democratic state convention.

Because illiteracy was rampant in the Gilded Age, many voters had little or no understanding of the issues involved. Party platforms were usually filled with platitudes and empty gestures that paid lip-service to unrealistic goals. Candidates intentionally made their position on issues vague, indefinite, and imprecise. Debates were often emotional, disjointed, and hard to follow. This political situation did not lend itself to an issue-oriented polity; symbols were used to evoke common meanings and common bonds. Various groups, in which social class, religion, and ethnicity were identifying features, transferred their rivalries and antagonisms into party conflicts. As Schudson notes:

> It is not that parties from 1870 to 1900 stood for nothing at all, but it is not easy to find consistency in their stands. The tariff issue over which parties regularly waged their campaigns was a patchwork of local protectionist rate schedules. When Democratic candidate Winfield S. Hancock in 1880 declared it a 'local' issue, he was certainly right, but a generally protectionist Republican Party and a generally free-trade Democracy made rhetorical hay out of what was not much more than special-interest politics on both sides. Similarly, in the 1880s and 1890s, when the currency question divided the parties, the symbolic weight of the issue (silver as the people's money, gold as the businessman's rock of security) provided a party rallying cry more than an ideologically coherent account of conflicting principles or interests.[16]

Class conflict between Democrats and Republicans in New Jersey probably reached its apogee during the last quarter of the nineteenth century. In his efforts to build a broader and more inclusive coalition, Abbett reshaped the state Democratic party, transforming it from the deference politics of the local gentry into an increasingly working-class party. This in turn pushed government into a more activist mode and involved putting together a diverse coalition of predominantly white Anglo-Saxon Protestants, urban ethnic immigrants, and newly enfranchised blacks. The governor achieved considerable unity among Democrats by blending anti-monopoly rhetoric with a class-conscious, antiaristocratic vocabulary that borrowed heavily from the Jacksonians. More often than not, this strategy proved successful in winning majorities in electoral campaigns.

The political class warfare that New Jersey Democrats waged against "monopoly" and "aristocracy" differentiated them from their Republican opponents who favored a free market along with sound money and a protective tariff. Abbett's policy positions favoring labor and the financially hard-pressed cities not only appealed to swing voters, but also defined the emergent majority within his own party. To keep this coalition intact and operating smoothly, Abbett had to maintain a class solidarity among blue-collar workers without driving the Protestant elite out of the party. Democratic leaders included some of the wealthiest men in the state, particularly large landowners and those who held stock in the railroads. Maintaining party unity among such diverse groups was at best a delicate balancing act.

The broad-based Democratic coalition that Abbett and his allies had put together included a wide variety of men—rich, poor, bankers, merchants, farmers, mechanics, laborers, and artisans. While Abbett declared his opposition to monopolies and his support of workingmen, he was no rabble-rouser. Nor was he an unrelenting critic of corporate power. He sought to preserve the essential character of the existing economic system by finding the means to make it more stable and humane. Contrary to the political propaganda distributed by his enemies, he was not the wild-eyed radical and anarchist that they falsely made him out to be. He brought about incremental social change, subtly paving the way for a remarkable transformation of the old social order.

In the 1870s and 1880s, the people of New Jersey were experiencing the shift from an agricultural to an industrial society. It was a very dynamic era: a time of prosperity and wealth, driven by innovation and technology. With the rapid growth of industry there was a tremendous demand for workers to operate textile mills, construct industrial and commercial buildings, manufacture great quantities of goods, and wrest from the earth the raw materials necessary for such economic expansion. From the 1880s on, new workers, most of whom were foreign immigrants, arrived by the thousands in New Jersey. The rise of big business and new technology robbed life, and therefore government, of the simplicity that had previously existed in a pre-industrial and pre-urban society.

Railroads changed the face of America during the nineteenth century. From Maine to California, they played an important role in state politics, but nowhere was that role assumed earlier or more pervasively than in New Jersey. The Camden and Amboy Railroad was chartered as a monopoly in 1830, and soon thereafter rail lines connected it with Jersey City. Other railroads subsequently crisscrossed the state, and railroad mileage more than doubled in each decade between 1850 and 1870. By 1860, every major city in New Jersey had a rail link with other parts of the state. The discovery of anthracite coal in neighboring Pennsylvania in the early 1870s enticed the railroads to enter the profitable coal industry. Before the expansion of the railroads had ended, there were more than 2,500 miles of track squeezed inside the narrow boundaries of the state, and every mile of it had political consequences.[17]

This "railroad fever" fired the entrepreneurial imagination. Given the state's strategic location, railroad construction was concentrated in the main corridor between New York and Philadelphia, the nation's two largest cities. As William Gillette observes:

> Railroads shaped and spurred growth in the state and the region by modernizing the economy. By building up the population of major cities, connecting them with satellite towns and outlying suburbs, and harnessing seaports, railroads created jobs by supplying raw materials to manufacturers, who in turn found larger markets by shipping their finished products. The Mid-Atlantic region became the core of the emerging northeastern megalopolis, whose cities were tied together by railroad tracks. New Jersey at one key crossroad commanded the main line and exploited its advantage as a major transportation hub.[18]

The old standing order was reeling from the impact of industry, burgeoning cities, and the constant arrival of new immigrants. It was a trying period in America and one that evoked deep anxiety. Several decades earlier, the Jacksonians had begun to question the idea of elite rule in a democracy. Since the early days of the Republic, elections were acts of deference, ratifying rule by the landed gentry and moneyed aristocracy who regarded political office as an obligation connected with social standing. In the 1830s and 1840s, political leaders built mass parties as the politics of affiliation gradually replaced the politics of deference. The age of Jackson introduced the common man theory of government, patronage and spoils, and the principle of rotation in office. Wherever a competitive, two-party system took hold by the 1840s, party loyalty assumed a major role in the behavior of the mass electorate. The electorate took its partisan passions seriously, and it was deeply divided on most issues of public policy.

For his part, Abbett began to see the ugly realities of the social order and made up his mind that the patrician class ought not to have an

exclusive right to govern. Consequently, he set out to break the stranglehold of power that this ruling elite maintained over state affairs. With mischievous relish, he sought to dislodge the moneyed aristocracy from their prominent positions of power. Since Abbett believed in meritocracy not aristocracy, he favored providing ordinary people with access to power. The notion of empowering nonestablishment groups remained largely unexplored, undefined, and even unrecognized. Abbett felt strongly that some tangible assistance had to be given to industrial workers and farmers to combat the general sense of alienation that existed among them. This was gesture politics on a big scale. He, of course, did not do all this by himself. Nor was he the only leader who recognized the need for such change. Other political actors were involved in bringing about the new social order, but Abbett was its principal architect in New Jersey. There were skeptics—in politics, in the press, and in the academic world—but he ultimately proved them wrong.

ON THE STUMP

With his good looks and resonant voice, Abbett used these personal assets to advantage, especially while on the stump. He was an articulate public speaker whose words were enlivened with populist denunciations. Those who heard him speak were captivated by his florid oratory that flowed effortlessly from behind his brown beard. His speeches were filled with the usual bombast and dazzling rhetorical flourishes that characterized public speaking in the Gilded Age. According to those who heard him speak, Abbett was not a polished orator in the flamboyant style of his time, but he could hold large crowds in thrall with his commanding stage presence and his colorful use of political prose. Newspaper stories indicate that the governor created an aura of excitement wherever he went. People flocked from far around to see and hear him speak; many came by horse and buggy, especially those who attended the local county agricultural fairs that were highly popular events. He drew even larger audiences in the cities.

Abbett ran for office on populist themes that aroused the electorate: the ideal of egalitarianism and equal opportunity. Political campaigns usually involved the traditional paraphernalia of mass democracy —volunteers, rallies, torchlight evening processions, leaflets, posters, and pin-on buttons. Inspirational oratory, interspersed with brass bands and martial music, provided lively entertainment that the general public enjoyed immensely. Party workers, especially those on the payroll, were eager to participate in an activist polity. Campaigning from the front porch was still feasible in those days, and class rhetoric and a simplified version of capitalistic ideology held sway.

Abbett was a determined and inveterate campaigner, whether on or off the ticket. When most people turned their attention to politics in the fall season, he could be found on the stump exhorting Democrats to unite behind their party. Party regularity and straight-ticket voting were more prevalent in those days.[19] When Abbett first ran for governor in 1883, he took his message about railroad taxation directly to the people and barnstormed the state appealing for votes. In rallying his loyal followers, the Hudson Democrat articulated a coherent party policy and encouraged them to jump on the party bandwagon before it was too late.

Whenever Abbett spoke, he appealed mostly to mainstream Democrats and those who felt alienated, marginalized, or left out. Despite his antimonopoly stance, he was by no means hostile or antagonistic toward business. On the contrary, Abbett had a good working relationship with the business community, which tended to temper his views and his tone. He played a major role in attracting industry to New Jersey and in developing its political economy. The governor was committed to saving capitalism rather than overthrowing it. He was no Marxist or radical socialist as some of his critics claimed. Like the immigrant city bosses who ran the urban machines, he came to terms with his business and industrial counterparts. As governor, he collaborated with city bosses and corporate leaders. Unlike previous governors, however, he did not allow himself to be captured or co-opted by the business community. He insisted that democracy not merely accommodate the interests of business, but that business accommodate itself to democracy.

ANTIMONOPOLY POLITICS

Where and when machine politics flourished, as they did in New Jersey beginning about 1870, the call for curbing the unbridled power of corporate monopolies and trusts was insistent. Ever since the Jacksonian era, the Democrats had resisted the supremacy of the business world. They railed against monopolies, banks, high tariffs, and entrenched social privilege. These long-standing economic and cultural grievances were instrumental in shaping Abbett's political philosophy. In his inaugural message of January 1884, the governor went after the railroads on the tax issue. In years past, they had been notorious for evading state and local taxes. He sent a clear antimonopoly message that resonated with voters. The public at large was concerned about the growing economic power of the railroads, especially true of the Pennsylvania Railroad that was the leading railroad in the country. Acquiring extraordinary power, it became the mightiest of the mighty, with its almost military-style discipline and organization and its vast resources of men and equipment. In the late 1880s, the Pennsylvania was racing to complete a rail route west to

compete with the New York Central, the Erie, and the Baltimore & Ohio, which were each pushing in the same direction.

As much as any politician in the country, Abbett understood the essence of the political game and his battle to tax the railroads provided the perfect illustration. The political stakes were high risk, high gain because it was considered political suicide for a New Jersey politician to even go near the railroad tax issue. Governor George C. Ludlow, who had preceded Abbett, had tried to tax the railroads, but he failed miserably. In retaliation, the powerful railroads made sure that Ludlow's public career ended abruptly. Fully aware of the fate that befell Ludlow, Abbett was still willing to put his power and prestige on the line.

It was an auspicious time for such a venture. This was truly the meeting of the moment, the man, and the place. At a time when public distrust of corporate monopolies ran high, the railroads brazenly flaunted their power. In the end, Abbett beat the railroads at their own political game. His smashing victory established him as a force to be reckoned with, but it came at a heavy price. In retribution, the railroads used their political clout to defeat Abbett in his bid to become a U. S. senator, apparently his most cherished ambition. Again, it is noteworthy that U.S. senators were not elected directly by the people in the Gilded Age; they were chosen by their respective state legislatures. In plain fact, Abbett never lost a popular election. He was truly a man of the people.

ABBETT'S PRIVATE LIFE

In his private life, Abbett was typically kind and gentle. He led a busy life, surrounded by close friends and affecting the lifestyle afforded only by those whose wealth was extraordinary. Politically he may have championed the poor and disadvantaged, but socially he gravitated toward the rich and powerful. He enjoyed dining at fashionable restaurants like Delmonicos in New York City. An avid yachtsman, Abbett sailed in the waters off Long Island Sound and was a member of the New Rochelle Yacht Club, serving as its commodore in the late 1880s. His ability to hobnob with the rich and famous was one of his many contradictions, but his constituents did not seem to mind. They secretly envied his strutting in public and mingling among high society.

By religion, Abbett was an Episcopalian. He and his wife Mary were members of Saint Matthew's Episcopal Church in Jersey City. Serious in their Episcopalianism, they attended church regularly. They also liked to socialize and were one of the most stylish and glamorous couples in New Jersey. They had three children and raised them in sumptuous upper middle class comfort. Abbett cared deeply about his family, and they in turn brought out the gentler aspects of his character.

According to local newspaper stories, he showed a tender, paternal warmth toward his children. Mary Abbett, as mentioned, died of cancer in 1879, five years before her husband became governor. Widowed at the age of forty-three, Leon never remarried. His solid marriage of seventeen years had provided him with all the emotional sustenance he needed.

Abbett's personality was as multidimensional as his leadership. He was a bundle of competing emotions. Friends sensed a burning inner drive and a relentless energy that fired his ambition. He had an enormous sense of self-worth and a large enough ego to be angered, profoundly angered, when things did not go the way he expected, or when he was otherwise adequately provoked. Under these circumstances, he could explode into a fierce rage and be vindictive and mean-spirited. This dimension unveiled his dark side. There is some indication that he detested this streak in himself, but his chafed ego sometimes got in the way. In public, he succeeded in masking his anger, at least to the extent that rugged individualism allowed. To harness these negative emotions, he developed a marvelous self-control that tempered his anger and aggressiveness.

Whatever his virtues and vices, Abbett struggled to deal with his own failings and human imperfections, but he did not allow them to interfere with satisfying his intense personal power needs. Psychologically drawn to politics at an early age, he had a temperament that was well suited for the political arena. He accepted the inherent messiness of the real world and displayed a tolerance for chaos and ambiguity. At the same time, he could efficiently sort out, accommodate, and integrate conflicting views. A flexible politician, Abbett was receptive to new ideas and always tried to keep his options open. Seldom did he allow himself to get rigidly boxed into a corner without finding some avenue of retreat. Although he was open-minded in discussion, once he made up his mind he clung to his opinions with unbending stubbornness. That stubbornness, however, did nothing whatsoever to diminish the fervor with which he worked to achieve his goals. Constant achievement was as necessary to his spirit as it was to the most industrious nineteenth-century capitalist. This personal element is essential to understand, because it was such a vitally important aspect of his power.

The governor was a creature of habit. Prone to wake early in the morning, he obtained daily exercise by taking brisk walks around Van Vorst Park in Jersey City, where he and his family resided. They had moved from Hoboken to Jersey City in 1866 and lived for awhile at 16 Sussex Place. Jersey City was the seat of county government in Hudson County. It also was an Irish stronghold. In the late 1880s, the Abbetts resided in a large brownstone mansion at 288 Montgomery Street that was furnished in the ornate and opulent style of the period. A portrait of his beloved Mary hung above the fireplace. At the time, this was an upscale, trendy neighborhood comparable in status to Gramercy Park in

New York City. Some of the most distinguished citizens in New Jersey resided there.

Conservative Bourbon Democrat Joseph D. Bedle, who served as governor from 1875 to 1878, lived at 473 Jersey Avenue, which was just around the corner from Abbett. Although the two men were friends, they came from rival factions and from sharply adversarial positions within the Democratic party. They had been neighbors since 1866, when they first lived next door to each other on Sussex Place. Abbett saw Bedle as an adversary, not an enemy. Further down Jersey Avenue was the residence of Republican Jonathan Dixon, a state supreme court justice who ran against Abbett for governor in 1883. In terms of commuting distance, Abbett's residence was little more than an hour's train ride to the State House in Trenton.

Abbett's closest friend, both socially and politically, was his other next-door neighbor, William C. Heppenheimer, who served in the dual capacity as state comptroller and inspector general in Abbett's second administration. Heppenheimer and Abbett were not far apart in age and became fast friends. They practiced law in the same office building at 229 Broadway in New York City. Descended from German aristocracy, Heppenheimer was a brilliant lawyer who had graduated from Columbia College and Harvard Law School. He provided a bridge to the world of finance and to the German immigrant community.[20]

In addition to Heppenheimer, dinner guests at the Abbett household frequently included Allan L. McDermott, chairman of the state Democratic Committee; William Brinkerhoff, Democratic state senator from Hudson County; Willard C. Fisk, the governor's private secretary; John McGill, his personal physician; and Alexander T. McGill, who served as chancellor of the New Jersey Court of Chancery. These were men with reputations for objectivity and wise judgment, and they advised the governor and constituted his kitchen cabinet.

CHALLENGING THE YANKEE ELITE

In the aftermath of the Civil War, the Yankee elite in New Jersey gradually began losing its long-standing political support. Apparently oblivious to the sea change that had already taken place in the state's social mixture, they failed to acknowledge the altered circumstances. Their objectives were minimalist government and a larger sphere for the workings of the marketplace. With the decline in the tight oligarchy of political power held by the Yankee elite on a statewide basis, Abbett and his followers sought to oust them from their prominent positions of power in the Democratic party. The former were a group of reactionaries protesting the disappearance of a bygone agrarian past, while the latter were mostly urban liberals seeking to mitigate the worst abuses of capitalism. The stresses and strains within the Democratic party were generating a contentious atmosphere. Internal dissension grew amid chronic factionalism. There was one internal party dispute after another. As time went on, the chasm between the two factions became wide and deep. The spotlight on Abbett's acrimonious dealings with the Yankee elite intensified when his feud with U.S. Senator Theodore Randolph broke into the open in 1875. The growing animosity and tension between Abbett and Randolph had been brewing for sometime, anticipating a formal break. Their relationship was now one of mutual contempt; they intensely disliked each other.

Almost simultaneously, a new breed of immigrant big-city bosses was emerging with a strong cultural and moral basis for transforming the political system. They were men who came predominantly from the working classes. They subscribed to Abbett's common man theory of government, but their rise to power and less-than-reputable status offended the established order. Yankee hegemony was beginning to give way to the Irish political ascendancy, at least in Hudson County where Abbett's brand of populism first caught fire. Rudolph Vecoli put it best when he observed, "Men of foreign stock now took their place in the councils of state with the scions of the oldest and most distinguished Jersey families, the Stevens, the Frelinghuysens, the Stocktons, the Voorhees and the Zabriskies."[21] Still the links between them were not strong. The old guard continued to embrace a laissez-faire ideology to the extent that Adam Smith had originally envisaged.

At first glance, it seemed like irreconcilable political difference between Abbett and Randolph, but their feud went much deeper than that. Much of this conflict reflected class differences within the Democratic party and created an intense scramble for party control that was both personal and ideological. These intramural battles set into motion a bifactionalism that pitted conservative Randolph Democrats against progressive Abbett Democrats. Theodore Fitz Randolph, no friend of Abbett, was the wealthy scion of the famous Randolph clan of Virginia. Elegant and pompous to the marrow of his bones, Randolph had impeccable Yankee credentials and was a member in good standing of the social aristocracy. A Rutgers graduate and former Know-Nothing, he was a dangerous and indefatigable opponent. Popularly known as "Old Moneybags," Randolph was president of the Morris and Essex Railroad. He had served as governor of New Jersey from 1869 to 1872 and then served one term in the U. S. Senate from 1875 to 1881.

Randolph and Abbett differed sharply in ideology and outlook. Their struggle for party control attracted much public attention and media coverage, because it pitted a blueblood aristocrat with a strong sense of privilege against an upstart commoner with a strong sense of

egalitarianism. It provided a classic match-up that accentuated their class differences. Bear in mind that New Jersey was a state where blue bloodlines and Yankee institutions still had a potent claim on the collective imagination.

Party leadership was controlled by relatively few men. The Randolph faction, commonly known as the State House Ring, was "a masterful coterie of party managers, who pulled the strings of politics behind the curtains of officialism."[22] They were also nicknamed the "Board of Guardians," because they used their power to minimize government interference with the railroads. Their tight grip on the state Democratic party stirred class and ethnic tensions between Randolph loyalists who favored business and rule by a capitalist-bourgeois elite and Abbett supporters who favored communal needs and the cause of the common man. Although both men were Democrats, they were far apart ideologically and eventually broke with each other politically. Randolph did not like Abbett for any number of reasons, including Abbett's successful efforts to deny him party control. There was bad blood between them.

A talented young newspaperman by the name of William Edgar Sackett, who was born in New York City in 1848, watched these battles at close range. He was one of the most perceptive commentators on the New Jersey political scene during the Gilded Age. A muckraking political journalist, Sackett described Abbett's style and strategy as a public person in masterly fashion:

All through his legislative career Mr. Abbett's course had been one of unfaltering opposition to the domination of the State House magnates. He had hauled them to the bar of public opinion as purse-proud aristocrats who had no sympathy with the masses; and springing always to the defense of the common people, he had posed as the Great Commoner of the state. The State House people were indeed a trifle overstrained and high-toned, and Abbett was specially obnoxious to them from the two points of view that he had made himself their political enemy, and that he was "not of their set."[23]

It is in this twin context that Abbett's rise to power and his subsequent behavior as governor is best understood. He defined the class struggle in New Jersey by defending the working poor who endured demonstrable hardships. Aware of these fundamental shifts in the underlying economic strata, Abbett set about to remedy the situation. He faced difficult contradictions among competing forces within the Democratic camp and his choices in policy were seriously constrained by the realities of economic life. Still, Abbett understood the stakes involved and recognized that the time was ripe for major legislative initiatives. Under his leadership, the Democrats enacted a series of labor laws that improved conditions of industrial employment. As governor, he personally intervened in labor disputes and found new ways of resolving them. Notable was his intervention in a violent strike at the Clark Thread Mills in Newark, and in a lockout at the Oxford Iron and Nail Company in Warren County. To control labor violence and to protect public safety, the governor created the first state police force in New Jersey, but he was careful to do so without being labeled a strike-breaking governor. That was quite a feat.

A complex and controversial personality, Abbett was filled with contradictions and ambiguities. Ambitious for himself as well as for his adopted state, he combined opportunism with principle to advance his cause. He was the epitome of the pragmatic man of action and practical thought, responding to issues of social injustice not so much as a warm-hearted liberal but more as a tough-minded, very self-centered, self-oriented man. Abbett positioned himself correctly on most issues, moved toward the middle of the political spectrum, and projected multiple images that enabled him to be all things to all people. He had a passion for change and inclusion. Moreover, he enjoyed the job of being governor tremendously and successfully conveyed that impression to the general public. He instinctively knew that having the support of the people of New Jersey was extremely important. All his life he took pleasure in his daily work, in using his power and celebrity to help others less fortunate than he.

ENDNOTES

1 William E. Sackett, *Modern Battles of Trenton* (New York: The Neale Publishing Company, 1914), 12:13.

2 Personal data and physical characteristics of Leon Abbett are taken from his U. S. Passport issued on May 9, 1874.

3 See Leslie Lipson, *The American Governor from Figurehead to Leader* (Chicago: University of Chicago Press, 1939).

4 John F. Reynolds, *Testing Democracy: Electoral Behavior and Progressive Reform in New Jersey, 1880-1920* (Chapel Hill: University of North Carolina Press, 1988), 54.

5 *Ibid.*, 61.

6 Biographical information about Leon Abbett can be found in standard sources such as Charles Robson, *The Biographical Encyclopedia of New Jersey of the Nineteenth Century* (Philadelphia: 1877), 316-317; Mary D. Ogden, ed., *Memorial Cyclopedia of New Jersey* (Newark: 1915), 2:28; William H. Shaw, *History of Essex and Hudson Counties* (Philadelphia: Everts & Peck, 1884), 2:1078; *The National Cyclopaedia of American Biography* (New York: 1898), 458; and *The Dictionary of American Biography* (New York: 1956), 1:23. These biographical sketches, however, must be used with some degree of caution, because they contain errors and specific inaccuracies. Abbett's personal history is found in the annual edition of the *New Jersey Legislative Manual* (compiled by Thomas F. Fitzgerald) for each year that he presided as governor. The earliest biographical sketch is found in the *Jersey City Herald*, April 22, 1871.

7 Duane Lockard, *The New Jersey Governor: A Study in Political Power* (Princeton: D. Van Nostrand, 1964), 9.

8 Lockard, *The New Jersey Governor*, 6-7. See also Paul A. Stellhorn and Michael J. Birkner, eds., *The Governors of New Jersey 1664-1974* (Trenton: New Jersey Historical Commission, 1982).

9 See Robert F. Williams, "New Jersey's State Constitutions: From Ridicule to Respect," *New Jersey Lawyer* 185 (June 1997): 8-11.

10 Robert C. Wood, *The Metropolitan Governor* (unpublished dissertation, Cambridge: Harvard University, 1949), 164.

11 Stellhorn and Birkner, *The Governors of New Jersey*, 127.

12 Lockard, *The New Jersey Governor*, 7.

13 Morton Keller, *Affairs of State: Public Life in Late Nineteenth Century America* (Cambridge: Harvard University Press, 1977), 522.

14 See Michael Schudson, *The Good Citizen: A History of American Civic Life* (New York: The Free Press, 1998), 145.

15 Arthur M. Schlesinger, Jr., *The Cycles of American History* (Boston: Houghton Mifflin, 1986), 260-261.

16 Schudson, *The Good Citizen*, 166.

17 For a fascinating account of the development of the railroads in New Jersey, see Wheaton J. Lane, *From Indian Trail to Iron Horse* (Princeton: Princeton University Press, 1939). See also Map of the Railroads of New Jersey 1890 (Copyright 1887 by Van Cleef and Betts).

18 William Gillette, *Jersey Blue: Civil War Politics in New Jersey 1854-1865* (New Brunswick: Rutgers University Press, 1995), 11-12.

19 See John F. Reynolds and Richard L. McCormick, "Outlawing 'Treachery': Split Tickets and Ballot Laws in New York and New Jersey, 1880-1910," *Journal of American History* 72 (1986): 835-858.

20 Daniel Van Winkle, *History of the Municipalities of Hudson County* (New York: 1924), vol. 2, 141-142.

21 Rudolph J. Vecoli, *The People of New Jersey* (Princeton: D. Van Nostrand, 1965), 162. This book provides an interesting historical analysis of the transfer of power in New Jersey during the late nineteenth century.

22 Sackett, *Modern Battles of Trenton*, 12:13.

23 William E. Sackett, *Modern Battles of Trenton* (Trenton: John L. Murphy, Printer, 1895), 1:144.

Understanding Abbett's Political World

To understand Leon Abbett more thoroughly as a political actor, we need to reconstruct and examine the political world in which he operated. He had to deal with a host of difficult social problems that were fundamentally caused by the rise of urban industrialism. In what would become a powder keg of the labor movement, New Jersey had all the essential ingredients: a large industrial workforce, the increasing concentration of economic power in large corporations, the exploitation of immigrants, violent labor strikes, the divisive issues of race and religion, and bitter and unyielding conflict between Yankee Protestants and Irish Catholics. These societal and economic forces combined to make the forging of public policy by the governor a hard job.

For a generation or two, no other Democratic leader in New Jersey had so consciously and successfully developed a strategy for helping the working classes. Staying the course, Abbett built his career around them, especially among urban, immigrant Catholics who became his core constituency. The business titans, whose wealth controlled capital, dominated the men, women, and children whose hands did most of the labor. These workers groped for ways to escape an almost suffocating ideology of laissez-faire economics and its companion Protestant work ethic. They cried out for human rights as well as for better working conditions. Their sense of grievance and deprivation was legitimate. Desperation sanctioned new approaches to labor-management problems.

Workers experienced long hours, low wages, harsh working conditions, and great fluctuations in employment opportunities. They constantly struggled with the reality of sudden wage cuts, job layoffs, and unemployment. Their niggardly wages actually fell as industrialization progressed. They could be dismissed from their jobs without any notice or due process, and with no recourse. Nor was much attention paid to

worker safety. Dangerous occupational health and safety hazards resulted in injuries and fatalities suffered at the workplace. Women and children toiled in loft sweatshops under deplorable conditions. To reduce the costs of production, businessmen contracted with state prison officials to get convicts to do piecework. The company town, with its substandard company housing and high-priced company store, exploited workers and degraded their human dignity. Company towns were usually located in isolated and remote rural areas. Such isolation facilitated control over the town by excluding outside troublemakers and alternative employment. It allowed management to impose discipline through eviction from the community as a penalty for breaking the rules—such as prohibitions against joining a union or trying to promote one.

Not surprisingly, labor unrest was prevalent in New Jersey during the Gilded Age. Strikes, unionizing efforts, socialist agitation, violent confrontations between workers and police, and the systematic suppression of union leaders by corporate detectives were regular occurrences. A conservative judiciary restricted the freedom of unions to strike, picket, or boycott. The courts generally favored capitalists over trade unions, creditors over debtors, and railroads over farmers and consumers. Too often, human rights were subordinated to property rights. The labor movement was still in its nascent stages and trying to flex its political muscle, but union power paled by comparison to corporate power. Without a level playing field, labor had little say or clout at the bargaining table. The workers' main weapon was the strike. Employers countered strikes by hiring replacement workers, usually blacks, which then exacerbated racial tensions. They resorted to various tactics to keep the unions out. Many employers insisted that employees sign "yellow dog contracts" as a condition of employment; workers had to swear they were not members of a labor union and that they would not join one while in the employ of the company. If they did join, they were subject to immediate dismissal.

The giant national corporations threatened to put democracy itself at risk. A major source of anxiety that hovered like a dark cloud over democracy was the gnawing fear that the urban masses were mere pawns in the hands of those who controlled corporate wealth. The antimonopolists railed against the evils of these big corporations and trusts. Leading thinkers, such as Henry Demarest Lloyd, were alarmed by the threat that the large conglomerates posed to democracy. In his book *Wealth Against Commonwealth*, published in 1894, Lloyd argued that the power of the trusts was pervasive and it corrupted every aspect of American life. The social critics were concerned that democracy would not endure if private concentrations of wealth were permitted to become more powerful than the state. Henry Adams, a proper Boston Brahmin, had raised this question in 1870 and cited the Erie Railroad as a prime example. Adams had no political aspirations, so he said whatever he pleased, but in this case he

was right. Businessmen disliked competition and did their best to avoid it. They set up gentlemen's agreements, pools, and holding companies to control production and prices.

Such conditions as business cycles of boom-and-bust, poverty, illiteracy, ill health, and racial intolerance were viewed largely as situations to be endured. Widespread unemployment, bankruptcy, and labor unrest followed the depression of 1873, but these phenomena did not seem to deter long-range economic growth. Two decades later, in 1893, the nation was again convulsed in depression. In the mid-1890s, an unregulated boom had given way to an unregulated bust. Political leaders regarded economic depression as a natural calamity beyond human control. The aftermath of the Civil War brought with it alluring economic opportunities, at least for those with the vision, cunning, and strength to seize them. Improved technology, some of it produced before the war, opened new fields of endeavor. The invention of the telegraph, the telephone, the reaper, and the Kelly-Bessemer method of processing steel were all major advances that changed the way people did things. Almost everyone living in the cities had electricity or natural gas in their homes. There were typewriters in most offices, and many people bought one of the new Kodak cameras.

People generally believed that the virtues of hard work, diligence, and thrift would reward anyone with social and economic mobility. The contemporary Horatio Alger novels that glorified the work ethic were more myth than reality. There were exceptions, of course, but most people did not reap the financial rewards of the emerging industrial order. Those who failed commonly blamed themselves for their difficulties rather than the political or economic system. The tensions produced by failure and penury disrupted family life. Charity programs were few in number and those that existed offered only meager help. The settlement house movement, legal aid programs, and professional social work were just beginning to appear. Poverty and squalor, along with the spread of cholera, typhoid, tuberculosis, and mental illness, ultimately forced local governments to take care of their poor. The results were modest at best because such efforts did not take into account the ways in which economic power made poverty a consequence of the way the system worked. When everything else failed, the only alternative was the awful fate of the county workhouse or public asylum. Perhaps more than other social institutions, the orphanage symbolized the welfare state in the nineteenth century.

The sudden modification of normal conditions posed a threat to one's individual security. People had been subjected to a succession of technological shocks, each of which evoked deep emotions that ranged from fear of the new to maintaining things as they were. Improved communication made it possible for people to send messages and to talk with one another over long distances. With the invention of the telegraph, the telephone, and the incandescent electric light bulb, anything was possible from instant communication to instant illumination. Central power plants, paved city streets, and arc lamps for outdoor lighting were all added to the municipal infrastructure. Rapid transit technology progressed from the horse-drawn car to the cable car, to the electric trolley, to the elevated railway, and finally to the subway. These new emerging technologies kept pace with changing social conditions and provided the amenities that made central cities more livable.

Among the more spectacular engineering feats was the construction of the Brooklyn Bridge that opened in 1883, the year Abbett first ran for governor. This magnificent suspension bridge, considered a technological marvel, was designed and built under the supervision of German-born John Augustus Roebling. His steel mills, located in Trenton, provided the wire cables for the Brooklyn Bridge.[1] At the same time, Thomas Alva Edison was fast becoming America's premier inventor. He had assembled a small but immensely talented research team in Menlo Park, New Jersey. They grappled with the complex design problems of the light bulb, the electrical power generator, and the grid system necessary to distribute this power economically over a large area. They perfected the first commercially viable light bulb in 1879 and the world's first central electric light power station in 1882. Technology not only made contemporary life more convenient, but it also made it more complicated.

In this modern world of complexity, relative freedom existed to advance the interests of various social groups. There were few formal restraints on the organizing of group interests, but the freedom to organize was not the same thing as the capacity to do so. Profits were to be made and fortunes accumulated by those who were not overly prudent or scrupulous in their financial and political dealings. Money represented power, and poverty was a sure sign of powerlessness. People were spurring themselves to excel and some took their acquisitive behavior to extremes. Ruthless and arrogant businessmen—robber barons—made their fortunes in railroads, coal, steel, oil, shipping, and stock manipulation. Gilded Age entrepreneurs like John D. Rockefeller and Andrew Carnegie believed the hurly-burly of the marketplace sorted out gifted, farsighted leaders, men who would "administer surplus wealth for the good of the people."[2] The post-Civil War boom stoked the economy and enabled American captains of industry to amass great wealth, but it also created a propertyless and dependent laboring class.

Andrew Carnegie, who ruled the steel industry in a ruthless manner, became the wealthiest man in America, while philanthropy made him respectable. He pushed upward and onward in his relentless pursuit of wealth and without much concern for the common man. The "gospel of wealth," as articulated by Baptist minister Russell H. Conwell, became the dominant ethos of the business community.[3] The creed of Carnegie was

reinforced by the theories of Charles Darwin, the English biologist. Both laissez-faire economics and Darwinian evolution fostered the belief that "survival of the fittest" through free competition in the marketplace was the best way to achieve progress in the commercial and industrial world. Darwin's theories clashed with traditional religious beliefs. Herbert Spenser, who was Darwin's disciple, took it upon himself to spread the word. He articulated the philosophy of Social Darwinism in his work *Social Statics* that conveyed the message he brought from biology to politics. During a celebrated trip to America in 1882, Spencer introduced Social Darwinism to Gilded Age scholars and pundits.[4] No other English thinker, except Darwin himself, exerted a more powerful influence on American thought.

POLITICAL ORGANIZATIONS AND PARTY AFFILIATIONS

Generally speaking, political parties represented coalitions of people united by ethnocultural loyalties and tended to embody the stances or styles of different religious and ethnic groups. They recruited a wide variety of men, but in each a certain type clustered and predominated. The Democratic party was a mixture of native Protestants, immigrants, farmers, and small businessmen. The party's rank-and-file, however, was mostly industrial workers, but its leadership was dominated by the Yankee elite. The Republicans, who formed their party in the mid-1850s, appealed to similar constituencies and their leaders were mostly Protestant businessmen. Because the Republican party absorbed remnants of the Know-Nothings, this new party would not have much claim on Irish Catholic affections. As the party of the native farmer, small town businessman, and skilled tradesman, the Republican party was not one in which the immigrant, urban, wage-earning, unskilled laborer could feel comfortable or at home.

Voters were psychologically attached to their parties and passed party loyalty from fathers to sons. Women were legally denied the right to vote, but candidates were well aware of their influence and courted them assiduously. Both Democrats and Republicans had "ladies" auxiliaries that participated in campaigns. However, the female exclusion from suffrage kept them from the inner circles of party life. Ironically, women had been granted the right to vote in New Jersey as early as 1790, but their enfranchisement did not last long. It was rescinded by statute in 1807, and then it was revoked in the state constitution of 1844. Women were barred from running for public office and they were also denied the right to own property, practice law, and testify in court. If they divorced, they were often denied the custody of children. Until the late 1840s, women had been prohibited from attending college, and those who subsequently did so were expected to fulfill only submissively domestic roles, as dictated by the cult of true womanhood.

Running for public office was considered men's work and politicians were mostly white males. Political parties, with their local clubhouses, provided a gathering place for men and male-bonding. Under the state constitution, only white men were allowed to vote. Universal male suffrage was not achieved in New Jersey until 1874. To comply with the Fifteenth Amendment, the legislature passed a law that removed the earlier restriction and permitted black men to vote.

In 1894, the year Abbett died, Mary Philbrook of Newark, then twenty-two years of age, was the first woman to apply for admission to the New Jersey bar. The state supreme court denied her application, refusing to interpret either constitutional or statutory language as granting permission for women to practice law. The court ruled that such a radical change of public policy had to come from the legislature. Undeterred, Philbrook then lobbied it and secured passage of a statute in 1895 that opened the practice of law to women. She had broken through the glass ceiling of her day.[5]

Since women were barred from voting, the size of the electorate was reduced accordingly. In 1890, white females in New Jersey outnumbered white males 699,842 to 696,739. The same was true of people of color. The federal census recorded 24,272 colored females as compared with 24,080 colored males. The largest concentration of people of color was in Newark, where 4,141 of them resided. It should be noted that the "colored" census category included nonwhites other than blacks (mostly Chinese, Japanese, and Native American Indians).

In 1890, the total New Jersey electorate numbered 413,530 adult males of voting age. A breakdown of this figure reveals that 254,633 were native-born whites; 144,333 were immigrants; and the remaining 14,564 were men of color.[6] It was strictly a man's world and one in which politics was controlled exclusively by white males. Blacks had recently won their freedom and the right to vote, but they were ideologically written off as being inherently inferior. Politics for black men was not the same as politics for white men. Blacks were a despised subculture, and as such they were treated as second class citizens. "The institution of slavery," writes historian James Horton, "formed our understanding of race and the relationships between races in America."[7] That was certainly true in Abbett's time.

The oppression of blacks served the economic as well as the class interests of those comfortably ensconced in the white power structure. Segregated churches, schools, cemeteries, and public accommodations were the accepted norm. In 1896, the U.S. Supreme Court, in the landmark case of *Plessy v. Ferguson*, ruled that "separate but equal" was constitutional and thereby reinforced segregation. The College of New Jersey (now Princeton University) was controlled by conservative Presbyterians. Considered a rich man's school, Princeton was a socially conservative institution that admitted only white male Protestant students. Among the

clusters of denominational colleges, Princeton was the most favorably disposed toward Southerners. Woodrow Wilson, a son of the South, who was born in Virginia and reared in Georgia, graduated from Princeton in the class of 1879. He later became president of Princeton (1902–1910) and used this position as a stepping stone to become governor of New Jersey and then president of the United States.

In March 1863, Rutgers was designated as New Jersey's public land-grant institution. Its trustees established a scientific and agricultural department that opened in 1865. In 1888, James Dickson Carr was the first black student to be admitted to Rutgers; whereas Princeton, with its strong Southern influence, did not admit a black student until the 1940s during World War II. Meanwhile, the neighboring states of New York and Pennsylvania each established a separate college for blacks. New Jersey did not do so. Illiteracy was a way of controlling blacks; higher education for women and blacks was not encouraged.

New Jersey was a racist society, and most white people blatantly displayed their racism. With the end of Reconstruction and the emergence of the Ku Klux Klan, the Gilded Age witnessed the high tide of racism in America. White supremacy, which espoused racial purity and condemned interracial marriage, pervaded its social and economic life. The intellectual respectability of racism simply added to the suffering of blacks. Hostility toward them was overt and hardly concealed. Although many Republicans had been opposed to slavery, they accepted black inferiority as a fact of life. Few Republicans accepted black intellectual equality with whites. Most Democrats were racists.

In the early stages of his career, Abbett was an avowed racist. He towed the party line when it came to race and race policy. As a Copperhead Democrat during the Civil War, he had opposed federal efforts to advance blacks, which earned him the support of most whites. For nearly twenty years, he defended white supremacy and voiced racial prejudice. So did most other Democrats in New Jersey. In a stunning reversal, however, Abbett abruptly changed his position on the race issue when he first ran for governor in 1883. He appealed to blacks and promised to secure passage of civil rights legislation. This was a radical stance for his time. Critics charged that he did so solely as a matter of political expediency. They could see him manipulating the issue for votes. This criticism may have been well taken, but no one could deny the fact that he forged an alliance with blacks that helped Democrats win close elections. By participating in the baptism of a black child in Newark, he, in effect, built a bridge to the black community. This was another instance in which he felt the potential gains outweighed the political risks.

Intense partisanship was the order of the day. Political parties performed valuable functions that made them indispensable during the Gilded Age. They served as a vehicle for mass mobilization, a transmitter

of information and communication, and an agency that provided welfare for the urban poor. City bosses supplied the links between government and the people—a linkage that meant jobs, food, shelter, medical care, and various other kinds of practical assistance. They dealt with the problems of poverty and immigrant assimilation by acting as employment agencies and by dispensing welfare. The basket of food and the bucket of coal served as the currency of exchange. All the party asked for and received in return were their votes on election day.

PARTY MEMBERSHIP AND PARTY COMPETITION

Since the two major parties in New Jersey were of comparable strength numerically, they were highly competitive. Voters often elected a governor of one party and a legislature of another. The Republicans dominated the small rural counties, which gave them almost continuous control of the state senate; whereas the Democrats, with large majorities in the big cities, usually won control of the general assembly. The Democrats had a virtual lock on the governorship during the Gilded Age. Patronage and party loyalty were too important to be taken lightly. With this objective in mind, Abbett distributed the plethora of public jobs and state contracts to keep his supporters happy. He consolidated his power through patronage, attention to the demands of competing ethnic groups, and the provision of public services through partisan channels. He made sure that political power was concentrated in the governor's office, where he maintained tight control of the party apparatus and played a major role in policymaking. Politics and policy were for him inseparable. Abbett believed that good public policy made good politics. Patronage in Hudson County was the equal opportunity employer of its day. Immigrants, who sought public employment, had little choice but to become beholden to local politicians. As the power of such politicians grew, so did corruption as a means of their holding onto that power.

Party politics played its part, for the cities in the 1880s were becoming increasingly Democratic, the split between urban and rural was well established, and practical considerations of party control figured prominently. Since elections for governor in New Jersey normally fell in off-presidential years, state politics had considerable latitude to chart its own course without being unduly influenced by the impact of national tides. Gubernatorial elections were closely contested and the margin of victory was usually very small. Of the eleven elections conducted for governor between 1865 and 1895, six were won by margins of less than two percent of the total vote and only once did the winner get more than fifty-four percent.[8] The Democrats captured the governorship nine times in

those eleven elections. This meant that the Republicans controlled the executive branch only six of those thirty years.

The Republicans worked hard to convey a posture favorable to business and free enterprise. They countered Democratic strength in the cities by attracting voters in the Protestant suburbs and rural farming communities. Several commanding personalities set the tone for New Jersey's Republican party. John W. Griggs, George A. Halsey, Garret A. Hobart, John Kean, Jr., Charles S. Olden, William W. Phelps, William J. Sewell, and Marcus L. Ward were among the major Republican leaders. They made their own competitive egalitarian appeals to the electorate, but they pitched their message more toward the middle and upper classes. Their supporters were mostly mainline Protestants who tended to be pro-business, antiunion, anti-Catholic and pro-temperance. The vast majority of Civil War veterans remained loyal to the party of Abraham Lincoln, their fallen hero. They also admired General Ulysses S. Grant, an inept president, who catered to the rich, no matter how often they tried to fleece him. The Grand Army of the Republic, formed in 1866 to represent northern veterans, was a powerful special interest group.

The Republicans recruited men of wealth and status into their ranks. They viewed the Irish with contempt and often used them as a negative reference group. As a result, they wrote off the Irish as being hopeless to recruit. Much of this had to do with the interplay of religion and politics, but some of it could be attributed to the unwavering Irish support of the Democrats. The Republicans deliberately played the Germans and Irish off against each other. By exploiting these ethnic rivalries, the Republicans were able to make inroads on German Democratic voting strength. They did so by casting German Protestants in a favorable light, at the same time denigrating the Irish as drunkards, hotheads, troublemakers, and incorrigibly lazy people.

Once these parameters were established, the Republicans fought to hold their own in the cities, but they fared much better in the suburbs and small rural towns, where the impulses of temperance and evangelical Protestantism worked in their favor. Religious leaders were fond of intruding into partisan politics. Preserving the Sabbath from desecration was an important evangelical cause. Protestants steadfastly observed Sunday as the Lord's Day that, in their view, was to be devoted strictly to church going and prayer. Manual labor was strictly forbidden. The passage of Sunday "blue laws" by a Republican legislature met this goal. Such legislation forbade any kind of commercial activity, especially the sale of alcoholic beverages. No other question did more to place the Republicans on the side of morality and religion.

Independent third parties, fed by the discontents that came with industrial and agrarian crises, appeared intermittently. Their leaders engaged in class protest that tended to focus on single-issue public

questions. The Granger and Greenback movements of the 1870s and the Labor Union party of the 1880s were manifestations of this phenomenon. The Greenback party was concerned mostly about antimonopoly issues and currency inflation. The depression of 1873 took its toll in the big cities and lingered on in the countryside. In addition to currency expansion, the Greenbackers called for railroad regulation, a graduated income tax, and the protection of American workingmen through restrictions on immigration, child labor, and prison labor.[9] The postwar Greenback movement reached its peak in 1878, but small pockets of Greenback support could be found in New Jersey throughout the decade of the 1880s.

The Socialist Labor party was organized in Newark in 1877 by a group of radicals who had definite Marxist leanings. There was a great deal of socialist unrest and agitation during the great railroad strike in 1877. Misery and desperation were causing workers to take drastic action in the face of spreading unemployment. Friedrich A. Sorge of Hoboken, who was a disciple of Karl Marx and general secretary of the International Workingmen's Association, spearheaded this third-party movement. He received considerable help from Joseph P. McDonnell, a left-wing Irish socialist and editor of the *Paterson Labor Standard*. These two socialists organized the International Labor Union among the silk workers in Paterson and led a successful textile strike in 1878.[10] Amid this labor unrest and socialist ferment, they spread the ideology of socialism to the urban proletariat, but the doctrines behind it were born of the continental Marxist model, and that did little to promote its popularity. The Socialist Labor party did not grow into a viable political force. In the United States there was no fertile soil for that seed to germinate, and it withered and died. Most Irish labor leaders wanted no part of a leftist third-party movement. They preferred to back candidates from the two major parties who endorsed labor's goals. Even Joseph McDonnell later switched his party affiliation and supported Abbett for governor. The influence of the Catholic church also retarded the growth of Marxism.

The avowed purpose of the Prohibition party, as its name suggests, was to outlaw the manufacture and sale of liquor. Party activists sought to stop the flow of alcohol and to restrict the proliferation of saloons and breweries. But the temperance movement clashed with the norms and customs of German and Irish immigrants who sold and drank alcohol. As brewers and saloonkeepers, the Germans and Irish opposed restrictive liquor legislation as an infringement of their personal liberty. These battles pitted nativist "drys" against immigrant "wets" or what seemed to some observers as Protestants fighting Catholics. As historian Ronald Formisano explains, "Temperance everywhere tended to be nativist and anti-Popish as reformers frequently associated immigrants, especially Irish Catholics, with drunkenness."[11] Yet, politicians could hardly ignore the

demands of these immigrants, who differed in the way they preferred to spend their leisure.

Prohibitionists in New Jersey were mostly evangelical Protestants, who firmly believed that most of society's ills could be attributed to the abuse of alcohol. Their rallying cry against the evils of whiskey and "demon rum" struck a responsive chord among rural, church going people, especially among Baptists and Methodists. They recruited men like Stephen B. Ransom and Clinton B. Fisk to run for governor in 1880 and 1886, respectively. They received valuable electoral support from groups like the Women's Christian Temperance Union (founded in 1874) and subsequently from the Anti-Saloon League that was organized in 1894. The WCTU, one of the most feared, most powerful, and most important social movements of the age, was the first effective mass movement of American women: making inroads in both urban and rural areas, terrifying saloonkeepers, threatening the social peace, and upending the social order. In 1888, New Jersey's Clinton Fisk ran for president on the national Prohibition ticket. But the national party was too narrowly based to become a viable political force. It would be decimated in the 1890s by the Populists and by William Jennings Bryan, who appealed to many of its supporters.

Independent third parties appealed mostly to alienated and disaffected voters. Perpetual third-party men like Clinton Fisk made their voices heard above the roar of the crowd, but their "single-issue" protest politics had limited appeal. Such men did not have the ability to compromise, and in the world of politics, compromise is necessary to maintain broad-based coalitions. Except for the election of governor in 1886, when the liquor question waxed hot and heavy in New Jersey and Clinton Fisk garnered nearly 20,000 votes, fringe candidates did not pose a serious threat to the two major parties. Nevertheless, in a tight election, they could siphon off enough votes to play the role of spoiler. But both Democrats and Republicans made it very difficult for upstart third parties to get their candidates on the ballot.[12]

RELIGION AND POLITICS

Protestantism remained the dominant form of Christianity throughout nineteenth-century New Jersey. The white church steeple that towered above the skyline symbolized its dominance. Religion and politics were often intertwined. Of all religious groups, the Presbyterians were the most active politically. They were conveyors of that puritan New England culture in which religion pervaded all spheres of life. Seven Presbyterians, imbued with a "new light" evangelicalism, had founded the colonial College of New Jersey in the city of Elizabeth in 1746. This institution then moved to Newark and subsequently to Princeton, where it changed its name. Its founders were all disaffected alumni of Harvard and Yale who felt that these New England schools had been moribund during the eighteenth-century religious revival known as the "great awakening." They resolved to establish a more spiritually alert college. The Princeton Theological Seminary was later founded to prepare young men for a career in the Presbyterian ministry.

A bastion of Presbyterianism, Princeton was a center for anti-Catholic literature and antipapist propaganda. The Reverend James McCosh, a Scot Presbyterian and Free Churchman, educated at the University of Edinburgh, presided as president of Princeton from 1868 to 1888. Although the Princeton trustees saw fit to award Leon Abbett an honorary degree in 1884, McCosh personally disliked him because the governor was a spoils politician who was too closely identified with Irish Catholics and with the liquor and racetrack interests. After all, the saloon was the place where political favors, contracts, and city and state jobs were dispensed by emergent Irish political bosses. The propensity of Democrats to court these tawdry and disreputable interests must have seemed shocking to staunch Presbyterian moralists like McCosh.

Protestant hatred of Catholics, based mainly on the fear of a dominant papacy and a centralized church authority in Rome, played a large part in generating and energizing American nativism. This was especially true after the First Vatican Council in 1870 that promulgated the dogma of papal infallibility. The religious divide provided a source of constant conflict in New Jersey. This intolerance of each other led to various attempts by native Protestants to prevent Catholics from participating in the political process. As historian John Higham writes, "Anti-Catholic nativism, aiming at stiff naturalization laws and exclusion of Catholics and foreigners from public office, completely overshadowed every other nativist tradition."[13]

Hatred of Catholics ran deep in New Jersey, especially among evangelical Protestants. Conflict between these two religious traditions was bitter and unyielding. Much of it had to do with the accommodation of old world grievances as it did with disputes over religious dogma and sectarian doctrines. Romanism, the code word for Catholicism, inevitably clashed with the Protestant concepts of free inquiry and liberty of conscience. Playing on fears of popery became a chief means of raising funds and reducing internal strife among Protestants.

These tensions and resentments continued unabated in a sea of political discord. The Catholic drive to obtain public funding for parochial schools infuriated Protestants, who felt strongly that such a practice violated the constitutional separation of church and state. Correspondingly, Bible reading in the public schools inflamed Catholic passions. These were not minor disputes. Most Catholics saw Bible

reading as a blatant attempt to proselytize their children and to indoctrinate them in the tenets of Protestantism. Morton Keller sums up the endless fountain of religious controversy:

> By far the most substantial religious issue of the post [Civil] war years was the place of Roman Catholicism in America. The Catholic church was widely perceived to be a major threat to the society. Irish Catholics in particular, whose politics were overwhelmingly Democratic, whose Negrophobia was raw and overt, and whose concentration in cities and heavy use of alcohol were sources of social concern, irritated Protestant Republican sensibilities.[14]

Under these circumstances, religious antagonisms played an important role in the formation and adherence of party loyalties. In New Jersey and other states, Catholics were almost always Democrats, whether they were rich or poor, urban or rural, French, German, or Irish. Jews, who arrived mostly from Germany, Poland, and Russia, showed a similar proclivity. Some Germans were either socialists or free thinkers, and as such they, along with avowed atheists, were hostile toward organized religion. Congregationalists, Disciples of Christ, German Reform Protestants, and English Quakers were typically Republican. Among the mainstream Protestant denominations, those who adhered to an evangelical fundamentalism—such as Baptists, Methodists, and Presbyterians—tended to be Republican; whereas those who were more ritualistic in matters of faith—such as Episcopalians and Lutherans—were likely to be Democrats.

An increasing number of Catholics and Jews began to challenge the Protestant majority. By 1890, when Abbett began his second term as governor, 281,801 Protestants lived in New Jersey compared with 222,274 Roman Catholics. Jews (estimated to be around 25,000) made up a smaller segment of the electorate.[15] Presbyterians, whose membership reached 59,464, took their sense of civic duty and responsibility to the secular state seriously. Many of them were concerned about the social and moral welfare of the community. As a religious group, they wielded political and social influence disproportionate to their numbers. Most of the governors in New Jersey during the Gilded Age were Presbyterian. The New Jersey Synod regularly published position papers on various issues of public policy that were intended to inform lawmakers in Trenton.

A revival of spiritual yearning translated into a large increase in membership for mainline Protestant denominations. Numerically, Methodists were the largest single religious denomination with 96,377 members. They were strict in their morality and frowned on the sensual pleasures of dancing and drinking. They held their revivalist summer camp meetings in the dry communities of Asbury Park and Ocean Grove. There, gathered under large white canvass tents, these born-again Christians listened to sermons, sang spiritual hymns, and prayed for eternal salvation.

Whenever moral issues like gambling and drinking arose, the Protestant community could be expected to descend en masse upon the State House in Trenton to lobby for or against specific legislation. Spurred on by Protestant clergymen, they often staged protests against proposed laws that they found objectionable. Clearly, their intent was to legislate morality, but their good intentions did not always succeed.

POPULATION GROWTH AND SHIFTS

During the second half of the nineteenth century, the population of New Jersey showed a pattern of continued growth. It climbed steadily from 672,035 in 1860 to 906,096 in 1870, and then it soared during the next two decades, rising from 1,131,116 in 1880 to 1,444,933 by 1890. Changes in distribution of population showed the big cities gaining residents, while rural areas remained relatively constant or else declined. The five cities with the largest numerical increases were Newark, Jersey City, Paterson, Camden, and Trenton. Overall, this explosive population growth amounted to a 465 percent increase that represented 2.31 percent of the nation's population. Natural reproduction, of course, accounted for some of this growth.

The foreign-born had arrived in numbers that far exceeded everyone's expectations. Until 1880, ninety percent of the immigrants came from northern Europe, especially Great Britain, Germany, and Ireland. Beginning in the 1880s, a massive flood of "new" immigrants poured into the United States from southern and eastern Europe—from Italy, Hungary, Greece, and the Balkan countries as well as from Poland, Lithuania, and Russia. Their assimilation was slow and painful. They mixed uneasily with the British, Germans, and Irish who had immigrated earlier. Strangers in the land and unable to speak English, they were mostly unskilled and illiterate peasants, ready to take any job that was available. They came when physical labor was in great demand, and they were specifically recruited for that purpose. Almost half the population of Jersey City was foreign-born, more than in any other New Jersey city.

These urban newcomers faced a harsh life, especially in cities that showed little compassion for their immigrant poor. Still, their situation was hopeful. Industrialization of urban areas in conjunction with greater access to transportation and factories fostered good job prospects for city residents. The travails of tenement life shortened the existence of many immigrants, but they shared a spirit of common struggle that kept their hopes alive. It was an era when child labor was rampant. Too often these children were needed to help support the family. They went to work as early as possible. Speaking little or no English, the parents depended on

their children to learn the ways of their new country. The second and third generations followed the tenement trail and moved onward and upward in the way of the Germans and Irish. The Irish had two things going for them: they did not have a language barrier and they were familiar with the workings of county government.

Such massive population flows produced a profound change that was accompanied by far-reaching culture shock. Most of the new arrivals were Catholic immigrants who crowded into the tenements of the teeming cities. The fear and antipathy toward these immigrants reached new heights, because this was a way of expressing social anxiety. The Know-Nothing movement that flourished in the late 1840s and 1850s was fueled by anti-Catholic hate mongering. The same was true of secret fraternal societies such as the Order of United American Mechanics, the American Protestant Association, and the Patriotic Order of the Sons of America. Protestant fear of a papist takeover of civic institutions stirred such hatred. Virulent anti-Catholicism reappeared in the early 1890s with the formation of such groups as the American Protective Association. These hate groups were mostly anti-Catholic and antiforeigner in their outlook. Since Jews were much smaller in number, they posed less of a threat to the established order. Nevertheless, the populism of the 1890s produced a virulent strain of anti-Semitism.[16]

The Know-Nothings had used anti-Catholicism to win public favor. The pontificate of Pius IX (1846–1878) furnished native Protestant Americans with some grounds for their anti-Catholic feelings. Pope Pius IX's reliance on reactionary forces to preserve the papal states, his opposition to republican institutions in Italy, and his ultraconservative views enunciated in his Syllabus of Errors simply added fuel to anti-Catholic attitudes in America.

In 1860 slightly over eighteen percent and in 1890 nearly twenty-three percent of New Jersey's population was foreign-born—some 328,975 people to be precise. The vast majority of immigrants gravitated toward the urbanizing northeastern counties, but many dispersed across the state, moving from towns to farms to mining and railroad camps. Counties with the largest number of foreign-born in their population were Essex, Hudson, Passaic, and Union. As the state's fastest growing region, this area had a great deal going for it, including its proximity to New York as well as its large workforce. Other counties with a high percentage of foreigners included Mercer, Middlesex, Camden, and Bergen. Camden County absorbed the spillover of newcomers from nearby Philadelphia. The number dropped sharply in each of the remaining thirteen counties. Cape May County had the fewest immigrants with only 493. Hudson County, Abbett's political base, topped the list with 97,603 newcomers.[17]

FARMS AND FARMERS IN THE GARDEN STATE

Fertile land, lakes, and rivers had always attracted settlers to the south-ernmost counties. The coastal terrain with its dark loamy soil made this rural area ideal for farming. Many English Quakers, Swedes, and Dutch farmed in the southern counties of Atlantic, Cumberland, Gloucester, and Salem. The small rural town of Swedesboro, located in Gloucester County, was typical of such farming communities. Even the rocky north-western counties, with their glacier-made lakes and upland hardwood forests, drew relatively dense settlement. This glaciated farm country was difficult to plow, but the hilly terrain provided grazing for cattle and sheep. There was also some iron and zinc mining in this area. Few people chose to settle in the lower central region in Burlington and Ocean coun-ties, where heavy pine growth and sandy soils discouraged farmers. The Pine Barrens remained sparsely settled. The bog iron industry that had once prospered there died out in the late 1840s when high-grade bitumi-nous coal was discovered in western Pennsylvania.[18]

Open farmland still dominated New Jersey's landscape. Everywhere in the state from 1860 to 1890 new farms were freshly plowed and planted. There were 34,307 farms in 1890 with the average farm comprising eighty-five acres. Over seventy-five percent of them were family-owned and operated. These family farms inculcated conservative values and bred Republicanism to a large extent, but in rural counties like Sussex, Somerset, and Morris, they served as a wellspring of the old Jacksonian philosophy. Monmouth and Warren counties were tradition-ally Democratic. Many farmers had been hurt financially by the panic of 1873 and they were still recovering from its lingering effects. It was an age in which most of them could survive on the produce of their own farms. Even so, they felt that a way of life they had known for generations might be in jeopardy. Farm failures were fairly common. Faced with postwar inflation, increasing operating costs, and high railroad rates, they sought a better break for the average farmer. The farmers were already a power-ful special interest group, and they sought to use government to improve their competitive position.

What emerged from the Civil War were important institutional arrangements that brought technical assistance to farming communities. With the passage of the Morrill Act by Congress in 1862, each state was granted 30,000 acres of land for every member of its congressional dele-gation. In some states, like New Jersey, the land went to existing private schools. Vying for this federal subsidy, Rutgers won out in the competi-tion over its intrastate rival Princeton, and it was designated as the pub-lic land-grant college in 1863. A decade later, in 1872, the state Board of Agriculture was created. This agency sought to help farmers maximize their group objectives. The federal and state governments cooperated to establish an agricultural experiment station at Rutgers in 1880 that became involved in research and extension work. The focus was on the improvement of agricultural practices and production through the county agent who assisted farm families in an outreach capacity. These institutional arrangements were woven into the social fabric of rural agricultural life.[19] Farmers began to use the latest methods of fertilizing crops and breeding livestock as well as improved plows and harvesters to increase output and cut labor costs. Several counties in the state became highly productive, and profitable truck gardens supplied the metropolitan markets in New York City and Philadelphia.

Meanwhile, New Jersey had gone from being largely rural and agricultural to being largely urban and industrial. In 1840, most New Jerseyans (334,347) lived in rural areas, while the remaining 38,959 resided in urban communities. Fueled by immigration and urban growth, these demographics changed dramatically over the next forty years. By 1880, city dwellers (610,071) surpassed those (521,045) living in the countryside. For a state small in size, New Jersey became even more highly urban and more densely populated during the ensuing decade.[20] As higher paying jobs lured farm hands to factories, the number of workers engaged in agriculture gradually declined. Despite these demographic shifts, agriculture still played an important role in the state's economy. In the 1880s, New Jersey ranked as the nation's sixth largest industrial state. The booming production of its factories and sweatshops showed no signs of slowing down. Ten years of uninterrupted economic growth and development lay ahead.

THE RISE OF URBAN INDUSTRIALISM

By 1890, the five major manufacturing cities of Camden, Jersey City, Newark, Paterson, and Trenton accounted for one-third of the state's population and more than one-half of its 150,000 factory workers. These central cities were characterized by a few dominant industries. Newark, the state's largest city, was the exception. Its major products included ironware, food and beer, clothing, sewing machines, and leather goods. Railroads and shipping gave Bayonne, Hoboken, and Jersey City their special character. The giant Standard Oil refineries towered over Bayonne, while Jersey City thrived on its large sugar refineries as well as its Colgate soap and Lorillard tobacco factories. George P. Lorillard, the tobacco mogul, located his plant there. A few industries, ironmaking in North Jersey and glass production in South Jersey, were located in the countryside because of its raw materials. Trenton had its iron and steel mills, but the city was especially known for its potteries that made it a center of American china and dishware. Proud of its manufacturing industries, the

Works of the
CLARK THREAD COMPANY, Manuf's of **CLARKS "O.N.T." SPOOL COTTON** – Newark, N.J.

FIG. 7
Clark Thread Company,
Newark, New Jersey.

city boasted a banner logo that read, "What Trenton makes, the world takes." Camden was known for its iron mills and shipyards; the city of Orange specialized in making hats. Silk and textile production put Paterson on the map. Workers there also found employment in its locomotive, iron, and machine shops.

Rural folk, who lived far removed from the corrupting influences of city life, resented the growing power of the immigrant vote in the cities, but they had little or no cause to complain. On the contrary, the state constitution of 1844 guaranteed one state senator per county, regardless of size or population. It was a political compromise that had been struck in 1776 in the glory days of an agrarian society and still persisted in the Gilded Age. This was an era when farm "cow" areas dominated in legislative representation, particularly in the northwestern counties where conservative Democrats outvoted more liberal Hudson

County. Such malapportionment resulted in legislative districts of unequal populations.

The lopsided apportionment formula favored the small, sparsely populated rural counties. Overrepresented rural interests could easily block or kill legislation in the state senate, which was usually dominated by conservative Republicans. Conversely, legislators from the large, populous urban counties that were underrepresented often found their interests thwarted. With an influx of multiple cultures and diverse traditions, the electorate not only became more pluralistic, but it also became more polarized on most issues of public policy. The voting population was closely divided by party affiliation, and Governor Abbett had to live with that fact. There was a sharp division between urban and rural voters. New Jersey was a state divided as much by geography as by political party.

Continuing throughout the 1870s and 1880s, it was mostly the private sector that assumed the task of building New Jersey's industrial cities. The free market remained the preferred instrument for urban development. Public officials and businessmen worked closely together to generate business activity. Motivated by greed and corruption, they built cities that lacked aesthetics and drained municipal and county treasuries. Businessmen, who were always willing to make a deal, embraced the local political machine. Machine politicians produced the cynical politics of spoils and plunder. Scandals in public franchises and contracts were endemic in the late nineteenth century; bribery and kickbacks were a way of doing business.

City councilmen and mayors were enriched by the bankrollers of these business ventures. Corruption was rampant in Camden, Essex, and Hudson counties, where city ward bosses and precinct captains lined their pockets with petty graft. Venality ranged from influence peddling to kickbacks on municipal contracts, dishonest elections, and vote fraud. The herding of illiterate immigrants to the polls to do the bidding of the ward bosses was a common scene. On election day, the Irish drank and brawled, disrupting the democratic process and intimidating other citizens. Charges of fraudulent vote counts meant that some candidates were counted out of office. Upright, law-abiding citizens were outraged by what they saw and reacted strongly.

Patronage and corruption lubricated the friction between the world of equality and the world of privilege. The big city machines usually picked men of stature to run for office, but behind them was the county boss. Nowhere did this process operate more smoothly than in the industrializing cities of New Jersey. In several cities, Jersey City being the best known example, businessmen regularly rejected appeals for reform. Upper class, silk-stocking Republican reformers, who were popularly known as Mugwumps, saw city machines as a threat to democracy. Abbett could not escape being tarnished by such patronage and corruption. Nor could he elude the intricate web of power relationships that he had established. He found political company and support from labor leaders, liquor dealers, racetrack owners, and immigrant city bosses. These men were regarded by the upper classes as the unsavory and disreputable elements of society. One can speculate about the governor's motives for assembling such a motley following, but he no doubt needed their support if he was to counteract the entrenched power of the railroads.

For many people, the very idea of being a machine politician smacked of corruption. Journalists, who tended to be pessimistic about anything good coming out of politics, anointed instant heroes and villains. As the head of a corrupt and boss-ridden party machine, Abbett was cast mainly as a villain. He was chastised as much for his associations as for his personal philosophy. Scorned especially by reformers and journalists, they saw him courting people with no social standing and they wrote off his political cronies as being incorrigibly corrupt. Throughout his two administrations, Abbett had to contend with a mounting drumbeat of abusive criticism. Publicly, he tried to put a positive spin on the situation, but he could not overcome a barrage of bad publicity.

TWO CONTEMPORARY VIEWS OF ABBETT

William E. Sackett, a clever and competent journalist, first told the story. He profited from the flood of revelations uncovered by the Voorhees Committee that investigated widespread graft and corruption in New Jersey shortly after Abbett died. This investigation stained many reputations and foreshadowed the nascent power relations in post-Abbett New Jersey. Between 1896 and 1911, the Democrats experienced a prolonged dry spell during which no Democrat would sit in the governor's chair for the next fifteen years. A Republican resurgence and domination marked most of the Progressive era in New Jersey. The Democrats did not recapture the governorship until Woodrow Wilson appeared on the political scene in 1910.

A veteran political reporter, Sackett is best known for his delightful two-volume work aptly titled *Modern Battles of Trenton*. Published in fall 1895, the first volume chronicles New Jersey politics from 1868 to 1894. Written in a few months, his book is best understood as a scathing indictment of machine politics and boss rule. It was the type of slashing expose on political corruption soon referred to as muckraking. As such, it deals with the two Abbett administrations, but only in a superficial way. Rushing to meet his deadline, Sackett did not analyze in depth the political realities and complexities that Abbett had to deal with as a politician. At any rate, the critics loved it. A reviewer for the *Somerville Unionist-Gazette* remarked, "To those who have watched the exciting scenes which have transpired in the legislative halls this work is

a real romance." The subject of an ecstatic review in the *New York Times*, the book was an instant success and quickly became a best-seller.[21] Today, it ranks as a classic in muckraker literature. The second volume, published in 1914, covers the period from Governor George Werts to Governor Woodrow Wilson.

Sackett was not Abbett's biographer, though Abbett fascinated him as a political phenomenon, but the evidence that led him to see Abbett as a rogue politician is mixed. He wrote in a florid style of the new muckraking journalism and his purple prose captivated readers. Although Sackett respected Abbett for his more reputable achievements, he developed a jaundiced view of the man and was very harsh in his judgment of him. While watching the plundering of Abbett's political cronies and the endemic municipal corruption, Sackett had become disillusioned with machine politics and boss rule. Whatever inconsistencies in his argument, his book had a profound impact on public opinion. With his penchant for gossip and exaggeration, Sackett detailed what happened when big-city bosses found themselves possessed of political power and enticing economic opportunities. Even if one discounts the more one-sided passages in his unbalanced but fascinating account of Abbett, the story Sackett tells reveals much about the way in which power was centralized when developmental public policies were at stake.

Much of Sackett's criticism of Abbett was no doubt justified, but his account is marred by inaccuracies and must be cited with caution. Typical of muckraking journalists, Sackett had a tendency to exaggerate, misinterpret, and oversimplify events. What is more, he viewed the political system through the prism of his Protestant Victorian morality and with an antimachine and antiboss bias. In his rush to publish, Sackett judged Abbett too quickly. His first book suffers from both a lack of objectivity and a lack of historical perspective. Repulsed by the excesses of machine politics, Sackett leaves out a big piece of the story and thereby does him a disservice.[22]

In cutting through Sackett's misinterpretation, we find the source of Abbett's constantly renewed power was the steady stream of immigrants who came to New Jersey and the local Democratic machines that he controlled. The governor also had great reach within the business community. As long as his power base and resources were constantly expanding, so was his political reach. Because of incessant business activity, Abbett could act with secrecy and dispatch, gain the favor of one New Jersey mayor after another, and build an awesome political network. For Sackett, the essence of Abbett's power resided in his personal ambition, his mastery of ethnic and class politics, and his use of machine tactics in the name of reform. Abbett seems guilty on all counts, but these techniques were not the only source of his power. The mainstay of his influence was his party machine. Had Abbett not been the key figure in the

development of the state's urban industrial economy, he never would have commanded the great influence he enjoyed.

Perhaps no public figure in New Jersey history has aroused more controversy or evoked more contradictory emotions than Abbett. He was either revered or reviled, with precious little middle ground. To his many loyalists, the Hudson County Democrat was a dynamic leader, who was tempered in the fires of politics. He survived three decades of political combat, bloody but unbowed. To his equally numerous detractors, Abbett was an unscrupulous machine politician, who got his way through naked power and intimidation. They saw him as domineering, vindictive, secretive, and frighteningly authoritarian. In a campaign of vilification that never seemed to cease, they demonized him. Throughout his career, the governor had to contend with rough editorial comment of the slash and burn variety. Abbett bashing became a favorite pastime.

Despite these attacks, the Abbett phenomenon had roused the interest of magazine editors outside New Jersey, and in 1905, an article appeared in *McClure's Magazine* that gave him something like the treatment he would receive today. "New Jersey: A Traitor State," written by Lincoln Steffens, the dean of American muckrakers, was sympathetic and surveyed Abbett's career in a fairly even-handed way. Intrigued by the governor's political style and methods, Steffens offered a more measured judgment and helped transform the image of Abbett from that of political hack to principled visionary. As Steffens wrote:

Abbett had to go to the people. It seems to me that this most interesting man was an instinctive Democrat, and would naturally have campaigned the state, county by county, as he did. But no two Jersey witnesses agree about him now any longer, and it is certain that when he ran for governor he was forced by the fury of the attacks on his imperfect record to fight on the stump. But he was called a 'politician,' a 'demagogue,' an 'anarchist'; and I find that 'business' reserves these bad names for men who are brave enough to challenge and able enough to beat bad business; and that was Abbett. There was another charge against the man, however: ambition. His enemies said he cared nothing for the state; which was not true; or for the governorship, which was partly true. They said he wanted to be a United States Senator, and believed that by taxing the railroads he could achieve his ambition. Here was the outrageous truth: Leon Abbett was one of those "unscrupulous politicians" who want, not money, but office, and who think to rise, even to the United States Senate, by serving not the special, but the common interests of the state. This makes the man interesting to all of us; his career was an experiment in democracy.[23]

Even allowing for Steffens' expansiveness, this is a remarkable portrait of the Hudson Democrat as a versatile and mature politician. Steffens knew Abbett well and often spoke to men who knew him better. A classic political insider, Abbett knew how state government worked

and how to get things done. He was every bit as ruthless as the railroad oligarchs he fought. More important, perhaps, he believed that there was no point in holding power unless it could be used effectively. As chief executive, he played his various roles to the hilt and understood the potential uses of the office. In personality he had force and style, conveying an image of dedication and competence, controlled energy and rationality, and a gift for seizing the initiative and holding firmly to his objectives. He believed that the executive should use power vigorously. He grew into the job over the six years that he held the office, crafting a persona and record that his enemies could not diminish no matter how much they denounced him.

During his thirty years in state politics, Leon Abbett had come to thoroughly understand the strengths and weaknesses of the political system in which he operated. He recognized the social ferment brewing in New Jersey and understood the reasons that caused people to press for social change. Looking back at the social and economic conditions that existed in the 1880s and early 1890s, we can see the political situation was clearly manipulable by someone like Abbett. Abundant evidence suggests that constituency and leader were attuned to each other's calculations. Abbett was a centrist Democrat, who had a keen knowledge of the culture. Neither a liberal nor a conservative, he was an operator of quick intelligence and strong ambition who stated many principles eloquently and convincingly, even though his actions did not always match. The politician had become a legend; the man had become a myth. In sum, he was a dangerous and courageous foe.

ENDNOTES

1 See David McCullough, *The Great Bridge* (New York, Avon Books, 1976).

2 Ron Chernow, *Titan: The Life of John D. Rockefeller, Sr.* (New York, Random House, 1998), 49.

3 Alpheus T. Mason and Richard H. Leach, *In Quest of Freedom* (Englewood Cliffs, Prentice-Hall, 1959), 352.

4 For an account of the Spencer tour, see Richard Hofstadter, *Social Darwinism in American Thought* (Boston: 1955), 48-49. See also Gerald Garvey, *Constitutional Bricolage* (Princeton, Princeton University Press, 1971), 105.

5 Robert F. Williams, "The New Jersey Equal Rights Amendment: A Documentary Sourcebook," *Women's Rights Law Reporter*, 16 (Winter 1994), 79.

6 These statistics are taken from the *Compendium of the Eleventh Census: 1890* (Washington, D.C., U.S. Government Printing Office, 1892), 230.

7 Quoted in the *Boston Globe*, June 5, 2000.

8 Lockard, *The New Jersey Governor*, 74-75.

9 For a good analysis of the Greenback movement see Irwin Unger, *The Greenback Era: A Social and Political History of American Finance 1865–1879* (Princeton, Princeton University Press, 1964).

10 Vecoli, *The People of New Jersey*, 97-98.

11 Ronald P. Formisano, *The Birth of Mass Political Parties: Michigan, 1827–1861* (Princeton, Princeton University Press, 1971), 233.

12 See Richard P. McCormick, *The History of Voting in New Jersey: A Study of the Development of Election Machinery 1664–1911* (New Brunswick, Rutgers University Press, 1953), 180. See also W.J. Rorabauch, *The Alcoholic Republic: An American Tradition* (New York, Oxford University Press, 1979).

13 John Higham, *Strangers in the Land* (New York, Atheneum, 1978), 6.

14 Keller, *Affairs of State*, 137.

15 *Compendium of the Eleventh Census: 1890*, Part II, 298-305. The census takers officially recorded 4,276 Jewish congregations, but many Jews were not affiliated with synagogues. The estimate of 25,000 Jews is found in Vecoli, *The People of New Jersey*, 130.

16 Vecoli, *The People of New Jersey*, 147-51.

17 *The Eleventh Census of the United States* (Washington, D.C., U.S. Government Printing Office, 1892), 653.

18 See John McPhee, *The Pine Barrens* (New York, Farrar, Straus and Giroux, 1968), 38; Arthur D. Pierce, *Iron in the Pines* (New Brunswick, Rutgers University Press, 1957), 10-19.

19 For a history of New Jersey agriculture and the social institutions that were created during this period, see Ingrid N. Waller, *Where There Is Vision*, (New Brunswick: Rutgers University Press, 1955). See also Fred A. Shannon, *The Farmer's Last Frontier: Agriculture, 1860–1897* (New York, Harper & Row, 1945).

20 These statistics are found in the *New Jersey Legislative Manual of 1892* (Trenton: 1891), 417. See also Gillette, *Jersey Blue*, 13-14.

21 See book review in the *New York Times*, December 1, 1895.

22 See William Sackett's obituary, which is found in the *New York Times*, November 19, 1926. Politically, Sackett was a reform Democrat who eventually became fed up with machine politics and political bossism. He made a futile attempt to seek his party's nomination for governor in 1913, during the high noon of progressivism. Governor Woodrow Wilson, who had just left office, was his ideal and role model. Seeking to follow in his footsteps, Sackett ran on a reform platform that attacked machine politics and urged the overthrow of the immigrant city bosses. The celebrity-journalist spouted his antiboss rhetoric, but to no avail.

23 Lincoln Steffens, "New Jersey: A Traitor State," *McClure's Magazine* (New York, April 1905), 24:658-659.

Coming of Age in Antebellum Philadelphia

In the 1830s, Philadelphia was the center of art, beauty, refined taste, and culture in America. The city was also a thriving manufacturing, shipping, and commercial center. During the three decades before the Civil War, the city grew from a lively commercial town into a large industrial metropolis. Much of this urban growth could be attributed to a municipal consolidation that took place in 1854. This merger joined the original center city with several other suburban municipalities in Philadelphia County. The city-county consolidation merged 29 separate localities into a single municipality.[1]

Convulsive social upheaval that unhinged traditional loyalties accompanied this expansion of the city. Immigration on a large scale had produced multiple cultures and fierce rivalries among ethnic communities. The city was torn asunder by religious conflict between native Protestants and Irish Catholic immigrants. Moreover, the birth of the labor movement spawned its own conflict. Disputes over wages and control of the work process provoked labor strikes that erupted into violent riots. The urban riot was a common form of protest in the age of Jackson. Few cities experienced more social turmoil and upheaval than the City of Brotherly Love. Nativist riots, labor strikes, temperance crusades, anti-railroad protests, and sporadic racial violence were all part of its ever-changing political landscape. The very different mix of cultures contributed to the increasing civil unrest as disturbances continued.[2]

The turbulence of Jacksonian Philadelphia provided Leon Abbett with a training ground for what he would later encounter in New Jersey politics. While growing up there, he became familiar with the dynamics of city life, along with its class resentments and ethnic tensions. What he learned shaped his subsequent thinking: the way he looked at the world, at the public, at duty, at responsibility, at democracy, and at the cruel

caprices of life. To understand what motivated him, we need to reconstruct the urban environment in which he was raised and to specify the various people who influenced his personal, intellectual, and social development. The obvious ones include his parents, his siblings, his school teachers, and his classmates. Less obvious, because they are less well recorded, were his mentors.

THE ABBETT FAMILY HISTORY

At the outset, we first need to examine Leon Abbett's family history. He was descended from four generations of Pennsylvania farmers. His ancestors came to America from England sometime around the middle of the eighteenth century. The exact date in unknown. It is believed that William Abbett, the family patriarch, emigrated to America in the early 1750s. Identified in biographical material as English Quakers, the family settled in Montgomery County, Pennsylvania, where they established themselves as tenant farmers and subsequently as millers.[3]

There is no record of William Abbett having served in the American Revolution. His Quaker pacifism may have kept him from joining the Continental Army. Since the Abbetts lived near Valley Forge, they probably witnessed the movements of George Washington's troops who were encamped there during the bitter cold winter of 1777. After the war, the names of William Abbett and his son, who went by the same name, were recorded on the tax rolls of Whitemarsh. In 1783, their names appeared on the militia muster for Whitpain Township, where they rented a farm on the outskirts of Blue Bell, located 25 miles north of Philadelphia.[4]

Montgomery County, with its fertile soil and rolling hills, was an early center of Quaker settlement. But one gets the impression that the Abbetts were only lukewarm Quakers; they did not join the Society of Friends, or at least there is no record of their having attended either the Gwynedd or the Plymouth monthly meetings.[5] Nominal Quakers, who married out of meeting, were "disowned" or disassociated. Presumably, this is what happened to the Abbetts. In any event, they lived among Quaker farmers and were influenced by them. The austere Quakers, with their intense pietism and rigid moral code, had a significant influence on the social and economic life in the Delaware Valley.

As tenant farmers, the Abbetts adapted to a rural style of living. For them, agriculture was a preferred way of life with its pastoral virtues of thrift, hard work, faith, sobriety, and self-reliance. Prayer, Bible reading, and Protestantism permeated these small family farms. The Abbetts blended into the god-fearing yeomanry who made their livelihood on the subsistence farmlands in southeastern Pennsylvania. Like most tenant farmers, they dreamed of owning their own farm someday. Attracted to

the concepts of Jeffersonian democracy, the Abbetts became ardent Democrats, who valued rural life and the virtues of independence that went with it. They embraced Thomas Jefferson's ideas of social equality and individualism.

These values and core beliefs were passed on from one generation of Abbetts to the next. Property deeds and land records indicate that they moved around quite a bit in those days, but they stayed within the confines of Montgomery County. Because land was plentiful in relation to the sparse population, farm ownership eventually came within reach of William Abbett senior. In 1797, he purchased a sixty-four-acre tract of land in Norriton Township from innkeeper Joseph Tyson. The Abbett farm was smaller than most, but it had a grist mill, a saw mill, and a stone farmhouse. It contained the necessary tools and machinery for grain and milling operations; the saw mill produced lumber for barns and village homes.

The third generation of Abbetts remained at the homestead in Blue Bell. Their names and occupations are recorded in the tax assessment books preserved at the Montgomery County Historical Society. They are listed as Miles, a farmer; Jonathan, a mason; and David, a millwright.[6] Working together as a family unit, they put their combined skills to good use. Miles managed the farm, while Jonathan and David plied their trades in the local village.

The Abbetts continued to farm the land until the mid-1820s. Year in and year out, they plowed, planted, and harvested their crops. In addition to rye, wheat, and oats, they raised five horses, seven cows, and twelve sheep. These animals were kept in a large barn that was filled with hay.[7] At the end of the harvest season, Miles and his brothers bedded down the livestock for the winter months. The women prepared food, tended gardens, marketed produce, milked cows, and produced butter, cheese, soap, and candles. They were also responsible for making cloth. The Blue Bell farmers ground their own grain, cut their own lumber, and did their own masonry work. They did not own any slaves. Quakers believed that slavery was immoral and against God's will. The governing body of the church decided in 1776 that members who did not free their slaves would be expelled. Slavery was abolished in Pennsylvania in 1780, thereby making it a free state.

Ezekiel Maddock Abbett was born at the Blue Bell homestead in 1808. He grew up on the farm where he lived a normal rural boyhood. Like most Pennsylvania farmboys, Ezekiel walked behind his father's plow, took care of the cows, and did the chores afterward. He received a few years of common schooling and learned how to read and write, but he remained largely self-taught.[8]

Life was an unrelenting struggle for the Abbetts. They found it increasingly difficult to survive in an agricultural market swayed by new technology and new economic forces. Depressed farming conditions and

the lure of industrial jobs in the city resulted in a large number of people leaving Montgomery County. A syndicate of real estate agents purchased farms abandoned by descendants of original settlers and sold the property at inflated prices. In 1813, the Abbetts sold forty-one acres of their family farm in Norriton Township to Jacob Weiss of Philadelphia. This sale left them with twenty-three acres of tillable land. Inheritance practices made it difficult for sons to acquire farms and tenancy was no longer economically feasible.

Slowly but surely, the Abbetts were being pushed off their land. When economic depression struck in 1819, they joined the exodus of people who left their farms in Montgomery County to toil in the textile mills and factories of nearby Philadelphia. These working people played a vital role in the Industrial Revolution. The rise of industrial capitalism not only disrupted rural life and its traditions, but it also created a demand for cheap labor. The lure of the city was hard to resist: ambitious young men who would have never strayed more than twenty miles from their home now deserted their family farms for jobs in the city.

AN ARTISAN CULTURE

A similar fate befell Ezekiel Abbett. In 1824, he left the hardscrabble existence of his father's farm and apprenticed himself to a master hatter in Philadelphia. Given the contemporary dress code, there was a demand for hats, bonnets, and other types of head cover. Ezekiel spent three years learning his trade and progressed from apprentice to journeyman hatter. Most hatters made between twelve and fifteen hats a week and worked by hand with their own tools. Depending on their rank and seniority, they earned a weekly income between $12 and $20. The demand for master craftsmen was great enough to provide an enterprising journeyman with the opportunity to set up his own shop.

The transportation revolution was revamping the economy from market craftsmanship to industrial capitalism. Nothing dramatized this economic transformation more than the opening of the Erie Canal in 1825. Several states constructed canals and other public works to facilitate the transport of goods to major markets. These states also granted special charters to private corporations such as turnpike, bridge, and railroad corporations, and they assisted them by granting subsidies and monopoly rights. The railroads soon surpassed the canals as a more efficient means of transportation. All of which meant that the distribution of manufactured goods was no longer confined to a specific locale. Once the railroads were in operation, such products could be shipped to market faster and over far greater distances. The shift of manufacturing from household to central shop or factory was part of this transformation.

Industry and commerce drew its manpower from within walking distance of the workplace.

Among Philadelphia's wage-earning class, the hatters enjoyed the image of fierce individualists. They believed in the dignity of labor and valued their independence as workmen. They took great pride in their craftmanship and saw it as an expression of their own individualism. The hatters controlled their work schedule. On any day, they decided for themselves whether to work or not; they were their own bosses. Not only did they exercise a great deal of control over the work process, but they were also fiercely proud of their status as artisans. Meticulous men by nature, many of them were literate and well read. They were inspired by the writings of Thomas Paine, who had come to America in 1774 as a common man and a laboring man. He urged them not to forget the democratic ideals of the American Revolution. They believed that they had the power to control their own destiny and to shape the world around them.

By the early 1830s, the hat industry was undergoing drastic change. With the advent of power-driven machinery and factory production, the hatters faced an uncertain future. Machines displaced some of them and downgraded their skills. This new mode of production led to a division and specialization of labor. It also brought about other changes such as standardization of product, greater discipline of the labor force, improved efficiency, higher volume, and lower costs. The hatters in Philadelphia fought these economic changes that they saw as threats to their individuality and autonomy. Their fears were soon confirmed: increased competition, larger-scale production, and advance of technology relegated many skilled workers to a future as lifelong wage earners. At the same time, they lost a good deal of control over their workplace. The craft skills that set artisans apart from common laborers were being eroded by these changes and by the increased use of machinery. As a consequence, the hatters formed a trade union and strongly resisted the new machines and new methods. These workers were at the cutting edge of labor protest in the antebellum era.[9]

Urban workers in Philadelphia constituted a self-conscious political subculture in the age of Jackson. Spontaneous protests were organized into a political movement. In 1828, they formed their own Workingmen's party that advocated the abolishment of imprisonment for debt; the regulation of apprenticeships; the restriction of female, child, and convict labor; the prohibition of chartered monopolies; and the creation of a public school system. But their party did not last very long. When it folded in 1832, many workers switched their allegiance to the Democratic party that eagerly sought their support. Their intellectual spokesmen provided the rationale for the Jacksonian coalition. Jackson Democrats opposed the public agenda set forth by the Whigs, who favored banks, protective tariffs, corporate monopolies, and federal internal improvements. Much

Jacksonian rhetoric played variations on these themes. The hatters of Philadelphia were very much a part of this political subculture.

THE JACKSONIAN INFLUENCE

The presidential elections of 1824, 1828, and 1832 were focused more on personalities than issues. The Democrats portrayed Andrew Jackson as a man of the people and a military hero. He was by nature and training a frontiersman and a soldier, who expressed his faith in the common man and his disdain for elitism and entrenched special privilege. Ushering in a new era of American politics, Jackson encouraged ordinary men to become active in party politics. The Jacksonians accepted parties as essential to the workings of democracy and to the safeguarding of liberty. They set up party organizations in every state in the Union. As historian Ronald Formisano points out, "Although Jacksonian Democrats professed a passion for laissez faire in government and society, they combined this with a pragmatic ability to submit to organization, to an authority which functioned at least as much by oligarchic as by majority rule."[10]

Jacksonianism, as an organized political movement began in 1828, lasted well into the 1840s. Jackson favored strong government, active on behalf of the common people as opposed to the landed and moneyed aristocracy that flourished in the absence of such an intermediary. To open public offices to a greater number of the people, Jackson proposed a system of rotation in office. The vested interest in government jobs by a few officeholders would thus be prevented. It was a period marked by an increase in democracy, including universal manhood suffrage, direct election of public officials, short terms of office, and a political system in which the victors of electoral campaigns were entitled to reap the spoils of office.

The genesis of mass democratic politics began to take primitive form during the decades of the 1830s and 1840s. Campaigns were now characterized by appeals to the common man, mass meetings, torchlight parades, and the distribution of literature and other paraphernalia. Communications to the electorate were filtered through parties and through partisan propaganda. These efforts were designed to mobilize voter support for party candidates. All of which placed greater emphasis on party organization and party loyalty.

On December 7, 1833, Ezekiel Abbett married Sarah M. Howell, a country girl who came from southern New Jersey. She was born in 1809 in the tiny village of Mauricetown, located in Down Township along the banks of the Maurice River in Cumberland County. At the time, the village was no more than a landing, a small shipyard, and a few scattered farms. By 1880, or a half century later, Mauricetown only numbered 575 people. Most were farmers, but some engaged in commercial fishing.

Very little is known about Sarah Howell's family history. More information would no doubt be available if the birth records for Down Township had not been destroyed by fire. As a result, the identity of Sarah's parents will likely remain a mystery forever. She apparently came from old New Jersey stock on her father's side, but she was not "to the manor born" as some accounts suggest.[11] What we do know about her is gleaned from her obituary that appeared in the *Trenton Times* on July 21, 1900. It indicates that Sarah Howell was raised in a rural Baptist family, but she was not a richly endowed bride. It was probably the dowry of a Protestant English family that had sold off its ancestral farm. A spry and diminutive woman, Sarah had strong evangelical leanings and remained a devout Baptist throughout her life.[12]

THE BIRTH OF LEON ABBETT

Ezekiel and Sarah Abbett took up residence in Kensington, then a separate township adjacent to old Philadelphia. They lived in a triple-decker house at 14 Beach Street, near the intersection of Shackamaxon. Leonidas Abbett was born there on October 8, 1836. A fifth-generation English-American, he was a native-born son of native-born parents. Family legend claims that his birthplace was within 100 yards of the towering elm tree under which William Penn had signed a peace treaty with the Delaware Indians in 1682.[13] Wrapping himself in the mantle of the "log cabin" myth so popular in his day, the future New Jersey governor did little to dispel the romantic gloss. He had a talent for putting his own spin on events to suit his particular needs.

Kensington was a blue-collar, working-class community that stretched along the banks of the Delaware River. It was also a port-of-entry for foreign immigrants and a center for hand-weaving. Most of its hand-loom operators were Irish, both Catholic and Protestant. With the advent of the steam-powered loom, their days as hand weavers were numbered. The new machines put many of them out of work. Labor leader John Ferral led a general strike in 1835 to protest their deteriorating working conditions.

While Kensington voted Democratic, old Philadelphia remained a Whig stronghold as the Whigs were the ruling power in the central city. Many were descended from prominent Quaker families that had earned their fortunes in the eighteenth century: the Biddles, Binneys, Cadwaladers, Ingersolls, Mifflins, Morrises, and Whartons. New money was to be made in commerce, publishing, and manufacturing. The *nouveaux riche* included men like Girard and Drexel, Curtis and Bok, and the locomotive manufacturer Matthias Baldwin. They were all Whigs who represented Philadelphia's social and economic elite.

When the Republican party replaced the Whigs in the mid-1850s, most of them became Republicans. For the moment, however, they were worried about protecting their property. Sixteen riots had taken place in 1834, and another thirty-seven riots occurred the following year. Most of these riots erupted in the working-class suburbs, but they were too close for comfort. The small local police force did not have enough manpower to adequately patrol the entire city. Some 24 day constables and 120 night watchmen were on duty in 1833. This amounted to 1 patrolman for every 3,352 inhabitants.

As fate would have it, Leon Abbett entered the world in the midst of a presidential election in 1836. Martin Van Buren, born in the small upstate New York town of Kinderhook, headed the Democratic ticket. Standing only 5 feet, 6 inches tall, he was known as "Little Van" and "Old Kinderhook." Having previously served as secretary of state and vice president under Andrew Jackson, Van Buren was the president's hand-picked successor. He was an evasive politician who avoided taking a stand on most issues whenever possible. While many suspected him of being a closet abolitionist, Van Buren later opposed the extension of slavery. Despite his evasiveness, he won the presidency against a disorganized Whig party that fielded several candidates. Although not an original thinker, Van Buren took Jackson's concept of laissez-faire a step further and insisted on a minimum of governmental interference in national economic life. He occupied the White House from 1837 to 1841. The inflationary effects of Jackson's veto of the recharter of the Second Bank of the United States and his subsequent deposit of government funds in state banks combined to produce an economic depression of serious proportions. Labor strikes, public debt, and inflation were the troublesome issues that concerned most Philadelphians. The banking controversy remained the most polarizing issue in Pennsylvania for the next decade, pitting probanking Whigs against antibanking Democrats.[14]

The obscurity and poverty into which Leon Abbett was born entailed the unremitting regimen of manual labor. He was raised in a close knit, working-class family where individual worth was valued more than material possessions. Ezekiel Abbett was an able and active man, who encouraged his children to make something of themselves. Their mother was an indomitable woman, sustained by a strong Baptist faith and her sense of family duty. Sarah was a dominating influence in their lives.

As urban working people, the Abbetts were very much a part of their social class and political environment. Leon grew up in a nurturing family that gave him a strong sense of self. Since the Abbetts did not keep any family records, or at least there are none that have survived, the formative years are only vaguely documented. Using the work of anthropologists and historians, we can place Leon Abbett in a historical context and reconstruct much of his early life.[15] Fragmentary signs suggest that he was raised in an artisan culture, where money was tight and the Protestant work ethic was emphasized more by parental example than lecture.

Ezekiel and Sarah Abbett had five children—four sons and one daughter. In birth order, Leon was the second child. Albert, the firstborn, died in infancy from a cholera epidemic in Philadelphia in 1834. This dreaded pestilence struck the city repeatedly, and it took hundreds of lives with the ravages that it inflicted. Albert's death made Leon the oldest child by default. His younger brothers were Franklin and Edwin. The three boys were devoted to one another, and yet they were fiercely competitive. They more than fulfilled their parents' expectations. All three boys became lawyers, and all three entered public service. Franklin went on to become a state legislator in Pennsylvania, while Edwin became a city attorney in New York. Little is known about their sister Emily who lived a quiet and obscure life.

A HATTERS' TRADE

With an upsurge in the demand for hats, Ezekiel worked hard to support his growing family, laboring for long hours at low wages. By the late 1830s, he had opened his own shop in which he was assisted by his wife and children in sewing and trimming hats. The family constantly strove to improve its standard of living. The parents followed the Quaker way of self-disciplined, noncoercive childrearing. Sarah assumed responsibility for socializing and educating the children. She ran the house, read the Bible to them, made their clothing, and instilled values of pride and ambition. Sarah was a small, brisk woman, who not only outlived her husband but also outlived four of her five children. Edwin was the only son who survived her. She died in July 1900 at the age of ninety-one.

Shortly after Leon was born, the Abbetts fell on hard times. When the financial panic struck in 1837, most artisans suffered wage cuts, but those in the hatter's trade were especially hard hit. Mills closed, jobs disappeared, and unemployment increased. The next six years were lean and filled with hardship. The depression, which lasted until 1843, went from bad to worse; nine states defaulted on their debts. The hatters suffered periodic reversals. "Men who were getting $12 a week in 1835," says labor historian Norman Ware, "could make only $8 a week in 1845, and while, at the earlier date they could depend on constant employment, they later lost one third of their time."[16]

In this trying setting, the Abbetts experienced varying shades of poverty from poor to nearly poor. Regardless of how Leon Abbett's life is reconstructed, his hardships were genuine. He was poor but all the kids in the neighborhood were poor, and none of his subsequent successes in

life could erase those boyhood memories. His reflections in later years reveal a deep and abiding love for his parents that was grounded both in personal feeling and a healthy sense of filial duty. We imagine that he derived strength of character from his stoic and stalwart parents.

At the appropriate time, Ezekiel introduced his sons to the workplace. Leon's relations with his father were not always easy, especially when they worked together in Ezekiel's shop, which was a routine part of the boy's life. The intimate bonding between father and son took place there. Leon sometimes chafed under his father's discipline, but he had tremendous respect for him. He learned a lot about the labor movement and politics and unions from his father who passed his Jacksonian convictions along to his son. Ezekiel would live long enough to see Leon complete his first term as governor of New Jersey, but not his second term. He died on January 1, 1889, at the age of eighty-one. At the time of Ezekiel's death, Leon looked back on his family life with fond memories of warmth and affection.[17] His whole outlook on life was fundamentally shaped by his Jacksonian upbringing.

In the presidential election of 1840, Martin Van Buren, the Democratic incumbent, was challenged by Whig candidate William Henry Harrison, who was a decorated military veteran of the Indian wars. Harrison had become a national hero (and got a nickname) when he defeated the Shawnee tribe at the battle of Tippecanoe in 1811. His running mate was John Tyler. Each candidate claimed to have the right answers to such contentious questions as how to improve the economy, reorganize the military, regulate trade, and define the role of the federal government in national life. It was the first modern political campaign, complete with catchy slogans, rousing songs, colorful parades, and political symbols. Whig crowds chanted slogans such as "Van, Van, he's a used-up man!" and "Tippecanoe and Tyler too!" The Whigs promoted Harrison as a plainspoken, rustic military hero. They portrayed Martin Van Buren as a guileful, effete aristocrat. In the end, Harrison won the presidency.

AN ANTIMONOPOLY RIOT

Meanwhile, Kensington residents took direct action whenever their community was threatened. In the early 1840s, the Philadelphia and Trenton Railroad began constructing its tracks down the middle of Front Street, which created a public nuisance. The railroad obstructed horse-drawn vehicles, endangered pedestrians, and posed a serious fire hazard. Residents feared that the hot coals spewed from its locomotives would ignite their wooden-frame houses. They voiced their complaints and pressured city officials to abate the nuisance. The latter ducked the issue,

claiming that the state had jurisdiction because it granted the railroad its special charter and right-of-way.

By 1842, as confrontation loomed, Kensington residents mobilized for action. Rebuffed by local officials, the angry protesters decided to take matters into their own hands. Women stoned construction crews during the day, while men destroyed the tracks at night. News of this violence reached the state capital in Harrisburg. A few weeks later, the state legislature withdrew the railroad's right-of-way, thereby halting construction.[18] Ordinary working people had discovered their power.

Antebellum Philadelphia was hardly the City of Brotherly Love that William Penn had envisioned in his utopian experiment. With a rising tide of nativism, the city became the scene of religious bigotry and racial intolerance. The source of the anxiety was the large number of pre-famine Irish who had arrived in large numbers around 1833. Fresh off the boat, these urban newcomers encountered a hostile environment. They were numerous enough to frighten nativist Protestants, who saw them as slavish followers of a Roman Pope. In Protestant eyes, Irish Catholic immigrants appeared alien, uncouth, and menacing. These ethnic tensions were most pronounced in Kensington and Southwark, which were fast becoming Irish enclaves.

The nativists were mostly Protestant fundamentalists who saw the Catholic church as the handiwork of Satan and superstition. They were highly organized and fielded a variety of spokesmen. Intellectuals argued that Catholicism was incompatible with American democracy; while ethnocentric cultural purists advocated that the United States should be reserved exclusively for Anglo-Saxons. Some genuinely believed that it would be difficult to integrate so many culturally diverse immigrants. The nativists in other sections of the nation included among their number such illustrious Americans as John Jay, John Quincy Adams, John Calhoun, Stephen Douglas, and P. T. Barnum, all of whom spoke out publicly against the Catholic church and warned of the dire consequences that would happen if Catholics were allowed into the country. Samuel Morse, the inventor of the telegraph, spread rumors of Catholic conspiracies against liberty. Scurrilous books, depicting salacious stories about concupiscence in convents and sex in seminaries, were widely circulated. This sort of hate-mongering continued throughout the nineteenth century.

Ship traffic into the deep-water port of Philadelphia and the tonnage of cargo handled by its dock workers grew steadily. So did the large influx of Irish immigrants. As people with a strange brogue, peculiar clothes, wrong religion, willingness to work for long hours and low wages, and other distinctive but unloved traits, the Irish were an object of xenophobia long before the famine. Many had the further disadvantage of lacking all but rudimentary English. Most were illiterate peasants. By the late 1830s, they filled most of the unskilled occupations in the city:

stevedores, coal heavers, hod carriers, laborers, draymen, and carters. The pittance they received in wages barely sustained their families. Because they arrived in such staggering numbers, the city was woefully unprepared to receive them. Poverty, discrimination, unemployment, and a crippled economy exacerbated their vulnerability. As Dennis Clark points out, "The Irish immigrants, jammed into overcrowded housing, laboring under a memory of oppression in Ireland, and confronted by nativist hostility in the city, were appropriate tinder for intergroup conflagration."[19] Nowhere was this tinder more flammable than in Kensington.

The Catholic church, with its foreign immigrant priests, its medieval religious dogma, and its centralized authority, became a symbol of distrust and hatred to most Protestants. To them, Catholicism seemed so blasphemous, idolatrous, superstitious, and ostentatious compared with the stark simplicity of their religion. Worse, they saw Catholics as owing their primary allegiance to a foreign power in the Vatican in Rome. Suspicions between the two traditions ran deep. In the coded language of the day, Protestant clergymen placed much emphasis on "liberty of conscience," which was a way of alerting their adherents to the dangers of Catholicism. Such concepts captured the fears and anxieties of most Protestants, who saw the Catholic church as a direct threat to American democracy.

Protestants elsewhere were equally alarmed by the rapid spread of popery. Fear and antipathy toward Catholics had reached new heights in Massachusetts in 1834, when an angry mob of nativists set fire to a convent in Charlestown where Ursuline nuns ran a boarding school for children. This mob was incited by Lyman Beecher, a Congregational minister and father of Harriet Beecher Stowe. Secret Protestant societies were formed to combat the Catholic menace. They included groups like the Sons of the Sires, the United Sons of America, and the Order of the Star Spangled Banner. These fraternal groups copied Masonry in their hierarchical degrees of membership, initiation rites, and secret oaths of allegiance. Before long, they coalesced into the Native American party, or what became known as the Know-Nothing party. Caught up in this popular hysteria, the Know-Nothings exploited the growing animosity toward Catholics and foreigners.[20] With an anti-immigrant agenda, they recruited their leaders primarily from the white middle class, but they also attracted a large following among skilled Protestant workers. Kensington soon became a hotbed of nativist politics and a breeding ground for Know-Nothings.

Native Protestant workers felt threatened by the growing pool of cheap, immigrant labor. They felt that they were witnessing the destruction of their traditional American way of life. Their hatred of the Irish became fused with their fear of Catholicism. Confronted by events they could not fully comprehend, they took their prejudices into the streets.

"Like the working-class Irish," historian Michael Feldberg writes, "native artisans were quick with their fists or paving stones in debates over religion, politics, economics, or personal and group honor."[21]

Ordained a Catholic priest at Saint Mary's seminary in Emmitsburg, Maryland, in 1826, the Irish-born John Hughes was assigned to the diocese of Philadelphia where he became an eloquent and courageous crusader against religious bigotry. He did not want Catholics to become second-class citizens in America as they were under British rule in Ireland. Moreover, he felt it his duty not to repeat the mistakes of the clergy in Ireland, who had been remiss in not speaking out more forcefully against British oppression. Resistance to the hate groups, in his view, was imperative. During the 1834 cholera epidemic in Philadelphia, which nativists blamed on Irish immigrants, Hughes worked tirelessly among the sick and dying, while many Protestant ministers fled the city to escape infection. After the pestilence subsided, he wrote the *U.S. Gazette* that Protestant ministers were "remarkable for their pastoral solicitude, so long as the flock is healthy, the pastures pleasant, and the fleece lubricant, abandoning their post when disease begins to spread dissolution in the fold."[22] He praised the work of the Catholic Sisters of Charity, who had cared for cholera victims without regard for their own personal safety, and he wondered out loud where all the people who spoke about perversion in the convents had gone during the epidemic. The object lesson was clear.

RACE RIOTS

Religion was not the only source of social conflict and violence. Philadelphia was a racial time bomb waiting to explode. White supremacy was prevalent throughout Pennsylvania, which had rescinded the vote to blacks at its state constitutional convention in 1837. The power of the vote would not be restored to black male voters until 1870, five years after the Civil War. In 1838, an angry mob set fire to Pennsylvania Hall, then hosting a convention of the Women's Anti-Slavery Society. This was an interracial event. The sight of black and white women walking together arm-in-arm had inflamed the racist mob. Volunteer firemen, who were summoned to the scene, protected the surrounding buildings but allowed the hall to burn to the ground. In the aftermath of this fire, race relations became increasingly strained.

Most of the dockworkers and stevedores in Philadelphia were Irish. They found their jobs threatened by blacks, who lived in the wretched slums near the wharves. Shipowners often played black and Irish dockworkers off against each other to obstruct union organizing. Intimidation and fighting were endemic to the waterfront. The Irish

underclass fought desperately to protect jobs; this was a fight for economic survival.

The Irish fear of degrading competition with black labor no doubt contributed to their Negrophobia. They were envious of a black elite who prospered in the city. Philadelphia had the largest and most distinguished African-American population of any city north of the Mason Dixon line.[23] In an ostentatious display of their economic success, some blacks hired white drivers for their carriages. Racial tensions were exacerbated by economic competition for low-paying jobs. The Irish nightmare of blacks moving North to steal their jobs seemed to be coming true. Blacks continued to arrive almost daily via the Underground Railroad, a loosely connected network of routes originated in the South, intertwined throughout the free North, and often extended into Canada. The northern migration of blacks set off a wave of attacks on black neighborhoods.

One of the most violent race riots erupted on August 1, 1842. The riot began in Moyamensing, a working-class suburb that boasted 450 liquor dealers, most of whom were Irish. A group of emancipated slaves from the British West Indies had organized a temperance parade to celebrate the anniversary of their emancipation. When the black marchers took a wrong turn in their parade route, they inadvertently strayed into an Irish neighborhood. The unfriendly Irish were spoiling for a fight. A temperance march casting the British in a favorable light provided sufficient provocation. The blacks were severely beaten, their homes destroyed, and a black church was burned. Since the blacks and Irish were the two most impoverished groups in the city, it was a case of "the poorest of the poor" fighting each other.

Frictions in the workplace often flared into rioting. In 1836, Philadelphia longshoremen joined in a strike that tied up most of the ports along the eastern seaboard. Weavers in Kensington and Moyamensing went on strike in 1842 to protest a cut in the piece rate. They marched through the textile districts, entered the homes of nonstriking weavers, and threw their unfinished work into the street. The strikers then broke up a meeting of master weavers by threatening to destroy the house in which their meeting was taking place. In January 1843, weavers armed with bricks and two-by-fours drove off a sheriff's posse that tried to arrest a strike leader.

A MOVE TO THE CENTER CITY

For whatever reasons, the Abbetts decided to move from Beach Street in Kensington to center city Philadelphia, where the respectable shopkeepers lived. City directories indicate that this move took place in 1842. They purchased a modest house at 109 North Fifth Street, just a few blocks

from Independence Hall. It stood on what is now the site of the U. S. Mint, which put them in the heart of the city. It was not a fashionable section of the city, but one that was attractive in terms of desired city services and proximity to the fledgling public schools.

The Pennsylvania Anti-Slavery Society, headquartered across the street from the Abbetts, was where abolitionists, both black and white, mounted their attacks against the slave power. They viewed slavery as sinful, and in their opinion slaveowners were no better than common criminals. One of their fiery orators was a black named William Still, born into slavery but who subsequently bought his freedom. He went on to become a successful coal and lumberyard dealer in Philadelphia. A courageous man, Still had dedicated himself to freeing blacks who remained in human bondage. He masterminded and coordinated the covert operations of the Underground Railroad.

For the next eighteen years, Leon Abbett grew up watching the comings and goings of these abolitionists. How much their activities rubbed off on him is hard to say, but his contact with them did not make him sympathetic to their cause. On the contrary, it probably had a negative effect on him. A segregated city no doubt influenced his early views on race, which were decidedly antiblack.

Movement up and out of the working class via an artisan proprietorship was becoming increasingly difficult for those Philadelphians at the lower end of the economic scale.[24] Few artisans achieved such success. Ezekiel Abbett was one who did. He kept abreast of the division of labor taking place within the hat industry by shifting to the more specialized task of pressing women's bonnets. From 1843 on, he was listed in the city directory as a bonnet presser.[25] He was gradually moving from wage labor to self-employment as an entrepreneur.

Although Ezekiel and Sarah had received little formal schooling themselves, they encouraged their children to obtain as much education as possible. This required considerable sacrifice on their part. Sarah opened a millinery shop at the intersection of Callowhill and North Fifth Street, where she retailed women's bonnets. At the time, it was frowned on for a married white woman to enter the workforce, even if she came from the laboring classes. Yet, it was not unusual for the wife of an artisan to sell his products. The Quaker emphasis on family life, combined with the cult of domesticity, put pressure on women to stay at home. Sarah defied this cultural norm. She saved most of what she earned to help defray the expense of educating her children.

At age six, Leon Abbett was enrolled in the Fulton Grammar School within walking distance of where he lived. He attended this neighborhood school from 1842 until 1849. The building, which stood on the south side of New Street, had been a former Quaker Meeting House. It was converted for school purposes in 1838, when Thaddeus Stevens, a

dedicated abolitionist and state legislator from Gettysburg, led the charge for free public education in Pennsylvania. The public school movement was launched under the mantle of civic virtue.

At the Fulton School, Leon obtained the conventional education offered at the primary level in the 1840s. He learned the basic skills of reading, writing, and arithmetic. The hatter's son worked on his math problems, memorized his multiplication tables, and perfected his graceful, free-flowing penmanship. Students were taught the Palmer method of handwriting. They also learned the fundamentals of grammar, spelling, history, and world geography. Much of this learning was done by rote, whereby students were required to recite lessons from their textbooks and to write compulsory exercises. The *McGuffey Eclectic Reader* had been recently introduced in the public school classrooms across the country. This famous textbook was named after its author, William McGuffey, who believed in teaching moral values and individual responsibility. The object of the *McGuffey's Reader*, the preface stated, was not only to "present the best specimens of style in the English language" and "to impart valuable information," but also to "exert a decided and healthful moral influence."

By the age of ten, an intelligent and impressionable Leon Abbett was fascinated with books. Encouraged by his parents, he became an avid reader, enjoying the dime novels and adventure stories that were popular in his day. He read just about everything he could get his hands on. These reading habits stirred his imagination and excited his boundless curiosity. He dreamed the normal boy's dreams and aspired to make something of himself. His mother taught Sunday school and counseled Leon to take worthwhile risks.

BIBLE READING AND THE NATIVIST RIOTS

While Leon was attending the Fulton School, Bible instruction in the public schools became a volatile political issue. The school day began every morning with the reading of passages from the Protestant King James Bible. Most of the school teachers were Protestants who used textbooks that were blatantly anti-Catholic. Some indoctrinated their pupils with the idea that Protestantism was synonymous with the American way of life. Irish Catholic parents objected to such religious instruction on the grounds that it put pressure on students to conform to that religious belief. They felt their children were threatened by values that they abhorred. More precisely, they objected to the compulsory reading of the King James Bible, which conjured up in their minds the Protestant Reformation and hostile British oppression in Ireland.

In 1842, a Catholic teacher in Southwark had been fired for refusing to start the school day with readings from the Protestant Bible. Bishop

Francis P. Kenrick, the Catholic spiritual leader, met with school officials to resolve the dispute. Kenrick negotiated an agreement whereby Catholic children would be allowed to read their own Douay Bible or else be excused from the religious exercises. This compromise did not sit well with die-hard Protestants. Suspicious of Kenrick's motives and incensed by his bold initiative, they attacked him as a foreign prelate who was interfering in American public education. They accused Catholics of trying to remove the Bible from the schools. Although bogus, this accusation was nonetheless inflammatory.

With both sides stockpiling weapons, an air of violence hung over the city. The dispute reached a flash point in 1844, when Catholic alderman Hugh Clark, a member of the Kensington school board, ordered an immediate suspension of Bible reading in public schools. This action intensified fears on both sides and sparked an outburst of violence. For several days bands of armed men roamed the streets and fought pitched gun battles. The nativists attacked Irish neighborhoods, where they met with return gunfire. Most of the rioting took place in Kensington and Southwark. When the local police arrived, they were unable to subdue the combatants, and the rioting raged out of control. At the request of city officials, the governor of Pennsylvania called out the state militia, whereupon the riots turned into a bloody massacre. Sixteen people were killed and others wounded. Philadelphia was in flames. Two Catholic churches were burned along with a Catholic library.[26]

Saint Augustine's Catholic Church, at Fourth and Vine streets, was destroyed by fire. The Abbetts lived just around the corner from this church, and they probably watched it burn, or at least they saw the smoldering remains. It was a sight hard to forget. The torching of churches was a favorite tactic used by the Protestant majority to intimidate the Catholic minority. But the arsonists did not succeed. It only hardened the Irish resolve. The church burners were unable to drive them out of the city. Black churches, which hid fugitive slaves, also were the targets of arsonists. Some blacks, who feared for their lives, quietly slipped across the Delaware River to New Jersey. They resettled there in rural communities like Burlington, Mount Holly, and Swedesboro.

The causes of the religious riots in 1844 extended beyond Bible reading. In a faltering economy, the crosscutting issues of nativism and anti-Catholicism were inextricably linked with unemployment. After the riots, the religious conflict defined a central fault line in American politics for years to come. The downtrodden Irish, whose plight was unending, were blamed for everything that went wrong in Philadelphia. By blaming the victims, the nativists found a convenient scapegoat to express a passion for political retribution that far exceeded Bible reading. This social divisiveness split the laboring classes along religious lines and undercut the class solidarity that Jacksonian Democrats had worked hard to achieve.[27]

The Second Awakening was a religious revival that prompted evangelical Protestants to redirect their energy to the temperance movement. It was an effort on their part to use government to make people virtuous.[28] Temperance caught hold in Pennsylvania, attracting serious commentators and public figures as well as finding considerable support, even if under close scrutiny, it turned out to be illusory. Appealing to deepening frustration and righteous indignation, the temperance advocates sought to persuade the lower classes that alcohol was the root of all evil and immorality. A clash of cultures was the inevitable result. As Arthur Schlesinger notes, "The German fondness for beer gardens and jolly Sundays excited puritanical disapproval. The Irish were regarded as shiftless and drunken; moreover, they were papists, and their fealty to Rome, it was said, meant they could never become loyal Americans."[29]

Temperance preachers spoke about the moral failure of those who succumbed to the temptations of alcohol. They also sought to prevent the desecration of the Sabbath that in their view was the Lord's day and to be observed as a day of rest and spirituality. Blue laws were passed to ensure such behavior. Stores and taverns were not allowed to do business on Sunday.

These militant efforts produced impressive results. A large number of Philadelphians took the pledge. Adult per-capita consumption of alcohol diminished accordingly. Because of its moralistic fervor, the temperance crusade heightened ethnic tensions. Resistance came mostly from German and Irish immigrants, whose beer gardens and taverns were centers of social and political life. Their contempt for temperance advocates was hardly concealed.

Economic recovery from the depression lessened the conflict between native and foreign-born workers to some extent, but as the flood of immigrants increased, so did resentments among the nativists. By 1850, Catholics from Ireland comprised twenty percent of Philadelphia's population. More were still to come. Such rapid growth caused many problems, especially with regard to housing, policing, public sanitation, and health care. Crime and welfare costs soared. Protestants attributed these problems to Irish immigrants, whose arrest rate and share of relief funds were higher than their percentage of the population. They were particularly incensed by Catholic efforts to obtain public funding for parochial schools. Catholic priests, who tended to the spiritual needs of their flock, were denied access to local hospitals and prisons.

Clannish by nature, the Irish turned inward and sought solidarity among their own. They overcame nativist hostility by creating an awareness of their shared destiny and by forming powerful social institutions like the parochial schools and the Knights of Columbus.[30] To alleviate their suffering, they turned to their religion and parish life for solace and

comfort. They relied on the role that family, church, school, and neighborhood played in their lives.

Even before the nativist riots of 1844, the Irish had voted Democratic. They were offended and put off by the Whiggish nature of nativism. The more the Whigs insulted the Irish with their ethnic slurs and papist invectives, the easier it was for Jacksonian Democrats to lure them into their party. By the same token, the Whigs drew substantial support from native Protestant workers with their anti-Irish appeals. Many of them deserted the Democratic party and joined the Whigs. Not surprisingly, the Know-Nothings competed with both the Whigs and the Republicans for the anti-Irish vote. In the early 1850s, the Know-Nothings were the fastest growing party in states like Massachusetts, Pennsylvania, and New Jersey. They supported their own candidates as well as those who shared their goals of restricting officeholding to native-born Protestants and preventing immigrants from voting by lengthening the period of naturalization and allowing only citizens to vote. The Know-Nothing movement not only scrambled American politics, but it also produced favorable results at the polls.

The tides of popular support that shifted back and forth between the parties in these years resulted in a realignment of voters. Impressed by the electoral gains of the Know-Nothings, the Republicans exploited the religious animosity of Protestant workers. Some historians contend that the Republicans became a major political force during this era by recruiting anti-Irish workers into their party. These same scholars argue that the Irish question was even more important than slavery in terms of the party realignment that took place during the 1850s.[31] The common denominator that united Know-Nothings and Protestant immigrants was their hatred of Catholics. The Quakers were almost always Whigs and later Republicans.

As a teenager, young Leon Abbett continued to be exposed to a large dose of anti-Catholic, anti-Irish, and antiliquor sentiment, and even a larger dose of Protestant evangelicalism. Following the racial violence of 1842, a seven-year period of racial peace existed between blacks and whites. This racial peace was shattered by an election-day street fight on October 9, 1849, when an angry mob of whites attacked blacks on the corner of Sixth and Saint Mary streets in Moyamensing. It was the site of a popular tavern known as the California House, owned by a black man who had recently married a white woman. It was rumored that the tavern was a front for a brothel. Outrage over prostitution and miscegenation sparked the rampage. What started as a barroom brawl quickly erupted into a full-scale race riot. Blacks retaliated and fought back. One black and three whites were killed. Nine whites and sixteen blacks were hospitalized, and many more were injured.[32]

THE CENTRAL HIGH SCHOOL YEARS

Shortly before this race riot occurred, Leon Abbett had entered the Central High School, then located on Juniper Street. He passed its rigorous entrance examination on July 18, 1849. Of the 189 white boys who took the exam that day, 125 passed it while 64 failed. The stringent admission requirements were based on merit and the admissions process was highly competitive. In the words of Franklin Edmonds, the school historian, "To be admitted was a great honor, and correspondingly great was the sting of defeat."[33] From its beginning, the school was animated by an egalitarian spirit and the academic environment was challenging. Students were drawn from almost every segment in society. Black students, however, were not admitted until 1881, when the school was desegregated.

Founded in 1836, Central High was the precious crown jewel that stood at the apex of the city's public educational system. Here Leon Abbett would obtain a classical education and be groomed for future leadership. The school, known for its academic rigor, was modeled after the Boston Latin School that had been established 200 years earlier in 1635. The all-white, male Central High reflected the rigid gender and racial segregation of the time. It never occurred to anyone then that such an admissions policy was discriminatory. It seemed a natural order of things as God had ordained them. The school was established with surplus federal funds that had been left over from the second Andrew Jackson administration. This was a time when the national government raised more revenue than it could spend—a result of high tariffs and low federal expenditures. The surplus money was returned to the states for their discretionary use.

By the time Leon Abbett entered Central High, this elite exam school already had made a name for itself. It compared favorably with the military academy at West Point when it came to teaching mathematics and the natural sciences. As a result of its high academic standards, the Pennsylvania legislature conferred degree-granting power to the school in 1849. This was the same year that Leon was admitted. Popularly known as the "People's College," Central High educated boys whose parents could not afford to send them to college.[34] Wealthy Philadelphians sent their sons either to the University of Pennsylvania or to Princeton. A private college education in this era was only for the privileged few. The public land-grant college movement would not begin for another decade.

Working people, like Ezekiel and Sarah Abbett, saw Central High as the great lever of upward mobility. The 400 places in its student body were highly coveted. Its curriculum was classical and fully prescribed; every course was required of every student. Not only the courses, but even the textbooks were rigidly prescribed. Classes consisted for the most part of recitations based on home work assignments. Most everyone knew

what a classical education meant—Latin, Greek, the Bible, mathematics, English literature, and ancient history.

It would have been hard to find a person better suited to run the school than John Seely Hart, its influential and widely respected principal. During his tenure as principal, which lasted from 1842 until 1858, he turned a good school into an outstanding institution. The principal urged the faculty to challenge and inspire their students, and to prepare them to go out into the world as educated and informed citizens. Many of its graduates went on to distinguish themselves in their chosen fields of endeavor. Sociologist Digby Baltzell claims that the school produced more leaders of real distinction than any other educational institution in the city, including the University of Pennsylvania.[35] Among its famous alumni were U.S. Senator Charles F. Manderson of Nebraska, Governor Robert E. Pattison of Pennsylvania, and Representative Ignatius Donnelley of Minnesota. Henry George attended Central High for a brief period, but his family moved away before he could finish. Later, George ran unsuccessfully for mayor of New York and proposed his single-tax idea in 1886. Another distinguished alumnus, Jeremiah P. O'Connor, became a Jesuit priest and served as president of Boston College from 1880 to 1884.

A Princeton graduate and ordained Presbyterian minister, John Hart was a man of exemplary rectitude. He attended the Tenth Presbyterian Church in Philadelphia, where he was active in the Sunday School movement and carried forward into this new era the best tradition of evangelical Protestantism. Hart looked after his students in much the same way that a pastor tended his flock. He prepared his charges for life's serious purpose by stressing the importance of character and encouraging them to develop habits of hard work, self-reliance, and perseverance. An energetic and somewhat evangelical pedagogue, Hart was a stern disciplinarian who knew how to turn unruly boys into refined gentlemen, and insisted on civility and tolerance. He also taught courses in Anglo-Saxon and English literature. His favorite author was Edmund Spenser. When lecturing in class, he quoted passages from Addison, Byron, Chaucer, Pope, and Milton, and he expected his students to do likewise.[36]

As an educational reformer, Hart was comparable in stature to Horace Mann and Henry Barnard. He tackled the thorny issue of school reform, concluding that major changes and innovations in curricula were necessary if Central High was to provide a trained workforce and meet its commitment to the larger community. As a result, the principal revised its admission requirements, tightened its academic standards, and revamped its curriculum. Retaining classical studies as its core, Hart felt that it was possible to conceive of entirely new paths for learning experiences, fitting modes of instruction to preprofessional training while preparing students for the workforce. He introduced new courses in trigonometry, surveying, navigation, bookkeeping, and phonography. These courses not only

enriched the curriculum, but they also provided students with practical hands-on skills that the marketplace demanded.

Tensions at the school surfaced in the early 1850s when nativist Know-Nothings threatened to lower its standards and make it mediocre. Alarmed by these prospects, Hart fought hard to defend the school from such political interference. He also lobbied for more public funds. Over and beyond that, he dispensed with the traditional written final examination for seniors. As an alternative, he invited prominent citizens to examine the boys orally. Intrigued by this innovation, the examiners responded with great interest. This novel experiment proved successful, especially when it came to job placements. Employment notices that appeared in the press frequently stated that a Central High graduate was preferred.

By all accounts, Leon Abbett was a bright student, high-spirited, and somewhat mischievous. During his freshman and sophomore years, he struggled academically and earned only mediocre grades. Under Hart's guidance and discipline, Leon settled down and displayed a willingness to learn and achieve. In terms of overall academic performance, he was a good student—not great—but very good.[37] While he preferred to mask his intelligence, he sometimes allowed it to shine through. The principal sensed, from the very beginning, that the hatter's son was talented and promising, but a little too rambunctious and undisciplined for his own good. Hart took a special interest in the boy and had a discernible influence on him. Leon in turn became a more active and constructive participant in class. Hart encouraged him to believe in himself and to take his studies seriously. Indeed, it was Hart's faith in Abbett that helped the boy emerge from his adolescent trials with his confidence strengthened rather than broken. Hart would be the most important influence in his life.

The best of Leon's teachers were intellectually stimulating men who nourished and expanded young minds. They encouraged critical thinking and cautioned against received wisdom, prejudice, and dogmatism. In James Rhoades, the students had an inspiring rhetoric and history teacher who linked the past with the present. It was in his classroom that Abbett first learned about American history and government. Standing 6 feet 9 inches tall, Professor Rhoades towered over his students and intimidated them with his stern manner and rigorous standards. He insisted on original work in their assigned term papers and was a stickler for proper grammar and punctuation. Under Rhoades' tutelage, the hatter's son realized his academic potential and blossomed as a student. Leon would astonish his father and mother and even his closest friends. Most of all he would surprise himself.

Abbett had the benefit of other learned men like Martin H. Boye, Ezra O. Kendall, and William Vogdes, who taught chemistry, astronomy, and mathematics, respectively. Only a few students could actually follow Professor Vogdes' demanding lectures on calculus. The school had one of the best equipped astronomical observatories in the country and the quality of its German-made telescopes were superior to those at Harvard. The return of Halley's Comet in 1835 had ushered in a new age of astronomy that stimulated a renewed interest in teaching the subject. The popularity of this course depended as much on Professor Kendall's exuberance as a teacher as it did on his lectures in cosmology. In taking this course, Abbett was motivated by a city boy's innate curiosity to learn more about the solar system and the beginnings of the universe, but his burning ambition was to rise above his station in life.

Nor were the other teachers any less demanding. Henry McMurtrie taught courses in anatomy, physiology, medicine, and surgery and impressed his students by lecturing without notes. Another inspiring teacher was Henry Haverstick, who taught Latin and Greek. He had his students read Ceasar, Cicero, and Virgil as well as Dante, Homer, and Petrarch.

Foreign language study suffered at Central High, partly because of the lack of instruction at the lower elementary schools. Part of this deficiency was due to political interference by Know-Nothings who branded foreign language teachers as subversive and un-American. Between 1853 and 1856, the Know-Nothing movement swept the farms and villages of rural Pennsylvania. Party leaders also swept the city elections in 1854, and they captured most of the state's congressional seats. In 1856, they won control of the state legislature. Once they gained power locally, the Know-Nothings promptly fired the foreign language teachers at Central High solely for political reasons.

In 1850, when Leon was a sophomore, the admissions policy at the school came under attack. Working people complained that the composition of its student body reflected an inherent class bias that favored the middle and upper classes. A special blue-ribbon committee was appointed to investigate the matter. Its members included Craig Biddle, Jesse R. Burden, Thomas K. Finletter, and Fayette Pierson. They found no evidence to substantiate such charges, and ignoring the gender and racial segregation, they concluded that the school was sufficiently diverse in its admissions. They further noted that "no graduate had ever been arraigned before our courts on a criminal charge."[38]

A group of British educators, who had visited Central High in 1845, were very much impressed with the school. They wrote as much in their report:

> We see in it four hundred boys selected from all classes of society, without respect to rank or patronage, whose only certificate of admission is superiority of talent and capacity for learning—whose only certification for continuance is industry and good conduct. Here are seen, side by side, the child of the judge and the child of the laborer, the children of the physician, the merchant, the lawyer, and the manufacturer, in the same class with those of the bricklayer, the carter, the cordwainer, and the

blacksmith, studying without distinction, under masters and professors of the same attainments, in the halls and classrooms equalling those of many of our colleges.[39]

Four years at Central High had a significant influence on Leon Abbett, who attended the school from 1849 to 1853. These were some of the happiest years of his life. He wanted very much to be liked by the other boys and formed some lasting friendships. Among his boyhood friends were Willard Blair, John Campbell, Thomas Davis, Gerald DeCoursey, George Ford, and Charles Higgins. They had all attended the Fulton Grammar School together before moving on to Central High.

Always clever and resourceful, Leon won the respect of his teachers and peers both in the classroom and on the playgrounds. He had an attractive personality and a strong motivation to succeed. From puberty onward, he had been testing the parameters of his existence, stretching them at times to see how far he could go. At times, his hyperactivity landed him in trouble. The whole pattern of faculty control and discipline was designed to reward obedience and punish aggressiveness. The student code of conduct was rigidly enforced. The number of demerits that a student received as punishment for disciplinary infractions was subtracted from his grade-point average. Evidently, Abbett was a high-spirited lad who did not conform to the tyranny of such harsh discipline. No one could tame his restless spirit, not even John Hart. But all who dealt with him were captivated by his contradictions and won over by his boyish charm.

By the time Abbett had completed Central High, his distinctive ways had set him apart. Three decades later, when Abbett was inaugurated as governor of New Jersey, an anonymous classmate remarked, "Leon at school was one of those bright boys who always know their lessons, yet are relegated to the rear because of their unruly spirit. Young Abbett was the leader of his class in all their sports and games, and when he went to the High School he was head and shoulders above the rest."[39] These qualities yielded a personality that was aggressive and prone to take risks. During his adolescent teenage years, the hatter's son displayed the genesis of leadership that he would later evince as governor.

The faculty placed a great deal of emphasis on public speaking and debating. Declamations, disputations, and orations were regular fare and there was keen competition for public speaking prizes. Congressmen John C. Calhoun, Henry Clay, and Daniel Webster were the great speakers in this "golden age of oratory." The Central High boys emulated their speaking style as best they could.

Inspired by the oratorical prowess of his American heroes, Abbett excelled in public speaking and debating. When it came to debating skills, Leon learned how to frame an argument, reason logically, support his position with evidence, and anticipate the opposition. He was good at

dialectic and became one of the best declaimers in his class. Seldom did he get tripped up on questions of fact and general knowledge.

One such incident occurred when Leon was participating in an oratorical contest. Upon hearing the name of the person about whom he was assigned to speak, Abbett drew a mental blank and froze momentarily. On his way to the podium, the befuddled hatter's son asked the boy next to him for help. His classmate whispered the man's occupation. Aided by this scant prompting, Leon recovered sufficiently and proceeded to deliver a speech that won the first prize.[41] Such was his ability to speak extemporaneously. His oratorical capabilities would eventually take him into law and politics.

The competition to obtain good grades at Central High was intense. Every student was graded on his daily recitations, his term papers, and his test scores. Some students dropped out and did not complete the full four-year program. While the school accepted students on the basis of merit, it also meticulously weeded out those who could not meet its rigorous standards. Of the 125 boys who started with Leon Abbett, only 23 completed the four-year program. At the end of four years, Leon Abbett had compiled a grade-point average of 74.3 (a grade of 60 was passing). The grade-point averages in his class ranged from a high of 94.3 to a low of 61.8.

For the first two years, Abbett's grades were just average. As to his mediocre performance, that is impossible to fathom. Some of it no doubt was due to his poor conduct and unapplied ability. He was an underachiever as well as a late bloomer. During his junior and senior years, his grades improved substantially. By his senior year, he had raised his term average to 86.5, which earned him distinction.[42] This was quite a feat for a working-class boy. Central High contributed both to his intellectual growth and social development. His education there transformed his life by enabling him to contemplate the future in ways that would otherwise have seemed unattainable.

Leon Abbett graduated from Central High on July 21, 1853. Commencement exercises were held at the Musical Fund Hall, which was large enough to hold the huge crowds who wanted to watch some twenty-three young people walk across the stage for their degrees. The Right Reverend Alonzo Potter delivered the invocation. Faculty, alumni, trustees, and relatives sat listening to the dignified flow of senior oratory. Abbett was chosen as one of ten commencement speakers. The valedictory was given by Orlando G. Wagner, the son of a bookbinder. Evan W. Thomas, who had a grade point average of 94.3, was the top student academically. He was the son of a farmer in Kingsessing.

Most students looked on their world and their lives as a competitive ladder. The commencement program listed the place of each graduating senior in the competitive class standing. Leon Abbett ranked eighth in

his class of twenty-three members.[43] As was his custom, John Hart presented him with a bachelor of arts degree along with a handsome, leather-bound copy of McIlawain's *Evidences of Christianity*.

BECOMING A PHILADELPHIA LAWYER

On graduation, the not quite seventeen Leon Abbett was still undecided about his future. He had no desire to take up his father's trade and wanted to escape the drudgery of hatmaking. Isaac Ashmead, a trustee at Central High, persuaded him to work as an apprentice engraver in his print shop. A master engraver, Ashmead was active in the labor movement and had established an apprentice training program for young men in Philadelphia.[44] Leon had gone to school with his son Henry Ashmead. The trade of engraving was a step up from Ezekiel's occupation as a hatmaker, and one that was less threatened by mechanization. But Leon did not stay long enough to complete his apprenticeship. His brimming ambition would not be satisfied by the tedious work of engraving. Isaac Ashmead saw in him qualities more suited for a legal career.

At this point, Abbett got his first big break. Isaac introduced him to his relative John Wayne Ashmead, who was the U.S. Attorney for the eastern district of Pennsylvania. The latter offered him a chance to clerk in his law office. This was a defining moment in Leon's life. Here was a career cut out for him. The hatter's son had already exhibited that brand of gusto and flowery speech commonly used by the lawyers of his day. This coveted clerkship provided him with a rare opportunity; he would make the most of it.

John Ashmead was a Whig, who became a Know-Nothing in the early 1850s. He had been involved in nativist politics in Kensington and was a member of the Order of the Star-Spangled Banner. He also abstained from alcohol and was active in the temperance movement. Ashmead did not rank among the top attorneys in the city, nor was he part of its economic elite. In 1844, the year of the nativist riots, Ashmead had run unsuccessfully for Congress on the Whig ticket. It was the same year that Henry Clay, a well-known Whig, lost the presidency to Democrat James K. Polk. For the first time, territorial expansion became a major national issue. Polk was an enthusiastic expansionist, who believed that it was America's "manifest destiny" to expand westward to the Pacific and absorb the Oregon territory (then in dispute with Britain) and southward to the Rio Grande, adding Texas (over Mexico's protest) to its continental domain.

Four years later, in 1848, John Ashmead campaigned for Zachary Taylor, who defeated Democrat Lewis Cass for the presidency. Taylor promptly rewarded Ashmead for his party loyalty by appointing him U.S.

Attorney, a position he held from 1849 until 1854. Pro-slavery and pro-Southern in his thinking, Ashmead was strongly opposed to abolition.[45] The slavery question would split the Know-Nothing party in 1855.

In November 1851, Ashmead prosecuted a high profile murder case in the small town of Christiana in Lancaster County. While attempting to capture his runaway slaves, Edward Gorsuch, a Maryland plantation owner, was shot and killed. Castner Hanway, a Quaker sympathizer, who had hidden the slaves in his house, was tried for murder and treason. The government charged that he had participated in an armed rebellion. Before the trial began, the slaves had escaped to Canada. Abolitionist Thaddeus Stevens defended Hanway and succeeded in creating a reasonable doubt in the minds of the jury. Nobody knew for sure who had fired the shots that killed Gorsuch. The jury acquitted Hanway on both counts. But the Christiana uprising was a foreshadowing event that foretold the coming of the Civil War.[46]

At the time, most American lawyers trained by clerking in private law offices and educating themselves by reading the law. Leon Abbett did both in John Ashmead's office at 74 South Fifth Street, not far from where he lived. He spent his time reading case law in the law libraries. There he read the great authorities—Blackstone's *Commentaries*, Chitty's *Pleadings*, and Greenleaf's *Evidence*. Law clerks in those days seldom had firsthand contact with court opinions. The case method of teaching law was still another decade away. So Abbett read the law and absorbed as much knowledge as he could from watching his mentor in action. For the next three years, from 1853 to 1857, he absorbed knowledge of agency, torts, contracts, equity, and replevin. What he did not know, he learned by dint of hard work and on-the-job training. His clerkship in the U.S. Attorney's office enabled him to gain an understanding of federal law and procedure.

Although John Ashmead did not rank among the top lawyers in the city, he was still influential. Admission to the Philadelphia Bar Association depended on being a respectable person and having the support of a prominent sponsor. A committee of lawyers examined the applicants and asked questions that required factual answers. Rejections were common. With Ashmead's sponsorship, Leon Abbett passed the city bar exam on February 5, 1857.[47]

On his admission to the bar, the twenty-year-old Leon Abbett came of age. Still young, he was now a serious professional man. Notable changes in his personal appearance were beginning to take place. He dressed in a manner to impress people; along with more suitable attire, he began to grow a moustache and beard. A bearded face would soften his well-formed features and make him look more mature. The personality traits that would characterize his later life also came into sharper focus. He showed a strong desire to accomplish whatever he set out to do, a stubbornness to adhere to his own point of view, and an unwillingness to concede anything in

argument. These personal traits suggest that his strength as a lawyer depended as much on his advocacy skills as it did on his legal reasoning.

Economic depression struck again in 1857, whereupon Abbett decided to return to Central High to pursue a masters' degree. The combined income of his parents was sufficient to enable him to obtain more education. By this time, Central High had moved from Juniper Street to a new building located on the southeast corner of Broad and Green streets. A year of graduate study enhanced Leon's knowledge and his natural bent toward inductive reasoning. It likewise afforded him an opportunity to polish his skills in rational argumentation and oratory. He received his masters' degree at the commencement exercises at the Academy of Music on July 15, 1858. It was then the largest hall in North America. Also graduating was his younger brother, Franklin Abbett, who received his bachelor of arts degree. Principal John Hart presented both of them with their respective degrees.[48] The Abbetts finished Central High the same year that Hart made his own departure. The principal left to become president of the New Jersey State Normal School in Trenton. Later, Hart was invited to join the Princeton faculty, where he finished his distinguished career as a professor of English.

Shortly after receiving his masters' degree, Abbett opened his own law office at 243 South Fifth Street. Clearly he was conscious of the legal world into which he had entered and of its class implications. His first year of lawyering started inauspiciously. For a young man just entering professional life, he did not fare too well. His practice seemed ill-fated from the start. In the cyclical flow of the economy, times were hard. Although the depression of 1857 turned out milder than expected, Abbett had difficulty attracting clients. Those people who could afford to hire an attorney were more likely to retain an aristocrat rather than a commoner.

Philadelphia teemed with lawyers hungry for cases. Many of them belonged to established father-and-son law firms that made it difficult for someone like Abbett. By 1859, the economic recovery was almost complete, but Leon's law practice did not render him depression-proof. That same year John Brown concocted his raid on the federal arsenal at Harpers Ferry. A fanatical abolitionist, Brown was obsessed with the notion that the slavery issue could be settled only by violence and bloodshed. The specter of civil war loomed large.

ROMANCE AND THE WINDS OF CIVIL WAR

With the winds of war swirling, Leon Abbett met and soon fell in love with the woman he would soon marry. Mary Ann Briggs was a gorgeous and intelligent female who knew and spoke her own mind. Born in Philadelphia to a patrician family, she was truly aristocratic in appearance

and bearing. During their romance, she delighted in teasing and flirting with Leon. Class differences obviously separated them socially, but they were very much attracted to each other. If Leon's intentions were to marry up, he certainly chose the right person.

Mary's father, Amos Briggs, was a prominent Republican lawyer, who later became a judge in the court of Common Pleas. A courtly and elegant gentleman, he had been a Whig before he became a Republican. His dignified Episcopalian demeanor concealed his Quaker origins. Some of the prominent, and most of the socially ambitious, Quakers found it advantageous to become Episcopalians. Amos Briggs, who supported Abraham Lincoln for president in 1860, became one of the founders of the Union League Club in 1862. Established by business and professional men of substance and influence, the Union League became an auxiliary of the Republican party.

Mary, a blonde beauty and a belle of the city, was a cultured and refined young lady, who displayed the social graces and sophisticated ways of a well-bred urban life. She was an 1850s feminist. The Briggs family owned a summer home in Tullytown, where they vacationed. As devout Episcopalians, they had the social status and financial security that Leon Abbett lacked. At first, Mary's parents did not approve of him for reasons that seemed obvious to them. He had no money or social standing. In their eyes, he was beneath their class. They wanted their daughter to marry a wealthy gentlemen, preferably an Episcopalian. As time went on, they gradually came to accept Leon. He talked with them about everything—politics, religion, music, law—and listened attentively when they spoke. Although they felt that Mary could have done better, they reluctantly gave her permission to marry him.

Leon courted Mary Briggs ardently for the next few years. In his efforts to win her hand in marriage, he joined the Episcopal Church and moved up to a more socially prestigious denomination. He did so more for social reasons than from any profound spiritual need or religious experience. Although he may initially have felt uncomfortable with the splendor and formality of a high church denomination, it nonetheless gave him respectability. More important, perhaps, he ingratiated himself with his fiancée as well as her parents. Membership in the Episcopal Church also enabled him to escape from his social class, something few men managed to do in those days.

Philadelphia was a segregated city. Abolitionism was not nearly as strong there as it was in both Boston and New York, although the *Philadelphia Telegram* was the oldest black newspaper in America. As early as 1783, the supreme judicial court in Massachusetts decided that no person residing in the Bay State could be held as a slave. Among its ardent abolitionists were William Lloyd Garrison, Wendell Phillips, Harriet Beecher Stowe, and former slaves Frederick Douglass and Harriet

Tubman. Pained by the injustices of slavery, Stowe wrote her famous novel *Uncle Tom's Cabin*, which was published in 1852. Tubman, who had been abused and cruelly mistreated as a slave in Maryland, was a heroine of the Underground Railroad. Outraged by the evils of slavery and fiercely self-righteous, Garrison penned blistering editorials that condemned this social institution and relentlessly attacked the slaveowners. Known as the "Thunderer," he had founded *The Liberator* in 1831, a militant antislavery newspaper that he used to promote abolitionism. Imbued with an ideological fervor and the moral rectitude of his cause, Garrison was one of the most radical and influential abolitionists in the country. Small wonder that blacks looked upon the Bay State as a beacon of freedom and liberty.

The Liberator had wide appeal. It was the only abolitionist newspaper to survive thirty-four years of continuous publication. Garrison's ability as editor to create and hold a readership impressed and attracted supporters. Even when the abolition movement had splintered into several factions, *The Liberator* remained (despite its idiosyncrasies) the publication that people most closely associated with the cause. Black abolitionist newspapers suffered for their radicalness, and some folded because of lack of advertising and economic failure. Not so for *The Liberator*; a paper that exploited the black cause for its appeal and capitalized on its radicalism.

Run by a white man, the paper tapped revenues not readily available to black abolitionist newspapers. For one thing, the paper geared itself toward a white readership while it also enjoyed the support and attention of blacks. As a result of its appeal to readers on both sides of the color line, the paper offered access to a broader spectrum of the population, and thus could attract advertisers interested in expanding the marketplace beyond the racial limits that held sway during the period.[49]

Many Quakers in Philadelphia were Garrisonians, but most were moderate in their opposition to slavery. A person risked serious repercussions if he or she became too outspoken or too openly identified with the antislavery movement. It was considered a socially disruptive thing to do. Consequently, most upper class gentlemen tended to be either indifferent or complacent. They also opposed women's suffrage and worried that the abolitionist harangues might lead to war.

Few white wage-earning people in Philadelphia favored abolition, and those who did rarely viewed slavery as part of the labor question. Frederick Douglas, a former slave turned impassioned abolitionist, fought tirelessly in his efforts to eradicate slavery. He observed that racism was most prevalent among the city's artisans and mechanics. Reflecting on his own experience in 1862, Douglas remarked, "There is not perhaps anywhere to be found a city in which prejudice against color is more rampant than in Philadelphia."[50]

It was virtually impossible for someone of Abbett's generation not to be caught up in the political agitation over slavery that was sweeping the country. His prejudice against blacks was due mostly to the racist society and segregated city in which he lived, and not because of any personal experience involving race. Although Abbett disapproved of slavery, he had no love for abolitionists or their cause. He saw them as a group of fanatics, who were obsessed with the idea of freeing the slaves and intent on provoking a disastrous war. Like most northern Democrats, Abbett favored a middle course of national reconciliation. He professed a passionate commitment to states' rights, but he did not go so far as to endorse John Calhoun's theories of nullification and secession. While Abbett favored preserving the Union and the Constitution, he was opposed to the national government using its power to compel an end to slavery. That is what he believed the Republicans were trying to do.

As tensions escalated between North and South, Congress was unable to find a satisfactory solution to the problem of slavery that had spread to the new territories. Most Republicans were calling for greater federal responsibility in dealing with this problem. Their shrill voices could be heard in the halls of Congress and state houses throughout the North. The Democrats took a diametrically opposite stand. They believed that each state had a right to determine its own destiny, and that settlers in the new territories should decide the slavery question for themselves. Congress had attempted to settle the controversy with the passage of the Missouri Compromise of 1850 and the Kansas-Nebraska Act of 1854. These legislative remedies were crafted by Henry Clay, John Calhoun, and Daniel Webster, all trying to avert civil war. Centrism was simply inadequate. The most glaring examples of its shortcomings were these doomed efforts at compromise over slavery. They merely postponed the armed conflict.

MOVING TO NEW YORK CITY

In the antebellum America that the French aristocrat Alexis de Tocqueville observed, men who were dissatisfied with the communities into which they were born could simply leave and start over elsewhere. If a young lawyer had what it takes, he could make it on his own. Upward mobility was the great American dream. Never was that dream stronger than on the eve of the Civil War.

Yearning to escape his origins, Abbett had long felt the gravitational pull of New York. In 1860, he decided to leave his native Philadelphia and move to Manhattan. This was a bold decision on his part, because most Philadelphians scoffed at New York as being crass and vulgar. They looked on New Yorkers as being too pushy and overly aggressive. To those who knew him, Abbett's move seemed somewhat puzzling. Surely, his prospective marriage into a highborn Philadelphia family would have gained him entry into a respectable law firm. Both Amos Briggs and John Ashmead could have helped him in this regard. What exactly impelled him to move cannot be ascertained today, but move he did. The only explanation that survives is provided by Hugh McDermott, the editor of the *Jersey City Herald*, who later recalled:

Young lawyers generally seek new territory. No matter what their talents are, they are afraid of entering into competition with men whose fame is established. This was not the case with Mr. Abbett. He felt conscious of his own abilities, and all he desired was a fair opportunity. Like a little giant, unhearlded and unknown, he entered the great metropolis of New York to carve out his own fortune and establish a name.[51]

With boundless faith in his ability to succeed, Abbett saw New York as a place of unlimited opportunity. He also saw it as a place that would give him more freedom and independence. He apparently found class-bound Philadelphia too stodgy and too restrictive. He was determined to go as far as his legal talent would take him.

The presidential campaign of 1860 was a critical election. Abraham Lincoln, who was pro-Union, ran against Democrats Stephen Douglas in the North and John C. Breckinridge of Kentucky in the South. John Bell of Tennessee ran on the National Union ticket. Douglas, author of the Kansas-Nebraska Act in 1854, stumped the nation widely, but he lost mainly because the rival southern Democratic candidate Breckinridge split the vote. Capturing only forty percent of the popular vote, Lincoln was elected president. He carried all the free states except New Jersey, which divided its electoral college vote.

As war approached in the weeks after Lincoln's election, southerners saw his victory as a sign that the Union was about to be radicalized. Feelings ran high. All the pent-up hostility and tensions of the past decade were now unleashed. In Baltimore, anti-Lincoln men rioted in the streets. The emotions of Democrats in New York were no less explosive. In reaction to Lincoln's election southern states began to secede. On February 4, 1861, they formed the Confederacy in Montgomery, Alabama. Any prospects for peaceful reconciliation with the South had vanished. War could no longer be averted. Abolishing slavery was no longer the top priority; preserving the Union, which began falling apart in earnest, had replaced it.

The Civil War began in the early dawn of April 12, 1861, when Confederate artillery batteries, under the command of General Pierre Beauregard, commenced firing on Fort Sumter in Charleston harbor. With the outbreak of hostilities and the fall of Fort Sumter, President Lincoln immediately issued a call for 75,000 volunteers. At the time, the Union Army suffered a severe manpower shortage. Drawn by the lure of the soldier's bonus, hundreds of Pennsylvania farm boys and those in the

cities responded to this call and rushed to defend the Union, but Leon Abbett was not among them.

Military operations and ground fighting commenced in the Great Valley, lying between the Allegheny and the Blue Ridge mountains, running roughly northeast-southwest from Pennsylvania through a corner of Maryland and into western Virginia and down to Georgia—thus crossing the Mason-Dixon Line, the traditional dividing line between North and South. Harpers Ferry lay in the valley where the Shenandoah meets the Potomac. It was the scene of some of the most important events and some of the fiercest fighting of the Civil War. Union and Confederate forces soon became engaged in prolonged bloody conflicts. At Malvern Hill, Antietam, Fredericksburg and Gettysburg, the Wilderness and Spotsylvania Courthouse, the list of battles multiplied as the war progressed and casualties on both sides mounted well beyond normal expectations. The death toll skyrocketed as human bodies were strewn across the battlefields. The carnage was appalling.

As a fledgling states' rights Democrat, Leon Abbett, of course, was strongly opposed to the war. Therefore, he did not respond to Lincoln's call for volunteers. Virtually all those who ducked military service were Democrats. The painful reality of what turned out to be a long and gruesome war struck home when Abbett learned that Central High classmate Fletcher Clay had been killed at Fredericksburg.

MARRIAGE AND A LAW PARTNERSHIP

Returning from New York to Philadelphia, Leon Abbett married his fiancée Mary Ann Briggs on October 8, 1862. Their wedding took place on the groom's twenty-sixth birthday. They were married by the Reverend Robert C. Matlack at the Episcopal Church of the Nativity: a handsome Gothic structure that stood on the corner of Eleventh and Mount Vernon streets. A high spirited and vivacious young woman, the bride was described as "lovely, charming, and gracious." Like many women of her era, Mary wanted to be someone and not something, but she was noticed more for her physical beauty than for her intelligence, although she was a smart and talented woman.

The couple decided to live in Hoboken, New Jersey, which sat on the cliffs overlooking the Hudson River. With the spacious parkland and Elysian Fields that bordered the river, Hoboken was then a fashionable suburb of New York. It was only a ferryboat ride to Abbett's law office in Manhattan. The couple thought about living there, but they opted instead for what New Yorkers viewed as the "wilds" of New Jersey.[52]

Through a mutual friend, Abbett was introduced to William J. Fuller, a New York lawyer whom he had wanted to meet. Before long, he

and Fuller formed a legal partnership. Then forty years of age, Fuller was a much older and a more experienced attorney than Abbett. Born in Boston in 1823, Fuller had been raised by his paternal grandfather, the Reverend Daniel Fuller, who was a prominent Congregational minister. William attended Harvard as a freshman, but he did not do well in his studies and was placed on academic probation. He never finished. Shunning the ministry, he clerked in a law office and became a lawyer instead.

Fuller and Abbett were an odd couple. Skeptical by nature, Fuller specialized in admiralty and patent law, whereas Abbett specialized in municipal and corporate law. They differed in ideology and outlook. Fuller was a Republican and a staunch abolitionist. He was outspoken, forceful, and smart, but he lacked Abbett's aggressiveness and intellectual power. Before the Civil War, Fuller had made a name for himself as an antislavery speaker in his native state. During the war he commanded a regiment of Massachusetts volunteers. After the war, Fuller moved to New York where he joined the Union League Club and founded the Whist Club in 1885. He and his family lived at 117 East Thirty-fifth Street.[53]

Fuller recognized Abbett as a man with a bright future in the law, a dynamo bursting with energy and ideas. They combined their considerable talents and established a law office in the vicinity of Battery Park at the lower end of Manhattan. Their address was 229 Broadway and near Barclay Street in the heart of the city's financial district. It was across the street from the Astor House that was a favorite haunt of bankers, stockbrokers, and professional men. Given the profiteering that took place during the Civil War, they had no trouble attracting clients. The bipartisan nature of their law firm contributed to their success. The initial bond between the two men was their commitment to the law.

Abbett and Fuller were both strong-minded lawyers with enough practical experience to master the details of litigation and the burdens of trial practice. In due course, a personal affinity evolved between them that ripened into a close friendship. Their future relationship was one of mutual respect and cooperation. Their law partnership lasted for twenty-six years, or until March 11, 1889, when William Fuller died. But the pattern was already set for the immediate years ahead.

ENDNOTES

1 For the best account of how Philadelphia grew and developed, see Sam Bass Warner, Jr., *The Private City: Philadelphia in Three Periods of Growth* (Philadelphia, University of Pennsylvania Press, 1968), 49-157.
2 For a stimulating case study see Stuart Blumin, "Mobility and Change in Ante-Bellum Philadelphia," in Stephan Thernstrom and Richard Sennett, eds., *Nineteenth-Century Cities* (New Haven, Yale University Press, 1969), 165-208.
3 For a thumbnail sketch of the Abbett's family history see, Charles Robson, *The Biographical Encyclopaedia of New Jersey of The Nineteenth Century* (Philadelphia,

Galaxy Publishing Company, 1877), 316-317. See also *Jersey City Herald*, April 22, 1871.

4 This information about William Abbett's family is found in *Pennsylvania Archives*, series 3, vol. 16, 723. See also "Militia Rolls of Whitpain Township" (1783-1790) *Pennsylvania Archives*, series 6, vol. 3, 1339-40.

5 Records of the Gwynedd and Plymouth Monthly Meetings, housed at the Friends Historical Library at Swarthmore College, show no entries for the senior William Abbett or any of his progeny.

6 Information about the third generation of Abbetts is taken from the *Tax Assessment Books*, stored at the Historical Society of Montgomery County in Norristown, Pennsylvania.

7 See *Pennsylvania Archives*, series 3, vol. 16, 723.

8 Obituary of Ezekiel M. Abbett is found in the *Philadelphia Public Ledger*, January 2, 1889.

9 Bruce Laurie, *Working People of Philadelphia* (Philadelphia, 1980), 14-17.

10 Ronald P. Formisano, *The Birth of Mass Political Parties: Michigan, 1827–1861* (Princeton, Princeton University Press, 1971), 58.

11 Fitzgerald and Gosson, eds., *New Jersey Legislative Manual* (1884), 45. Because the birth records for Down Township (now Commercial Township) were destroyed by fire, it is virtually impossible to trace Sarah Howell's genealogy. Even so, given the prominence of Leon Abbett, it is puzzling that her family history remains shrouded in mystery. Jean C. Jones, a professional genealogist and president of the Maurice River Historical Society, attempted to trace the elusive Howell family for me but without much success. She thinks that Sarah Howell might have been either the illegitimate daughter of a prominent Howell, or else she may have been adopted. There is no evidence, however, to substantiate such unfounded speculation (Jones, letter to author, March 7, 1977).

12 Biographical information about Sarah M. Abbett is taken from the obituaries found in the *Trenton Times*, the *State Gazette*, and the *Daily True American*. All three obituaries are dated July 21, 1900.

13 For a biographical sketch of Leon Abbett, see Robson, *The Biographical Encyclopedia of New Jersey of the Nineteenth Century*, 316-317. See also *Jersey City Herald*, April 22, 1871.

14 Charles M. Snyder, The *Jacksonian Heritage* (Harrisburg, 1958), 82-95.

15 For an explanation of placement theory, see Richard E. Neustadt and Ernest R. May, *Thinking In Time: The Uses of History for Decision Makers* (New York, The Free Press, 1986), 181-85.

16 Norman Ware, *The Industrial Worker* (Chicago, Quadrangle Books, 1964), 65.

17 At the time of Ezekiel Abbett's funeral, the *Newark Journal* commented: "Ex-Gov. Abbett has met a severe personal bereavement in the death of his aged father, who expired on Tuesday in his home in Philadelphia at the ripe age of 81 years. In all his active professional and public life the ex-governor has affectionately cherished the associations of his boyhood home and been a loving and loyal son." See *Newark Journal*, January 4, 1889.

18 For a detailed analysis of this protest, see Michael Feldberg, "The Crowd in Philadelphia History: A Comparative Perspective" 15 *Labor History* 330 (1974).

19 Dennis Clark, "Urban Blacks and Irishmen: Brothers in Prejudice," in Miriam Ershkowitz and Joseph Zikmund, eds., *Black Politics in Philadelphia*, (New York, 1973), 21.

20 For the anti-Catholic nature of the Know-Nothing party, see Paul Kleppner, "Defining Citizenship: Immigration and the Struggle for Voting Rights in Antebellum America," in Donald W. Rogers, *Voting and the Spirit of American Democracy* (Urbana and Chicago, 1992), 43-52.

21 Michael Feldberg, *The Philadelphia Riots of 1844* (Westport, CT, Greenwood Press, 1976), 38.

22 Quoted in William J. Stern, "Urbanities: How Dagger John Saves New York's Irish," *City Journal* (Spring 1997), 88.

23 Julie Winch, *Philadelphia's Black Elite* (Philadelphia, Temple University Press, 1988). See also Roger Lane, *William Dorsey's Philadelphia and Ours* (New York, Oxford University Press, 1991).

24 Stuart Blumin, "Mobility and Change in Antebellum Philadelphia," in Stephan Thernstrom and Richard Sennett, eds., *Nineteenth-Century Cities*, (New Haven, Yale University Press, 1969), 190-200.

25 *McElroy's Philadelphia Directory* (Philadelphia, 1843), 1.

26 For the most detailed and comprehensive analysis of these riots, see Feldberg, *The Philadelphia Riots of 1844.*

27 Michael Feldberg, The Turbulent Era: Riot and Disorder in Jacksonian America (New York, PUBLISHER, 1980), 9-32; Bruce Laurie, *Working People of Philadelphia*, 130-133; and David Montgomery, "The Shuttle and the Cross: Weavers and Artisans in the Kensington Riots of 1844," *5 Journal of Social History*, (1972) 411-446.

28 For a history of the origins and development of the temperance movement in America, see W. J. Rorabaugh, *The Alcoholic Republic* (New York, Oxford University Press, 1979).

29 Arthur M. Schlesinger, Jr., *The Disuniting of America* (New York, 1992), 29.

30 Feldberg, *The Philadelphia Riots* of 1844, 14.

31 Michael F. Holt, *The Political Crisis of the 1850s* (New York, John Wiley & Sons, 1978), 156-181. See also William E. Gienapp, "Politics Seem to Enter into Everything: Political Culture in the North, 1840-1860," as found in Stephen E. Maizlish, et. al, *Essays on American Antebellum Politics, 1840–1860* (College Station, Texas A&M University Press, 1982), pp. 13-69.

32 Noel Ignatiev, *How the Irish Became White* (New York, Routledge, 1995), 156. See also Winch, *Philadelphia's Black Elite*, 21; and Warner, Jr., *The Private City*, 140-141.

33 Franklin S. Edmonds, *History of the Central High School of Philadelphia* (Philadelphia, J. P. Lippincott, 1902), 70.

34 David F. Labaree, "The People's College: A Sociological Analysis of the Central High School of Philadelphia, 1838-1939," (unpublished doctoral dissertation, University of Pennsylvania, 1983). See also Michael B. Katz, *Reconstructing American Education* (Cambridge, Harvard University Press, 1987), 45.

35 E. Digby Baltzell, *Puritan Boston and Quaker Philadelphia* (New York, the Free Press, 1979), 273.

36 The most detailed biography of John Seeley Hart can be found in Robson, *The Biographical Encyclopaedia of New Jersey of the Nineteenth Century*, 425-427. A published scholar, Hart wrote on various topics that included English authors, contemporary American themes, and women writers. In 1851, he published his most famous work entitled *The Female Prose Writers of America*. Hart was also managing editor of both the *Common School Journal* and *Sartain's Magazine*.

37 Letter to the author from Rudolph Sukonick, acting president of Central High School, September 26, 1977.

38 Edmonds, *History of the Central High School of Philadelphia*, 128, 145.

39 Quoted in Edmonds, *History of the Central High School of Philadelphia*, 125.

40 Quotation in the *Newark Evening News*, January 12, 1884.

41 This incident is chronicled in Leon Abbett's obituary as printed in the *Philadelphia Record*, December 5, 1894.

42 Controllers of the Public Schools for the City and County of Philadelphia, *35th Annual Report*, (Philadelphia, 1853), 129-131.

43 *Ibid.*, 129.

44 *Dictionary of American Biography* (New York, 1957), 1:392.

45 Information about John Wayne Ashmead is taken from his obituary that was published in the *Philadelphia Public Ledger*, April 11, 1868.

46 Charles L. Blockson, "The Underground Railroad," *National Geographic*, July 1984.

47 John Hill Martin, *Martin's Bench and Bar of Philadelphia* (Philadelphia, 1883), 243.

48 Controllers of the Public Schools for the City and County of Philadelphia, *40th Annual Report*, (Philadelphia, 1858), 124.

49 See letter by Augusta Rohrbach, *Boston Globe*, October 8, 2000.

50 Quotation from Ignatiev, *How the Irish Became White*, 165.

51 *Jersey City Herald*, April 22, 1871.

52 *Jersey City News*, December 7, l894.

53 Biographical information concerning William J. Fuller is drawn from his obituaries printed in the *New York Tribune*, March 12, 1889, and the *Boston Evening Transcript*, March 12, 1889. Records regarding Fuller's undergraduate years were provided by the Harvard College Archives.

4
The Political Apprenticeship

When the Abbetts arrived in Hoboken hardly anyone knew them. They were introduced to people locally by their in-laws William and Martha Dodd. Within less than a year, Abbett was appointed city attorney in 1863. This position gave him a chance to get to know people and to become familiar with the problems of local government. In 1864, he threw his hat in the ring and entered the open race for a state assembly seat in the fourth legislative district of Hudson County that included the municipalities of Hoboken and Weehawken. Abbett was prepared to fight for the position in the face of intraparty opposition. In a closely contested Democratic primary convention, he won his party's nomination by defeating Augustus O. Evans, editor of the *Hudson County Democrat*. Gracious in defeat, Evans showed his party loyalty by endorsing Abbett in his newspaper, the local party organ.[1]

As a fresh face on the political scene, the twenty-eight-year-old Abbett ran against Republican Charles Chamberlain, who was a gauger by trade and worked as a customs inspector for the port of New York. Chamberlain served on both the Hoboken city council and the local draft board that paid cash bounties to those who enlisted in the Union Army. With commutation and substitution existing as alternatives to being drafted, many men avoided military service by paying $300 or finding a substitute to enlist for three years. Hoboken was one of several induction centers spread across the state. At these camps, officers trained enlisted men and quickly whipped them into shape for military combat. More experienced and better known than Abbett, Chamberlain was a capable opponent who could not be taken lightly.

Since presidential politics made 1864 an important election year, Abbett decided that it would be in his best interest to campaign for General George McClellan, who headed the Democratic ticket. William

Fuller, Abbett's law partner, was a close friend of Randolph B. Marcy, who was McClellan's father-in-law. Fuller encouraged Abbett to stump for McClellan, but the young lawyer needed little encouragement.[2] After all, McClellan, like Abbett, was a native Philadelphian, and he was also a powerful symbol of opposition to Lincoln's war policies. The president had relieved him of his command, because of his failure to pursue the war more aggressively and to commit his troops to all-out combat.

The presidential election of 1864 turned out to be a referendum on the war. Although the overwhelming strength of the Union army was bearing down on the Confederacy, the prospects of victory still seemed bleak. The invasion forces headed by General Ulysses Grant were bogged down in Virginia, while those under the command of General William T. Sherman were stalled in Georgia. Unlike McClellan, however, Grant was an offensive-minded general who tenaciously pursued Robert E. Lee's Confederate troops and engaged them in bloody battles. Newspaper accounts listing heavy casualties eroded public support for the war. The Democrats in New Jersey were split into two distinct factions: one of war supporters, the other of peace advocates. The latter were nicknamed "copperheads," and they saw the opportunity to win power by promising a quick end to the war.

BAPTISM OF FIRE AND DESIRE IN PARTISAN POLITICS

Campaigning as a political neophyte and sensing a war weariness among his constituents, Abbett identified with the antiwar Democrats and came out boldly against conscription as being unjust and unfair. He likewise opposed Lincoln's policy of emancipation. Abbett recognized that racism, states' rights, and fear of a coercive federal government would prevent many New Jerseyans from accepting the moral arguments that Republicans put forth for freeing the slaves. Most Democrats before the war did not support abolition. Those who did switched to the Republican party. In northern states, the Democrats were less likely to call for an end to slavery; in neighboring Pennsylvania, for example, the party had led the fight to take the vote away from free blacks at the 1837 state constitutional convention. As a loyal Democrat, Abbett's conservative position on race was consistent with his party throughout the Civil War and Reconstruction era. In short, he was a racist.

Despite their patriotism, many men of military age worried about the draft. Their fear mounted substantially when they heard of the horrendous casualties at Gettysburg and Vicksburg. Draft riots erupted in nearby New York City in July 1863. Most of the rioters were angry working men, notably but not entirely Irish, who saw the Civil War as "a rich man's war and a poor man's fight." The rioters were too poor to buy their

way out of military service. They feared for their employment if thousands of freed slaves appeared on the labor market. Rumors circulated that once the slaves were freed, they would take Irish jobs. This was sufficient provocation for them. Mobs rampaged through the streets on the east side of Manhattan for four days, terrorizing city residents.

A class-driven rage fueled the New York City rampage and fed the fires of racism that escalated into wanton destruction, killing, and looting. Mobs wrecked draft offices, an armory, the homes and offices of Republican officials and editors. Some of the worst violence occurred in black neighborhoods, where the rioters vented their fury, burning a black orphanage and a church, hanging blacks from trees and lampposts, setting them on fire, and bashing the heads of black infants on fire hydrants. On the fourth day, after much destruction of property and loss of life, police and federal troops with rifles and cannons mowed down the rioters, dispersed them, and restored some semblance of order. Before the rioting ended, 105 people had been killed and many were wounded.[3]

Shocked by the barbarous nature of the New York riots, many New Jerseyans were repulsed by such civil disobedience and mob violence. On July 15, Governor Joel Parker, a war Democrat, issued a stern warning discouraging such lawlessness. He advised the citizenry to refrain from acts of violence and to maintain trust in law and elections. In response to Parker's plea, Lincoln agreed to delay the draft in New Jersey until the spring of 1864. In return, Parker, not wanting to undermine the president in his conduct of the war, offered to make a concerted effort to fill the state's quota through volunteers. Pressed on one side by war supporters and on the other by peace advocates, Parker steered a difficult but courageous path.

Beset with difficulties in raising troops and harassed by the activities of southern sympathizers (doughfaces) in the border states, Lincoln suspended the writ of habeas corpus in a number of states. Alarmed by these antiwar protests, Secretary of War Edwin M. Stanton rounded up antiwar activists and draft resisters and threw them in jail. Among the thirty-seven citizens arrested in New Jersey was James W. Wall, a well-known Burlington lawyer and politician.[4] He was a copperhead who allegedly had encouraged the residents of Maryland to secede. He came from a prominent political family in New Jersey; his father, Garret D. Wall, who was connected with the railroads, had served as U.S. senator from 1835 to 1841.

Federal marshals imprisoned Wall at Fort Lafayette in New York Bay for nearly two weeks, or until he swore allegiance. On his release, he returned to his hometown of Burlington in triumph as a martyr for the cause of civil liberty and a free press. As a symbolic gesture and seeking some measure of revenge, the Democrats in the legislature promptly elected him to the U.S. Senate to fill an unexpired term of six

weeks. This vacancy was created by the death of John R. Thompson, who had been president of the Philadelphia and Trenton Railroad. Serving briefly from January 14 to March 3, 1863, Wall hardly had time to make much of an impression. In addition, he was an antiwar Democrat from a prowar state.[5] Not surprisingly, Wall failed to gain reelection to a full six-year term.

Contrary to popular belief, most New Jerseyans supported a vigorous prosecution of the war. In his excellent book *Jersey Blue*, historian William Gillette provides ample evidence to disprove the claim of some observers that New Jersey was supposedly "a southern state, a border state, a doughface state, or a copperhead state." He argues quite convincingly that these views are inaccurate and do not square with political reality. Gillette goes on to conclude, "New Jerseyans regarded their interests as similar, if not always identical, to those of New York and Pennsylvania. Like their neighbors, New Jerseyans wished to preserve the peace and to maintain the Union. They might disagree about how best to accomplish this goal—and their elected representatives reflected this disagreement—but they shared a broad consensus."[6]

Nonetheless, peace Democrats in New Jersey opposed further prosecution of the war of rebellion. Copperheads tried their best to take advantage of military setbacks and unpopular policies to break the will of the people and their government to wage a successful war. They attracted considerable attention, but they did not succeed in sabotaging the state's war effort and military recruitment. In 1863, they failed in their attempt to pass a legislative resolution calling for a unilateral armistice.

Racist appeals continued in New Jersey. As racists, the Democrats opposed federal efforts to advance blacks, although only a few copperheads explicitly denied the principle of racial equality. They realized that race had much to do with the way New Jersey citizens voted. This was especially true in Hudson County, where the Irish were intensely antiwar and antiblack. Fearing the worst, the Irish did not want to sacrifice their lives for the sake of freeing slaves, only to have them take their jobs later on. Yet, many of the Irish fought valiantly on the bloody battlefields. They, of course, did not have a monopoly on racial prejudice. Many English and Germans were racists, only they did not display their Negrophobia as openly as the Irish. By 1860, there were 62,006 Irish and 33,266 Germans residing in New Jersey. Both war and peace Democrats were adamant in their opposition to wholesale emancipation. Appealing to both factions within the Democratic party, Abbett stressed the importance of restoring the Union, while at the same time opposing the draft and emancipation.

Abbett found a common enemy in the Republican president and a common battle cry in states' rights as he campaigned throughout Hudson County. From his perspective, the Republican war aims, as objectionable as they were, fitted into an even more dangerous pattern of centralizing power

FIG. 8
*Remnants of Leon Abbett's
residence in Jersey City,
corner of Montgomery and
Jersey Avenues.*

in the federal government at the expense of the states. By definition, states' righters were localists. They saw the danger of increased federal power as posing a serious threat to the states. Abbett played on these concerns in his maiden political speech from the steps of the old City Hall in Jersey City. Speaking mostly to low-income working people, he appealed to their racial fears and their desire for local control of government. Reiterating these themes, Abbett then spoke at the Napoleon Hotel and at the Otto Cottage Garden in Hoboken, a favorite place for German immigrants to socialize. Here, too, he struck a responsive chord. Abbett was a hard-hitting speaker and a powerful logician. According to those who heard him speak, the handsome New York lawyer made a big impression and got his message across convincingly. "He was not a polished orator in any sense of the word," writes William Sackett, "but he was a vigorous and earnest and logical talker. He never failed to carry the throng with him."[7]

Despite his oratorical prowess, Abbett did not have an easy time. His antiwar stance offended those who supported the war. Not all New Jerseyans were states' righters. Most Republicans were Unionists, not

hardened abolitionists intent on destroying slavery and the social system that it sustained. Charles Chamberlain fell into this category. He took Abbett to task for his errant defeatism and for his failure to support the war effort. The Hoboken Democrat not only faced stiff opposition from Republicans, but he also encountered cleavages within his own party. A faction of war Democrats in Hoboken had clashed with peace Democrats over their divergent loyalties. Unable to resolve their differences, the war Democrats deserted McClellan in the presidential race and crossed party lines to embrace Lincoln in his bid for reelection.[8] Abbett had all he could do to prevent such defections and to make sure that the ire of the war Democrats was not directed at him. But he could not escape unscathed. Hurt by this intraparty discord, Abbett defeated Chamberlain by only 215 votes. He received 866 votes out of a total of 1,517 votes cast, while Chamberlain polled 651 ballots.[9] Significantly, New Jersey was the only northern state that McClellan carried in 1864.

The outcome was not exactly an overwhelming mandate, but it spelled victory for Abbett. Getting elected to the General Assembly gave him his voting base; now he attempted to solidify that support. The divisiveness of the Civil War and the widening of class differences

FIG. 9
View of Jersey City from the river, 1857.

VIEW OF JERSEY CITY, N. J., FROM THE RIVER.

overshadowed much of his early career. As he saw it, the Republicans, whose fanaticism had provoked the disastrous war, were fighting more for abolition than for preservation of the Union. He considered himself more pro-Union than they were, and he criticized Lincoln for his suspension of the writ of habeas corpus and for his imposition of martial law to carry out the draft. Irish and German immigrants, who made up the bulk of his constituents, were the strongest opponents of these measures. Abbett catered to antiwar sentiments by making conscription a partisan and class issue. The seeds of populism were evident.

Coming from Hudson County, Abbett was in a unique position to lead his party's fight against ratifying the Thirteenth Amendment. A vote against it was not only a vote to uphold racial distinctions, but also a vote for states' rights, and it was a vote strictly according to party line. "As localists who viewed national powers narrowly and state rights broadly," William Gillette observes, "the Democrats insisted that the institution of slavery came under the exclusive control of the states. They contended that no amendment prohibiting slavery in the states could be adopted legally and that no such change could be made without the consent of all the slave states."[10] This bitter fight over ratification of the Thirteenth Amendment thrust Abbett into the political limelight. As a racist Democrat, he opposed federal efforts to advance blacks. As a proponent of reconciliation, he saw abolition as a roadblock to reunion and declared that the North should not "punish the South; we would endeavor to heal old wounds by kindness and a spirit of conciliation."[11]

A few weeks before the Confederate forces surrendered at Appomattox, Abbett delivered a major speech opposing the Thirteenth Amendment. Careful to make known his aversion to slavery and his desire to preserve the Union, he condemned the amendment as an unconstitutional curbing of state authority.[12] Although he spoke about the need for healing the nation's wounds and for reconciliation with the South, he argued that slavery should be abolished by state law, not federal law. He wanted more state latitude in governing, not more federal encroachment. Shrewdly couching his argument so that it appealed to ardent Unionists and copperheads alike, he was able to present a cogent and logical position on the question. Newspapers throughout New Jersey carried his speech verbatim. Even some Republican newspapers acknowledged his political acumen. The *Trenton Monitor*, for example, made the point succinctly:

> The Democratic leader, Leon Abbett, delivered the speech of his party against the measure. Cold, plausible, consecutive, well delivered, it won attention by its richly-glossed copperheadism, by its free professions of personal dislike to slavery, and love for freedom and the Union. His speech, considering his position, was the ablest made on either side; and it is a regret that so much labor and nice sophistry were wasted on an untenable subject.[13]

Far from being wasted, Abbett's carefully calibrated speech reached out to all segments of his party. Indeed, the speech was classic Abbett. Recognized for his capable leadership, he was already looked on as a rising political star with a bright future ahead of him. In relatively short order, Abbett's diplomatic talents had made him the chief broker between the two factions within his party. He helped to unite them in resisting Republican war aims. Although New Jersey ratified the Thirteenth Amendment, it failed to ratify the Fifteenth Amendment that gave black males the right to vote. Later on, the state attempted to withdraw its ratification of the Fourteenth Amendment that guaranteed blacks equal protection of the law.

Abbett maintained a hard line on states' rights and race issues when he helped defeat legislation proposed in March 1865 that would have allowed Union soldiers the opportunity to vote in the field. Keenly aware that most Union soldiers were Republicans, the Democrats did not want to grant them an absentee ballot. These servicemen fought under the command of Republican officers who made sure they understood which party supported their cause and which party opposed it. New Jersey was one of the few states that did not permit absentee balloting.

In a similar vein, Abbett played the race card and joined his fellow Democrats in defeating legislation that would have paid the widows of black soldiers the same war pensions that white widows received. During the war, black soldiers were expected to fight for less money than their white counterparts. Once again, the vote was strictly along party lines. The Democratic victory reflected a racist reality.

On April 4, 1865, as the war of rebellion neared its end, the Confederate capital of Richmond fell. On that same day, Abbett, recently chosen chairman of the Democratic legislative caucus, showed his partisanship and vented his cordial distaste for Lincoln. He argued that Lincoln had nothing to do with achieving victory; in fact, he had been an impediment to the war effort, and the war could have ended much sooner without him in the White House.[14] To show his distaste, Abbett sponsored a motion that deleted Lincoln's name from a joint resolution that expressed the gratitude of New Jersey to the commander-in-chief and the gallant Union soldiers for a hard-fought victory. The General Assembly passed Abbett's motion by 27 to 20. "While they apparently approved of the military victory that preserved the Union," writes historian William Jackson, "the majority of legislators again rejected the war's higher purpose as exemplified in Lincoln's leadership."[15] Party politics dictated such a stance, especially if Abbett wanted to get ahead and stay around for any length of time; those who held office the longest in New Jersey tended to be those who went along with their party. Obviously, Abbett was a fiercely loyal partyman.

War Democrats and copperheads could agree on many questions related to the war, such as the unpopularity of emancipation, the

inequities of conscription, the corruption and inefficiency in the military, and the suppression of civil liberties. Abbett's success in brokering the political differences between the two party factions led to his chairmanship of the Democratic caucus. He was also named a member of the state Democratic central committee in September 1865.[16] These rewards came quickly and were all the more remarkable when one considers that he was still a junior member of his party. With these two appointments, the Hoboken assemblyman was definitely on his way. Proof that he had arrived was that, in the complex realities of New Jersey Democrats, he emerged a popular rather than a hated figure at the end of the war.

LOCAL RIGHTS AND IMMIGRANTS' RIGHTS

In fall 1865, with the Union forces having won the war, Abbett sought reelection to the General Assembly. Once again, he faced Charles Chamberlain, who attacked him for placating the rebels and for seeking peace at any price. Republicans saw Abbett's antiwar stance as tantamount to treason because it had played into Confederate hands. In a concerted attempt to vindicate his patriotism and to offset a Republican surge, Abbett campaigned for the restoration of state power and against the nationalist principles on which the war had been fought. No longer a greenhorn and somewhat better known, he continued to play the race card. He considered his position on race a winner in Hudson County with its large Irish population, but he underestimated the opposition. When the polls closed on election day, he barely eked out a victory, defeating Chamberlain by a substantially smaller margin of ninety-five votes.[17]

The Hoboken Democrat had dodged a bullet, but his confidence was severely shaken. Amid the jubilation of a Union military victory and the release of pent-up tensions, 1865 turned out to be a banner year for New Jersey Republicans, whose ranks were bolstered by returning servicemen. The Republicans needed their support to win the governorship. Marcus L. Ward, the Republican candidate, who was an ardent Unionist, campaigned as "the Soldier's Friend." His opponent, Newark Mayor Theodore Runyon, was more of a peace Democrat rather than a war Democrat. In addition to winning the governorship, the Republicans captured control of both the state senate and the assembly. The vote count for governor reveals the closeness of the competition between the two major parties. Ward received 67,525 ballots, whereas Runyon received 64,736 votes; only 2,789 votes separated them.

The Democrats were fighting a Republican tide in 1865, but why was New Jersey so evenly divided when much of the North became so Republican? In Pennsylvania, for example, the Democrats remained out of power for the rest of the century. The competitiveness of the two major

parties in New Jersey had a lot to do with it. Because gubernatorial elections usually occurred in nonpresidential years, there was ample opportunity for state politics to take its own course and be less dependent on national tides. Another probable effect of the competition was the incentive it gave party leaders to fashion strong party organizations with which to win elections. Returning servicemen had swelled the ranks of the Republican party and contributed to its victory in 1865. The newly formed veterans' organization, the Grand Army of the Republic, soon became a virtual adjunct of the Republican party. It set up local chapters throughout the state.

By adopting more confrontational tactics, Abbett was able to regain some of the momentum his party lost in New Jersey at the end of the war. He attacked the Republicans as "the corrupt and revolutionary party," usurping state power as they embarked on a course of national supremacy. Having opposed the use of federal power during the war, the Hoboken Democrat remained consistent in opposing military rule in the South and the expanded role of the federal government in Reconstruction. On this and a series of other issues, ideology and the sweeping changes taking place in American federalism played a part. When President Andrew Johnson vetoed the Freedman's Bureau bill in 1866, Abbett introduced a resolution that expressed gratitude to those congressmen who had voted to sustain the veto and directed the state militia to fire a 100-gun salute at sunrise. He also introduced two other resolutions, both extending an olive branch to the South. One expressed a conciliatory position on the readmission of the conquered southern states as they returned to the Union, while the other one urged that these former slave states were entitled to representation in Congress.[18]

But these issues of ideology and federalism played a secondary role in determining Abbett's political future. He was more concerned about what was happening locally. Throughout the 1860s, the cities and towns in Hudson County were undergoing rapid demographic change. Situated at the entrance to New York Harbor, Jersey City was fast becoming an "immigrant city." Ships filled with Irish and German immigrants continually unloaded their passengers at nearby Castle Garden, which was a ramshackle depot used for processing. More would arrive later, when Ellis Island became the new processing center. By 1860, Catholics from Ireland comprised forty percent of Jersey City's population. Native-born Protestants accounted for another forty percent, while English and German immigrants each made up ten percent.[19] The Protestant elite deeply resented being displaced by the Irish horde.

Because these foreigners were largely Democratic, Catholic, and wet, the nativists viewed them with suspicion and distrust. The onrushing Irish tidal wave alarmed Protestants, Republicans, and temperance advocates, some of whom were the same men. Since the Irish had won the

mayoralty of Jersey City in 1869, the nativists feared an imminent Irish takeover of the city government. Even Protestant Democrats were alarmed at this prospect. "Home rule" meant Irish rule, and resentment against them intensified. By the same token, however, it insulted ethnic pride. In view of these realities, those concerned about the "Catholic menace" began a concerted drive to disempower the Irish. Temperance and nativism that had flourished as reform movements in the 1850's were now revived. This reform impulse had a definite anti-Catholic ring to it. Temperance, of course, was an anti-Irish issue.

Indeed, the Irish became a prime target for scapegoating. They were blamed for everything that went wrong: the local press compiled statistics that showed the Irish at the top of the list with regard to the incidence of crime and pauperism. They were depicted as illiterate peasants who could not hold steady jobs because they drank too much and were unreliable. To offset these negative stereotypes, the middle-class (or lace curtain) Irish in Jersey City launched their own temperance movement that sought to reaffirm the dignity and self-worth of their fellow countrymen. The shanty Irish had to deal with religious prejudice, discrimination, persistent poverty, illiteracy, unemployment, disease, and illness—some of which lingered from the famine era. Living in filthy tenements and ramshackle shanties, they were a culture under stress, facing the conflicting pressures of ethnic identity and assimilation. Confronted with such overwhelming adversity, they struggled to survive, and many stubbornly refused to bend to the ways of the Protestant nativists.

Always seeking to enlarge his base, Abbett continued to court the Irish and German immigrants whose numbers were constantly being augmented by new arrivals from their homelands. Their political demands were simple: they sought greater recognition from and parity with other groups in society. Beginning in the mid-1860s, the rural-based, Republican-dominated state legislature had made one incursion after another on Jersey City's administrative and fiscal autonomy. In 1866, Abbett opposed the passage of "ripper" legislation that removed the police in Jersey City from local control and placed them under the centralized authority of a state-appointed commission. Irish immigrants believed this partisan mischief was aimed at them. Usurping control of the police from a city controlled by the Irish and granting it to a state agency had been used before in New York City and Boston. The New York episode resulted in the same kind of battle that developed in Jersey City. The Republicans attempted to impose state control, while the Democrats favored a locally run police force.

In Jersey City, Protestant supporters of the police takeover were clever enough to mask their anti-Catholicism, but they could not conceal their intent. One of the motives behind such action was indirectly expressed by City Republican Obadiah D. Falkenbury who spoke on the

floor of the General Assembly. "Life and property," he declared, "are unsafe in Jersey City. The police are a politico-religious society. Pass this bill and it will put down 700 rum holes."[20] Taking their cue from Falkenbury, the Republicans made temperance and liquor control their objectives. Although they carefully avoided any mention of Irish Catholics, they were determined to rid the city police department of its Irish influence. The *Jersey City Times* branded those who opposed the new police commission as "opponents of good government and reform."[21]

Abbett, who recognized the incongruity of nativism with his own ideology, opposed the police reorganization bill for much the same reason that he opposed Reconstruction of the South: it violated fundamental principles of democracy and home rule. "Don't trample on the rights of the people," he warned his fellow legislators. "Don't allow this gradual attempt to centralize power."[22] When it was clear that this goal was unattainable, Abbett then offered two amendments to the bill. The first would have made the office of police commissioner elective; the second would have delayed the implementation of an appointive board until it had been first approved by the voters of Jersey City in a public referendum.[23] But Abbett's warning went unheeded. Both his amendments were soundly defeated by the Republicans who passed the legislation in its original form. Soon after its passage, Irish cops were summarily dismissed from the Jersey City police force, and the antiliquor laws were rigidly enforced. The Republicans gloated over the outcome.

The fight was hardly over. Abbett was not a man to take defeat lightly. When the Democrats regained control of the legislature in 1868, he resumed his partisan fight. Lobbying the Democratic legislative leadership behind the scenes, he persuaded them to pass a bill that abolished the Republican-appointed Hudson River police commission and replaced it with a Democratic-appointed Jersey City police commission. This time it was the Democrats' turn to gloat. Such an outcome greatly pleased the Irish, who now looked on Abbett as their champion. This continuing conflict between Protestants and Irish Catholics provided the central dynamics of the home-rule controversy that rocked Jersey City over the next eight years. As the city continued to change demographically, many nativists genuinely feared for the future of local democracy. Their fears were as strongly held as Abbett's concerns over the loss of home rule and community control.

As political power in Jersey City shifted inexorably from its wealthy Protestant elite to its predominantly working-class Irish, the election of Charles O'Neill in 1869 as its first Irish-born mayor was a historic turning point. Between 1860 and 1870, the population of the city had more than doubled, climbing from 29,226 inhabitants to 82,546. While the Protestant population increased 72.9 percent, the Catholic population soared by 115 percent.[24] There were also 696 blacks living in the city.

These numbers clearly favored the Irish. Abbett may have foreseen this demographic change; at least he staked his political future on it and seldom missed an opportunity to support the Irish political community.

Not unexpectedly, Abbett was inevitably drawn into the partisan intrigues, jealousies, and hatreds of the Reconstruction period. When fellow Democrat John P. Stockton was expelled from the Republican-controlled U. S. Senate in 1866, he immediately came to his defense. Stockton's ouster, which was of dubious legality, amounted to hardball partisan politics. The reasons behind his expulsion soon became obvious. The radical Republicans in Congress had passed the Civil Rights Act of 1866, but President Andrew Johnson vetoed it. They fell one vote short of overriding his veto. By ousting Stockton and replacing him with a Republican, they would gain the necessary vote for an override, though their legal authority to do this was questionable. Politics had become a blood sport.

In September 1866, Governor Marcus Ward called a special session of the state legislature for the dual purpose of ratifying the Fourteenth Amendment and electing a U.S. senator. Ratification passed in the General Assembly by a vote of 34 to 24 with Abbett voting against it. The Republican-controlled legislature chose Alexander G. Cattell of Camden County to replace Stockton.[25] Cattell, a wealthy Philadelphia banker and grain dealer, wanted to become a kingpin in state politics. After receiving firm pledges of support for his senatorial bid, Cattell and his people had worked hard to elect Marcus Ward governor. Some considered Cattell more a Philadelphian than a New Jerseyan.[26]

Abbett understood only too well the stakes involved in Stockton's expulsion. He sternly rebuked the Republicans for using an unconstitutional means to achieve a partisan end.[27] Such rhetoric inflamed tensions, but his speech gained front-page headlines. He also gained a valuable political ally. John Stockton was the scion of a first family of New Jersey, whose ancestry dated back to the American Revolution and whose business interests were tied to transportation. He had served as the American ambassador to Rome during President James Buchanan's administration. The significance of first families varied from state to state, but in New Jersey this sort of blue-blood status meant a great deal politically. At the earliest opportunity, the Democrats returned Stockton to the U.S. Senate in 1869. Abbett's alliance with Stockton would prove crucial to him when he later became governor.

THE MATURE POLITICO

At the expiration of his second term in the state assembly, Abbett sought to broaden his voting base. He moved to Jersey City, which was the seat of county government in Hudson and the place where most of the Irish

were concentrated. Continuing to curry favor with the wealthy Protestant elite, Abbett purchased a house at 16 Sussex Street, next door to conservative Democrat Joseph D. Bedle, a rising political star in the party. Bedle was already being touted as a possible candidate for governor. Even though the two men were good friends personally, they were still political rivals. Bedle was a railroad attorney and closely identified with the State House Ring.

Abbett now continued to acquire allies among the rich even as he expanded his support among the working poor. In September 1868, he was asked to chair the state Democratic party convention that selected Theodore Randolph as its candidate for governor. The Democrats actively courted Randolph, a business titan and president of the Morris and Essex Railroad. He had rescued the financially troubled rail line from near bankruptcy. Under Randolph's adroit management, the value of the company stock had doubled within two years. He then leased the line to the Delaware, Lackawanna, and Western Railroad (DL&W) that hauled coal and freight to seaboard. This lease gave the parent company direct access to a deep-water coal terminal in Hoboken.

Like his father, Theodore Randolph had been a Whig, a states' righter, and a vigorous opponent of abolition. After the demise of the Whigs in 1856, he switched to the Native American party and remained a Know-Nothing until the end of the decade. In 1860, he joined the Democratic party and was elected to the General Assembly from Jersey City by a coalition of Democrats and Know-Nothings. The next year they elected him to the state senate. In 1862, he purchased a spacious ninety-acre farm in Morristown, where he raised livestock and crops as a gentleman farmer. As a railroad president and one of the largest coal operators in New York City, he became known as "Mr. Moneybags of Morristown."

Most Know-Nothings had been absorbed by the Republican party, but the fact that Randolph and some of his friends joined the Democrats suggests that in New Jersey differences between the two parties were influenced by ethnic and religious considerations. The loyalty of Catholics to the Democratic party can be attributed to their perceived threat of Protestant evangelicalism. Most Whigs, with the notable exception of William H. Seward, had taken an anti-Irish position and thus were susceptible to Know-Nothingism. Discontented Protestant workers, who could not abide the courtship of the Irish, played a large role in both the break-up of the Whig party and the formation of the new anti-Irish Republican party.

In his pursuit of the governorship, Randolph had the backing of the State House Ring, a coterie of party managers whom he had personally recruited and brought together. Thus all were part of a social elite whose private and public lives intersected regularly. They represented the Bourbon or conservative wing of the Democratic party and were

determined to maintain the existing system of power in New Jersey. Also known as the "Board of Guardians," they all had financial interests in the railroads that they protected from governmental interference. These aristocrats were intensely anti-Irish, anti-Catholic, and antilabor. Although they were willing to accept Irish votes on election day, they excluded Catholics from leadership within the structure and hierarchy of the Democratic party.

This political situation inevitably forced Abbett to break with the State House Ring, but not before he had consolidated his power within Hudson County. For the moment, however, he was content to bide his time and to go along with the Randolph faction largely as a matter of political expediency. He was deceptively cooperative. In fact, he seemed increasingly comfortable practicing pragmatic politics and trying to broker the political differences between the nativists and the urban newcomers. As time went on, a more serious and potentially more damaging chasm surfaced among the Randolph Democrats.

In 1868, the Democrats in Jersey City picked Leon Abbett to run for the General Assembly. This time he ran from the first legislative district in Hudson County, the same district that Theodore Randolph had represented in 1860. It encompassed the city's first and second wards that were those nearest the Hudson River docks where the ferryboats departed for New York City. Abbett ran against Republican John Edelstein, a cigarmaker who was closely identified with the liquor interests. Edelstein served as a city alderman and later as a commissioner of finance. It was a lackluster campaign, but Abbett could now depend on the Irish to come through for him. When election day arrived, he won by a comfortable margin, polling 1,342 ballots compared with Edelstein's 957.[28] His win was part of a much larger victory. As the voters expressed their disapproval of the harsh Reconstruction policies imposed by the Republicans, the Democrats swept New Jersey in 1868, including both the presidential and gubernatorial elections. These two offices were filled simultaneously every twelve years when the four-year cycle for president coincided with the three-year cycle for governor.

During the same campaign, Abbett endorsed fellow Democrat Orestes Cleveland in his successful bid for Congress by reminding New Jerseyans that Cleveland "would never vote a dollar for the Freedman's Bureau or to keep an occupying army in the South."[29] A prominent politician in his own right, Cleveland had served as a local alderman in Jersey City from 1861 to 1864 and then as mayor from 1864 to 1866. From 1856 to 1859 he, like Randolph, had been active as a Know-Nothing. That tensions would arise between Abbett and Cleveland was almost inevitable. They were both ambitious men, and their political careers evolved in parallel fashion. But they differed in style and substance. Cleveland showed disdain and contempt for the Irish while accepting their votes, whereas

Abbett genuinely embraced them. Both men had their sights set on the governorship. Similar tensions arose between Abbett and Randolph, but their dislike for one another would not surface publicly until 1875 because, though they had differences, they also had common needs.

Abbett, however, did not let personal feelings cloud his political judgment. With his return to the general assembly, he continued to climb onward and upward as a party leader. By this time he had become adept at political bargaining and compromising. Many times when he argued, the argument would turn as a consequence of the way he argued it. Recognized for his command of the issues and for his leadership in building coalitions, the Democrats elected him speaker of the assembly for both the 1869 and the 1870 legislative sessions. The speakership was an important leadership position that he used to great advantage, never losing a crucial vote during his tenure. The key to his success lay in his instinctive ability to gauge what would be acceptable to his own party, to the Republican opposition, and to Governor Theodore Randolph. Seldom would Abbett risk intraparty strife if he could possibly avoid it. Like most politicians who move to the front ranks, he discovered that the political system within which he had to operate was not only shaping his decisions, but also formulating the options from which he could choose.

Meanwhile, Abbett had to stand for reelection in fall 1869. This time he ran against Republican Stephen S. Sparks, a sacrificial candidate the Republicans offered because they believed they had no chance of beating Abbett. Sparks had a checkered career as store clerk, liquor dealer, and bartender. In early August, Abbett launched his campaign by speaking at New York's Tammany Hall that was an Irish stronghold. In his speech before the Tammany Democrats, he deplored the tyranny of British rule in Ireland, identified with the Irish struggle for independence, and called for the abolishment of all naturalization laws.[30] To woo the Irish further, he endorsed John Kennedy of Hoboken for county clerk and Patrick Harrington of Hudson City for sheriff.[31] When the votes were tallied, on election day, Abbett received 1,067 ballots to Sparks' 654.[32]

New Jersey political leaders and the economic interests they represented demonstrated an overriding commitment to laissez-faire capitalism in its purest form. Perhaps there is no better evidence of this than the treatment accorded the Camden and Amboy Railroad (C&A) that during the 1830s laid track between Camden on the Delaware River and South Amboy on the Raritan River. The legislature encouraged this effort by granting the railroad a lucrative, long-term monopoly of rail traffic between Philadelphia and New York, the nation's two largest cities. In return, the legislature expected the state treasury to receive a guaranteed annual income without risking cash or credit for new transportation and without having to tax residents for it. Income from railroads and canals, seventy percent of which came from the Camden and Amboy Railroad

and the Delaware and Raritan Canal, paid the expenses of the state government.

To prevent the financial collapse of the canal and to avoid ruinous competition between the canal and the railroad, the state also approved the merger of the Delaware and Raritan Canal and the Camden and Amboy Railroad into the Joint Companies. Robert F. Stockton, who headed of the Delaware and Raritan Canal Company, was the power behind the Joint Companies. After 1844, the railroad formed a political alliance with the Democrats, who in principle were opposed to monopolies but in practice aided the C & A's monopoly. Conversely, the Whigs, who in principle favored monopolies, in practice tended to oppose this particular monopoly because of its alliance with the Democrats.

From the 1830s onward, the Joint Companies built a powerful political organization whose agents worked in election campaigns and whose lobbyists made financial contributions to particular candidates. They in turn pressured governors to appoint state judges who were friendly to the railroads. In the antebellum period, the railroad magnates had made requests and worked for their attainment; now with the courts packed in their favor and other sources of power firmly established, they made demands and insisted on compliance. Legislators found it hard to disregard such threats for fear of political reprisal.[33]

The C & A monopoly was eventually broken in the 1870s, and as a result, it no longer paid a subsidy to the state. This was important because in the eighteenth century the state financed most of the costs of government through the interest on paper money loaned out and in the nineteenth century by using the railroad subsidy. The end of this subsidy surely had something to do with Abbett's desire to find other fiscal resources for the state. With the monopoly broken, other railroads appeared on the scene, but most politicians still accorded them differential treatment.

In New Jersey, almost every major prewar politician survived financially by acting as a lawyer for corporations, particularly the railroads. Sometimes railroads had the support of politicians from rival parties. While Garret Wall served as counsel for the C & A, his chief rival in state politics, Samuel Southard, also served as its lawyer. The Fitz Randolphs were connected with both the Morris Canal and the New Jersey Railroad Company.

No crusader, Abbett collaborated with the railroads and came to their defense when the federal government made demands on them during the Civil War. For reasons not altogether clear, he used his influence as assembly speaker in 1869 to defeat legislation that would have chartered a fast train known as the New Jersey Air Line Railroad. The incorporation bill had been introduced by State Senator Noah D. Taylor of Hudson County. Both Orestes Cleveland and William Fuller (Abbett's law

partner) were listed among the proposed incorporators. [34] Something similar happened in 1870, when the speaker used his position to defeat a bill that would have made the Millstone and Trenton Railroad part of a larger competing railroad running from New York to Washington. Surely this corporate buyout would have benefited the railroad capitalists. [35]

Obviously, Abbett sought to stay in the good graces of the railroads as much as possible. As his private law practice grew in size, he represented railroad companies in various land and financial deals. Some of his critics claimed that he could always be found on the side of the largest retainer. Among his more lucrative railroad clients were the Erie, the Baltimore and Ohio, and the Pennsylvania. The Pennsy leased the lines of the United New Jersey Railroad, and it soon overshadowed the Camden and Amboy. Lobbyists for these rail carriers knew that Speaker Abbett was well-connected politically and that he was in a good position to help them. They wanted to avail themselves of his political influence as well as his legal talent. He was considered to be a better lawyer than Theodore Randolph and his professional colleagues.

Whatever benefits or shortcomings may have accrued from Abbett's legal work, it had immense political advantages from his point of view. Absorbed in his busy double life as attorney and politician, he had the ability to play both sides, depending on the circumstances. He not only represented the railroads in court, but he also opposed them in litigation. His freedom from railroad harness is suggested by the fact that the local communities of Bayonne, Hoboken, Union, and Jersey City all retained him as counsel, a role that frequently required him to oppose the railroads. Abbett won a series of court cases against them. [36] This duplicity did not seem to bother him. On the contrary, although his railroad clients were not particularly pleased with his behavior, it seemed to satisfy the political maverick in him.

The speaker assisted business interests in various ways. He introduced legislation to attract venture capital to New Jersey by exempting from personal property taxes business corporations engaged in manufacturing, banking, and shipping. [37] In his view, what was good for business was good for the commonwealth. After Randolph was elected governor, Abbett opposed his idea to tax business corporations one-half of one percent on their gross earnings on the grounds that it would have discouraged economic development and placed local industries at a competitive disadvantage with those in neighboring states. [38] A less subtle or more effective way of endearing himself to the business community is hard to imagine. Developmental politics, aggressively pursued, made him electorally popular, because it meant the creation of more jobs.

Almost everything Abbett did was calculated for effect, especially when it came to local politics. In 1869, he got himself elected to the Jersey City Board of Education and served for two years as its president. In this

capacity, he succeeded Bennington F. Randolph, a hard-line Protestant and a temperance advocate. At the time, the local school board was embroiled in a two-pronged controversy over Bible reading in the public schools and Catholic demands to obtain public funding for parochial schools. Catholic students, who refused to participate in the compulsory Protestant-oriented religious activities, were subjected to harsh discipline.[39] Their parents objected to what they saw as religious coercion and the systematic proselytization of their children.

Feelings ran high on both sides of the religious divide. Because tax money for parochial schools would divert existing school funds and place an added tax burden on propertyowners, Protestants viewed the Catholic demands as an assault on their cherished public school system. The most vociferous objector was Zebina K. Pangborn, editor of the *Evening Journal*, who voiced his concerns in a volley of anti-Catholic diatribes, mostly expressing his belief that Catholics were trying to get elected to the local school board.[40] "They never neglect any chance of crowding a Roman Catholic into the school board," Pangborn warned, "To what end? With what motive? Their only possible purpose is to injure and destroy the schools, and yet they forsooth, cry out to us to let them alone. It is only surprising that so many friends of the system of common school education are so slow as they are in appreciating the danger of this Roman Catholic assault on our most important and valued American institution, and in resisting it." [41]

While serving as president of the school board, Abbett showed a willingness to face this unpleasant and disruptive issue. He attempted to soften the religious controversy by placating both sides. Mindful of the Bible-reading dispute that had erupted into violence in Philadelphia in 1844, he met with representatives of both groups to pave the way for workable compromise. After numerous conferences, it was agreed that Catholic pupils would be allowed to read from their own Douay Bible, but they would be required to participate with everyone else in the common prayers. Furthermore, Abbett was able to persuade the school board to sell city land to the Catholic church for its own school purposes, while at the same time coaxing Catholics to pull back from their demands for obtaining public funding.

Abbett's actions illustrated the honest broker role he sought to play. Before stepping off the school board, he laid the groundwork for the creation of the first public high school in Jersey City, which became a reality in 1874. He also pushed for the hiring of bilingual teachers who could speak both English and German.[42] There were approximately 1,500 German children between the ages of five and eighteen enrolled in the city's public schools.

By such actions, Abbett supported both Irish and German drives for political equality, especially in cities most resistant to recognizing

minority needs and rights. He left the local school board in June 1870, when the cities of Bergen and Hudson were consolidated with Jersey City. The new school board resembled the Board of Aldermen in its ethnic and religious makeup: almost half of its members were Irish Catholics, a fact that did not sit well with Zebina Pangborn's *Evening Journal*.[43]

A SOURCE OF CONSISTENCY: THE IRISH ALLIANCE

The Republicans scored significant gains in the elections of 1870 and recaptured the state legislature. Abbett may have sensed what was coming, because he did not seek reelection. In Hudson County, the Democrats were divided and suffered a galling defeat. The middle-class Irish, who were led by Aeneas Fitzpatrick, rebelled at what they saw as an unholy alliance between the old Know-Nothing leadership and the working-class Irish. As a result, they bolted the Democratic party and ran their own independent slate of candidates. In a futile attempt to head off this lace curtain revolt, Abbett tried to bridge the rift. The dissidents were upset because the lone Democrat to lose in 1869 was their political hero, Patrick Harrington, who ran for county sheriff. They blamed Protestant Democrats for sabotaging Harrington's chances. Native-born Republicans and Democrats closed ranks whenever the Irish seemed likely to increase their power. As payback, the Fitzpatrick faction retaliated with its own sabotage. By splitting the Democratic vote, they contributed to the defeat of incumbent Representative Orestes Cleveland, a former Know-Nothing.[44]

Frightened by the insurgent Irish, who made repeated attempts to wrest political power from them, the Protestants in Jersey City concocted ingenious schemes to prevent effective Irish political participation. Spearheading this movement were men whose previous involvement in the Know-Nothing party was well known. Unwilling to share power with the Irish intruders, they now conspired to put the city government beyond their reach by drafting a new city charter. The charter removed the Irish from elected office and replaced them with commissioners appointed by the state legislature, a body dominated by rural Protestants. The conspiracy was well conceived and well executed. The Republican legislators appointed only nativist Protestants with token representation from the German Protestant community. In essence, they responded to the threat of an Irish takeover by abolishing city government.

Most Protestant Democrats played a role in the conspiracy by keeping silent or by offering only passive resistance. The charter movement was much larger than just a ripper issue. It was steeped in nativism and driven by anti-Catholicism. "Commission government was advanced in the name of efficiency," historian Douglas Shaw writes, "but is best

understood in terms of class, ethnicity, and religion. The purpose of the charter was to restore native-born Protestants to office, and purge the city of lower-class Irish and Catholic influence."[45] Jonathan Dixon, a Republican lawyer who would run against Abbett for governor in 1883, drafted the charter. Dixon's role in this nefarious affair would eventually come back to haunt him.

On this politically charged issue, Abbett decided to lead the fight in behalf of his Irish constituents. If he was going to take on the political establishment, he knew he would need help. Noah Taylor, the state senator from Hudson County, was the only other major Democratic leader who joined him. Conspicuously absent was Orestes Cleveland, who was as much responsible for the charter as the Republicans. Nor did Democrat John R. McPherson raise his voice in protest. A political star on the horizon, McPherson lived as a bachelor in Taylor's Hotel at Exchange Place, the political and financial hub of Jersey City. He courted the Irish, but he was reluctant to alienate the nativists. Together, Abbett and Taylor opposed the charter movement and worked hard to defeat it, but the veto-proof Republican legislature rammed through the statute despite their best efforts. Governor Randolph's veto of the bill, token opposition based only on legal defects in its drafting, was promptly overriden.[46] The new charter became law on March 29, 1871, and took effect immediately.

The Irish were furious. The new charter not only subverted local democracy, but it also robbed them of their legitimate right to govern. It turned over the city government to three five-member commissions, all appointed by the Republican-controlled state legislature. The Irish saw the newly established governing process as being closed, secretive, undemocratic, and unresponsive; they charged that it left large discretionary power in the hands of a few well-placed people without placing any political checks on them whatsoever. Hugh McDermott, the editor of the *Jersey City Herald*, aptly dubbed the new legal document the "thieves charter."

Adding insult to injury, the Republicans exploited their control of the legislature by redistricting the state for the next decade. They drew a set of legislative districts that included a horseshoe-shaped constituency in Jersey City. Into this small area they packed as many Irish voters as possible. By concentrating the voting strength of the Irish into one compact district and by diluting the remainder of it among several other districts, the Republicans assured themselves at least three safe legislative districts in Jersey City. At the same time, they denied the Irish the additional representation that their numbers warranted. It was a gerrymander worthy of Elbridge Gerry, who as governor of Massachusetts invented gerrymandering in 1812. The infamous "horseshoe district" encompassed the tenements along the Hudson River docks and the make-shift shanties at the base of Bergen Hill. Into this odd-shaped area, chortled the Republican *State Gazette*, was crowded "the political filth of the city in one spot." [47]

The Irish, who were accustomed to such ethnic slurs, knew that the whole elaborate scheme was intended to deny them fair representation and to diminish their voting power.

During his tenure as governor (1869–1871), Theodore Randolph was no friend of the Irish. Despite their party loyalty, he failed to appoint them to any significant positions within his administration. In 1870, Governor Randolph intervened in a bitter railroad strike and used state troops to suppress the rioting of Irish laborers. A year later, he put the New Jersey National Guard on alert when Irish Catholics threatened to disrupt the parade of the Orange Order in Newark, a Protestant fraternal group that sought to commemorate the victory of the Protestant forces in Ireland's Battle of the Boyne in 1690. No antagonism was more intense than the kind that drove apart Catholic and Protestant Irish. To let the Irish know that he was serious, the governor issued an executive order directing the guardsmen to carry live rounds of ammunition in their rifles; blank cartridges were normally used for riot control purposes.[48] The Irish Catholics got the message and refrained from any violence.

Randolph received much praise and media coverage for preventing a potential sectarian clash, but his actions exposed the raw nerve of ethnic tension running throughout New Jersey. A Protestant hard-liner who clung tenaciously to his Know-Nothing ideology, Randolph harbored an intense hatred of Irish Catholics and their radical labor leaders. As one disgruntled Irishman expressed it, "Scratch Governor Randolph until he bleeds, and you will be sure to come upon a Know-Nothing in the full regalia of the order."[49]

Abbett soon came to see Randolph as a rigid and inflexible party leader who was becoming increasingly unpopular with the urban masses. He now began to distance himself from the governor and the State House Ring. Abbett envisioned the emerging Democratic party as a broader coalition of businessmen, shopkeepers, urban industrial workers, and small farmers. Some of the battles within the party were based on this demographic division, with Randolph representing the older rural areas. By marked contrast, Randolph remained subservient to the railroads, while Abbett began to reassess his position toward them. Unlike Randolph and other nativists who maintained the status quo, Abbett wanted to recruit new party members. Inclusion rather than exclusion was his formula for electoral success.[50] Clashing personalities and ambitions sharpened these factional rivalries and divisions. The two men could barely conceal their hostility toward each other, and their feud simmered for years before it flared openly in 1875.

For his part, Abbett seemed less anxious and better equipped intellectually to handle ethnocultural and religious questions than the Randolph faction. Consequently, he was able to overcome the narrow-minded nativism so common among Protestant leaders during this

period. Abbett felt comfortable and mingled freely with both Catholics and Protestants and frequently played the role of broker between them. What mattered most is that he understood and accepted the idea of what is now called cultural diversity, in part because he had grown up among Irish immigrants in Philadelphia. Abbett's actions and other statements evinced respect for the Irish, and they in turn respected him. In every situation in which they needed his help, Abbett acted as they hoped he would. To quote Douglas Shaw again, "During the 1870s, Abbett was one of the few people who succeeded in holding the confidence and trust of both the native-born and Irish Democrats."[51] With his ability to work together across religious and class lines, he won the support of both groups; the Protestant nativist press as well as the Catholic press endorsed him.

Abbett won the support of the Irish because he was willing to share power with them, which explains in large measure why he was so successful in holding the Hudson Democratic party together when he needed it in later years. Party machinery above the ward level remained a tenuous Yankee preserve; nativist Democrats held most elective offices at the state level, such as assemblyman and senator. But at the local level, Abbett let the Irish ward bosses settle their own differences. By permitting them a certain degree of autonomy, he skillfully maneuvered through this difficult and at times treacherous political terrain.

Simon Kelly, who ran the local Democratic machine in Weehawken, was a typical Irish immigrant boss. Born in Ireland in 1848 during the worst of the famine, his immigrant parents brought him from Kildare to Weehawken in 1849. In 1868, Kelly became involved in local politics. A colorful and flamboyant politician, he held a variety of municipal jobs in Weehawken, ranging from local postmaster, fire chief, justice of the peace, president of the school board, police chief, and finally mayor. Sometimes mockingly called "King Kelly," he developed a large supportive following by distributing favors, jobs, and welfare services. The *Boston Pilot* remarked, "Simon never allows Weehawken to go Republican, and he never takes more than $21,000 to run the township. When people need money, he gives them money tickets good in any store in Weehawken, Hoboken or Jersey City. Kelly always pays and hence has unlisted credit. He is most frequently called on to pay for funerals."[52]

Abbett took an immediate liking to Simon Kelly and found himself increasingly taking his new friend into his confidence. Abbett also supported the cause of Irish nationalism, whether it be the Fenians or the Land League. Jeremiah O'Donovan Rossa and a group of Fenians, who had been imprisoned and exiled by the British, visited New York in 1871. Abbett made sure that he was on hand to greet them, and then attended a reception given in their honor in Jersey City.[53] O'Donovan Rossa, who

FIG. 10
Simon Kelly, local Demo-
cratic boss known as "king
Kelly" from Weehauken, NJ.

came from West Cork, was the founder of the Phoenix Society in 1858 and a leader of radical Fenianism.

In the elections of 1871, Abbett worked hard at mending political fences and persuading the dissident lace curtain Irish Democrats to return to the party. Although he did not run for office that year, he was much in demand as a speaker. An inveterate campaigner whether on or off the ticket, he blasted the Republicans at rally after rally for circumventing local democracy. Abbett focused on their abolishment of local government and singled out Jonathan Dixon as the main culprit who had drafted the "thieves charter" and masterminded the scheme. He also reminded his audiences of Dixon's caustic public comments that the Irish were incapable of governing Jersey City.[54] Abbett was indefatigable. The editor of the *Jersey City Herald* described him in action in April 1871:

> We have known Leon Abbett since his first entry into political life, which was during the McClellan campaign of 1864. We heard his first speech on that occasion. He was quite young, and the excellence and soundness of his remarks surprised us. Everybody warmed to the "young New York lawyer," as he was called on the evening of that speech, and he was applauded to the echo. Since that time, there never has been an election in this county which did not find him on the stump every night, whenever he was called—one night at Hoboken, another at Union Hill, another at Union Township, and Weehawken, West Hoboken, Hudson City, South Bergen, Greenville, Bayonne, and back again to Jersey City, often meeting pressing engagements to speak two or three times in one night. Where the battle was hottest there was he to be found, bringing victory often out of pending disaster, exhorting wavering and dissatisfied Democrats to unity of action, and, in a word, doing the best political fighting ever done in this county since the days when the late General Edwin R. Wright was at the zenith of his political glory. Abbett is the very bulwark of the Democratic party of Hudson County today. He is an indefatigable worker. He often had important cases in which he was engaged postponed by the courts that he might give his valuable time to the success of the Democratic party as its eloquent advocate on the stump.[55]

With such prodigious efforts, Abbett was able to bring the Fitzpatrick dissidents back into the Democratic fold. When it came to rallying the party faithful and building the party, he spared no effort. He also demanded strict organizational discipline. In addition to electing four state assemblymen in 1871, the Hudson Democrats elected John McPherson as state senator and John Rhinehart as county sheriff. They also contributed substantially to Joel Parker's gubernatorial victory that year. Nothing could have pleased them more. They succeeded in spite of the Republican horseshoe gerrymander that had diluted the voting power of the Irish.

WIDENING ALLIANCES: THE POLITICS OF THE 1870S

After the 1871 election, Abbett formed an important political alliance with local Democrats John McPherson and Robert Gilchrist that would prove mutually beneficial in the years ahead. This triumvirate represented a new breed of insurgent Democratic leaders: all three men were Protestants and all were political stars of equal magnitude in the Hudson galaxy. Gilchrist was the attorney general of New Jersey and was very popular with the Irish in Hudson County. While serving as mayor of Jersey City from 1850 to 1851, Gilchrist had earned their respect and confidence.

Both Abbett and McPherson came from humble origins, and both appealed to similar constituencies. They competed for the same bloc of votes. Rather than run against each other for the position of state senator in Hudson County, they cut a deal. For purposes of party harmony, Abbett agreed to step aside in favor of McPherson but with the understanding that he would run for the same office when McPherson's term expired in 1874. By combining their political forces, this trio was determined to break the stranglehold that the State House Ring held on the state Democratic party organization. What united these men was a desire to broaden the base of the party and a mounting dissatisfaction with Randolph Democrats who seemed interested only in protecting their own economic interests. Outside of Hudson County, other alliances were also forming that would prove helpful to their cause.

If there was any unifying theme in Abbett's public life during this busy period, it was his fight against nativism and his efforts to recruit more urban ethnics into the Democratic party. Like the Grant administration in Washington, commission government in Jersey City was awash in scandal. A gang of Republican boodlers headed by William H. Bumsted, who served on the Board of Public Works, were involved in bribery and other forms of corruption. Spending the city almost bankrupt, the Republicans awarded city contracts without competitive bidding, accepted kickbacks, and dunned city employees for campaign contributions. Bumsted, the ring leader, had tipped off Garrett Vreeland, a private real estate agent, about the city's plans to build a new reservoir on Bergen Hill. Acting on this insider information, Vreeland purchased the property under consideration and resold it to the city at a substantial profit. The price seemed rather high. After this sale, the two men split the $30,000 in profit. Bumsted awarded the reservoir contract to Democrat Jeremiah B. Cleveland without advertising for bids. The brother of Orestes Cleveland, Jeremiah Cleveland had a financial interest in the *American Standard* newspaper and was an important figure in Jersey City politics.

When Sheriff John Rhinehart uncovered such official misconduct, a county grand jury indicted the men involved in January 1872. Robert

Gilchrist prosecuted the Bumsted Ring. Much to everyone's amazement, Abbett decided to defend them. If politics made for strange bedfellows, this episode provided a case in point. William Bumsted had been born in England. His father, a staunch Baptist, came to America in 1836 after refusing to pay church tithes in his native Norfolk. In Jersey City he founded a contracting business. His son soon followed in his father's footsteps and established his own firm that specialized in sewer and street repairs. The son eventually moved to the more affluent suburb of Bergen, where he served as a local alderman before consolidation. Bumsted neither smoked nor drank, and he contributed to the Baptist church. As a prominent Republican, he had promoted the new charter in Jersey City. His personal net worth was estimated to be well over $100,000.

Abbett had a business relationship with Bumsted. The two men jointly owned property located in the Jersey City meadowlands.[56] Abbett's peculiar behavior can be explained in part by his business connection with Bumsted. After lambasting commission government and Jonathan Dixon on the stump, he suddenly switched sides. Even more bizarre, Abbett teamed up with Republican Jonathan Dixon and Democrat Charles H. Winfield to defend the Bumsted Ring. Because those indicted were all Republicans, he ran considerable risk of jeopardizing his reputation.

At the trial, the three defense attorneys based their case on the argument that there was no intent on the part of their clients to defraud the city. Conducting the trial amid much fanfare and negative publicity, they attempted to discredit the court proceedings as a political witchhunt and a media circus.[57] Bumsted was steadfast in his denial of any wrongdoing, but in the end he was the only one convicted of the charges. Judge Joseph Bedle fined him $500 and sentenced him to nine months of hard labor at the state prison in Trenton. After his release from prison, Bumsted lived in disgrace and died a broken man.[58]

In 1872, Abbett attended his first Democratic National Convention, which was held in Baltimore. He supported for president his good friend U.S. Senator Thomas F. Bayard whom he had first met in Philadelphia. Bayard later served as secretary of state in the Grover Cleveland cabinet. At the convention, the Democrats picked Horace Greely as their candidate. The celebrated newspaper editor was chosen as a fusion candidate with liberal Republicans. This selection shocked many party regulars, including Abbett, who had grave doubts about it. Arrogant and unpredictable, Greeley had castigated the Democrats for years in his Republican newspaper. He said anything he pleased and offended many Democrats. Greeley ran a poor campaign, and his ineptness as a candidate brought disaster to the Democratic party, just as Abbett had predicted. General Ulysses Grant, who had failed to carry New Jersey for the Republicans in 1868, had no trouble doing so in 1872. It was difficult for local Democratic politicians to hold their own against

such a national tide. The Republicans captured control of both houses of the New Jersey legislature.

In 1873, inflation and the mad dash for riches that followed the Civil War ended in a prolonged slump that dragged on for six long interminable years. On Black Thursday—September 18, 1873—the banking house of Jay Cooke and Company failed because of problems in financing the Northern Pacific Railroad. This event triggered a panic, leading to a stock exchange shutdown, a string of bank failures, and widespread railroad bankruptcies. During the next few years, deflated by massive unemployment, daily wages plunged twenty-five percent, exposing many Americans to the horror of downward mobility.

The Panic of 1873 struck Jersey City with devastating impact. Its negative effects were felt for six lean years. Because of costly capital improvements necessitated by the recent consolidation with Bergen and Hudson, the enlarged city found itself in serious financial trouble. The street and sewer contracts let by these localities before consolidation created a large debt that required funding. Since Jersey City was built largely on reclaimed land just above the water line, the sewers had to be extended and relaid. In less than three years after the merger, the city's tax rate had more than doubled and its public debt had increased from $5.1 million to $13.2 million. Adding to its woes, the city treasurer had embezzled $87,000 in municipal bonds and then absconded to Mexico with the stolen money. Unable to sell its bonds and to collect its taxes, the city government teetered on the brink of bankruptcy.[59]

Meanwhile, the railroads were frantically buying whatever land they could in order to expand their terminal facilities. By 1873, the railroads owned virtually the entire Jersey City waterfront. Because of special irrepealable contracts that granted them certain tax exemptions, they removed through purchase more and more property from the city's tax rolls. As its taxing capacity became more circumscribed, Jersey City taxed its residents and business firms at higher rates to maintain public services. Its effective tax rate was two or three times higher than the tax rate in suburbia and rural towns. Other cities and towns in Hudson County, experiencing resource limitations of their own, were suddenly faced with fiscal crisis as well. Something had to be done if the distressed cities were to remain solvent. Hudson County taxpayers clamored for tax relief.

The convergence of these forces gave rise to the equal tax movement that began in Jersey City in 1873. This grass-roots protest would eventually grow into the most fundamental challenge to the railroads that New Jersey had ever witnessed. Over the next decade, the tax revolt gained momentum and spread to the far corners of the state. It led eventually to the formation of the Anti-Monopoly League in 1880. But initially it was centered in Hudson County, the largest terminal site in the state. Much of its real estate was owned by the railroads.[60] The prime

FIG. 11
Home of the Union League
Club, Jersey City. From Free
Library of Jersey City, NJ.

movers behind the protest were Steven B. Ransom, James Flemming, and Isaac N. Quimby—all of whom were somewhat leery of Abbett. They viewed him as having sold out to the railroad power because of his activity as a railroad attorney and what they perceived as his compromising stand on the tax issue. As speaker of the assembly in 1869, Abbett had supported legislation that abolished transit duties and substituted a state railroad tax of one-half of one percent. This act allowed the so-called "exempt companies" to pay a fixed sum in commutation of the ad valorem state tax.

In spring 1874, the Hudson Democratic organization asked Abbett to run for state senator, but he was about to leave with his family on an extended tour of England, France, and Germany. After the Civil War, many Americans flocked to Europe for vacations. Abbett told the party that he wished to defer his decision until his return in September.[61] While abroad, he learned that he had been nominated for the position, curtailed his travel plans, and hastily returned home to accept the nomination. It is tempting to suggest that Abbett deliberately cut short his vacation so that

FIG. 12
Fuller Building, Jersey City.
From Free Library of Jersey City, NJ.

the nomination would be a surprise to him. Surely he knew about these plans well in advance of his sailing for Europe. Moreover, he had already cut a deal with John McPherson to succeed him when the latter's senatorial term had expired.

On returning to New Jersey, Abbett lost no time in launching his senatorial campaign against Republican James H. Startup, a Jersey City grocer. Abbett attacked Startup for favoring commission government. William Startup, the candidate's brother, had served on the city's Board of Public Works, was a member of the Bumsted Ring, and had been indicted in the reservoir scandal. Whenever Abbett spoke, he revealed this family connection, while promising to restore home rule to Jersey City and to compel the railroads to pay more local taxes. To improve his chances of winning, he asked his good friend U.S. Senator Thomas Bayard of Delaware to come to New Jersey and campaign for him. Bringing in someone from out of state for such an endorsement was a new technique in political campaigning. Bayard gladly obliged.

Startup counterattacked by hitting Abbett where he seemed most vulnerable. He reminded voters that his Democratic opponent had defended the Bumsted Ring in court and had received $18,000 for his legal services. Whether or not Startup knew of Abbett's shady business dealings with Bumsted remains unclear. If he did know, for some unexplained reason, he chose not to expose them. In any event, Startup received substantial support from English Protestant nativists in Jersey City. Staunch Republicans, they formed the British-American Association in 1874 that functioned as a Republican political action committee. But after a bitterly contested election split along class and ethnic lines, Abbett emerged victorious with 13,131 votes against Startup's 8,191.[62] Abbett's carefully cultivated alliance with the Irish machine in Hudson County had delivered for him. In the horseshoe district, he received 2,285 votes; Startup gathered only 550 there. The voters also elected Patrick H. Laverty as county sheriff and Patrick Sheeran as a state assemblyman. Both were Irish immigrants.

New Jersey politicians had played ethnic politics long before the 1870s, but Abbett worked hard in perfecting this strategy. Ronald Formisano and other scholars have maintained that mass politics began in the 1830s, and it is evident that in New Jersey during that decade, both parties resorted to ethnic politics as soon as the Irish began voting.[63] Led by Governor Peter D. Vroom and Senator Garret Wall, the Democrats took pro-Irish positions, while the Whigs worked to enact voting restrictions even before 1840. This was a stirring issue at the New Jersey constitutional convention in 1844. But Abbett took ethnic politics to a higher level in the 1870s, when New Jersey was home to 86,784 Irish and 54,001 Germans. He managed party nominations and distributed public jobs to urban ethnics in exchange for their votes at election time.

Patronage, in his view, was the glue that held the party organization together. Critics now depicted him as an unsavory spoils politician, but his skill in playing ethnic politics accounted for much of his success as a politician.

THE CONSUMMATE DEMOCRAT

In 1875, Abbett returned to Trenton refreshed and energized for the issues confronting him in the senate. He now sought to fulfill his campaign promise by filing a municipal charter reform bill for Jersey City. The central political task was to restore the city to self-governance. Because the legislature was then divided, with the assembly in the hands of the Democrats and the senate strongly tilted toward the Republicans, the circumstances were not favorable. Arguing with renewed vigor, Abbett pleaded his case and the assembly passed his bill, but he was rebuffed in the senate by obstructionist Republicans.

Although Abbett was not successful in getting his home rule measure passed, he did succeed in getting a general law passed to incorporate businesses. To that end, he drafted the Corporations Act of 1875 that put a stop to the abuse and favoritism inherent in drafting special laws for individual companies. The statute had an antimonopoly ring to it that enhanced his popularity among the working class. With his sights set firmly on the governorship, Abbett continued to appeal to the Irish and Catholic vote. He played subtly on the religious and ethnic issue in 1875 when he sponsored his "Liberty of Conscience" bill that was designed to give Catholic priests access to inmates at state reformatories, prisons, and mental institutions. The problem had recently surfaced at the state reform school in Jamesburg. Catholics were disturbed by the fact that the Reverend Luther H. Sheldon, an ordained Protestant minister in charge of the reformatory, conducted compulsory chapel and instructed the boys in the basic tenets of Protestantism.

This highly charged issue came to a head when a delegation of Catholic laymen, headed by Democrat James Smith of Newark, visited the Jamesburg Reform School. After their inspection of the facility, they wrote a letter to the trustees requesting that Catholic boys be excused from Protestant religious instruction and that a Catholic chaplain be assigned to minister to their spiritual needs. Principles of equity and fairness demanded as much in their view. The trustees flatly rejected both requests. As a result of this setback, Bishop Michael A. Corrigan, the spiritual leader of the Newark archdiocese, purchased a large tract of land in Denville on which he opened a Catholic Protectory for destitute children in 1874.[64] Many of these wayward boys and girls wandered in packs around the cities, not attending school, not working, and not under any

adult supervision. They were exposed to all the allurements of vice and street crime. A similar Catholic Protectory had been established in Westchester, New York, where it received some city and state money.

At this stage of the controversy, Assemblyman Patrick Doyle of Newark, desiring to please his Irish constituents, introduced a bill that authorized the commitment of Catholic children to church institutions and provided for state funds to help support the Protectory. A native of Ireland, Doyle was a big, brawny laborer who worked at the Atba Steel Works in Newark. While his bill made it through the general assembly without much difficulty, it engendered militant Protestant opposition in the senate, where it was soundly defeated. Assemblyman William H. Kirk of Essex County led the attack on the bill in the lower house. Presenting the protest of the Newark Methodist Episcopal Conference, he declared that the bill violated the constitutional doctrine of separation of church and state. "Not a Protestant in the land," Kirk argued, "would have the unblushing effrontery to propose such a bill."[65] Kirk's address was printed in most newspapers and was the main theme of Sunday sermons in Protestant pulpits across the state. The Order of United American Mechanics held a public meeting in Newark at which Kirk's position was strongly endorsed.

Unlike the Doyle bill, Abbett's statute cleverly avoided any use of public funds, thereby skirting the thorny issue of separation of church and state. Concerned about not offending hard-line Protestants, he titled his bill Liberty of Conscience—cover words that sent a cryptic double message. To Republicans this was carefully coded language that meant protection from Catholic designs and a guarantee to the right of individual interpretation of the scriptures. Alternatively, Democrats interpreted it to mean the right of Catholics to be free to practice their religion as they deemed proper and without any interference from the state. The confusion was intentional. In both language and tone, Abbett continued to broker the political differences between the two religious groups. Nonetheless, his proposed legislation aroused anger among Protestant conservatives and stirred doubts in the minds of many moderates.

With Protestant opposition so aroused, Abbett realized that his bill stood little chance of passing in the senate in which he could muster only five votes for it. Yet, even in defeat, Abbett turned the issue to his advantage. Speaking on the senate floor, he told his fellow lawmakers that Catholic priests in Hudson County were allowed to minister to members of their faith in the local jails, poorhouses, hospitals, and sanitariums.[66] Such sentiments were warmly received by the Irish who continued to view Abbett as their champion in the face of nativist attacks. Over and beyond that, his speech sent a powerful message to the growing number of Catholics throughout New Jersey who saw him as a stand-up leader on whom they could count to represent their interests. Roundly condemning

Abbett for his efforts, Republicans called him a Catholic sympathizer. Ethnocultural and religious animosities continued to influence the voting behavior of the electorate.

Breaking sharply and completely with the State House Ring in 1875, Abbett decided to support Attorney General Robert Gilchrist for the U.S. Senate rather than back Theodore Randolph, who wanted the seat for himself. Gilchrist by now was one of Abbett's principal allies. As attorney general, he had gained fame in prosecuting the Bumsted Ring. Randolph, however, was not about to relinquish his command; his leadership was at stake. Abbett did not have to go it alone as he tried to push aside the titular party leader. He was joined in this high-risk venture by Gilchrist and John McPherson. These three Democratic leaders realized that to win elections the party must temper its nativism and continue to appeal to blue-collar workers and Catholic immigrants.

At a time when the Irish in Jersey City were being stripped of their power, the insurgent Democratic leadership—as represented by the triumvirate of Abbett, Gilchrist, and McPherson—courted the Irish and provided a means for accommodating the narrowly political aspects of their demands. Conversely, the Randolph faction abhorred the Irish courtship and staunchly resisted such demands. As they strove to maintain control of the state party organization and preferential treatment of the railroads, they staunchly resisted the demands of organized labor. If nothing else, the senatorial race brought these intraparty differences into sharper focus.

But the attempted coup failed. With Henry C. Kelsey and Henry S. Little operating behind the scenes, the State House Ring secured the Democratic caucus nomination for Theodore Randolph. He then went on to defeat Republican George M. Robeson of Newark before a joint session of the state legislature. While these efforts ended in failure for the Abbett faction, they had at least thrown down the political gauntlet and served notice that Abbett and his allies were to be taken seriously. Angered by the abortive coup, the Randolph faction retaliated. Governor Joseph Bedle promptly removed Robert Gilchrist as attorney general for what he considered treachery and betrayal. Not only were the old differences between the two factions still very much alive, but new differences were being created. The Randolph Democrats were intent on disabling the labor movement, not in helping it survive, but this fight was being waged primarily outside the state government. Pressures supporting the rights of labor were building against the reactionary State House Ring.

On April 13, 1876, Abbett was named by the local Board of Finance as corporation counsel for Jersey City. In this capacity, he began to reexamine the city's legal position on railroad taxation and to press its case. The financially distressed city was hurting for revenue. In 1875, Abbett had drafted and pushed for the adoption of the equal tax amendment to the New Jersey constitution to require real property to be

assessed according to its true value under general laws and by uniform rules. Heretofore, the railroads had taken advantage of a tax loophole that permitted them to be taxed either on the basis of their capital stock or on the "cost, equipment, and appendages" of the railroad, or whichever was less. By introducing a bill that substituted the new assessment standard of true value for that of cost, Abbett showed his interest in closing this loophole.[67] Abbett's increasing involvement in the equal tax movement and his growing criticism of the railroads put him at odds with his party's leadership, but he did not misjudge the potency of the issue or his ability to espouse it. The amendment was adopted, and an alert sense of the popularity of the equal tax trend continued to shape Abbett's strategy.

In a dramatic shift of his position, Abbett opposed a large subsidy (by way of tax abatement) that the United New Jersey Railroads and Canal Companies sought to obtain from the state in 1876. He personally led the attack against this legislation. When it looked as if the bill might pass, he fought a valiant delaying action. He conducted a thirteen-hour filibuster that assured its defeat and demonstrated his increasing willingness to take on the railroad power. But there was not much he could do about the irrepealable contracts that gave certain railroads tax exemptions because the federal and state courts had upheld them. These actions on Abbett's part hardly pleased the railroad companies or the State House Ring, but they endeared him to his Hudson County constituents.

In June 1876, Abbett attended the Democratic National Convention in St. Louis and was named chairman of the New Jersey delegation. He placed Governor Joel Parker's name in nomination for president as a favorite son candidate and gave a stirring speech in his behalf. The Democrats chose New York Governor Samuel J. Tilden, who had sent Boss William Tweed and his cronies to jail and was credited with smashing the corrupt Canal Ring. Meanwhile the Republicans, meeting in Cincinnati, picked Ohio Governor Rutherford B. Hayes as their candidate. In the presidential campaign that followed, Hayes and Tilden agreed on most of the major issues—hard money, withdrawing federal troops from the South, and civil service reform.

Although Tilden carried New Jersey and won the national popular vote, he wound up losing the election. The electoral votes of four states were in dispute. With Congress unable to agree on the counting of the electoral votes, a fifteen-member commission was appointed to adjudicate the disputes, including several U.S. Supreme Court justices. Seven were Republicans, seven were Democrats, and the fifteenth, Judge David Davis, was widely regarded as an independent. When Davis was elected a Democratic senator from Illinois, Justice Joseph Bradley of New Jersey was chosen to replace him. Up to that point, the commission had been deadlocked. An ardent Republican, Bradley joined his fellow

Republicans and cast the deciding vote that broke the deadlock. In a strict party line vote (8 to 7), the commission awarded the disputed electoral votes from Florida, South Carolina, Louisiana, and Oregon to Hayes.[68]

The Republicans apparently had cut a deal. They agreed to Democratic demands that federal troops be pulled out of southern states and stop enforcing the civil rights of blacks. Hayes won the White House by the margin of one electoral vote. The freed slaves were shoved back into oppression. Most historians agree that this election was stolen. The net result was a hobbled president known to all as "His Fraudulency," unprecedented partisan warfare, and a cloud over national politics for a generation.

After Reconstruction, and with the far-reaching issues of American federalism gradually receding, Abbett was chosen president of the state senate in January 1877. He had risen in his party because his colleagues and constituents perceived him as an outspoken advocate for the common man. The new battles that Abbett would face involved issues dealing with railroad and labor politics heavily mixed with those of urban growth and economic development. At this stage of his political career, the Hudson Democrat fully understood the ethic of the senate and the intricacies of the legislative process. As its presiding officer, he knew how to advise without becoming patronizing, how to bargain without promising more than he could deliver, and how to appeal to personal honor or party unity without becoming overly solicitous. Moreover, he knew where each of his colleagues in both parties stood, or wavered, and what each wanted or feared. He disguised his own position until it was absolutely necessary to divulge it. Few people knew what he really wanted, other than to come out on the winning side.

Changing labor-management relations, especially in New Jersey's glass, pottery, silk, and cotton industries, required new approaches on the part of policymakers. As senate president, Abbett pulled off a major coup by sponsoring a statute that required management to pay employees in cash rather than in scrip or company store merchandise as was the custom in such rural areas as South Jersey. Glass workers located in remote company towns were dependent on their employers for food, housing, and the other basic necessities of life.

In keeping with the fiefdom motif, companies had their own monetary system, issuing their own scrip. Some would advance scrip in anticipation of earnings, thus putting the glass workers in debt, while others granted scrip only if the income had already been earned. Scrip was good at face value only in the company store. Since prices were higher in company stores, scrip's value was inevitably less than that of cash. Trapped in these feudal circumstances, the glass blowers were being paid in "shin-plasters" refundable only at the company store.

After the company deducted rent and staples from their wages, employees often found themselves destitute and without any cash saved from their labor. "Three fifths of the 7,000 workers in Bridgeton," claimed the *Paterson Labor Standard*, "never handle a cent of their earnings in cash."[69]

A delegation of glass blowers called on Abbett at the State House to win redress of their grievances. He listened carefully and expressed sympathy for their plight. Afterward, he drafted a statute that presented a solution to the problem. During the acrimonious debate, when his bill appeared in trouble and looked as if it might be defeated, the senate president took the floor and gave a rousing speech. "It is a fraud on the workingman," he declared, "to compel him to take shinplasters for his pay."[70] Abbett's real work then began as he persuaded a majority of his colleagues to pass the bill by converting seven votes to his side.

Abbett scored a second major coup with labor in 1877, when he helped employees from the bankrupt Jersey Central Railroad recover back wages. In dire financial straits, the Jersey Central arbitrarily had imposed a drastic wage cut amounting to $401,362 and failed to pay its employees what they had legitimately earned. The senate president engineered the passage of a law that made workers' unpaid wages a prior lien on the assets of the bankrupt company. The law seemed like adequate protection. Ordinarily, it would have been except that Francis Lathrop was the court-appointed receiver. Lathrop, a close friend of Randolph and the presumed brains behind the State House Ring, was a lay judge on the New Jersey Court of Errors and Appeals. As a member of the state Riparian Commission, he had helped the Jersey Central Railroad gain access to tidal property in Jersey City. Lathrop believed that any law or procedure could be evaded in one form or another, and by citing a provision in the statute that referred to employees as "laborers," he narrowly ruled that it only covered those men who worked on the railroad bed and tracks. Hatred of the Jersey Central was fueled when the receiver refused to pay the conductors, locomotive engineers, firemen, brakemen, freight agents, passenger ticket clerks, and various other personnel.

No sooner had Lathrop issued his ruling than litigation ensued. On March 22, 1877, Abbett took the case to the New Jersey Court of Chancery, where he sought injunctive relief. In the course of the court proceedings, he argued his position before Chancellor Theodore Runyon and persuaded him that his cause was fair and just. Runyon issued a court order requiring the receiver to make full restitution to all the railroad workers. His decision was a stinging rebuke to Lathrop. Such a move on Abbett's part was, of course, extremely good politics. Refusing to accept a fee for his legal services, he then sent a telegram to Bartholomew Murtaugh, the track master for the Jersey Central: "Chancellor signed

order directing money to be paid. Men get $80,000 this month and balance will be paid in monthly installments until they are fully paid. Receiver will send out printed copies of the order so that the men can read it. Tell men I charge them nothing."[71] When the news of this court victory came over the ticker tape, the railroad workers were jubilant. They would never forget what Abbett had done for them.

Once again, Abbett was drawn into conflict with Randolph and the State House Ring over the election of a U.S. senator in 1877. The two men now loathed each other, their forced smiles barely concealing their fundamental disagreements. Randolph backed Ashbel Green for the position, while Abbett supported his ally John McPherson, who was favorably viewed by labor as a strong protectionist on the tariff issue. Green came from a first family in New Jersey, whose economic interests were connected with the canals and railroads. The power struggle between the two party factions took place in the Democratic caucus, where the Abbett forces now had the votes that they lacked in the previous senatorial contest. As a result, McPherson emerged victorious as the Democratic candidate. He went on to compete against Frederick T. Frelinghuysen, the Republican incumbent, before a joint legislative session.

The general assembly was evenly divided between Democrats and Republicans, while the Democrats held a one-vote advantage in the senate. Abbett knew the race would be extremely close. When friendly Democrats appeared to waver, he kept the pressure on. Assemblyman Gottfried Krueger, a German brewer from Newark, whose vote would be the linchpin to victory, was in trouble with the Internal Revenue Service over payment of beer stamps. He was pressured by the Republican administration in Washington to break ranks and support Frelinghuysen. Appealing to Krueger's sense of party loyalty, Abbett convinced him to stand fast. In the end, McPherson won by a single vote; it was a major victory for the Abbett faction.[72]

This fighting for control of the party organization was both personal and ideological. After McPherson's senatorial victory, Abbett settled a political score with Governor Joseph Bedle for having removed Robert Gilchrist as attorney general. He now blocked Bedle's appointments of Bennington F. Randolph and John S. Blair as state judges to the district court in Hudson County. Bennington Randolph was Bedle's father-in-law; John Blair was a railroad attorney and a prominent Republican. Abbett criticized the governor for nepotism and party disloyalty. Invoking the privilege of senatorial courtesy, he blocked the judicial appointments until the last weeks of the Bedle administration.

Most important of all was Abbett's quest to enact a law restoring home rule to Jersey City. The legal task had become more complicated

than when he had originally filed his bill in 1875. Since then, the New Jersey electorate had approved a state constitutional amendment that prohibited the passage of special laws for individual cities. This local government amendment was intended to prevent ripper laws that permitted gangs like the Bumsted Ring to take over a city government by legislative fiat. Only Jersey City had been subjected to such treatment. The constitutional amendment made it virtually impossible to pass legislation for a specific city.

Faced with what seemed like an insoluble dilemma, Abbett demonstrated a rare capacity for translating complex problems into politically viable and understandable statutory language. He overcame the constitutional problem by making all municipal commissions elective rather than appointive. Thus, he framed the statute as a general law. Jersey City was never once mentioned in his bill, and yet it applied to no other city. The technical skill of Abbett's legislative craftsmanship did not pass unnoticed.[73] The thieves charter had been abolished, home rule was restored, and Abbett had fulfilled his original campaign promise.

When his senatorial term expired in 1877, Abbett completed the legislative phase of his career. In so doing, he had emerged as a major figure in state politics. The durability of his convictions had been amply tested. He showed decisiveness in moving deliberately toward his goals and in steeling himself against the monopolistic power of capitalists. During this period, Abbett led the fight for the common man and built a reliable political base. Battling nativists in his state for more than a decade, he defended ethnic minorities from the attacks of intolerant bigots. He felt secure in his ability to marshal the power of reason against the pull of prejudice. The same was true with regard to labor. Against formidable odds, he had helped workers obtain some degree of social and economic justice. Such actions placed him in a unique position to mediate those conflicts and to continue to build a more cohesive Democratic party organization.

At this point, Abbett's main problem was that he had alienated some very powerful interests. It was inevitable that public policy decisions touching on such explosive issues, especially when most of them went against the grain of both the political philosophy and economic interests of the dominant ruling elite in New Jersey, would have serious repercussions. Since Abbett's enemies could not outmaneuver or outsmart him, they attacked his character and reputation. Nonetheless, Abbett's success in building a large personal following made him a force with which to be reckoned. He was viewed as a likely contender for his party's gubernatorial nomination in 1877. The political apprenticeship was now over and a new phase of his career had begun.

ENDNOTES

1 See *Hudson County Democrat*, November 5, 1864. This endorsement gave Abbett a much needed boost in publicity. Two years later, he would return the favor by endorsing Evans, who succeeded him in the general assembly in 1866.

2 Sackett, *Modern Battles of Trenton*, 1:223.

3 Adrian Cook, *The Armies of the Streets: The New York City Draft Riots of 1863*, (Lexington, KY, 1974), 193-94. See also Iver Bernstein, *The New York City Draft Riots* (New York, 1990).

4 *Biographical Directory of the United States Congress 1774–1989* (Washington, D.C., U.S. Government Printing Office, 1989), 1998.

5 For the best treatment of James Wall as a copperhead leader, see William Gillette, *Jersey Blue* (New Brunswick, Rutgers University Press, 1995), 226-228.

6 *Ibid.*, 8-9.

7 Sackett, *Modern Battles of Trenton*, 1:223.

8 *New York Times*, November 1, 1864.

9 *Hudson County Democrat*, November 19, 1864.

10 Gillette, *Jersey Blue*, 302.

11 *Debates of the Eighty-Ninth General Assembly of the State of New Jersey on the Bill to Ratify an Amendment to the Constitution of the United States*, 49, 23-103. See also Gillette, *Jersey Blue*, 302.

12 *Hudson County Democrat*, April 8, 1965.

13 *Trenton Monitor*, March 2, 1865.

14 Gillette, *Jersey Blue*, 306.

15 William J. Jackson, *New Jerseyans in the Civil War* (New Brunswick, Rutgers University Press, 2000), 214.

16 *Hudson County Democrat*, September 30, 1865. At the local level, Hoboken residents elected Abbett to the city's water commission.

17 *Hudson County Democrat*, November 11, 1865. Of the 1,165 votes cast, Abbett collected 630 as compared with 535 for Chamberlain.

18 *Minutes of the New Jersey General Assembly for 1866* (Woodbury, 1866), 37-38, 101-2, and 369-70.

19 For a detailed analysis of these demographic changes in Jersey City, see Douglas 5. Shaw, *The Making of an Immigrant City* (New York, Arno Press, 1976), Chapt. l.

20 *American Standard*, February 15, 1866.

21 *Jersey City Times*, February 14, 1866.

22 *American Standard*, February 15, 1866, and August 10, 1868; *Newark Daily Advertiser*, February 7 and February 23, 1866.

23 *Minutes of New Jersey General Assembly for 1866* (Woodbury, 1866), 211-212.

24 Shaw, *The Making of an Immigrant City*, 44.

25 *Trenton True American*, September 12, 1866.

26 Gillette, *Jersey Blue*, 312-313.

27 For a verbatim copy of Abbett's speech in defense of John P. Stockton, see the *Hudson County Democrat*, September 15, 1866.

28 *American Standard*, November 12, 1868; *Evening Journal*, November 11, 1868. Voter turnout in this contest was lower than the previous year, because it was an off-year election.

29 *American Standard*, April 11, 1868.

30 *New York World*, August 2, 1869.

31 *American Standard*, October 29, 1869.

32 *American Standard*, November 3, 1869; *Evening Journal*, November 3, 1869. Voter turnout in this contest was lower than the previous year, because it was an off-year election.

33 For a fascinating and detailed history of the Camden and Amboy Railroad, see Wheaton J. Lane, *From Indian Trail to Iron Horse* (Princeton, Princeton University Press, 1939), 321-25.

34 *Evening Journal*, March 19, 1869.

35 *Trenton True American*, February 18, 1870; *Trenton State Gazette*, March 11, 1870.

36 Abbett was opposing counsel to the railroads in at least seven cases that reached the appellate courts and were recorded in the New Jersey law and equity reports. See *Central Railroad Co. v. City of Bayonne* 35 N.J.L. 332 (1872); *Bennett v. New Jersey Railroad and Transportation Co.* 36 N.J.L. 225 (1873); *Sanford and Wright v. Newark and Hudson Railroad Co.* 37 N.J.L. 1 (1874); *Williamson v. N.J. Southern Railway Co.* 28 N.J.E. 277 (1877); *Coe v. New Jersey Midland Railway Co.* 30 N.J.E. 440 (1879); *Jersey City v. Lehigh Valley Railroad Co.* 41 N.J.L. 66 (1879); and *New Jersey Midland Railroad Co. v. Jersey City* 42 N.J.L. 97 (1880).

37 *Trenton True American*, February 15, 1870; *Minutes of the New Jersey Assembly* (1870), 47.

38 *Trenton True American*, March 16, 1870.

39 For a contemporary account of this controversy, see the *New York Herald*, April 21, 1873; the *Irish World*, May 10, 1873.

40 *Evening Journal*, May 18 and 29, 1869.

41 *Evening Journal*, May 11, 1869.

42 See *Annual Report of the Board of Education of Jersey City for year ending March 31, 1869* (Jersey City, 1869), 43-45; *Annual Report of the Board of Education of Jersey City for year ending March 31, 1870* (Jersey City, 1870), 32-33.

43 *Evening Journal*, July 13, 1870.

44 *Evening Journal*, November 1, 1870. See also Shaw, *The Making of an Immigrant City*, 170-183.

45 Shaw, *The Making of an Immigrant City*, 217.

46 Governor Randolph's veto message is printed in full in the *Newark Daily Advertiser*, March 25, 1871. A careful reading of his veto message reveals that the governor agreed with the substance of the bill.

47 *Trenton State Gazette*, April 3, 1878.

48 This profile is drawn from Charles Robson, *The Biographical Encyclopedia of New Jersey of the Nineteenth Century* (Philadelphia, Galaxy Publishing Company, 1877), 558; Rudolph J. Vecholi, *The People of New Jersey* (Princeton, D. Van Nostrand, 1965), 134-135; and Paul A. Stellhorn and Michael J. Birkner, *The Governors of New Jersey* (Trenton, New Jersey Historical Commission, 1982), 137-141.

49 Quoted in the *Irish World*, August 12, 1871.

50 Abbett's inclusive tendencies did not at this stage of his career embrace African Americans, of whom there were 38,853 in the state by 1880. Of these, 10,670 were males of voting age.

51 Shaw, *The Making of an Immigrant City*, 106.

52 *Boston Pilot*, June 30, 1885.

53 *New York Times*, February 22, 1871.

54 *American Standard*, November 7, 1871.

55 *Jersey City Herald*, April 22, 1871.

56 Evidence of their joint ownership of the Jersey City meadowlands property is found in the legal jacket of Leon Abbett's last will and testament (No. 15084) as recorded in the Hudson County Surrogate's and Register's offices.

57 *New York Times*, March 26, 1872; *New York Herald*, March 27, 1872.

58 Alexander McLean, *History of Jersey City* (Jersey City, 1895), 84.

59 *Ibid.*

60 Shaw, *The Making of an Immigrant City*, 251-252.

61 See U.S. Passport of Leon Abbett issued on May 9, 1874.

62 F. L. Lundy, *New Jersey Legislative Manual* (Morristown, 1875), 65-66.

63 See Ronald P. Formisano, *The Birth of Mass Political Parties: Michigan, 1827–1861* (Princeton, Princeton University Press, 1971).

64 Joseph M. Flynn, *The Catholic Church in New Jersey* (Morristown, 1904), 422-29.

65 Quoted in Sackett, *Modern Battles of Trenton*, 1:113.

66 A synopsis of Abbett's speech promoting his "Liberty of Conscience" bill is found in the *Jersey City Herald*, April 10, 1875.

67 New Jersey Laws for 1876, Chap. 101.

68 For a balanced treatment of Joseph Bradley's role in the resolution of the disputed 1876 presidential election, see Jonathan Lurie, "Mr. Justice Bradley: A Reassessment," 16 *Seton Hall Law Review* 343 (1986), 353.

69 Quoted in Rudolph Vecoli, *The People of New Jersey*, 90.

70 *Newark Daily Advertiser*, February 28, 1877.

71 Quoted in *The Record of Leon Abbett as Assemblyman, Senator and Governor* (Jersey City, 1889), 14.

72 Sackett, *Modern Battles of Trenton*, 1:124-130.

73 *Jersey City Herald*, March 3, 1877.

5

The Elusive Quest for Governor

In the spring of 1877, the economy was still in the throes of a bad depression that was getting worse. Unemployment remained high as people were laid off. There was no end in sight to the economic hard times. The rights of labor were being trampled by wrongs that were done to workers—unsteady work, low wages, disease, unsanitary housing, dangerous working conditions, and the wanton waste of human lives in accidents and violent sudden deaths. Management's insistence that employees sign yellow dog contracts as a condition of employment not only made workers angry enough to want to unionize, but it also incited them to retaliate. The ruthless eviction of workers and their families from company housing was another grievance in a long list of grievances. Criminal conspiracy laws made organizing efforts of legitimate unions more difficult than ever. As unemployment increased, the relationship between capital and labor became explosive. In city after city, violent race riots erupted, and many blacks were lynched. Street crime, teen-age gangs, and lawlessness spread across America. During the troubled summer of 1877, these conditions led to a nationwide railroad strike that resulted in widespread rioting and civil disorder. The pot was boiling over and the country was near revolt.

Against this background of labor unrest, Leon Abbett decided to make a run for governor. By this time, he had a built-in constituency and a statewide political base from which to launch his campaign. His supporters saw him as a time-tested, proven leader who could claim a record of having fought for more equitable treatment of workers and immigrants. They admired him for supporting numerous causes. Although Abbett had ambitions for national office and thought about running for the U.S. Senate, that option remained closed to him for the time being. Fellow Democrats John McPherson and Theodore Randolph already

occupied New Jersey's two senatorial seats. The opportunities for political advancement were limited for even the most ambitious local politicians. So Abbett decided to seek his party's gubernatorial nomination instead. He believed that his plans could best be advanced if he could present himself to the state Democratic convention as a proven leader who could unify the party, settle internal differences, and get important legislation enacted.

Obtaining his party's nomination would be a daunting task. The winds of political change were swirling. Hardly anything could have prepared the residents of New Jersey, in the fourth year of a depression, for the economic and fiscal disasters that would befall them in the years between 1873 and 1879. Throughout most of the 1870s, inflation and unemployment had risen together. Abbett's pursuit of the governorship depended a great deal on whether he would be able to unite and focus the political power of discontented farm and labor groups. His populist image as an authentic hero of the "little guy" had made him a popular Democrat. If Abbett's optimism proved premature, it still mirrored the hopes and aspirations of farmers and blue-collar workers. They directed their hostility at special interest groups fattening themselves at public expense. Their disenchantment and discontent with the railroads would soon erupt into a massive national strike.

Few businessmen engaged more actively or more conspicuously in New Jersey politics than the railroad coal magnates. Men like John I. Blair, Henry S. Little, William W. Phelps, Frederick A. Potts, Theodore Randolph, and William J. Sewell were among the more notable activists. They all made their fortunes in railroading. At the same time, the railroads were entering the coal industry, especially the anthracite fields in Pennsylvania. Coal production grew as industrial expansion accelerated. Smelting of ore into iron used increasing amounts of anthracite coal and in time hard coal took over the home-heating market. Expanding demand encouraged investors to enter the race to produce more coal and the investment paid off handsomely; the profits made from the mining and shipping of coal became increasingly lucrative. As the economic case for railroad expansion grew stronger, those groups with local tax and land use concerns that conflicted with the goals of the railroad developers also gained in political strength and momentum. The antimonopolists had become a viable political force, and they used their political clout to place railroad issues on the public agenda. Such issues were now shifting from the developmental to the allocational arena, and the politics of railroads took on a different character. The rapacious railroad coal operators took corporate greed to new heights during this period.

While Abbett felt confident about his pursuit of the Democratic gubernatorial nomination in 1877, he knew it would be a difficult task. Vicious scrutiny awaited him as he neared his goal. Since he had

antagonized both Republicans and Democrats alike, his foes were pre-pared to stop him. Such antagonism was to be expected because politics in New Jersey was intensely personal.

The Democratic party in New Jersey was plagued with chronic fac-tionalism, internal disputes, and personal jealousies, which meant that the Democrats maintained a shifting and at times uneasy coalition. Intraparty differences and squabbles continued to surface. Internal dissension between the Randolph and Abbett factions had grown worse in the two years from 1875 to 1877. They were clearly estranged. But the Republicans suffered from the same sort of party factionalism and inter-nal discord. The goal of achieving party unity proved difficult for both major parties. As Morton Keller observed: "The closeness of the party balance nationally and in many states, and the constant jockeying for power within each party structure, made organizational stability a prized but elusive goal."[1]

As a gubernatorial aspirant, Abbett had a lot going for him includ-ing his attractive wife, Mary Abbett, who was fully devoted to her hus-band. She brought warmth and grace to their household. Throughout their marriage, they had made many friends and acquaintances. They entertained a great deal and hosted sparkling dinner parties. Always the consummate hostess, Mary charmed her dinner guests with her social grace, beauty, and elegance. She was very supportive of her husband's political ambitions. Thirty-eight years of age, Mary was a smart Victorian woman, sweet and charming, who behaved in a dignified but unaffected manner. Her blend of native Philadelphia charm and sophistication made her an ideal candidate's wife. This gentle brown-eyed woman adored her husband and believed implicitly in him, but she was bothered by some of the charges hurled against him.

At this stage of his career, Leon Abbett kept his family apart from politics as much as possible. He had followed a basic rule of providing for his wife and children before stepping into politics. They lived in a family-owned brownstone on Sussex Street in Jersey City, where three Irish female domestic servants took care of the household and children. During the summer months, the Abbetts sought to escape the unbearable heat and humidity of Jersey City by vacationing at the Jersey seashore. They sum-mered at the fashionable resort towns of Long Branch, Spring Lake, and Sea Girt, where they socialized with the rich and powerful. Atlantic City, only sixty miles by train from Philadelphia, had built its famous boardwalk in 1870, and many people went there for health reasons and the "curative powers" of breathing the salt air and bathing in the ocean surf. President Ulysses S. Grant used Long Branch as the summer White House.

For her part, Mary Abbett moved with ease among various groups and constituencies. She had a style and presence that were rare. One newspaper reporter described her as "calm, thoughtful and sympathetic

—a lady of rare and conspicuous gifts" who impressed all who knew her "with a sense of admiration, respect and deference." Elaborating on this description, the reporter went on to say that she was endowed with "great intellectual powers, clear perceptions, and almost unerring judgment."[2]

From every indication, Mary Abbett encouraged her husband to seek the governorship, and she worked diligently behind the scenes on his behalf. Rumor had it that she longed to become the state's First Lady. Unfortunately, she would not live to see that day. While performing a routine medical checkup, her family doctor discovered cancer of the uterus, but he was unsure of his diagnosis and did not want to tell her until he was certain. Soon to follow was a second medical opinion that confirmed the first diagnosis. The medical reports were distressing. The doctors delayed telling her until March 17, 1877. Without mincing words, they informed her that it was cancer and that the malignancy was incurable.

Their diagnosis struck like a thunderbolt in the night. When her husband learned that Mary's illness was terminal, he was totally devastated. He could hardly bear the thought of losing his young wife. Yet, the warning signs were unmistakable. As things turned out, Mary had a little more than two years to live. She accepted her fate stoically and went on with her life and lived it to the fullest without wallowing in self-pity. As the cancer spread and took its toll, Abbett found it extremely difficult to watch her suffer and waste away. For a person of his stature not to be able to do anything about it only added to his stress. It presented an intolerable strain. At times, it was almost more than he could bear.

THE LIBEL SUIT AGAINST THE *JERSEY CITY HERALD*

Despite his personal troubles, Abbett continued to pursue his quest for the governorship. Too much momentum had built up. He was a man on a mission and now seemed more determined than ever to please his wife. But he soon ran into trouble in trying to secure his party's nomination. His meteoric rise to prominence had provoked jealousy among those who did not want to see him advance to statewide office. They indulged in gossip, slander, and malicious falsehoods in an effort to sabotage his gubernatorial plans. Abbett had mused about how many groups he could antagonize and still be effective. The leading role that he had taken on the issue of railroad taxation, in support of labor's goals, and in support of Irish-American causes had made him a target of political sniping. Much of this backbiting came from within his own party. Those hidden antagonisms now surfaced in response to his drive for higher office.

On May 12, 1877, less than two months after he had learned about his wife's terminal illness, Abbett suffered a damaging blow politically. The editor of the *Jersey City Herald*, Hugh McDermott, who nursed

a personal grudge, wrote a malicious character assault of Abbett. Tipped off by a confidence man, the editor started the article by asking and answering a series of embarrassing questions about Abbett's political behavior when he had served as speaker of the assembly.

In this type of format, McDermott accused Abbett of having accepted a $16,000 bribe for allegedly using his influence to defeat seven redistricting bills. He also accused him of conspiring with Republicans in 1871 to elect their fellow Republican Frederick Frelinghuysen to the U.S. Senate. At the time, Frelinghuysen's Democratic opponent was Governor Theodore Randolph, whom Abbett disliked intensely. No insult was more keenly felt than to be charged with party disloyalty; these were serious accusations.

Abbett, so the story went, was supposed to have split the bribe money with Caleb H. Valentine, an assemblyman from Warren County. Instead, he allegedly gave Valentine $3,000 and pocketed the rest for himself. Nothing of this nature did transpire. Stretching his imagination to the limit, McDermott leaped to the preposterous conclusion that because the redistricting bills were defeated, Abbett was somehow personally responsible for the "horseshoe gerrymander" in 1870, the consequent plundering by the Bumsted Ring, and the public indebtedness saddled on Jersey City.[3] These answers to McDermott's own questions stretched the limits of credibility.

McDermott's sensational story spread like wildfire. Newspapers across the state ran it on their front pages. Upon reading the article, Abbett was shocked and angered. When angry, he was known as a man who did not pull his punches. As a politician threatened with scandal, he realized that the damaging story could ruin his political career. He took immediate steps to clear his name. That same day, Abbett filed a libel suit against Hugh McDermott and demanded a retraction. In this kind of litigation, the common law of libel prevailed: the plaintiff had to prove that the defendant had published a falsehood either knowingly or recklessly. Since Abbett had to show that there was something false in the publication, the burden of proof fell upon him. Truth was an incontrovertible defense.

However bad the timing of the article, Abbett could ill afford to let McDermott's accusations go unanswered. He promptly contacted the four men who were named in the article as having witnessed the alleged bribe. They included Newark Assemblyman David Anderson, Statehouse Superintendent Barney Ford, Hudson State Senator Noah D. Taylor, and Eben Winton, who was editor of the *Hackensack Democrat*. At Abbett's request, each wrote a letter to the editor of the *Jersey City Herald* in which they exonerated the former speaker. All four of them supported Abbett in varying degrees and each denied any wrongdoing on his part. Contrary to what McDermott had written, they insisted that Abbett had

done everything in his power as speaker to ensure that a vote was taken on the seven redistricting bills in question. Subsequent publication of the roll call votes in the local press corroborated their public testimony. Since the Republicans controlled the legislature in 1871, they were not about to elect a Democrat like Randolph. So the charge that Abbett had conspired with them to elect Frelinghuysen was at best specious. Other leading Democrats took the newspaper to task for its irresponsible statements. U.S. Senator John McPherson wrote a public letter in which he vouched for Abbett's good moral character and denied there was a serious rift between them as McDermott had further indicated.[4]

Capping a week of frenzied activity, Abbett was able to develop credible evidence and extricate himself from a precarious situation that imperiled his political future. In the next issue of his newspaper, McDermott, threatened by the libel suit, published a complete retraction.[5] He implicated William B. Rankin as his accomplice. A disreputable con man, Rankin had provided McDermott with the false information for an undisclosed sum of money. In addition to identifying his anonymous source, McDermott wrote a letter of public apology that was published in the *Jersey City Argus*. He also admitted that he had written the article while under the influence of liquor.[6]

Despite its drama, the libel suit ended in anticlimax. The case was never tested in the courts. Abbett had met the burden of proof without having to go to trial. By going public on the matter, he showed that he had nothing to hide, and that McDermott had combined ill will and vindictiveness with knowing and reckless falsity. There was no basis in fact to the accusations. While Abbett had been defamed by a mean-spirited libel, he was able to vindicate himself.

Shortly afterward, the press revealed that the editor had nursed a bitter grudge against Abbett. McDermott, who was hired as the city printer, had published the minutes of city board meetings in his newspaper. On April 12, 1877, he had submitted a printing bill for $8,500. As corporation counsel, Abbett felt that the city had been overcharged. So he refused to approve payment until the bill had been properly adjusted. McDermott refused to make any adjustment. Frustrated and angry, he wrote his libelous article in a drunken stupor.[7]

THE MOLLY MAGUIRE TRIALS

While this was happening, the murder trials of the Molly Maguires were taking place in neighboring Pennsylvania. This episode involved a group of Irish Catholic coalminers who were locked in a bitter and protracted labor dispute with their Protestant mine operators. Working for starvation wages and in grave danger to life and limb in the dark coal mines, the

Irish miners endured conditions that were as depressing as they were debilitating. Living conditions were worse in coal towns than they were around the country generally. Nearly all miners lived in dreary company row housing with outdoor privies and no running water. Their gaunt little frame houses were perched on a hill just back from the railroad tracks. They had to purchase their food and supplies from the company store. The company held all the cards: it owned everything, it controlled everything, and it kept discipline through a combination of paternalism and domination. The miners earned $2.50 a day, barely enough to feed and clothe their families. The ignominy and abuse heaped on families by the reckless behavior of eviction agents infuriated the miners.

Many of the Irish miners belonged to a secret society known as the Molly Maguires, who took their name from a band of Irish rebels violently opposed to the English landlords and oppressors for centuries in Ireland. The Molly Maguires were associated with the American version of the Ancient Order of Hibernians, although that society was in no sense a sponsor. Wayne Broehl, author of an insightful study of the Molly Maguires, attributes British oppression and neglect in Ireland along with the great famine as the underlying historical roots of the dispute. Millions of people had starved to death in the famine. As Broehl explains:

> By the hundreds of thousands the survivors walked to the ports around the coast of the island, got passage in whatever vessel they could find, and emigrated. And they carried with them the accumulated grievances of hundreds of years of serfdom, ill treatment, and degradation. They brought with them deep, bitter, black resentments, resentments that could only be erased by time. And before they were completely wiped out, these resentments were inexorably destined to come to the surface again.[8]

These buried resentments surfaced in response to the oppressive working and living conditions of the anthracite coal fields where the Irish miners took out their anger by harassing mineowners, coal company bosses, and the police. No longer willing to accept their plight passively, they retaliated by setting fire to company buildings, destroying expensive mine equipment, and slowing down production. Their retribution against their oppressors included the murder of mine superintendents in cold blood, often preceded by "coffin notices" that were sent to their intended victims. These tactics terrorized coal operators and area residents generally. No Protestant living in the coal patches felt safe during this reign of terror. They were petrified by such violence.

The Irish miners faced an entrenched, wealthy, and ruthless opponent in Franklin B. Gowen, a coal mogul and president of the Philadelphia and Reading Railroad. He had both the means and the political power for dealing with terror. To combat the Mollies, Gowen hired Pinkerton detectives, who specialized in infiltrating unions. Mineowners like Gowen felt justified in resorting to extreme measures because they perceived the union movement as a challenge to their right to profit from their investments. Unionists were equally convinced that the battle for recognition would determine a way of life for themselves and their progeny. The Irish miners were prepared to use almost any means to secure their right to participate in basic decisions about their work conditions and lifestyle. Both sides resorted to illegal and often lethal measures in pursuit of a vision of rights claimed and wrongs avenged.

In 1868, John Siney, a union leader, had persuaded a number of local unions in Pennsylvania to create the Workingmen's Benevolent Association. He led a successful strike against the coal operators in 1869. Four years later, Siney brought anthracite and bituminous miners together in a convention at Youngstown, Ohio, where they formed the Miners National Association of the United States. In due course Siney was charged with violation of the Pennsylvania criminal conspiracy law. Although he was acquitted, the mine operators resorted to criminal conspiracy laws under which organizing a labor union was considered a criminal offense. They also demanded that miners sign yellow dog contracts as a condition of employment. Since the political power of the operators gave them control over state laws and courts, the individual miner had little chance to prevail in either civil or criminal law matters. Under these adverse circumstances, early labor unions failed one after the other.

At the behest of Gowen, Allan Pinkerton assigned his best detective, James McPharlan, to the Molly Maguire case. Since McPharlan himself was an Irish Catholic immigrant, he was the perfect undercover agent. Disguised as a miner and using the alias of "James McKenna," he successfully infiltrated the Mollies, rose to a leadership position, fomented terrorist acts, and informed on the leaders. Before long, McPharlan had collected sufficient evidence to convict the Molly perpetrators. But he needed some inside help to crack the case. James Kerrigan, an informer, turned state's evidence, and in exchange for immunity from prosecution, he betrayed his fellow countrymen. McPharlan had also become romantically involved with Mary Ann Higgins, who was Kerrigan's sister-in-law. She provided the detective with inside information that proved harmful to the Mollies. Such deceit and treachery compounded the atmosphere of distrust and betrayal.

The high profile murder trials were infused with religious prejudice. Highly publicized in the strident tabloids, they played to nativist bigotry and anti-Catholicism. Public opinion ran strongly against the Mollies. It was trial by ethnic identity and a popular prosecution. The state sought the death penalty. Not unexpectedly, the accused Irish miners were found guilty of first degree murder. They were sentenced to death by hanging. The convictions were quick and certain. Although the Catholic church had denounced the violent actions of the Mollies and

publicly excommunicated them, nevertheless, its clergy pleaded for commutation of their sentences to life imprisonment. Such pleas for clemency were to no avail. On June 21, 1877, or what soon became known as Black Thursday, ten men were hung: six were hung at the Schuylkill County jail in Pottsville, while four others swung from a hangman's rope at the Carbon County Jail in Mauch Chunk. Ultimately, twenty Irish miners went to the gallows for the Molly Maguire crimes. In the words of Anthony Lukas, "It was a deliberate demonstration of the state's power to exact the ultimate penalty, a day of awful retribution remembered for generations in the coal patches of Pennsylvania, in mining camps, and Irish American communities across the land."[9]

Meanwhile, the plight of the miners remained the same and Franklin Gowen continued to use Pinkertons for union surveillance and union busting. Organized labor deeply resented these tactics and viewed them as unfair labor practices. Between 1871 and 1874, Gowen had acquired 100,000 acres of land for the Reading Railroad. He then organized a market-control scheme that secured him a dominant position. This "coal combine" engaged in price-fixing and limiting competition by control of production. Under Gowen's scheme, each railroad could mine all the coal it desired, but a tonnage limit was placed on the amount that it could ship to market. The Reading obtained 25.85 percent of the market, the Delaware & Hudson 18.37 percent; the Jersey Central 16.15 percent; the Lehigh Valley 15.98 percent, and the Lackawanna 13.80 percent. Although the Pennsylvania Coal Company was not formally a member of the combine, it agreed to abide by a quota of 9.85 percent. The upshot of this agreement was to fix prices at $5 a ton wholesale.

Dissension among the companies participating in the coal combine over production quotas soon led to its demise, and Gowen and the other railroad coal magnates ruthlessly dumped coal on the New York and Philadelphia markets. Prices tumbled, and wages fell below the $2.50 standard. One of the biggest coal companies, the Lehigh & Wilkes-Barre, went bankrupt in early 1877 and the market continued to sag throughout most of 1877. Each new corporate difficulty adversely affected the miners' lot. There were strikes in the northern and central Pennsylvania coal regions that turned ugly. Federal and state troops were sent to Scranton to quell the violence. To quote Wayne Broehl again:

> Compounding the tensions was a mushrooming dispute with the Brotherhood of Locomotive Engineers. Ever since Gowen had first sensed McParlan's effectiveness as a spy, he had employed other detectives on the railroad to keep him posted on any union activities. Thus he knew ahead of time the plan of his engineers in the early spring of 1877 to strike the Reading (engineers had carried off successful strikes earlier in the year on the Jersey Central and the Boston & Maine). Moving quickly, he gave the engineers on March 27 a choice of staying at work with increased

benefits or being fired if they continued their membership in the union. The union struck, and Gowen countered by aggressively hiring new engineers and giving bonuses to the engineers and firemen who stayed. The union tried to frighten the public by insinuating that the Reading was running unsafe trains. But the quick, decisive moves by Gowen easily won the day and the strike failed miserably. Gowen sailed for Europe in early May to meet with the English stockholders, confident that union trouble had been put down again.[10]

The dreadful ordeal of the Irish miners dramatized the plight of workers in general and immigrants in particular. The immigrant workers were often given the most dangerous jobs, assigned the worst housing, and denied chances for advancement. Disliked as potential or actual strikebreakers by native-born whites, immigrants were also denounced as inciters of radicalism by coal operators who were quick to suspect anyone of harboring antioperator views. When some turned out to be genuine radicals with Marxist leanings, coal company men leaped to the conclusion that immigrants were commonly inclined to be bomb-throwing anarchists.

THE GREAT RAILROAD STRIKE OF 1877

These were volatile times. The mood of the workers had turned angry and sour. Labor's protest, anticapitalist in tone, was directed at the corporate monopolies and the greedy titans of American capitalism. Most workingmen were fed up with this kind of treatment, and they decided to fight back. They used their only effective weapon—the strike. A series of strikes took place in New Jersey in 1877 beginning with a general strike by the silk ribbon weavers in Paterson. The potters in Trenton also went on strike and engaged in riots. By the summer of 1877, there was massive labor unrest and intensive socialist agitation.

These conditions sparked the great railroad strike of 1877. It all began in Martinsburg, West Virginia, where the employees of the Baltimore and Ohio Railroad walked off the job because of a reduction in wages. Workers on the Pennsylvania Railroad went out in sympathy as the strike quickly spread to the Middle Atlantic states, leaving railway traffic paralyzed. The strike turned violent as the workers seized trains and destroyed railroad property. The bloody nationwide railroad strike had set off a wave of violent riots and a class war that brought the country close to revolution. For the first time in American history, a Red scare was directed against the urban proletariat. The violence caused fear among the general public and forced state politicians to take action.

Most state governors viewed the strike as a communist menace and came down hard on the strikers. They activated their National Guard

units to combat labor violence. In Baltimore, the edgy troops fired into an unruly mob and killed twelve people. The mob retaliated by chasing the soldiers into a train station and then setting it on fire. In Pittsburgh, state troops, while attempting to disperse an angry crowd, opened fire and killed more than two dozen men. Violence and brutality by the state only provoked more violence. Outraged by such deadly force, the strikers ripped up tracks, burned roundhouses, and destroyed rolling stock.[11] On July 24, firemen and brakemen struck the Jersey Central Railroad. The strike then spread to the Lackawanna, the Delaware and Hudson, and the Lehigh Valley railroads. Franklin Gowen was able to avert a strike of the Reading railroad through the use of company police in dispersing a mob in Mahanoy City.

Faced with crisis, New Jersey Governor Joseph Bedle was determined to put a stop to the rioting. The railroad magnates relied on state government to protect their coal domains and economic interests. Clearly identified as a member of the State House Ring or what was more accurately known as the "Board of Guardians," Bedle was viewed by labor as a tool of the railroads. Unionists did not see him as being impartial. Under intense pressure from the railroads, Bedle proclaimed martial law and sent the state militia to Jersey City and Phillipsburg, where they joined local police in putting down the labor uprising. Because these two cities were the main railroad entrances into New Jersey, they were considered the trouble spots. Bedle personally took charge of the troops in Jersey City; while Civil War general William Sewell commanded the units that were dispatched to Phillipsburg. At the time, Sewell was a Republican state senator and political boss of Camden County. Phillipsburg, located along the Delaware River just below the Delaware Water Gap, served as the gateway to the anthracite coal fields. This military response was justified by conditions of extreme duress. The rich and powerful viewed the military option as a way of "keeping the rabble at bay."

Violence erupted in Jersey City, where 1,500 railroad strikers disrupted freight trains and threatened to derail a passenger train passing through from New England. State militia protection and some adroit maneuvering by the local police got subsequent trains through safely. The rioters then attacked a train driven by a strikebreaking engineer, hurling bricks and paving stones at the moving locomotive. Governor Bedle had the brick throwers arrested and thrown in jail. But the strikers had made their point. Most of the men arrested were Irish Democrats. A county grand jury indicted them for inciting to riot. Abbett could not resist playing a starring role in this national drama. He successfully defended the brick throwers. None was convicted.[12] Once again, Abbett refused to accept a fee for the legal services that he rendered. He was adept at using litigation as a form of political action.

The great railroad strike of 1877 was a defining moment in the divide between labor and capital. It galvanized the labor movement into a cohesive and unified force. The Knights of Labor now began to press their demands in the political arena. Abbett had learned a great deal from the bloody strike: it was a mistake to use the state militia to quell labor riots. The brutality and lack of training on the part of the soldiers only inflamed the rioters and escalated the violence. It raised some serious questions in Abbett's mind about the appropriateness of deploying state troops for such purposes. Most of all, he learned that the workers' violence was directly related to their poverty, their poor health, and their despair over their inability to earn enough money to sustain their families.

THE STATE DEMOCRATIC CONVENTION OF 1877

In early September 1877, Abbett suffered another blow to his ill-fated gubernatorial plans. For the past few years, Abbett had been feuding with former Congressman Orestes Cleveland, who had been the Democratic mayor of Jersey City a number of times. He disliked Cleveland intensely and considered him a pompous and hollow politician. Their power relationship was strained to the breaking point. Cleveland was mercurial, vain, and compulsively duplicitous. The break between Abbett and Cleveland was no doubt brewing for sometime. Abbett had promised to help Cleveland become a member of the Democratic National Committee, but he reneged on his promise. Cleveland fumed that he had been betrayed, and seething with anger, he sought revenge. However, Abbett supported Congressman Miles Ross of New Brunswick, whom he had been assiduously courting for the past several months. A budding political alliance had brought them together. Ross was the powerful Middlesex County boss who could help deliver the governorship to Abbett.

Among the array of Democrats seeking the gubernatorial nomination, Abbett was the acknowledged frontrunner. In a crowded field of candidates, he appeared to have a commanding lead over his nearest rivals. Media observers felt that Abbett was more electable than the rest of the field. With his lobbying activity in full swing, Abbett received endorsements from U.S. Senator John McPherson and Congressmen Augustus A. Hardenbergh and Miles Ross. Other prominent party leaders supported him as well. This situation prompted the *New York Tribune* to remark:

In the huddle of candidates, the most conspicuous is Leon Abbett. He was the earliest in the field, is working with an industry which never rests, and a courage which never falters, is brim-full of confidence, and it looks now as if he could only be beaten by a combination of all the forces in the state."[13]

Only the powerful State House Ring could stop Abbett at this point. The party's old guard was preparing to bushwack him, and it was not going to let the senate president waltz off with the gubernatorial nomination without a fight. A secretly convened gathering of Randolph Democrats met in New York City to see if they could plot such a strategy. The circle of secrecy extended to Orestes Cleveland who was invited to attend the meeting. They first contacted Congressman Frederick H. Teese of Newark to see if they could persuade him to seek the nomination, but he turned them down. A popular figure, Teese had been a former speaker of the general assembly in 1861.

When Teese refused to seek the gubernatorial nomination, they continued plotting. Orestes Cleveland suggested George B. McClellan as a man who could defeat Abbett for the nomination. He reminded his colleagues that McClellan had successfully carried New Jersey for the Democrats in the 1864 presidential race. Although McClellan's Civil War record had ended in failure, he was still regarded as a military hero. He was a complex general who, though gifted with administrative and organizational skills, was unable and unwilling to fight with the splendid army he had created.[14] Upon returning to civilian life, McClellan took up residence in Orange, New Jersey. Civil War veterans revered him as the leader who had molded them into a proud army. The Randolph faction in New Jersey liked the idea very much. They recognized that it would take someone with McClellan's stature and name recognition to stop Abbett. With this scheme in mind, they hoped to stampede the convention behind him. One of McClellan's biographers claims that the former general had no part in this party intrigue.[15] But that simply is not true. McClellan had to be involved. For one thing, Henry Kelsey had been in touch with him to make sure that he was available and that he would accept the nomination if it was offered to him. The State House Ring was determined to keep its plan secret until the last moment.

A few days before the 1877 Democratic state convention opened, the Randolph faction distributed a handbill to the 1,000 delegates in attendance. It conveyed a terse but clear message, "Hudson County wants everything. Anything to beat Hudson County. Anything to beat Abbett."[16] When the delegates met on September 19, counterfeit tickets enabled hundreds of McClellan men to pack the galleries of the Taylor Opera House in Trenton. Chairing the convention was Benjamin Williamson of Elizabeth, who was the former chancellor of the New Jersey Court of Chancery. He was also a member of the board of directors of the Jersey Central Railroad. Choice of the chair was in the hands of the Democratic state committee. But in this instance, at least, the selection had been carefully arranged. Williamson was the obvious man to work cooperatively with the State House Ring. By keeping its plan secret, the Ring hoped to catch everyone by surprise.

The two frontrunners were the commoner Leon Abbett and the patrician John Stockton. The social class differences between the two men were striking. Stockton's grandfather, Richard Stockton, was the aristocratic squire of "Morven," who had signed the Declaration of Independence. Both men were praised by their supporters; neither was openly criticized. The first ballot revealed Abbett's strength. With 430 delegate votes necessary to obtain the nomination, he had compiled 304 votes for a substantial lead. He was far out in front of his two nearest rivals. Stockton placed second with 175 votes, while George McClellan trailed in third place with 171 votes. The nomination appeared within Abbett's reach on the second ballot, but such appearances were deceiving. The strategy of the McClellan forces was simple—bring the outside world inside the hall and manipulate the audience. Offer the convention a montage of images and a range of emotions that would transcend the power of speechmaking.

At the beginning of the second ballot, an unidentified delegate from Essex County started the bandwagon rolling by praising McClellan's military war record and extolling his leadership of the Army of the Potomac. Then, at a given signal, a life-size portrait of McClellan, hung concealed in the rafters above the center stage, was unfurled, and, at that precise moment, a band started playing the stirring battle hymn, "See the Conquering Hero Comes." Delegates rose to their feet and waved "the bloody shirt," creating a sense of structured pandemonium. The convention hall was thrown into a wild uproar as emotions reached a fever pitch. This staged production had a resounding impact, blunting Abbett's momentum at least temporarily. Charles Winfield of Hudson County, who had placed his name in nomination, made a valiant attempt to stem the tide by shouting that McClellan was not a genuine resident of New Jersey. But his words were drowned out by all the pandemonium and bedlam.

When the initial wave of emotion subsided, the same Essex delegate moved that McClellan be nominated by acclamation. On cue, Benjamin Williamson, the presiding officer, did his part by allowing those with counterfeit credentials to dominate the convention. They staged the kind of ruckus that conveyed the impression of irresistible momentum. The Essex County delegation led the break, and several other counties followed swiftly behind as the euphoric wave of emotion erupted again. In the midst of this pandemonium, McClellan's nomination was consummated. The strategy worked to perfection. The State House Ring had in effect high-jacked the convention.

The Abbett delegates were aghast as they watched the contest slip through their fingers; they had been caught completely off-guard. Abbett discovered too late that he had been outfoxed and outwitted. He was pale and visibly shaken.[17] Delegates from Hudson County were angry that their candidate had been rejected by such contrived shenanigans. In the

shark-infested waters of New Jersey politics, astonishment quickly gave way to consternation. Never again would Abbett allow a rival to steal the nomination from him.

But the dictates of political reality could not be ignored. When Abbett had recovered sufficiently, he handled his defeat in a manner that ultimately strengthened his party leadership. Instead of giving McClellan the cold shoulder and sitting out the election—as some Democrats advised him to do—he actively campaigned for him. His willingness to put the interest of his party ahead of his own amounted to smart politics. In so doing, he protected his political future. Placing the good of his party above all else, Abbett swallowed his pride and urged his supports to work for McClellan.[18] The disappointed Abbett men followed their leader's example and most of them campaigned for the Civil War general.

A similar process occurred at the Republican convention, but without the palace intrigue and surreptitious maneuvering. The Republicans appeared harmonious and ready to make a comeback. For the gubernatorial race the Republicans again tapped William A. Newell, a physician from Allentown, who combined politics with his career in medicine. He had previously served as governor from 1857 to 1860. Despite his prior gubernatorial experience, Newell ran an inept campaign and managed to alienate Republican county bosses like William Sewell in Camden County and George Halsey in Essex County. Both counties were Republican strongholds that Newell needed to win by a large margin, if he ever expected to beat McClellan.

Newell had also incurred the wrath of the Irish political community. Back in 1857, as a sitting governor, he had presided over the court of pardons. That year the court heard the case of James P. Donnelly, a medical student, who had been convicted of murdering Albert S. Moses over a gambling debt at the Sea View House in Navesink. A Monmouth County court had sentenced Donnelly to death. After losing on appeal, he sought commutation to life imprisonment. The court of pardons turned down his commutation request with Newell voting with the majority of judges. He saw no grounds for executive clemency. As the *Jersey City Argus* remarked, "Newell's action toward poor Donnelly had been prompted by his intense hatred of foreigners."[19] The young man was therefore sent to the gallows. The Irish deeply resented Newell's lack of compassion and mercy. Whether or not Donnelly was responsible for the murder, he did not receive a fair trial, in part because of popular hysteria, a biased judge, and a flawed legal system. The Irish believed that Donnelly had been convicted on questionable evidence by a Protestant jury and before a Protestant judge. They viewed his execution as a travesty of justice. Small wonder then that in the election of 1877, the Irish voted overwhelmingly for McClellan.

Already known popularly as "Little Mac," the charismatic McClellan was held in high regard by Civil War veterans who had proudly served as his infantrymen. He was a moderate pro-business Democrat and a fiscal conservative. McClellan knew very little about the public policy battles that had been waged in New Jersey over the past several years. Disagreements and disappointments were papered over for the sake of party unity. Everything was subordinated to the primary goal of a unified party. For his part, McClellan was beholden to the Randolph Democrats and the railroad power. Relying chiefly on political operatives to run his campaign, he chose Francis Lathrop as his campaign manager who decided that the best way for the Democrats to win was for McClellan to be seen but not heard. He advised him to remain above the fray. They kept him under tight wraps. Their strategy was based entirely upon McClellan's popularity as a war hero. While the former general made whistle-stop appearances across the state and waved to the crowds, he did little speechmaking.[20]

Election day in 1877 brought the Democrats a smashing victory. McClellan won 51.6 percent of the vote to the Republicans' 44.9 percent, the Greenbackers' 2.6 percent, and the Prohibitionists' 0.6 percent. The Republicans took their worst beating since they had become an established party. Ticket splitting was evident. Many Civil War veterans, who normally voted Republican, crossed party lines and voted for their former commander. The Democratic vote increased from 1874 to 1877, going from 97,283 to 97,837. The Abbett men remained loyal, though some campaigned primarily for the party and its platform rather than for McClellan.

THE McCLELLAN GOVERNORSHIP

McClellan assumed office with no idea of what he wanted to do and without a clear public policy agenda. He had problems governing. His political leadership proved as inept as his military leadership. When a governor is passive, as McClellan seems to have been, the public agenda is light, and the pace of public affairs is slow. Few if any significant ideas were transformed into policy. McClellan, known for his cautious nature, played it safe and called for the reduction of taxes, the training of factory workers by the private sector, and better military discipline for the National Guard.[21] He also created a Bureau of Labor Statistics to gather and publish data on the wages and living standards of industrial workers. But this was not a new idea on his part. A few years earlier, Massachusetts had established such a bureau.

Possessed of a Napoleonic personality and exquisite manners, McClellan was more a ceremonial figurehead than either a party or policy

leader. He seemed enamored with the trappings of office. In one of his messages to the legislature, he noted with dismay that the salaries of public school teachers had declined. Yet he offered no solution to the problem. Meanwhile, he allowed the railroads to pay a paltry sum in taxes, a source of revenue that he might have tapped to increase the pay of teachers. McClellan for the most part remained a captive of the railroad lobby and the business community. Such political behavior was hardly surprising. Before the Civil War, he had resigned his military commission in 1857 to become vice president of the Illinois Central Railroad. Three years later, he became president of the Ohio and Mississippi Railroad. So his capture by the railroad interests could have been easily predicted. The antimonopoly forces had lost out decisively as the McClellan administration stumbled inconclusively to its end.

CORPORATION COUNSEL FOR JERSEY CITY

During the intervening years from 1878 to 1881, Leon Abbett played a secondary leadership role in the Democratic party. His future appeared somewhat cloudy and uncertain, stemming from the factionalism that fragmented the party. Even so, Abbett managed to stay in the public eye through his legal activities as corporation counsel for Jersey City. In February 1878, for example, he argued the case of *Van Riper v. Parsons* before the New Jersey supreme court. This was a high profile case with the constitutionality of the home rule statute that he had previously crafted for Jersey City at stake.

   Abbett was on to something. This litigation was a part of the political maneuvering for control of Hudson County. The basic conflict was approaching its climax. The trial was cast as a showdown between Democrats and Republicans. Both political parties recognized its importance. Opposing counsel, William A. Lewis and Cortlandt Parker, were two of the best and brightest lawyers in the state. A Rutgers graduate and valedictorian in the class of 1836, Parker was a former Whig and a founder of the Republican party in New Jersey. He had formerly served as prosecutor of Essex County and was president of the American Bar Association. As ardent a Democrat as Parker was a Republican, Abbett proved his match. Presiding at the trial were justices Bennet Van Syckel, Alfred Reed, and the implacable Jonathan Dixon. Dixon was the person who had drafted the "ripper" legislation that deprived Jersey City of home rule, but he did not disqualify or recuse himself from hearing the case. Perhaps only the Irish, whom Dixon had disempowered, could truly appreciate the irony.

   As the trial approached, the excitement grew intense. The media provided extensive coverage of the courtroom drama. Both sides came

well prepared. At the trial, Lewis and Parker argued that the disputed home rule statute pertained only to Jersey City, and therefore it was unconstitutional because it violated the provisions in the state constitution that prohibited special legislation for individual cities. In his reply, Abbett brushed aside the constitutional argument and concentrated on legislative intent. He argued that the intent of the law was to terminate all legislative commissions, and thus it was a general law because it applied to every municipality in the state, not just Jersey City. The potency of his argument did not go unheard.

The ultimate irony of the whole affair was that all three judges, including Jonathan Dixon, agreed with Abbett's legal reasoning.[22] They upheld the constitutionality of the statue in question. The ruling intensified the home rule debate. In winning this case, Abbett not only achieved a legal victory, but he also obtained an immediately desired political result. Besides, he had bested the likes of Cortlandt Parker, which won him further acclaim in legal circles.

Once again, Abbett had taken a complex issue and reduced it to simplistic terms. He had the uncanny ability to make complex things understandable. Litigation and political experience alike had taught him that public tolerance for "ripper legislation" was limited. Public opinion strongly favored home rule. In a state where local control was greatly valued, such a result was welcomed. Thus, Abbett accomplished three objectives at once: (1) by getting out in front on this key issue, he was seen as leading the fight to free localities from unwarranted political interference by the state legislature; (2) by portraying himself as a champion of the home rule movement, he showed that his ideas were not radical or outside the political mainstream; and (3) by successfully defending his own statute, he continued to win favor with his Irish constituents in Hudson County.

Surely this outcome of the court case delighted the Irish. They now regained the local governing power that had been stripped from them in 1870. The Republican legislature could no longer control Jersey City through legislative commission. Abbett's legal reputation soared, while Courtlandt Parker's plummeted. To add to his laurels, Abbett was appointed by Governor McClellan to a special blue ribbon task force whose assignment was to draft a general municipal charter law.

THE DEATH OF MARY ABBETT

Misfortune followed on the heels of Abbett's courtroom success. The moment that he had long dreaded finally occurred. On June 16, 1879, Mary Abbett succumbed to the spreading cancer that she had fought courageously for the past two years. Only forty years of age at the time

of her death, she left behind three young children and a grief-stricken husband. The children would have to grow up without her. The couple had been deeply devoted to each other during the seventeen years of their marriage. Throughout her illness, Mary Abbett maintained her composure and showed remarkable courage. According to the *Jersey City Herald*, she met her untimely death with "heroic resignation."[23] Funeral services were held at Saint Matthew's Episcopal church in Jersey City. She was buried in the family plot at the Greenwood Cemetery in Brooklyn.

The personal tragedy crushed Abbett whose life changed forever. The light in his life had been snuffed out. No one ever completely filled that void for him again. He was consumed in grief beyond measure. Widowed at the age of forty-three, Abbett never remarried. After his wife's burial, he had to make certain adjustments in his lifestyle. His sister-in-law Martha Dodd and her husband came to live with them for a short period. She helped with the children, while the three Irish domestic servants did the housework.

The Abbett children adored their father. William Abbett, the eldest son, was sixteen at the time of his mother's death. He became his father's frequent companion. Leon Abbett, Jr., the youngest son and namesake, was twelve. The two boys were educated at the Hasbrouck Institute in Jersey City. After graduating from this private school, they both attended Columbia Law School and entered their father's law firm. Mamie Abbett was the only daughter. Born in Jersey City on February 13, 1870, she was only nine years old when her mother died. She was the apple of her father's eye, and now spent much more time with him. Later on, during his second term as governor, when Mamie was twenty years old, she acted as his official hostess.[24] He was extremely proud of her, and she partially filled the void in her father's life.

A black depression settled over Abbett. Mary had been the sunshine of his life for almost two decades, someone to whom he could always turn to for comfort and support. Without her, his whole world seemed to fall apart, but his despondency was barely noticeable to the outside world. For the next few years, he maintained a low profile and substantially curtailed his political activities. It was his way of processing his grief.

The fires of ambition that burned inside him had been dampened but not extinguished. For the time being, however, there was hardly anything that stimulated his interest. It was the most difficult period of his life. To those who were close to Abbett, he appeared strangely indifferent and remote. Many of his friends thought that he had retired from active politics and returned to his private law practice. Instead of clarifying the leadership problem that existed within the Democratic party, his indifference in some respects had made it worse. For the first time in more than a decade, Abbett was not in the public limelight, but he had no intention

of staying away permanently. Preservation of his power was vital to the continued achievement of his goals. As corporation counsel for Jersey City, he continued to press the railroads on the tax issue, but the struggle was almost too much for one man. Abbett's inner turmoil would have to run its course before he could regain his equilibrium.

THE GUBERNATORIAL RACE OF 1880

Most Democrats expected that Abbett would be a candidate for governor in 1880. Over and over, he would think about running, put it out of his mind, and then come back to worry about it again. Some Democrats chided him for hurting the party by being indecisive. Urged by several party leaders to seek the nomination, he flatly turned them down. Still grieving over his wife's death, he was despondent and emotionally depleted. William Sackett put it all in proper perspective: "If Mrs. Abbett's ambition had spurred him to the struggle he had made for the governorship in 1877, her death since that memorable convention had robbed him of his inspiration."[25] In short, Abbett lacked both the desire and the fire to seek the governorship. To quash rumors and eliminate any doubt about his intentions, he wrote a public letter in which he removed himself from consideration. His letter of withdrawal cleared the way for other potential aspirants.

No sooner had Abbett's letter appeared in print than Orestes Cleveland decided to throw his hat into the ring. With Abbett having removed himself from consideration, Cleveland attempted to obtain the nomination. The former mayor of Jersey City, whose ambition made him a perennial candidate for public office, thought that he could capture the prize by rising with the antimonopoly tide. More plausibly, he recognized the leadership vacuum left by Abbett's withdrawal and had a large enough ego to think that he could fill it. Whatever Cleveland's motives, he lined up as many delegates as he could before the party convention.

The news of Cleveland's intentions caused quite a stir. When Abbett learned of the news, he was furious. The last thing in the world he wanted was to see was his old political rival become governor. He believed that Cleveland's candidacy would split the party and result in disaster for the Democrats. The Irish community disliked Cleveland, because of his previous Know-Nothing activism. Quite apart from that, Abbett had his own score to settle with him. Here was a ready-made chance for retaliation.

Abbett bitterly resented Cleveland for having ruined his bid to become governor in 1877. Punitive paybacks were part of the political game in the Gilded Age. In a retaliatory mood, Abbett sought revenge. Quickly grasping the situation, he came roaring back from his self-imposed exile. Born in upstate New York in 1829, Cleveland had worked in the jewelry business in Manhattan before moving to Jersey City in 1845. After

FIG. 13
Orestes Cleveland, US
Congressman. He was also
mayor of Jersey City.

serving as a city alderman and then as mayor in the early 1860s, Cleveland was elected to Congress in 1868, but he served only one term and failed in his bid for reelection in 1870. Meanwhile, he became president of the Dixon Crucible Company in 1869. This firm manufactured black lead, stove polish, and the brand-name Ticonderoga pencils. Cleveland had married the boss's daughter. His father-in law, Jonathan Dixon (not to be confused with the state supreme court judge), was the wealthiest man in Jersey City. Cleveland was a very shrewd businessman in his own right and a cunning politician whose paunchy physique and balding head gave him a shifty appearance that matched his personality.

Clever, cynical, and unscrupulous, Cleveland was hardly a man of upright character. He entertained lavishly and cultivated those people who could help advance his career. Later on, it was revealed that he had embezzled funds from the Dixon Company to finance his political activities.[26] As part of his nefarious scheme, he had made his brother, Job Cleveland, the company treasurer. With a compliant board of directors and his brother covering for him, the theft was concealed from the stockholders for more than two decades. By the time Cleveland's embezzlement came to light, the pencil company had fallen into bankruptcy. Meanwhile, Cleveland stayed in the political arena trying with moderate success to keep alive a personal faction in the Democratic party.

Abbett was determined to settle the score with Cleveland. So intense was his antipathy toward him that he made a deal with members of the Democratic state committee. Putting aside their past differences, they allowed Abbett to chair the party's convention in 1880 provided he would not seek the nomination himself. He persuaded Henry Kelsey who in turn persuaded a skeptical Theodore Randolph. The State House Ring was displeased with Cleveland for having ruined Joseph Bedle's chances to win the Democratic gubernatorial nomination in 1871. As part of the deal, Abbett had to promise that he would not accept the nomination under any circumstances, not even if it were offered to him from the convention floor. Cleveland was naturally distressed by Abbett's selection, but he had already lined up his political supporters and felt confident he could win the nomination. With a majority of delegates already committed to him, he was convinced that he had the nomination sewn up. As Sackett points out: "Only those who had seen Abbett dominate and overpower and bulldoze the Democratic conventions in Hudson from the chairman's desk were able to realize what an awful obstruction the State Committee had thrown in the way of Cleveland's success."[27]

As it happened, Abbett ran the convention with an iron hand. He refused to seat anyone who lacked proper credentials. The bitter memory of what had happened to him in 1877, when outsiders had invaded the Taylor Opera House and packed the convention for McClellan, was still fresh in his mind. This time a floor fight developed over the question of

whether or not the unit rule should apply. Since Cleveland's strategy depended mainly on each county delegation casting its vote as a unit, Abbett ruled against it. Delivering a one-two punch, he then refused to entertain an appeal of his ruling. The Cleveland delegates were furious with this adverse ruling and they objected vehemently, but Abbett knew exactly what he was doing and blandly ignored their shouts.

They were further angered when Abbett insisted on taking a second ballot even though it was apparent that Cleveland had more than enough votes to win on the first ballot. He did so on the flimsy excuse that one of the secretaries had found an error in the tally. During the recount of ballots that ensued, Abbett's supporters urged him to resign as chair and accept the nomination himself. Although ostensibly relishing the wild demonstration conducted in his behalf, he resisted their exhortations and kept his pledge. By the end of the fourth ballot, Abbett had singlehandedly steered the rowdy convention behind George C. Ludlow, who was an attorney for the Pennsylvania Railroad and a state senator from Middlesex County. A Rutgers alumnus, Ludlow was the hand-picked candidate of the State House Ring.

Meanwhile, the Republicans selected Frederick A. Potts as their candidate. He was a state senator from Hunterdon County and a wealthy businessman, who had made his money in the coal business. Potts was an influential stockholder in the Jersey Central Railroad. Other railroads were expected to assist him through the efforts of Garret A. Hobart of Passaic, who was named the new chairman of the Republican party. At the time, the railroads functioned as quasipolitical parties fielding a team of political agents whose duty it was to finance and assist in election campaigns. But they exacted an ideological and political price for their support.

The competition of railroads acting as political organizations resulted in an extremely close vote. When all the ballots had been counted, Ludlow beat Potts by the scant margin of 651 votes out of nearly a quarter million cast, or 49.5 percent of the total vote. The Democrats polled 121,666 votes as compared with 121,015 votes for the Republicans. Disappointed in losing, Potts blamed his defeat on the treachery of William Sewell, the Republican boss in Camden County. After the election, Potts learned that Sewell had instructed the employees of the Pennsylvania Railroad to vote for Ludlow.[28]

THE LUDLOW ADMINISTRATION

Like McClellan, George Ludlow came to office beholden to the State House Ring. But there was a crucial difference. While Ludlow was no enemy of the railroads, neither was he their tool. He vetoed two important railroad bills in 1882. One would have permitted the directors of the

Jersey Central Railroad to increase its capital stock without the approval of its shareholders. The other bill (S-167) would have allowed the Pennsylvania Railroad to close certain streets in Jersey City, thereby denying public access to a large portion of its waterfront property. Ludlow's veto of the first measure was quickly overridden by both houses.

The senate overrode Ludlow's veto of S-167 without much difficulty. Only the revelation of a bribery scandal and a legislative investigation that ensued prevented an override in the general assembly. Hudson Assemblyman William McAdoo mounted "tenacious opposition" to the attempted override in the closing hours of the session.[29] The legislature adjourned before a final vote could be taken. The railroads were furious at Ludlow for his vetoes. They made sure that his political career ended abruptly, or as soon as he left office.

Meanwhile, in 1881, Governor Ludlow appointed Leon Abbett to a special constitutional commission set up to study the controversial railroad tax question. The problem of railroad taxation was complex. Most railroads paid taxes directly to the state and were largely exempt from local taxation. They claimed that their early corporate charters amounted to legislative contracts that exempted them from such taxes. By removing valuable property from the local tax rolls, they increased the tax rate and thereby added to the burden of other property-owners. Unless something could be done to alleviate this situation, the problem would only grow worse. But making a legal argument to this effect faced an enormous obstacle.

Going back to 1819, the U.S. Supreme Court had ruled in the landmark *Dartmouth College* case that a state grant of a corporate charter was a contract protected by the federal constitution against state abrogation or modification. Nor was that all. More recently, in 1877, the Court had ruled in the case of *New Jersey v. Yard* that the charter of the Morris and Essex Railroad was a contract that shielded it from taxation. These two court decisions gave corporate charters the sanctity of contracts. The legal armor of the railroads seemed impenetrable. Stymied by these decisions, state officials could not do much about checking federal judicial power. Corporations were gradually brought under the protection of the Fourteenth Amendment and laissez-faire theories of substantive due process began to dominate judicial thinking. In essence, the railroads could count on the courts to protect their interests in almost all circumstances.

Confronted with this conundrum that lay at the heart of the policy paradox, Abbett favored amending the state constitution as the best way to resolve the long-standing public dispute. On May 17, 1881, he testified before a special constitutional commission and presented three countermeasures: (1) taxing corporations in the same manner as real estate and personal property; (2) prohibiting the legislature from passing

any law that impaired the taxing power of the state and its political sub-divisions; and (3) rescinding the railroad contracts by process of public condemnation and making restitution for their value.[30] The key conceptual notion was the so-called equal tax provision. That goal was the central thrust of the ensuing law, but it would take another three years to achieve. The equal tax movement that would flower in 1884 was struggling to be born.

Abbett's proposed constitutional amendment received serious consideration by the special commission, but it fell just one vote shy of adoption. The railroad lobby brought all of its power to bear in defeating it. Consequently, the amendment was never submitted for popular referendum as originally had been intended. Although his efforts ended in failure, Abbett had presented another challenge and served notice that he was serious about getting his policy goals enacted into law.

THE ANTI-MONOPOLY LEAGUE OF HUDSON COUNTY

Governor Ludlow tried to solve the problem of railroad taxation, but he could not break through the stalemate of forces surrounding him. His failure to do so did not deter the equal tax advocates. The issue would simply not go away. A coalition of forces led to the creation of the Anti-Monopoly League of Hudson County, a pressure group agitating for equal taxation. Organized in 1880 by the charismatic Thomas V. Cator of Jersey City, other prime movers in this grass-roots organization included Edwin O. Chapman, William Kuhn, and Edward T. McLaughlin. The cause that bonded these men was their desire to see railroad property valued fairly and taxed equally with other local property.

The time was ripe for such a movement. Railroads in New Jersey were notoriously undervalued and underassessed. At a time when public distrust of railroads ran high and state and local deficits, unheard of in the 1860s, were regular occurrences, Cator's courtship of the radical anti-monopolists was shrewdly timed. Running as a splinter party candidate on an antimonopoly ticket, he got himself elected to the general assembly in 1881.

Agitation for the equal tax concept gathered steam in the 1882 legislature. When Thomas Cator introduced a railroad tax bill, the general assembly passed it, but the bill was buried in committee in the state senate where the railroad interests were firmly entrenched. The bill never surfaced and was killed in committee. Nevertheless, Cator persisted in his efforts and introduced a similar bill in 1883, but it again met the same fate. Cator's actions, coupled with his economic views, had reinforced his public image as an antimonopolist. Much to everyone's surprise, he deserted the splinter party and soon became a Republican. Although the

main thrust of this grass-roots movement was aimed at taxing the railroads, the ultimate objective was to curb the power of corporate America and other concentrations of wealth that threatened individual liberty and democracy.

Once Abbett had regained his focus, the fires of ambition started burning again, and he now resumed the objectives desired by his constituents. Considering the nature of his constituency, he had a large personal stake in the equal tax issue that he perceived as vital to their political interests as well as his own. The same motivation that had moved Abbett to initiate a constitutional amendment now inspired him to do more. Because the railroads in Hudson County were located at the nodal points of fixed water and rail transportation networks, they controlled some of the most valuable land in the greater New York metropolitan region. In reality, Abbett had very little leeway on certain questions and railroad taxation was by far the most important. Political forces operating in Jersey City placed particularly strong pressure on local public officials to do something about the problem. Such pressures offer a clue to understanding both the motives of the antimonopolists and the Democratic party's response to them.

Feeling this intense pressure, members of the Jersey City board of finance asked Abbett, as corporation counsel, to prepare a report on the subject in 1882. Written in response to their request, his report, published in pamphlet form, itemized in great detail the vast amount of railroad property exempt from local taxation.[31] Searching for a solution, Abbett recommended the kind of equitable legislation that was finally adopted when he became governor. Abbett's report was accepted by the local board of finance without objection, but this acceptance did not solve any of the basic problems. At the time, however, Abbett had made a careful analysis of the problem and was on record as to what needed to be done. The report came off the presses in June 1882, just in time to be distributed as a Democratic campaign document. So twice, just before critical elections, Abbett took steps in shaping the public agenda. Moreover, he presented his ideas in a format that captured the media's attention.

THE PROSPECT OF MUNICIPAL BANKRUPTCY

The Ludlow administration had inherited a large public deficit that contributed to the negative growth and high taxes that were keeping the New Jersey economy depressed. Throughout the 1870s, inflation and unemployment had risen together. The federal census revealed that the state's population had grown from 906,096 to 1,131,116 during the 1870s. This increase in population growth caused spending pressures on the public sector to intensify while the supply of public revenues remained weak and

uneven in distribution. Governments at all levels were struggling with deficits because they had incurred too much debt during the previous decade. State and local debt had more than doubled since 1870. By 1882, the fiscal deficit facing New Jersey's state government had reached $49.5 million, a figure most people found staggering. This increase in its indebtedness exceeded all other states except New York.

Telltale signs were evident as early as 1873, when inflation, resulting inescapably from the way in which the Civil War had been financed, turned a recession into a full-blown depression. States in one region after another faced fiscal deficits and political crises. This was especially true in New Jersey, where the recession at least applied a brake on expansive tendencies. Because of the dire fiscal situation, no major capital improvements had been undertaken in New Jersey during the 1870s. Nor had any bond issues been floated to finance large-scale public works projects. There was no Brooklyn Bridge, no Hoosac Tunnel, and no Tweed Court House to show for all the millions that had been added to the state debt during the past decade.

The expenditures of local governments were reduced sharply. In 1879, the city of Elizabeth carried a debt that was one-half of its assessed valuation. Municipal debt and taxation in the postwar decade substantially outstripped other indices of growth. The threat of municipal bankruptcy was real. Urban populations continued to carry the burden of cuts in public spending. However suddenly New Jersey found itself in such dire fiscal straits, the forces pressing in this direction had been in place throughout the postwar period. These constraints all combined to heighten the uncertainty of the revenue base and to put public sector finance under considerable stress. This stress was intensified during the early 1880s. Optimization of scarce resources became the defensive attitude of local public officials and state politicians seeking to stay in office.

The time of genuine reckoning was at hand. By 1883, the cities of Elizabeth and Rahway had both declared bankruptcy. Other cities faced a similar predicament. The need to develop new revenue streams to relieve the burden of property taxes was readily apparent, especially if the cities were to cope in the long term. Jersey City's tax rate of 2.94 percent, while lower than Camden's at 2.96 percent and New Brunswick's at 3.63 percent, was still higher than the tax rate in most other localities.

In the rural countryside, the number of farm debtors had increased dramatically. Many marginal farmers faced financial ruin. Creditors wanted payment in hard money, while debtors wanted to pay off their obligations in depreciated paper. Questions of public control over the growing business corporations were very much alive. The Granger demands for state control of grain elevator and railroad charges had focused the discontent of farm and labor groups throughout the country. Cries of protest and outrage against the abuses of unrestrained capitalism

were heard in New Jersey. Amid this clamor, the equal tax issue was beginning to gain momentum and to shape the public agenda in the state. In 1883, hostility toward the railroads was the principal fuel that fired antimonopoly Democrats.

THE IMPACT OF CHARLES CORBIN

The equal tax proponents had recruited Charles L. Corbin to help them frame the debate. An eminent attorney who specialized in corporate tax law, Corbin was an expert on railroad taxation. His expertise was unrivaled. On June 11, 1883, Corbin delivered an illuminating lecture to the Kent Club of Jersey City, whose membership included prominent lawyers and law students who were studying for the bar. The Kent Club was well known for inviting distinguished speakers to discuss important matters of public policy.

Beginning his lecture with a history of how New Jersey found itself in its current predicament, Corbin reviewed the pertinent case law involved and explained what could be done to counteract the charter contracts that exempted the railroads from paying their fair share of taxes. Drawing attention to the scope of the problem, he pointed out that more than one-fourth of the property in New Jersey was exempt from local taxation, and that most of this property was owned by the railroads. Even more significant was the fact that of the $12 million collected annually in total state and local revenue, the railroads were paying less than $1 million in taxes. In other words, the railroad industry was being subsidized to the tune of $3 million a year in the form of nontaxable real estate.[32]

While Corbin took into account the legal protection that the U.S. Supreme Court had afforded the railroads in the case of *New Jersey v Yard*, he reminded his audience that the problem grew from deeper roots than mere displeasure with specific court decisions. In his view, the problem could be attributed to the prevailing political culture and the dominance of the railroads. Corbin went on to say:

Experienced politicians in this state have so often seen the strength of a railroad company put forth in elections with decisive effect, that they have come to look upon it as invincible. No doubt it is great. We have a concentration of some of the greatest railroads in the country in one of the smallest states. The exercise of political power by railroad companies for forty years has given the abuse the strength of an established system. Practiced agents willing to do political work for pay are to be found in every township and ward. The sentiment of the community upon the subject has become demoralized. The sense of dishonor which should attach to the acceptance, by a candidate, of political favors, from a corporation which has legislative favors to ask in turn, is hardly known among our

New Jersey political leaders. A candidate so far from concealing his intent to favor a railroad company, makes his relations with it a claim for the nomination, and is nominated because he can command its political support. Members of the Legislature permit themselves to be classed as "the men" of a company formed to carry freight and passengers.[33]

Corbin's sobering remarks were refreshingly candid. Given this deeply ingrained folk wisdom, it is easy to understand why politicians were so reluctant to tax the railroads for fear of reprisal. The lesson that drove home the point was the fate of Governor Ludlow, whose political career ended as soon as he left office. There seemed to be no remedy in sight without new leadership. The fact that the right experts appeared at the right time, in Abbett's view, sharply shifted the terms of the debate and the emerging dialogue.

At least 5,000 copies of Corbin's lecture were distributed to fraternal, business, and civic groups for purposes of influencing public opinion. If anyone could challenge the railroads and placate the antimonopoly forces, Abbett could. No other Democratic leader had developed such a coherent and feasible strategy for taxing the railroads. He was responsible for placing the question on the public agenda and for providing the leadership it needed when momentum lagged. The political climate in New Jersey was conducive for him to make equal taxation a campaign issue in the fall of 1883. Because of his influence and ambitions, Abbett would have a crucial role in determining the fate of railroad legislation. He would now try to answer the public call for fundamental change. It would no longer be politics as usual.

ENDNOTES

1 Morton Keller, *Affairs of State: Public Life in Late Nineteenth Century America* (Cambridge, Harvard University Press, 1977), 264.

2 See *Jersey City Herald*, June 21, 1879.

3 *Jersey City Herald*, May 12, 1877.

4 The letters-to-the-editor are found in the *Jersey City Herald*, May 19, 1877, while the roll call votes are reprinted in the *Jersey City Argus*, May 15, 1877. See also *Evening Journal*, May 14, 1877; *New York Daily Tribune*, May 16, 1877; and *New York Times*, May 13 and May 17, 1877.

5 *Jersey City Herald*, May 19, 1877.

6 *Jersey City Argus*, May 14, 1877.

7 *Jersey City Argus*, March 5, 1882.

8 For a complete and balanced account of this episode see Wayne G. Broehl, *The Molly Maguires* (Cambridge, Harvard University Press, 1964), 70.

9 J. Anthony Lukas, *Big Trouble* (New York, Simon & Schuster, 1997), 187.

10 Broehl, *The Molly Maguires*, 346.

11 For a detailed account of this strike see Robert V. Bruce, *1877: Year of Violence* (Chicago, Ivan R. Dee Publisher, 1989), 161.

12 A.E. Costello, *History of the Police Department of Jersey City* (Jersey City, 1891), 184-186. See also *Jersey City Herald*, September 29, 1883.

13 *New York Tribune*, September 8, 1877.

14 Thomas J. Rowland, *George B. McClellan and Civil War Hostory* (Kent, Ohio, Kent State University Press, 1998). See also Stephen W. Sears, *George B. McClellan: The Young Napolean* (New York, Ticknor & Fields, 1988).

15 William S. Myers, *A Study in Personality: General George Brinton McClellan* (New York, Appleton-Century Company, 1934), 497.

16 *Jersey City Argus*, September 20, 1877.

17 Sackett, *Modern Battles of Trenton*, 1:152-53.

18 *Monmouth County Democrat*, October 25, 1877.

19 Quoted in Paul A. Stellhorn and Michael J. Birkner, eds., *The Governors of New Jersey 1664–1974* (Trenton, New Jersey Historical Commission, 1982), 127-28.

20 See John R. Reynolds, *Testing Democracy* (Chapel Hill, University of North Carolina Press, 1988), 22.

21 Myers, *A Study in Personality*, 500. In evaluating McClellan's performance as governor, Myers says that it was "a good piece of work, 'solid,' but undistinguished."

22 *Van Riper v. Parsons* 40 NJL 123 (1878).

23 *Jersey City Herald*, June 21, 1879.

24 Letter to the author from Leon Abbett Post, September 28, 1970.

25 Sackett, *Modern Battles of Trenton*, 1:166.

26 See letter from Joseph P. Tempelton, president of the Joseph Dixon Crucible Company, to Owen Grundy, secretary of the Jersey City Historical Society, dated December 27, 1968. Tempelton says in his letter, "Records in our archives prove beyond any shadow of doubt that Orestes Cleveland had misappropriated company funds to such an extent that the company was forced into a bankruptcy proceeding." He goes on to say, "From old correspondence, it appears that Orestes Cleveland's downfall stems primarily from his political activities. Not contented with having been Jersey City's Mayor for several terms, followed by representing the state of New Jersey at Washington, Cleveland also aspired to become a cabinet member as well. This, of course, required that he move about in the highest social and political circles at the national level, necessitating lavish entertaining and spending. Orestes seemingly was unwilling to foot this expense personally and leaned on the company cash box for the needed funds, until diligent stockholders became suspicious that all was not well with their company." This letter remains on file at the Jersey City Historical Society.

27 Sackett, *Modern Battles of Trenton*, 1:169.

28 Reynolds, *Testing Democracy*, 46.

29 *New Jersey Legislative Manual for 1884* (Trenton, 1884), 58.

30 *New Jersey Legislative Documents*, (1881), 15.

31 Leon Abbett, *Report of Jersey City Property Exempt from Taxation* (1882), 1-46.

32 Charles L. Corbin, *Taxation of Railroads in New Jersey* (Jersey City, 1883), 8. In his letter of transmittal to the Kent Club, Corbin wrote: "The subject of railroad taxation in New Jersey involves considerations of constitutional law as well as of state policy, and affords the members of our bar an opportunity to render the state a signal service by using their knowledge to explain and their influence to reform the present system."

33 *Ibid.*, 26-27.

6

The 1883 Gubernatorial Campaign

More fundamental forces were at work in state politics. The upsurge of power in the labor movement, agriculture, and the newly formed antimonopoly coalition continued to make headway. More alliances—permanent and temporary, easy and uneasy—came into play in the 1880s. During the summer of 1883 most New Jersey politicians expected Leon Abbett would attempt to head the state Democratic ticket. Many rank-and-file Democrats encouraged him to seek the party's gubernatorial nomination again. Party activists believed that his strength of character, knowledge of the state, intellect, and passion made him the candidate most likely to capture the prize. After a hiatus of six years, Abbett had time enough to recover from the personal loss of his wife. Having been relegated to the sidelines, he was now rearing to go. His political adrenaline began flowing again. He yearned to return to the combat of the political arena and felt the timing was right for him to run for governor. Whatever his motivation, his return to an active role was liberating for him. More than anything else, he wanted to appear as a leader who could unite the party, not divide it. The first order of business for him was to energize his home base.

William McAvoy, the surrogate of Hudson County who ran its Irish-dominated political machine, was the first party leader to endorse Abbett for governor. Endorsements from other party notables soon followed. Congressman William McAdoo, who was highly popular in the antimonopoly movement, gave him his blessing. So did Hudson's state Senator Elijah T. Paxton and Assemblymen Joseph T. Kelly and Dennis McLaughlin. In fact, the entire Hudson County Democratic organization lined up solidly behind him.

However, there was the incipient danger of a fragmented party. The Randolph Democrats were still bitterly opposed to Abbett; they disapproved of him because of his alliances with Irish Catholics, labor

leaders, the racetrack interests, the liquor dealers, and the less-than-reputable elements of society. Most of all, they feared that he would pursue the railroads on the tax issue. These silk-stockinged aristocrats viewed Abbett as a dangerous demagogue, who had aroused the laboring classes against them. Ideology and ethnic group antagonisms generated by different status and class positions fueled their hostility toward him. The two factions were once again on a collision course. The Randolph faction hoped to stop Abbett in much the same fashion as it did in 1877 by party intrigue and surreptitious maneuvering. Only this time, there wasn't a candidate as attractive as military hero George McClellan, who had previously defeated him for the nomination.

Henry Stafford Little, a slightly built man with a stern face and a shaggy beard, devised the Randolph Democrats convention strategy. Tall, dour, ponderous in manner, Little was a Princeton graduate, a country squire, and a wealthy railroad coal magnate. It is worth examining his political career in greater detail. Active in Democratic party politics since the early 1850s, he had cast one of the state's electoral votes for James Buchanan in the presidential election of 1856. Avoiding military service during the Civil War, Little was elected state senator from Monmouth County in 1863. Reelected to the office for three consecutive terms, he served until 1871. At that time, Governor Theodore Randolph appointed him clerk of the Court of Chancery, a very lucrative position that paid a decent salary augmented by fees and commissions.

After graduating from Princeton in 1844, Henry Little studied law with Asa Whitehead in Newark and was admitted to the bar in 1848. Dividing his time between his country law practice and his father's business, he was outwardly stiff and seemingly humorless. Seeking to accomplish something on his own, Little financed the construction of a plank road or "turnpike" that provided farmers in Monmouth County with direct access to urban markets to sell their produce. After this successful venture, he developed the New York and Long Branch Railroad, which connected South Amboy with Point Pleasant, a distance of 38 miles.[1] This was a crucial rail link that hugged the New Jersey coastline.

On the death of Francis Lathrop on March 3, 1882, Little succeeded him as the court-appointed receiver for the bankrupt Jersey Central Railroad. Under a new reorganization plan, Little served as its president for the next five years. A dry Presbyterian, he not only refrained from alcohol and tobacco, but he also remained a bachelor throughout his life. Sackett described him in one crisp sentence: "Too active to be stout, he was tall, wiry and nervous, and a man upon whose face one could read the signs of intense activity."[2] Descended from Scots-Irish ancestry, the dour Presbyterian bachelor despised Irish Catholics and their ascendancy in the Democratic party. As a conservative Bourbon

Democrat, he was a close friend and political ally of Grover Cleveland, the governor of New York and former reform mayor of Buffalo, who at the time entertained presidential ambitions.

Working diligently behind the scenes, "Staff" Little, as everyone knew him, made a special trip to Freehold to persuade state supreme court judge Joel Parker to oppose Abbett for the Democratic nomination. A well-liked politician in his own right, Parker had been a popular two-term governor, serving initially from 1863 to 1866 and again from 1872 to 1875. He and Little were political allies who had much in common: both were Presbyterians, Princeton alumni, lawyers, and Monmouth County Democrats. Despite their alliance and long-time friendship, Parker turned Little down, preferring to remain on the state supreme court. Having already served two terms as chief executive, Parker was simply not interested in running for a third term.

Although disappointed by Parker's refusal, Little had two fallback candidates in mind. He separately contacted former Governor Theodore Randolph and Attorney General John Stockton and urged them to throw their hats in the ring, but they both declined as well. The two men wrote public statements removing themselves from consideration. This caused the State House Ring to look elsewhere, though they were hard-pressed to come up with a credible candidate. The only prospect they could find was Andrew A. Albright, a Newark businessman who had tried unsuccessfully to obtain the nomination for governor in 1880. Albright, a wealthy manufacturer, had never held elective office. He had run for Congress in 1878, but he lost that year to Republican John L. Blake of Orange.

THE STATE DEMOCRATIC CONVENTION OF 1883

Desperate to stop Abbett, Little resorted to a vicious personal attack against him. The Randolph faction could agree on only the most general and obvious plan of battle, but it followed a well-worn pattern. On September 13, 1883, when the Democratic state convention opened, they distributed a leaflet that urged delegates to vote against Abbett for several reasons. This leaflet listed seven charges: (1) he had never opposed legislation that was detrimental to corporate interests; (2) he had allowed the Pennsylvania Railroad to acquire valuable waterfront property in Jersey City for less than fair market value; (3) he had drafted the "five county act" that prohibited the mortgagor from negotiating with the mortgagee for a lower rate of interest; (4) he had opposed the "six percent interest" law that required the mortgagor rather than the mortgagee to pay the taxes as well as the interest on the mortgage; (5) he had voted in favor of the Catholic Protectory bill; (6) he had used his political influence to have Judge David J. Pancoast removed from the state supreme court and

replaced with Judge Alfred Reed; and (7) he had been indicted by a Mercer County grand jury for "legislative malfeasance."[3]

Given the element of surprise, there was no way Abbett could head off the scathing attack. These nameless allegations were purposely designed to wreck his plans. Some of these charges were fabricated and without merit, while others were accurate but grossly distorted. It is difficult to separate fact from fiction. It was true that Abbett had drafted the "five county act" and had opposed the "six percent interest" law, but every state legislator who came from the five counties of Bergen, Essex, Hudson, Passaic, and Union, whether they were Democrats or Republicans, had voted identically on these two bills. Drawing attention to Abbett's vote in favor of the Catholic Protectory bill obviously was intended to arouse anti-Catholic prejudice. With regard to the allegation that Abbett had influenced the judicial appointments in question, it should be noted that he did not act alone. Several Democrats had signed a petition demanding Pancoast's removal. They all supported Alfred Reed as his replacement. But it was Governor Joseph Bedle, a Randolph Democrat, who had appointed Reed. So the buck stopped with Bedle.

The allegation that Abbett had been indicted by a Mercer County grand jury for "legislative malfeasance" was patently false. No such charge had ever been lodged against him. Nor had he ever acted according to the alleged charge. Commenting on this malicious falsehood, John D. Chandlee, the editor of the *New Brunswick Times*, declared:

It is a wicked and malicious lie. Mr. Abbett never was indicted in Mercer County or any other county of the state. In 1866 there were three men indicted for bribery in the legislature. One of these men declared that if he were indicted others should be. They tried to shelter themselves behind the reputation of other and better men.[4]

The two other allegations—that Abbett had allowed the railroads to acquire waterfront property in Jersey City for less than fair market value and that he had never opposed legislation detrimental to the corporate interests—were likewise false.

The leaflet was unsigned and no one claimed responsibility for it. But the leaflet had been planted by someone with apparent political motives. Political insiders speculated that Henry Little had written the anonymous leaflet, but they could not prove it. Little's antipathy toward Abbett was well known. The two men loathed each other; countervailing egos and a clash of personalities were at work here. Abbett was the complete opposite of all that Little represented. He had none of Little's advantages of inherited family wealth, Princeton education, or privileged social status. As a political leader, Little lacked Abbett's ability to work with partisans of different views for the common cause. And in recent years, each man had been able to frustrate the other: Little through his influence

with the State House Ring and the railroad power; Abbett through his control of the Democratic machine in Hudson County and his popularity with labor and the antimonopolists.

Much to Little's chagrin and disappointment, his spoiling strategy did not work. The sour-grapes effort on his part failed to wreck Abbett's determined bid for his party's nomination. Abbett appeared unstoppable. He was master of the situation and left nothing to chance. Remembering the high-jacking of the convention that had occurred in 1877, Abbett insisted that his protege, Allan L. McDermott, chair the convention. Only thirty years of age, McDermott was intelligent, discrete, energetic, and politically astute. He proved a wise choice for this important assignment. Having served as Abbett's former law clerk, he could be trusted to represent Abbett's best interests.

Allan McDermott was the son of newspaper editor Hugh McDermott, who had perpetrated the libel against Abbett in 1877. Born in South Boston in 1853, Allan McDermott had worked as a typesetter and a reporter for his father's newspaper. In 1871, he began his legal apprenticeship by clerking in Abbett's law office. But he took a leave of absence the following year and traveled extensively throughout the western part of the country. On returning to New Jersey in 1874, McDermott entered New York University Law School and clerked in the law office of Alfred B. Dayton. The impassioned young lawyer was admitted to the bar in 1877, setting in motion his remarkable career. McDermott ran for the general assembly in 1878, but he was defeated by Republican Frank C. Fry. The next year he ran successfully for the same office and was elected to three consecutive terms. In 1879, Abbett hired him as assistant corporation counsel for Jersey City. It marked the beginning of a long, intimate relationship that would endure until the end of Abbett's life.

Like other special assistants, McDermott became a master enforcer, negotiator, and interpreter for Abbett's not-always-clear direction. An innocent face with a full mustache concealed an extraordinary capacity for insight, anticipation, and guile. When combined with boundless energy, articulate command of the language, and complete loyalty, McDermott was a priceless addition. From the moment the two men met, it was clear that they were destined to be not only allies in a common cause, but special friends. Each quickly recognized in the other that combination of pragmatic idealism and cunning guile that would bind them for years to come. Now this exchange of mutual respect paid off nicely.

McDermott ran a tight convention and did not allow it to get out of hand. On the first ballot, Abbett compiled 218 votes compared with 139 for Andrew Albright of Essex County, 116 for Jonathan S. Whittaker of Cape May County, 47 for Charles E. Hendrickson of Burlington County, 44 for Lewis Cochran of Sussex County, and 43 for Augustus W. Cutler of Morris County. Inherited memories of the past gave certain

candidates added weight and at the same time tended to exclude others. Albright was the one candidate who held his own against Abbett. The *New York World* reported that Albright maintained a suite of rooms at a Trenton hotel, where delegates were plied with an ample supply of liquor, food, cigars, and other more lubricious inducements.[5] At any rate, neither Albright nor Whittaker was able to generate any additional support; in fact, both lost delegate votes on the second ballot.

Meanwhile, Abbett picked up those votes that had previously gone to Cochran, Cutler, and Hendrickson. He had accumulated 349 votes out of a possible 608. The fight was over. Abbett was nominated. All except the diehard Albright delegates were convinced that they had selected the strongest candidate. Few could have known that they had chosen the best man for the difficult task that lay ahead. Before the convention adjourned, the Abbett Democrats selected U.S. Senator John McPherson as chairman of the state committee. Abbett was now securely in control of the party organization, while the State House Ring was in retreat. After the convention, Abbett chose Allan McDermott as his campaign manager.

THE REPUBLICANS NOMINATE DIXON

The Republicans toyed with the idea of nominating John Hill for governor. A former one-term congressman, Hill was a rough-hewn merchant who lived in the small rural town of Boonton that was nestled in the foothills of Morris County. Farmers in this part of the state wanted a plain, down-to-earth businessman like Hill to run for governor. Before going to Congress, Hill had served several terms in the state general assembly, where he became speaker in 1866. During the Civil War, he was active in raising troops for the Union army and providing aid to New Jersey soldiers who were imprisoned in the South. In 1874, Hill had been elected to the state senate, where he served with Leon Abbett.

However, Hill proved unacceptable to William W. Phelps, a fellow Republican. A silk-stockinged gentleman reformer, Phelps was a commanding personality and a man of great wealth and social standing. A graduate of Yale and Columbia Law School, he gave up practicing law at the age of twenty-nine to become an investment banker, railroad financier, and country gentleman. He served as a director of the Morris and Essex Railroad and lived on a large estate near Englewood surrounded by thousands of acres of deer park and mountain slopes. In 1872, Phelps served what would be his only term in Congress. He voted against the civil rights bill, claiming that it was "unconstitutional and a bad policy for the colored race." In his bid for reelection to Congress in 1874, Phelps was defeated by Democrat Augustus W. Cutler by only seven votes. President James Garfield then appointed him as ambassador to Austria. Because of

factional infighting in the Republican party, Phelps disliked Hill and blocked his bid to become governor. He wanted a Republican of a milder persuasion, preferably someone who was more sophisticated and polished than Hill.

In the end, the Republicans picked Jonathan Dixon of Jersey City, an icon of the local establishment and a judge who sat on the state supreme court. He was British by birth, accent, and demeanor. Born in Liverpool in 1839, Dixon came to this country at the age of nine, but his parents were unable to care for him. He was raised in New Brunswick under the foster care of Cornelius Hardenburg, whose family was active in nativist Whig politics. A distinguished lawyer who had lost his eyesight, Hardenburg tutored young Dixon and instilled in him a deep and abiding respect for the law. To earn his keep, the boy worked as Hardenburg's amanuensis.

All accounts indicate that Dixon, in growing up in New Brunswick, had experienced a difficult and unpleasant boyhood. The picture emerges of a shy, precocious, and introverted lad, who had been picked on and bullied by the older boys in the local neighborhood. As a result, Dixon went through his adolescence never quite feeling that he fit in with the other boys. Stephen Fiske, who had grown up with Dixon, recalled their boyhood years:

> Boys are of all human beings the most cruel, and Johnny Dixon was regarded by the New Brunswick boys as a pariah and a butt for malicious jokes. The young rascals knew that a blind man is usually led about by a dog, and so they insisted upon inviting Johnny to have old tin kettles tied to the tail of his round-about, and whistled to him, and maltreated him when he ventured into the streets alone upon Hardenburg's errands.[6]

After graduating summa cum laude from Rutgers in 1859, Dixon studied law for the next three years in the law firm of Dutton and Adrian in New Brunswick. The prodigy was admitted to the bar in 1862. Shortly afterward, he moved to Jersey City, where he clerked for Edward B. Wakeman, a well-known and established lawyer. When Dixon received his license as counselor in 1865, he went into practice for himself. From 1870 until 1875, he served as corporation counsel for Jersey City, and in that capacity, he had drafted the so-called "thieves charter," under which the Republicans usurped power from the Irish. He formed a partnership with Gilbert Collins, who was then a rising political star in the Republican party and a future mayor of Jersey City. To offset the fact that Dixon had avoided military service during the Civil War, he became president of the Union League Club. A Congregationalist and a teetotaler, he supported temperance reform and Protestant efforts at proselytizing Catholic immigrants.

On April 8, 1875, Governor Joseph Bedle, a Randolph Democrat, had appointed Dixon to the state supreme court. Only thirty-five years

of age at the time, Dixon was the youngest person ever to have been so appointed. His judicial appointment to the high bench was unusual in other respects. State judges came mostly from privileged family backgrounds, even though they had earned their positions through a meritorious record of lawyering. They were more likely to be offspring of well-to-do professional and business people, not someone raised in foster care.

As a judge, Dixon reflected the reactionary conservatism that held sway in New Jersey for decades before the century's turn. He brought to the court a powerful intellect, disciplined work habits, conservative values, and the Protestant ethic. His formal written opinions were crafted with careful logic and erudition. Harking back to colonial days, when property rights superceded individual rights, Dixon subscribed to a similar judicial philosophy. Because of his conservative leanings, he was highly regarded as a trial judge. His judicial circuit included Bergen and Passaic counties. Republican Assemblyman Edward Q. Keasbey of Newark, who had graduated from Harvard Law School in 1871, described him as follows:

He [Dixon] was one of the most active members of the courts in which he sat. His natural endowments were such as made him eminently able to cope with the duties of a judge— cool, patient, observant, quick of perception, profound in his appreciation of the distinctions between right and wrong, capable of the most exhaustive analysis, dispassionate in judgment, careful to do what was right according to his own convictions irrespective of public clamor, able to express himself with an arrowy directness in a few words and always dignified and courteous.[7]

Scholarly and taciturn, Dixon bore few outward signs of the ambition for power that burned inside him. He struck most people as being cold, reserved, distant and aloof, as well as vain and self-righteous. While seemingly accessible, he was fastidious and impressed with his own intellectual ability. Men attracted to the judiciary were not typically endowed with the extroverted personality of the successful politician. Oddly enough, Dixon had never run for elective office before. Although he had twice served in public positions, both were appointive. But he shared at least one thing in common with Abbett, namely, his availability.

Despite his idiosyncrasies, Dixon was a formidable opponent and tried to convey the impression of being an independent jurist, who was above the political fray. At the 1883 Republican state convention, the delegates made two demands of him. One was that he resign from the judiciary; the second was that he actively campaign for governor. He managed to ignore both demands. Instead, Dixon adopted the strategy that had worked for Democrat Joseph Bedle in the gubernatorial election of 1874. Refusing to resign from the state supreme court, Bedle had

won the election without actively campaigning. Dixon felt confident that he could do likewise. From his perspective, it was not his job to win votes.

In his letter accepting the Republican nomination, Dixon informed the party faithful that he currently held "a public office second to none in the state for opportunities of usefulness and consequent esteem."[8] This was the usual double-talk of a politician declaring his candidacy, but Dixon meant it. He was unwilling to give up a judgeship that paid him $7,000, or $2,000 more than the governor currently earned. Quite apart from the salary issue, Dixon genuinely believed that the prestige of the judiciary would help to get him elected. He understood the magic that the "cult of the robe" bestowed on judges. Held in great esteem by the general public, judges were widely revered in the Gilded Age as high priests who dispensed divinely ordained justice. However idealistic and exaggerated this portrait may have been, it was probably true that respect for the tradition of an independent judiciary played a part. Yet for all its strength, this myth of the judicial function was never universally accepted.

AN UNPRECEDENTED GUBERNATORIAL RACE

At the outset of the campaign, Abbett realized the he faced an uphill climb. The media considered Dixon the favorite. Over the years, Abbett had alienated more than enough people to make him vulnerable to Republican attacks. He had aroused strong opposition in both parties. Anticipating the worse, James Yard, the editor of the *Monmouth Democrat*, warned:

> Abbett is a man of pronounced views with regard to public matters, and has always been able and willing to defend them before the people. In common parlance, he is what is known politically as a good fighter. He has consequently antagonized the Republican party during the last decade as scarcely no other man in the state has done. The opposition to him will be vigorous and unrelenting. No effort will be spared, no means will be left untried, to defeat him.[9]

The editor's warning became prophesy all too quickly. It turned out to be a hotly contested and bitterly fought campaign in which the outcome remained very much in doubt until the very end.

For his part, Abbett felt that the Randolph Democrats were never genuinely on board. Without their help and cooperation, he would have a difficult time. Beyond the political compulsion of a close election, Abbett had every reason to be concerned about defectors, but he had three skills that would prove very beneficial: how to give a stirring speech,

how to repair intrapatry rifts, and how to campaign aggressively. In an exclusive interview with the *Jersey City Journal* on September 21, Abbett detailed the rationale for his campaign and outlined the strategy that he would pursue:

The Republican party has made a strong nomination. I am free to say that if Judge Dixon gets to work he will make this a lively and interesting campaign, just such a one as I like. He is an excellent nominee. I think that John Hill would have polled a very strong vote. There is a feeling in those districts against lawyers. Of course, it is not justifiable, but it exists. They want what they call a plain, simple man, one of themselves, as they express it, and John Hill would have filled the bill. That feeling would have worked me harm, but as my opponent is also a lawyer, that element of strength has vanished from the Republican canvass. I am not at all inclined, however, to underestimate Judge Dixon's strength.

I have already done some work, and am ready to go ahead with the canvass. I have laid out my work and know exactly what I am going to do, and I am going to carry out my plan to the end. I shall be in the field from now until election day is over. I shall visit every county and every town, and shall speak and organize constantly. I have gone into this canvass to win, and I shall win, if hard and unceasing labor can bring that result about. I shall be elected by a 5,000 [vote] majority. I will be the next Governor of New Jersey. I am going ahead regardless of [Henry] Little and [Henry] Kelsey. Of course I would like the support of every man, but if I cannot have it I must do without it, but I shall not forget who are my friends.[10]

While Abbett exuded self-confidence to the press, he fully realized that as the antiestablishment candidate, he had an uphill battle. So he decided to take the offensive right from the start. Aggressive as ever, he mounted a vigorous campaign that relied on extensive travel, speechmaking, and party organization. He was determined to barnstorm the entire state. His electioneering efforts were unprecedented in terms of personal energy and the number of public appearances. The usual partisan Democratic newspaper endorsements appeared.

On September 14, the day after he had been nominated, Abbett showed up at the Monmouth County agricultural fair in Freehold. This was not exactly promising political ground to plow. Fears of a party split and possible defections prompted him to launch his campaign in Henry Little's political stronghold. There was a twofold purpose to this appearance. On the one hand, he realized the value of placating an antagonistic faction in the party. On the other hand, he did not flinch from doing battle in the heart of enemy territory, even if the opposition came from within his own party.[11] Abbett's strategy was shaped largely by the strengths and weaknesses of the opposition. He sensed at the very beginning of the campaign that the Achilles heel of the opposition was its subservience to the railroad power.

Early on in the campaign, Abbett decided to confront the railroads on the tax issue. With equal taxation as his battle cry, he promised to make the rail carriers pay their fair share of taxes. He carried this message of economic populism to urban and rural voters alike.[12] It proved an effective strategy, one that was far more appealing than a state property tax or a broad-based tax. Indeed, it was the centerpiece of his campaign, especially in Hudson County that was shaping up as the crucial battleground of the election. Both Dixon and Abbett lived in Jersey City.

Urban workers liked what Abbett had to say, while farmers in the southern and northwestern parts of the state found him credible. He knew how to stir the imagination of blue-collar farm and working families. Burdened with heavy debts and property taxes, marginal farmers were concerned about their economic survival. Their concerns were well founded and a recent spate of farm foreclosures justified their apprehension. Abbett's populist message appealed to them.

On September 19, Abbett attended the state agricultural fair that was held in Waverly. People from all parts of the state attended this highly popular event. In a display of party unity, Abbett was driven to the fair in the carriage of Andrew Albright, who opposed him for the nomination.[13] In a state as small as New Jersey, with a population of 1.2 million inhabitants, politics was intensely personal. Conspicuous by his presence at the fairgrounds, Abbett enjoyed greeting people, and they in turn enjoyed talking with him. Mingling freely among rural folks, he worked the crowd with the skill and ease of a man who had been plying his political trade for almost twenty years. As one observer described the scene, "Fond mothers carried their children to be kissed by him, and for years afterwards, it was the proud boast of many a farmer that he had shaken a real live Governor by the hand."[14]

On September 25, an inspired Abbett spoke to a Democratic rally at the Academy of Music in Newark, where a huge crowd had turned out to hear him. Newark was the state's largest city. Here he set the tone for his campaign and talked about his goals. His stump speech was filled with the standard Jacksonian themes of antimonopoly and antiaristocracy. At the beginning of his remarks, he made an important campaign pledge. "I propose to visit every village in this state," he proclaimed, "and if I am to stump the state without an opponent, I propose to let the people know some Democratic doctrine."[15] This may have seemed a flight of rhetoric, but he meant every word of it.

Abbett was in superb form. Waving a handful of newspaper clippings above his head, he recited the litany of Republican charges made against him and refuted them one by one. "My enemies say that I am in favor of monopoly. If my record is as they say it is, they should at least be able to prove it. They make no direct charge and never can. I defy them to show me other than working for the people."[16] At the climax of the

rally, Abbett was endorsed by fellow Democrats Andrew Albright, former Governor George McClellan, and former Congressman Augustus W. Cutler. His campaign had gotten off to a good start.

On September 26, the Hudson Democrat attended the combined agricultural fair of Union and Middlesex counties held in Plainfield. Here he repeated the same performance that he gave at Waverly. Before the campaign ended, he would attend all of the county agricultural fairs. Working as hard as ever, the Democratic party leader canvassed New Jersey county by county, and town by town. Traveling mostly by train and horse-drawn carriage, he went from the top of Sussex County in the upper northeast to the tip of Cape May County in the lower south, crisscrossing the state several times and making good on his campaign pledge. All along the way he made whistle-stops, gave stump speeches, and attended countless receptions. The pattern was pretty much the same wherever he went. He met old friends and made new acquaintances, who pledged their support to him. Among the latter were many new immigrant voters.

Both parties used their well-oiled machinery to rally voters to their side. Although some Republicans remained less than enthusiastic about Dixon, they went to work for him with fervor and dedication. In advocating high tariffs to protect manufacturing, the Republicans had an issue that went over well with the business community. Abbett sought to downplay this issue by indicating that tariff policy was a matter for federal, not state, legislation. He made a point of acknowledging that a governor could do very little about the tariff question.

Hudson County Republicans achieved a coup by persuading Assemblyman Thomas Cator to switch his allegiance from the antimonopolist party and to run for state senator on their ticket. A talented and articulate New York lawyer, Cator was expected to offset Abbett's appeal on the equal tax issue in Hudson County. As a newly minted Republican, Cator was a strong drawing card. The Democrats countered this move by getting former Governor Joseph Bedle to endorse Abbett publicly. Bedle, a factional rival, praised Abbett for his "ability, independence, manliness, integrity and personal worth."[17] This was an important endorsement, both real and symbolic, because it provided visual reassurance to key voting groups. Specifics mattered less than symbols, and this was indeed a symbolic gesture. By contrast, Dixon, serving as a state judge, was unable to mobilize this kind of support. He could not invoke party loyalty or patronage in behalf of his candidacy the way Abbett could. Dixon had aligned himself with the voices of the status quo.

While Dixon dallied, Abbett acted. In one of the master strokes of the campaign, Abbett arranged to have an empty chair placed next to him on the platform wherever he was invited to speak. Pointing to the vacant chair, he taunted Dixon by saying, "I would like to ask the old champion of the Jersey City charter a few plain questions, but he sits silently on the

bench, and with the halo of his judicial office thrown around him, asks you to vote for him."[18] This ploy became standard campaign theatrics. It was a real crowd-pleaser and did much to debunk the mythical cult of the judicial robe that Dixon sought to exploit. It later gave birth to an axiom in politics that if a candidate didn't define himself for voters, his opponent would, and not in flattering terms.

As the pace of the campaign intensified, Abbett made a concerted effort to gain the support of labor. While he may have sidestepped the protective tariff issue, he could not duck the sensitive issue of contract convict labor. For decades, industrialists had been contracting with state prison officials in Trenton to have inmates manufacture certain products that were then sold on the open market. Labor leaders vigorously objected to this arrangement. Both the New Jersey Labor Congress and the Knights of Labor raised two important questions. Should the state put convicted criminals in competition with decent, law-abiding workers? Should the state allow capitalists to profit from exploiting convicts, at the expense of free labor? Under pressure from these two labor groups, Abbett decided to push for this reform. Public opinion, however, was deeply divided on the issue. While Abbett spoke out on convict labor, he was careful not to call for its complete elimination. Unwilling to go that far, he wanted to keep prisoners engaged in productive work, but not for the benefit of capitalists. To clarify his position, he went on to say,

> I am opposed to contracts which give the profits of the labor of criminals to contractors. All the profit that can be derived from their labor should be paid directly into the treasury. Such a policy would not only be just to the state, but it would also protect the manufacturer and the mechanic from unfair competition. Give criminals employment, but not at the expense of honest labor. I do not want in New Jersey busy prisons and empty workshops.[19]0

His position on this issue went over well with labor leaders and trade unionists.

DIXON PERCEIVED AS ANTILABOR

Meanwhile, Dixon had incurred the wrath of labor for what it perceived as his judicial bias. He had presided over the highly publicized libel trial of newspaper editor Joseph P. McDonnell in 1880. An exiled Irish Fenian and socialist, McDonnell became a prominent American trade unionist and labor reformer. He was the founding editor of the *Paterson Labor Standard* that was the voice of oppressed labor in New Jersey. Despite much difficulty, his newspaper survived its early troubled years and remained a weekly labor paper until McDonnell's death in 1908.

Historian Herbert Guttman writes, "Many persons new to the urban-industrial world did not settle easily into a factory-centered civilization. McDonnell was one of them. More significant, however, is the fact that McDonnell's survival, much less his success, depended on such tension and conflict."[20]

McDonnell had come to America in 1872. He started his Marxist newspaper in New York City and then moved it to Paterson in 1878. Emblazoned across its masthead were the words of Karl Marx: "The Emancipation of the Working Classes Must be Achieved by the Working Classes Themselves." Militant Irish nationalism and socialism had shaped McDonnell's political thinking. He had been raised in a middle-class family in Dublin and educated at its university. He studied for the Catholic priesthood, but he left the seminary to join the Fenians and spent ten months in Dublin's Mount Joy Prison. He left Ireland in 1868 to live in London for five years. There he lectured and organized public protests that called for independence for Ireland and amnesty for Irish political prisoners. He also joined the International Working Men's Association, got to know Karl Marx, became a socialist, and served as Irish secretary of the International's General Council.

Soon after his arrival in Paterson, McDonnell supported the women and young girls in their nine-month strike against the nation's largest cotton mosquito net manufacturer. To the outrage of capitalists, he castigated management and referred to strikebreakers as "scabs." For using such language, the company brought a libel suit against the editor. A jury found McDonnell guilty, and Judge Barkalow of Paterson fined him $500. Within two hours, his sympathizers raised the money to pay his fine and then held a celebration for him.[21]

In late 1879, McDonnell published a letter from Michael Menton, an itinerant common laborer, who exposed the dreadful working conditions at the Mountain View Brickyards in Singac, where the workers endured unfair, brutal, and inhumane treatment. The brick manufacturer brought suit against McDonnell and Menton for libel. A jury found the two men guilty, and Judge Dixon sentenced them to three months in the Passaic county jail. This time the judge did not impose a fine knowing full well that their sympathizers would pay it.

Two prominent lawyers, Socrates Tuttle and William Prall, defended the embattled newspaper editor during his second trial. Tuttle was Paterson's most respected Republican leader, having served as school commissioner, city clerk, mayor, and state assemblyman. He told the jury that silencing McDonnell would deny working people the right to complain. While sitting in his jail cell, McDonnell received a letter from Tuttle that read, "I congratulate you upon your martyrdom in the cause of truth. Your imprisonment does not, cannot degrade you. You stand higher in the estimation of the people today than before your trial. You

have committed no crime. You have wronged no man. You have only helped in the exposure of a great wrong to others."[22] On his release from jail, McDonnell was again lionized by the workers of Paterson.

With these painful experiences still etched in his mind, McDonnell accused Dixon of being a biased judge, who was antilabor and antiunion. He made Dixon the object of his disdain. Scrappy, tireless, and single-minded, the socialist editor was a fiery crusader and a symbol of unionism. He not only endorsed Abbett for governor, but he also actively campaigned for him and galvanized the labor vote. Writing blistering editorials in the *Paterson Labor Standard*, McDonnell drew a sharp distinction between the two gubernatorial candidates:

> In the contest between Abbett and Dixon it is not possible for the honorable or intelligent workingman to support the latter. It is to the interest of every workingman, of every Republican, of every Democrat, of every Greenbacker that Jonathan Dixon be defeated. Workingmen cannot afford to stultify themselves by voting for a man who has no sympathy with them and who is opposed to their direct interests. Every vote given for Jonathan Dixon will be a vote to stifle the liberty of the press and to drown the cries of suffering labor. To defeat this man, Dixon, the workingmen of the state must not fritter away their strength.
>
> We have looked into the antecedents of Abbett and we were agreeably surprised to find that during the years he sat in the Legislature he voted for every labor measure and never voted against one of them. His present utterances are in accord with his past record. How different with Jonathan Dixon, the father of the Bumsted charter, and a Judge who used the power given him by the people to muzzle the labor press and stifle the cries of plundered labor. It is not hard to tell how the workingmen of all parties, who believe in the rights of labor, will vote in the coming contest.[23]

These editorial endorsements from labor gave Abbett's campaign a much needed boost. On the evening of October 19, the Hudson Democrat spoke at a large Democratic rally in front of City Hall in Perth Amboy. Mayor John T. Garrettson and several other party dignitaries were on hand to welcome Abbett. Taking a thoroughly Jacksonian stance, the Democratic candidate promised to put a stop to selectively screening people who wished to see the governor. Requests for such appointments had been routinely denied by Joseph L. Naar, who was Governor Ludlow's private secretary. Abbett declared that common folks would no longer be subjected to such discriminatory treatment. "Every citizen of this state," he said, "whether he be high or low, whether he be rich or poor, can always see me personally without the intervention of any man."[24] The audience loved it and clamored for more. His remarks about access to the governor's office must be seen in the context of antiaristocracy.

To demonstrate his party leadership, Abbett vowed that he would streamline the party organization to put a Democrat in the White House in 1884. In closing, he invited everyone in the audience to climb aboard his bandwagon before it was too late. "If I am elected," he shouted, "I will give to the state a pure administration; and I will do more—I will see that the Democratic party shall come into the fight one year from now as an organized party, and not as a disorganized mob. There is ample opportunity for those who want to get into the fold before it is too late. The Bible says that a man may come in at the eleventh hour and receive his penny, but the man who is outside on the day after election will stay there, for when the door is closed it will close forever."[25] The audience was on its feet, shouting and applauding.

As soon as Abbett had finished speaking, he was whisked away in a horse-drawn carriage and taken to the train station at Perth Amboy. There he and his entourage boarded a waiting Lehigh Valley train that would take them to Phillipsburg at full speed. As night came, this special train, which had an Eastlake car attached to accommodate the campaign party, departed at 8:30 p.m. and sped across New Jersey (a distance of fifty-four miles) in the record-breaking time of seventy-three minutes. The details of the trip were chronicled by William C. Reick, a newspaper reporter for the *Newark Evening News*, who accompanied them. According to Reick:

It was evident from the start that the engineer was doing his best. The impenetrable darkness without rendered it impossible to see a foot from the car windows, but the steel rails outside upon the opposite track and the cross-ties, under the light of the car lamps, looked like one continuous board road. As the engine rounded curves the occupants of the car had to clutch the seats for support.[26]

Once the train arrived in Phillipsburg at 9:43 p.m., Abbett was driven by carriage to Parochial Hall, where he gave another rousing speech and attended a reception afterward. That same evening, he returned to Perth Amboy on the midnight train. By using improved rail transportation, he was able to speak in both cities. This was an astounding feat in the Gilded Age. It produced favorable newspaper headlines that dramatized his cause. Refreshed after a night's sleep, Abbett was off early the next morning to Keyport for another long day of campaigning. The raw energy that he displayed on the campaign trail accrued to his advantage, because it created the public perception that he wanted the governorship more than Dixon did. Not only that, it energized party workers who realized that their leader spared no effort in soliciting votes.

There were a few holdouts, especially former Governor Joel Parker. The absence of an endorsement from him was a serious gap because Parker was a highly popular Democrat. On October 23, Abbett

toured several industrial factories in Camden County, where he shook hands with workers at the plant gates and asked them for their votes. Afterward, he attended a reception at the West Jersey Hotel where he was able to repair some intraparty rifts. Among the party dignitaries on hand were former Governor Joel Parker, Congressmen Thomas Ferrell and John Hood, and Camden Assemblyman George Barton. In a visible display of party unity, they all endorsed Abbett enthusiastically.

These endorsements were important geographically, because Abbett was not as well known in southern New Jersey as he was in the northern part of the state. Congressman Ferrell was a glassblower by trade and a prominent labor leader. He had defeated Republican George M. Robeson for Congress in 1882. His victory was considered a stunning upset. Ferrell represented the First Congressional District, including Camden, Cape May, Cumberland, Gloucester, and Salem counties, considered Republican territory. Farrell, one of the best political organizers in the state, knew his endorsement carried a lot of weight with workingmen. The glassblowers were grateful to Abbett for what he had done for them in 1877. They remembered that he had successfully sponsored legislation requiring their employers to pay them in cash rather than in paper scrip or shinplasters.

Although most Democrats climbed aboard the Abbett bandwagon, Benjamin F. Lee and Henry Kelsy were holdouts. Both men were part of the State House Ring. Lee was clerk of the state supreme court and Kelsy was secretary of state. Finally discarding their factional baggage, they scampered aboard the party bandwagon toward the end of the campaign. Obviously, they wanted to hold on to their state jobs. Abbett considered them less dangerous inside his administration than outside.

Defiant throughout the campaign, Henry Little continued to believe that the Abbett bandwagon could be stopped, and he went to great lengths to try and do so. Little even attended the Republican convention and urged Republican delegates to nominate Jonathan Dixon.[27] He was joined in his efforts by other defectors such as Rufus Blodgett and Thomas Kays. As the railroad tax issue drove a wedge deeper into party unity, these three disgruntled Democrats persisted in their vituperative attacks and obstructionism. Defections were counterbalanced by letters displaying loyalty and devotion.

At a crucial stage in the campaign, Little published a letter in the *Trenton Times* that charged Abbett had been paid $500 by the receiver of the Jersey Central Railroad for the legal services he rendered in 1877, when he successfully fought to obtain the back wages of its employees.[28] This caustic letter was intended to destroy Abbett's credibility with labor, but it backfired. Most workingmen were offended by Little's letter, and they turned out in large numbers to vote for Abbett on election day.

Meanwhile, Jonathan Dixon ran a lackluster campaign in which he made few public appearances. Both parties, of course, did their share of

mudslinging. Republicans John Griggs, William Phelps, and John Taylor were adept at this sort of thing. Turning up the political heat on Abbett, they branded him "a candidate of the liquor saloons and the political strikers."[29] They cast him as favoring intemperance and lawless labor riots.

All the Republican invective was directed at Abbett. They had researched his legislative record and highlighted several of his votes as an assemblyman. Among them was his vote in favor of a bill that denied New Jersey soldiers an absentee ballot during the Civil War. They also dredged up his "yea" vote that sought to remove Abraham Lincoln's name from a joint resolution expressing the gratitude of the citizenry at the end of the war. In an obvious appeal to Greenbackers, they reminded voters of Abbett's vote in 1865 favoring the payment of state legislators in gold rather than in greenbacks. They also ridiculed his vote against a prison reform bill in 1866.

The Republican press smeared him with as much mud as it possibly could. Both the *Jersey City Evening Journal* and the *New Brunswick Fredonian* published a story that accused Abbett of being one of the bank directors who was responsible for the failure of the Mechanics and Laborers Savings Bank in Jersey City. The article stated that he had "swindled hundreds of widows, orphans and laborers of their hard-earned savings."[30] Soon afterward, these two newspapers were forced to print a retraction when it was proven that Abbett had resigned as a director eight years before the bank failed. But it was Garret Hobart, the Republican state chairman, who made the most blistering attack against him. He delivered a long political harangue in which he assailed Abbett's character and cast him as a person with "a shady and untrustworthy reputation." False rumors circulated during the campaign about Abbett's personal life.

These were harsh words, but Abbett was skilled in defending his integrity against these scurrilous attacks. The more Abbett emphasized his differences with Dixon, the more he was able to connect with voters who were drawn to his core values and beliefs. Countering the array of charges leveled against him, Abbett blunted the impact of the Republican accusation that he was beholding to the railroad power. He declared, "It is said that I am the attorney of the Pennsylvania Railroad, and would, if elected, be controlled by that corporation. The truth is I have never within the past six years acted in any capacity, either as counsel or agent for that company."[31]

One incident made a particularly strong impression on people in Jersey City. Dixon appeared at an outdoor bazaar that was held at the city's fairgrounds. The funds raised by this event were to benefit the German School Association. Some women who were selling raffle tickets asked Dixon to buy one, but he refused by saying he could not participate in any form of gambling. Such a response made him the butt of gentle

ridicule. The incident embarrassed some of Dixon's supporters and enabled the Democrats to poke fun at him. The *New York Times* later recalled the scene in similar fashion. "This caused considerable comment, and the general impression was that for a politician the judge had stretched things a bit too far, but he stood firmly to his position."[32]

DIXON STUMBLES WHILE ABBETT SOARS

Many of Dixon's problems were of his own creation. He was too reserved and too stiff for a candidate trying to win votes. When he did appear at public gatherings, he came across as being cold and aloof. In part this was due to his shyness, but his troubles were partly due to the tactical mistakes made by Garret Hobart, who managed his campaign. Simply ignoring organized labor was not a smart move on their part. It was calculated to offend. Both candidates were asked to fill out a questionnaire submitted by labor. One of the questions inquired as to whether they would appoint workingmen to positions in state government that affected their interests. Irritated by such an inquiry, Dixon flatly refused to make such a pledge. Abbett took the opposite approach and responded by saying, "The wage workers of the state are entitled to the highest consideration in all matters affecting their interests."[33] Their responses underscored their ideological differences.

As the campaign wore on Dixon stumbled by equivocating on the liquor question; he managed to alienate people on both sides. This was especially true in Bergen County, where his judicial record on enforcing the liquor laws hurt him. Even Republicans were upset at the stiff jail sentences he had given offenders.[34] Much to his dismay, Dixon did not go over well with the temperance-minded. Solomon Parsons, the Prohibition party candidate, won most of the temperance vote. Unmistakably identified as a wet, Abbett no doubt benefited from Dixon's equivocation on the liquor question.

When the counterattack was in full swing, the Democrats did plenty of mudslinging of their own. They painted Dixon as a cold-hearted judge who favored property rights over individual rights, corporations over consumers, and creditors over debtors. Moreover, they tarred him with having drafted the "thieves charter" in Jersey City. The Irish despised Dixon as the person most responsible for their disempowerment. They hated Protestants of English descent who vilified their religion and insulted their manhood. Quipped the *New Brunswick Times*, "The fact that Judge Dixon is an Englishman by birth will not endear him to the Irish voters of the state."[35] These sentiments were echoed by the Anglophobic *Jersey City Herald* that commented, "The people of this state want no cold-blooded, icy Englishman in the governor's chair. We have a Jefferson

and a Jackson in New Jersey's Little Giant."[36] As the saying in those days went, "The Irish bury the hatchet, but mark the spot." They didn't get mad, they got even.

By manipulating these symbols, Abbett softened the impact of a vicious smear campaign. To offset these Republican tactics, the Democrats renewed their courtship of Catholics and foreigners. Abbett was determined to win most of the Irish and German vote. By 1880, the 93,079 immigrants from Ireland made up the largest ethnic minority in the state, while the 64,935 German immigrants was the second largest ethnic group. Aware of these numbers, Abbett worked his old magic when it came to playing ethnic politics. At Hibernian gatherings, he talked about the need for an unrestricted immigration policy and endorsed the goals of the Irish Emigrant Society because it promoted assimilation. Abbett flattered the Irish by acknowledging their contributions to America. He paid similar tribute to German immigrants.

Both candidates tried to win the "Negro" vote, but here Dixon had a decided advantage over Abbett. Ever since black men had won the right to vote, they had identified with the Republican party, mainly because of Abraham Lincoln's policy of emancipation. They owed their loyalty to their fallen hero, whose memory they revered and cherished. In their minds, the slain president remained their "great liberator." Such symbolism was hard to counteract.

Nevertheless, Abbett reached out to nontraditional constituencies and avidly sought support from black voters in 1883. He actively campaigned in the black wards of Camden, Jersey City, Newark, Paterson, New Brunswick, and Trenton. Most blacks lived in these big cities.[37] While campaigning in Newark, he met and befriended William H. DeKalb, a prominent leader in the black community. One of Abbett's strengths as a politician was his ability to adapt to changing political conditions. It was not always graceful or pretty, but it showed his flexibility. What emerges is a new Abbett who ceases to play the race card and dramatically reverses his position on civil rights. Such abrupt turns were not uncommon for him, but this turnabout was extraordinary, especially for a states' rights Democrat. Discarding the political baggage that he had toted with him since his Copperhead days, Abbett knew only too well that in a close election black voters could make a critical difference. There were some 38,853 black citizens living in New Jersey in 1883. Of this number, 10,670 were black males of voting age. Unlike most white politicians, Abbett promised to help them in their drive for political equality.

Despite his clumsy blunders, Dixon remained a formidable opponent. He gained the White House endorsement of President Chester Arthur, but it came too late in the campaign to be of much help. The Republican managers tried to reduce the normal Democratic majority among German immigrants. They achieved some success among German

Protestants, but their dalliance with nativism and temperance kept the Catholic vote mostly Democratic.

Dixon received stout support from middle-class Republicans, artisans, and farmers whose party loyalties were unshakable. The white Anglo-Saxon Protestant majority was dominant in the rural and suburban areas where Republicanism flourished. The political culture of the suburbs and the distinctive rural towns was dramatically different from the political culture of the big cities. It was far more conservative and rock-ribbed Republican. This was especially true in southern New Jersey, where temperance, Protestant evangelicalism, and anti-Catholicism flourished.

Democrats met the Republican challenges as well as the ambivalence in their own ranks with more assertive demands for regularity. All over the

FIG. 14
State Capitol, 1890.

state Democratic organizers heralded the virtues of party. Fearing divisiveness, Abbett urged them to work hard and to get out the vote on election day. With the gubernatorial race still in doubt, he put on a strong stretch drive during the last two weeks of the campaign. Considering the close balance between the two major parties, Abbett took nothing for granted. The Republican *New York Times* described the intensity of his campaigning:

> Leon Abbett, the Democratic candidate for Governor, is hampered by no judicial restraints nor restraints of any other kind. In fact, he is making a campaign of unprecedented vigor. He was a conspicuous figure at the State Fair. He has neglected no County Fair. He has spoken in two or three places every day or evening for the last two weeks. A reception at the hotel at which he has been put up has followed each public gathering and he has probably shaken hands, since he started out, with more than half the people in the Commonwealth. Carriages and carry-alls of all kinds have been called into service to enable him to keep his engagements. Special trains have been chartered for his transportation when friends accompanied him, and he has not been above speeding over the country on locomotives when travelling alone. He has spent but little time at rest, and he has not probably averaged more than three hours out of every 24 in sleep since he achieved the nomination.[38]

By all accounts, the gubernatorial race in 1883 generated a fervor that was unprecedented in New Jersey politics. It evoked far more passion and excitement than previous elections for governor. People were impressed by Abbett's views, his grasp of detail, his intuition, and his capacity to send a message. He reached out and touched ordinary people. They admired what he had done and how he had gone about doing it. His stump speeches were filled with Jacksonian rhetoric and partisan enthusiasm. In the end, it was Abbett rather than Dixon who reflected the popular mood by pushing for equal taxation and by advocating legislation to protect the economic interests of farmers and factory workers. Drained emotionally and exhausted physically, Abbett concluded his grueling campaign in Jersey City, which remained the center stage of the drama.

A STUNNING ABBETT VICTORY

New Jersey voters went to the polls on November 6, 1883. With no national election at stake, the voter turnout was not as large as the presidential election of 1880. When all the ballots had been tabulated, Abbett defeated Dixon by 103,856 to 97,047. The Hudson Democrat won the election with 51.6 percent of the two-party vote. Some 6,809 ballots separated the two major candidates, which was almost 2,000 votes more than Abbett had originally predicted. Compared with Governor Ludlow's narrow victory of 651 votes in 1880, Abbett won by a much larger

FIG. 15
Henry Stafford Little, state
senator from Monmouth
County. Chancery Court
Clerk and president of the
New Jersey Central Railroad.

margin, but it was not an overwhelming majority. The closeness of party competition limited majorities in electoral campaigns.

Independent third-party candidates contributed to the outcome of the election. They appealed to voters on the fringes of the political spectrum. Solomon Parsons, the Prohibition party candidate, picked up 4,153 temperance votes, whereas Benjamin Urner, the Greenback party candidate, obtained 2,960 Greenbacker votes.[39] Because of Dixon's waffling on the liquor issue, he lost Bergen County that normally went Republican. In the rest of the counties, the dry vote was split between Parsons and Dixon, while the wet vote went almost entirely to Abbett.

Greenbacker Benjamin Urner, who hailed from the city of Elizabeth, was the candidate of the disaffected. He advocated the use of the initiative and public referendum as a means of achieving direct democracy. Urner, who had run unsuccessfully for Congress against Republican John Kean in 1882, felt that these instruments were the best hope for keeping government responsive to the people.[40] He drew protest votes from radical socialists, anarchists, and silver inflationists who preferred soft money to hard money.

A closer look at the election results reveal that Dixon won ten out of the twenty-one counties in New Jersey. Seven of them were the small rural and less populous counties: Atlantic, Burlington, Camden, Cumberland, Gloucester, Ocean, and Salem. This was rock-ribbed Republican territory, where farmers and Protestant evangelicals held sway. Dixon also won the more populated counties of Essex, Morris, and Passaic. Meanwhile, Abbett carried the remaining eleven counties that were mostly urban and industrial. Hudson County gave him 15,293 votes compared with 12,009 for Dixon. As expected, Abbett ran strong in the big cities, where the links between white immigrant voters and the Democratic party were almost inseparable. Since no data exist on voting returns by race, it is impossible to determine how black men voted. Presumably, a good number of them voted for Abbett.

Abbett's brand of populism held him in good stead in the big cities. He won the cities of Elizabeth, Jersey City, New Brunswick, Paterson, and Trenton. By contrast, Dixon won Atlantic City, Camden, Newark, and Passaic. The support Abbett received from the textile workers in Paterson helped him carry that city. He lost Passaic by only 389 votes. Counties with sizable urban populations, such as Bergen, Mercer, Middlesex, and Union, gave him comfortable majorities. Abbett also fared well in certain farm areas. He swept the northwestern tier of rural counties that included Hunterdon, Somerset, Sussex, and Warren in which lingering Jacksonian sentiment among farmers was still prevalent. Historically, of course, this was traditional Democratic country. Especially gratifying to Abbett was the fact that he won Monmouth and Sussex counties. Despite the backsliding of Democrats like Henry Little, Henry Kelsey, and

Thomas Kays, Abbett carried Monmouth by 1,723 votes and Sussex by 1,204 votes. Even tiny Cape May County gave him a plurality of 56 votes.

When the polls closed, Abbett was anxious to learn the results of the election. He stayed up most of the night at his brownstone home in Jersey City, where he received telegrams and telephone calls from party leaders across the state. As the editor of the Jersey City *Evening Journal* marveled:

> Had anyone asserted a few years ago that a gubernatorial candidate could receive complete returns through the medium of the human voice, while seated in his own residence, and afterwards receive the congratulations of his friends and supporters in distant sections of the state by personal conversation with them at their residence, he would have been regarded as a fit candidate for the lunatic asylum. Yet this was done by the Governor-elect last night.[41]

The news of Abbett's stunning victory flashed across the cities and towns of New Jersey via improved communication technology. Democrats were jubilant and celebrated accordingly. But the next day they were shocked to learn of the death of Theodore Randolph. In an ironic twist of fate, Randolph suffered a fatal stroke at his country estate in Morristown on November 7, 1883. A profoundly distressed man, he was fifty-seven years old at the time of his death. Randolph's intense dislike of Abbett, who was his ideological opposite, had consumed him in his final days. He had spent them brooding about the outcome of the election. Some people believed that the news of Abbett's triumph may have caused his stroke. In any event, the election amounted to a repudiation of Randolph, who was fixed in his ways and belonged to a bygone era.

Abbett's victory, juxtaposed with Randolph's death, paved the way for a new order. It was a genuine changing of the guard. Two decades of intraparty wrangling, conflict sharpened by personal friction, competing ambitions, and clashing dogmas had caught up with the Randolph faction. At a crucial hour, Abbett showed his ability to popularize his own cause. His supporters saw him as speaking with a common voice, a common vision, and a shared sense of purpose. The governor-elect now faced the biggest challenge of his political career in taking on the powerful railroads over the issue of taxation. He knew it was going to be a monumental task and a risky undertaking, but he decided that it was a risk well worth taking. The stage was now set for an epic struggle.

ENDNOTES

1 Biographical information on Henry Stafford Little is taken from the following sources: *New Jersey Law Journal* (1904), vol. 27, pp. 157–158; *Princeton Alumni Weekly*, April 30, 1904, pp. 489–490; *Trenton Times*, April 25, 1904.
2 Sackett, *Modern Battles of Trenton*, 1:34.

3 *Trenton True American*, September 17, 1883; *Monmouth Democrat*, September 27, 1883. See also Sackett, *Modern Battles of Trenton*, 1:211–213.

4 *New Brunswick Times*, September 20, 1883.

5 *New York World*, September 13, 1883.

6 Quoted in *Kickerbocker*, September 2, 1883.

7 Edward Q. Keasbey, *The Courts and Lawyers of New Jersey* (New York, 1912), vol. 3, pp. 324–326. See also Charles W. Parker, "Some Reminiscences of Leading New Jersey Judges and Lawyers of the Later 19th Century," 53 *Proceedings of the New Jersey Historical Society* 230–231 (1935).

8 *Princeton Press*, September 29, 1883.

9 *Monmouth Democrat*, September 20, 1883.

10 *Jersey City Journal*, September 21, 1883.

11 *Monmouth Democrat*, September 20, 1883.

12 Sackett, *Modern Battles of Trenton*, 1:222–223.

13 *Trenton True American*, September 21, 1883.

14 Sackett, *Modern Battles of Trenton*, 1:218.

15 *Trenton True American*, September 26, 1883.

16 *Ibid.*

17 Sacket, *Modern Battles of Trenton*, 1:217.

18 *Jersey City Herald*, October 13, 1883.

19 *Jersey City Herald*, September 29, 1883.

20 Gutman, "Class, Status, and the Gilded-Age Radical: A Reconsideration," as found in Herbert G. Gutman and Gregory S, Kealey (eds.), *Many Pasts: Readings in American Social History* (Englewood Cliffs, NJ, Prentice-Hall, 1973), vol. 2, 134.

21 Leo Troy, *Organized Labor in New Jersey* (Princeton, D. Van Nostrand, 1965), 67.

22 Socrates Tuttle's letter, dated February 20, 1880, appeared in *The New Brunswick Times*, November 2, 1883. See also Leo Troy, *Organized Labor in New Jersey*.

23 See *Paterson Labor Standard*, October 6, 1883; October 13, 1883.

24 Gutman and Kealey (eds.), *Many Pasts*, 143.

25 Quoted in Sackett, *Modern Battles of Trenton*, 1:220.

26 *Newark Evening News*, October 20, 1883.

27 *New Brunswick Times*, September 21, 1883.

28 *Trenton Times*, October 31, 1883.

29 *New York Tribune*, September 28, 1883.

30 *Evening Journal*, September 29, 1883; *New Brunswick Fredonian*, October 1, 1883.

31 *Jersey City Herald*, October 20, 1883.

32 *New York Times*, March 12, 1893.

33 *New Brunswick Times*, October 26, 1883.

34 *Bergen Index*, November 9, 1883.

35 *New Brunswick Times*, September 21, 1883.

36 *Jersey City Herald*, September 29, 1883.

37 *New Brunswick Times*, September 28, 1883; *Newark Evening News*, October 27, 1883.

38 *New York Times*, October 31, 1883.

39 Complete election returns for the 1883 gubernatorial race are found in the *New Jersey Legislative Manual* (1884), 195–228. See also Richard P. McCormick, *The History of Voting in New Jersey* (New Brunswick, Rutgers University Press, 1953), 185.

40 See Chester M. Destler, *American Radicalism 1865–1901* (Chicago, Quadrangle Books, 1966), 24. According to Destler, Benjamin Urner, who had run unsuccessfully for Congress in 1882, was the first Populist politician in America to press for the initiative and referendum as a way of reforming the political system and bringing corporate capitalism under democratic control.

41 *Evening Journal*, November 7, 1883.

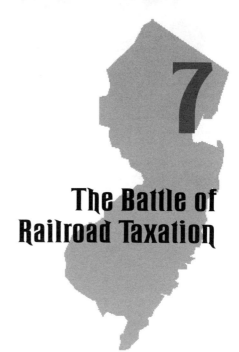

The Battle of
Railroad Taxation

Pressures on the new governor to overcome past tradition and cut through the complexities of railroad taxation to a prompt solution were strong. The trumpets for tax reform had been blaring in New Jersey for more than a decade. The political momentum generated by the Ludlow administration carried forward in the transition to Abbett. This was the context in which the new governor entered office and found a sizable fiscal deficit awaiting him. Flush with victory, Abbett was intent on fulfilling his major campaign promise. It was already documented that a major reason for the grievous shortfall in state revenue was the refusal of the railroads to pay an equitable tax on the property and mineral coal rights they owned. The impulse to tax them was almost irresistible, and it had considerable populist appeal. It would give the governor a new revenue stream without burdening him with the political necessity of imposing a broad-based tax. At the time, there was no income or sales tax, and indeed few taxes of any description. Vigorous gubernatorial action would be possible under these circumstances. What follows then, drawn from imperfect documentation, is a history of the battle to enact the railroad tax legislation and the trials and tribulations that accompanied its implementation.

Fresh from the campaign, Abbett brought his intense, sometimes bullying, but always dogged and resourceful style to a demanding job at a critical juncture. He was one of the few leaders who had a clear sense of himself and knew exactly what he wanted to do. Even the Republican press acknowledged as much. Zebina Pangborn, the editor of the *Jersey City Evening Journal*, had forewarned both political parties:

> Republicans, as well as Democrats, should take notice that Leon Abbett is a man who conspicuously exhibits the courage of his convictions, who does not hesitate to do whatever he decides to do. If he becomes our governor, he will be the governor, and it will be idle for anybody to attempt

to control him, or to prevent him from carrying out any purpose which he may entertain.[1]

As things turned out, this editorial comment could not have been more prophetic. From the moment he took office, on January 15, 1884, Abbett was ready to move on railroad tax reform and he gave almost single-minded attention to the task. He picked his inaugural ceremony as the appropriate occasion on which to sound his clarion. A propitious event in timing and location, the ceremony took place indoors at the Taylor Opera House in Trenton, while a blinding snowstorm raged outside. Chief Justice Mercer Beasley administered the oath of office to Abbett. As was the custom, outgoing Governor George Ludlow presented him with the "Great Seal of New Jersey."

The newly installed governor delivered his inaugural address in what the news media described as a "forceful and effective" manner. He devoted his inaugural message almost entirely to the subject of railroad taxes. Surveying the problem at hand, Abbett concluded that new legislation would be required to reform the tax structure. He clearly outlined the nature and extent of the problem:

Our tax laws demand immediate and radical reform. They impose unequal burdens. The only true rule in taxation is equality. All property should bear its equal share of the public burdens. This reform, imperatively demanded by the people, can only be secured by legislative action. In dealing with this question, I am aware of the complications that surround it. Courts have held that certain corporations have contracts which exempt valuable property from taxation. There are other corporations that claim to have contracts on this subject, the validity of which is still undetermined. These alleged contracts must be intelligently and practically dealt with in any legislation which we desire the courts to recognize as constitutional. The evil of bartering away the sovereign rights of the state over taxation is now apparent to all, but it is a doctrine which the courts have recognized and complete sovereignty can never be restored to the state until all contracts on the subject of taxation are extinguished.[2]

From all indications, Abbett intended his speech to be a call to action. The railroad industry, of course, interpreted his remarks as a call to arms, if not a declaration of war. The governor identified correctly the attributes of the tax problem and the options for its resolution. He clearly articulated his position and the substantive legal issues involved. Moreover, he fully anticipated the consequences of his policy and knew that his tax initiative would be a tough sell with the legislature, especially with the Republican-controlled senate. For the issue now was governing, not campaigning. There was a huge difference between the two.

New Jerseyans had long been struggling with the railroad tax problem but without much success. Since 1875, the legislature no longer

granted business corporations individual charters. They now operated under general incorporation laws. Because many railroads had been incorporated before the Civil War, they still operated under their original charters. As a result of a law passed in 1876, all railroad and canal companies were subject to the authority of a commissioner of railroad taxation. Yet abuses and irregularities in tax collection persisted: the railroads submitted their own property valuations. This loophole in the tax law had led to the rail lines being greatly undervalued and underassessed. Moreover, there was no way of verifying the accuracy or validity of their data.

Both the Morris and Essex Railroad and the Pennsylvania Railroad claimed that their corporate charters absolved them from paying taxes under the 1876 law. The issue of whether the Jersey Central Railroad was required to do so remained unresolved. State tax officials claimed that it was liable. The Jersey Central contended that under the terms of its corporate charter it could only be taxed on the cost of the road. The Erie Railroad, having already surrendered the special privileges previously possessed by its leased lines, paid taxes under an act of 1873. Several railroads were either delinquent in paying their taxes or evaded them altogether. Plainly, the state was not very efficient in collecting taxes under this hodgepodge of statutes. Such laxity and lack of uniformity contributed to a messy situation that was confusing and incoherent.

While the thrust of Abbett's legislation was aimed primarily at the railroads, the governor called for a comprehensive tax program. Only manufacturing firms were to be exempted under his plan. The governor created the impression that a painless solution—growth in public revenue without imposing a broad-based tax—was at hand. "I am in favor," he said, "of establishing a state policy which will forever obviate the necessity of raising any money from our people by a state tax."[3] Abbett then outlined the principal components of his plan: (1) increasing the tax rate on railroad property; (2) taxing the franchises of the railroads; (3) levying a tax on other classes of corporations; (4) imposing license fees on out-of-state business corporations; (5) placing a tax on the gross receipts of corporations; (6) imposing a collateral inheritance tax; and (7) increasing incorporation fees. This revenue package was designed to raise enough money to finance the entire operations of state government, which then included prisons, reformatories, public asylums, and normal schools or teachers' colleges.

In his inaugural speech, the governor also focused on the plight of New Jersey's financially distressed cities. "At the present time," he said, "our cities lose, for purposes of municipal taxation, not only all the improvements put upon property taken by railroad corporations having irrepealable contacts but they also lose the tax which was imposed upon the property before it was taken by the corporations."[4] To illustrate his point, Abbett cited the recent purchase by the Morris and Essex Railroad

of a parcel of land in Jersey City valued at $1.8 million that was then withdrawn from its assessment rolls. For the cities to deal with such a problem, the governor urged the legislature to delegate the power of condemnation to them. "I am also of the opinion," he added, "that not only can the state extinguish these contracts, upon compensation paid by it; but that the legislature can give to the cities of our state the same power to extinguish such contracts so far as they affect property within the territorial limits of such cities."[5]

TRANSLATING IDEA OF EQUAL TAXATION INTO POLICY

The political fallout from Abbett's inaugural message had the immediate effect of putting everyone on notice. The equal tax coalition was pleased with his remarks. He had accepted the challenge and responded to their concerns. Not unexpectedly, the railroads gave Abbett an exceedingly hard time and tried to persuade him to change his mind. Cross-pressured, the governor incurred the wrath of prominent Democrats like Henry Little, Joseph Bedle, and Rufus Blodgett. They argued that he would destroy the party, if he persisted in his course of action. Impervious to political pressure, Abbett concluded that they were "just plain wrong." As William Sackett recalled:

It was not an easy thing for him [Abbett] to withstand the pressure to which the railroad people subjected him for an abatement of his energies. The Democratic railroad partisans warned him that he would wreck the party if he persisted in his course, while other railroad people, who did not appeal to him on partisan grounds told him that his political future would be as black as that marked out for [George] Ludlow.[6]

Refusing to fold under this barrage of pressure, Abbett forged ahead and remained firmly committed to his tax initiative. He shaped the legislation largely on his own, but he did seek the advice and counsel of Charles Corbin and Allan McDermott. They actively participated in drafting the measure, and their input was given special consideration. His top aides were depicted in the press as being "wild men" who were arrayed against the state's railroads.

The governor's tax bill (A-253) was introduced by Assemblyman William Prall of Paterson. Prall came from a prominent political family; his father, Edwin T. Prall, had been a cotton manufacturer and former mayor of Paterson. Having lived abroad in Europe for several years, the son spoke German and French fluently. He had earned a doctorate at the University of Heidelberg in Germany and a law degree from Columbia Law School. An ardent Democrat and a highly competent attorney, he had won fame by successfully defending Joseph McDonnell, the socialist

FIG. 16
Rufus Blodgett. Engraving
by W.T. Bather, New York.

newspaper editor, in his libel trial in 1880. Viewed as a friend of labor, Prall was a man of great personal integrity and an ideal person to shepherd the governor's tax bill through the lower house. When his political career ended, Prall went on to become an ordained Episcopal priest.

The scope of Abbett's legislation was broadly defined to include all business corporations except for manufacturing firms. He wanted to avoid a subsequent court challenge that would invalidate the law as special legislation. The statute required the railroads to pay "a state tax on one-half of one percent upon the true value of all property owned, leased, used or occupied by them in the state, including the franchise."[7] Municipalities were allowed to tax the main stem of the railroads at the prevailing local property rate. By statutory definition, the main stem included the roadbed and track not exceeding 100 feet in width.

Abbett's bill was drafted in a manner to avoid being construed as hostile legislation. It did not contain a provision condemning the charter contracts. That solution, in his judgment, would have required an amendment to the state constitution. His bill did contain language that prohibited out-of-state corporations from doing business in New Jersey unless they surrendered their charter contracts. It also contained a provision that granted the attorney general sufficient power to force a corporation to pay its delinquent taxes. Hence, Abbett's bill did have some enforcement teeth with which to gain compliance.

The governor sought to circumvent the court decisions by taxing the franchise of the railroads, which granted them the privilege of doing business in the state. In addition to the vaunted efficiency of the railroads, Abbett duly noted their capacity to earn greater profits. He pointed out that the railroads were better off financially than any other industry in the state. While some had incurred increased operating expenses, the Delaware, Lackawanna and Western, the Pennsylvania, the Erie, the Reading, and even the Jersey Central showed sizable profits. Even so, they were not about to give up their "irrepealable" charter contracts. Both the federal and state courts had approved this arrangement and their judicial decisions made the existing political situation that much more difficult.

Faced with this seemingly insurmountable obstacle, Abbett decided that the only way to solve the problem was to tax the railroad franchises. The franchise was a license to do business and had a monetary value that could be taxed in a different way than terminal facilities or rolling stock. By adopting this strategy, the governor got around the legal constraints imposed by the courts. "If they are a contract," Abbett said, "and if that contract is irrepealable, it is a pretty valuable piece of property itself; we'll tax that."[8] He fully expected opposition from the railroads that considered his bill a form of socialism. The media also expressed some caution, not so much about the merits of Abbett's legislation but rather about whether he could get it enacted.

LEGISLATIVE COUNTERSTRATEGY

Seeking to upstage the executive, the legislature countered with its own tax proposal. The lawmakers formed a special joint committee on railroad taxation to study the problem. This six-member committee, which was chosen jointly by the two houses of the legislature, was bipartisan in composition. The three Republicans included state Senators John W. Griggs of Passaic County and Abraham V. Schenck of Middlesex County, and Assemblyman Edward A. Armstrong of Camden. The three Democrats were state Senator William Brinkerhoff of Hudson County, and Assemblymen James H. Neighbour of Dover and Edward S. Savage of Woodbridge. All six members were lawyers. Republican John Griggs, who aspired to become senate president, was named chair. He was intent on framing tax legislation that he considered less punitive than Abbett's bill. Brinkerhoff was the point man in the fight for equal taxation in the upper house. He made sure that the joint committee was not stacked entirely with railroad men.

After completing its study, the joint committee produced a rather conservative tax measure. Its bill (A-313), drafted by Assemblyman William H. Corbin of Elizabeth, introduced the concept of classifying railroad property for tax purposes. It divided this property into four separate classes: (1) the main stem; (2) all other real estate used for railroad purposes; (3) rolling stock and other personal property; and (4) the franchise. All four classes were to be taxed by the state at the rate of one-half of one percent, but property classified under the second category was to be taxed an additional one percent by local municipalities. The statute abolished the position of commissioner of railroad taxation and replaced it with a State Board of Assessors that was responsible for administering the law and determining property assessments. No longer would a railroad company be allowed to submit its own valuation figures without the new state agency verifying their accuracy. At the same time, the railroads won an important concession in getting the tax assessment function removed from the purview of local municipal assessors. Much controversy centered on the requirement of the franchise tax that Brinkerhoff insisted upon and fought hard to keep in the bill.

The Joint Committee's bill (A-313) was patterned after the Illinois railroad tax law that had been upheld by the U.S. Supreme Court. It differed from Abbett's bill (A-253) in at least five essential respects. First, it was more narrowly defined and applied only to railroads and canals, not to other business corporations. Second, it classified railroad property for purposes of taxation. Third, it exempted the main stem from local taxation. Fourth, it limited the local tax rate on railroad property to one percent. Fifth, it abolished the ten-acre terminal tax exemption. Tax experts estimated that this last provision would provide Jersey City with $200,000

in additional annual revenue. Contained in both the governor's bill and the Joint Committee's bill were certain provisions that the equal tax advocates had long been clamoring for as necessary to clarify and strengthen tax procedures.

Obviously, the Joint Committee adopted a conciliatory attitude toward the railroads. It acknowledged as much in its report: "We are convinced that these views, which are embodied in the bill herewith presented, ought to satisfy both the companies and the people concerned. Is it not better to deal conservatively with these great interests, which are so valuable to the state, than to enter upon a system of legislative warfare?" The report concluded:

The best that can be hoped for is to secure an honest effort at equalization. Such an effort can only be made when all mere sentiment and unworthy appeals to passion and prejudice are put aside, and the matter is treated on a basis of just dealing, as between man and man. For, after all, whether we speak of corporate property, or of individual property, the ultimate owners of it all are merely private individuals—our fellow citizens.[9]

The first public hearing was held on February 12, 1884. Chairman Griggs opened it with a brief history of railroad taxation in New Jersey. Citing figures obtained from the railroad tax commissioner, he pointed out that the railroads paid the state $677,557 in taxes for 1883. In addition, they paid $210,000 in local taxes. The total annual taxes paid by the railroads in 1883 amounted to $887,000. Griggs set the tone of the public hearing by saying:

These figures are given at present merely to indicate the importance of the subject of taxation when applied to these corporations. The very magnitude of the subject adds also to the responsibility that attaches to the effort to make laws that shall apply to this vast accumulation of property, and should make us cautious and deliberate in our attempts to equalize the burdens of public expenses between it and the remainder of the wealth of the state.[10]

Originally, the railroads presented neither a united nor a conventional front. They marched out their top brass to testify at the hearings. The lead-off witness was none other than U.S. Senator William Sewell, who represented the United New Jersey Railroad and Canal Company. Adopting a conciliatory stance, he came out in favor of the principle of equal taxation. Senator Sewell indicated that the company he represented paid $298,129 in state taxes and $30,000 in municipal taxes. It paid more than any other railroad operating in New Jersey. Following him was Robert Stockton, who represented the Erie Railroad. He surprised everyone by declaring that he was in favor of repealing the law that exempted the railroads from paying taxes on ten acres of land at their

terminal. Stockton, like Sewell, thought that the railroads should pay their fair share of taxes—no more, no less. This was a smart move on their part. Obviously, the railroads had preempted the high ground at the hearing. Yet they remained united in their opposition to the tax on the franchise.

Single-minded in his overriding commitment to capitalism, Henry Little, president of the Jersey Central Railroad, was good at projecting an image and provoking a reaction. He told the committee that he was not familiar with his company's tax returns, but that he had brought along his company treasurer, Mr. Watson, who could give pertinent figures. Little denied reports that his company was not paying its fair share of taxes. "How much taxes do you pay to Jersey City?" asked Chairman Griggs. Avoiding the question entirely, Little replied, " Well, you see our terminus at Communipaw is all land which we have reclaimed. We are not connected with Jersey City and receive no relief or protection from her fire and police departments." Suggesting the possibility of the state building a railroad bridge spanning the Morris Canal Tidewater Basin, Griggs asked, "Would you be willing to pay if we connect you with Jersey City?" Little responded affirmatively—an answer that drew derisive laughter from the other railroad executives.[11]

Former Governor Joseph Bedle testified for the Delaware, Lackawanna and Western Railroad. He argued that the main stem should not be subject to the "whims and caprices" of local tax assessors. In response to a question from the chair, Bedle replied: "We pay taxes in Jersey City to the amount of $5,000 and in Newark $2,000."

Chairman Griggs pursued this line of questioning further. "Governor, your company has an irrepealable charter contract. Now suppose the state offers you a just equivalent, will you surrender that charter contract?"

> Bedle replied, "I don't know what they can offer us." To this response, Griggs further inquired, "Well suppose the state agrees to give up its right to condemn your road and not buy it at its original cost at the expiration date of the contract of the charter?" "Well, well," said Bedle as he hesitated before replying, "I am not prepared to answer that. It is a question which requires serious consideration and I am not sure how far the right of the state goes."[12]

With this guarded comment, the first public hearing ended.

Hearings resumed on March 11. Lawyers and lobbyists filled the hearing room. Railroad witnesses brought reams of facts and figures, attempting to swamp the legislators with a mass of detail. Appearing for the Pennsylvania Railroad was Edward T. Green, a company vice president, who was verbally combative. Far less skittish about taking the measure of the governor, he openly attacked Abbett, claiming that he was a

stumbling block to solving the tax problem. Green described Abbett's bill as "an attempt at legalized fraud, with entire disregard for the sanctity of contracts. It was fostered by fanaticism."[13] Green then accused Abbett of making false public statements and of using scare tactics by raising the spectre of fiscal calamity and municipal bankruptcy.

The next witness was Cortlandt Parker, the distinguished Newark attorney, who had lost to Abbett in litigating the Jersey City home rule case in 1879. He represented three small railroads—the New York and Greenwood Lake, the Newark and Hudson, and the Paterson and Newark lines. Parker testified in favor of maintaining the current tax system that he felt was more than satisfactory. He saw no need for any further railroad taxes and cast doubts about whether the governor's bill would pass. These explanations may have had some merit, but they were not entirely convincing.

Allied with the railroads was an impressive array of other economic interests. A spokesman for the Mutual Benefit Life Insurance Company in Newark asserted that his company would be driven out of business if the governor's bill became law.[14] As the final hearing continued, it became obvious that certain business corporations were taxed lightly. For instance, the New York and New Jersey Telephone Company that reported gross receipts of $1 million paid only $527 in taxes for 1883. The American Cable Company, chartered in New Jersey by Jay Gould with capital assets of $10 million, did not pay any taxes whatsoever. Several companies had moved from Philadelphia to Camden to escape taxation in Pennsylvania. Since most business corporations, except for railroads and canals, were not affected by the Joint Committee's bill, they concentrated their fire power in trying to defeat the governor's proposal.

Testifying in favor of Abbett's bill were equal tax advocates from across the state. The Anti-Monopoly League of Hudson County sent a large delegation to Trenton to dramatize the issue and lobby in behalf of A-253. The charismatic Thomas Cator argued forcefully in favor of the governor's bill. Still others saw the solution of extinguishing the contracts through condemnation. All these people were vitally interested in reforming the tax structure. All favored increased rail taxes. Whatever the variance in opinion and perceptions, few informed observers could quarrel with the key fact that the railroads were taxed lightly.

Surprisingly, Abbett experienced little trouble in getting his bill passed by the general assembly. It had been put on the legislative fast track. The lower house was made up of thirty-four Democrats and twenty-six Republicans; many of whom were on record as favoring equal taxation. Both parties had adopted planks in their 1883 platforms endorsing the idea. After much debate, the assembly passed Abbett's bill by a lopsided fifty-six to one vote. The only negative vote was cast by Democrat Isaac Wildrick, an eighty-one-year-old assemblyman from Blairstown.

A cantankerous, die-hard railroad man, his vote showed how much he was out of step with public sentiment in the state.

Then the action shifted to the senate—the real battleground. There the railroad forces were prepared to exert their political clout. Railroad lobbyists, notably Culver Barkalow and George Dorrance, were hard at work trying to derail Abbett's tax initiative. They relied on the senate to defeat measures they opposed, because it only took eleven votes to do so; whereas it took thirty-one votes in the assembly. Although the legislature in 1884 was nominally Democratic, Abbett lacked a working majority in the senate that had twelve Republicans and nine Democrats. The governor's bill was referred to the Committee on Railroads and Canals, where it languished and never resurfaced. Stalled there for six weeks on the issue of the franchise tax, the bill eventually died in committee. Presiding over its burial were Republican Senators John J. Gardner of Atlantic County and John S. Applegate of Monmouth County.

With much of his legislative program thus blocked, Abbett relied on the counsel of Charles Corbin, whose lecture on railroad taxation in New Jersey had been widely distributed. Conventional wisdom suggested that both parties courted the railroads because they believed they could not win elections without their support. Corbin emphasized the fallacy of this argument in his analysis:

> The existing political parties have sought railroad support simply because it contributed to success. The railroad companies have supplied aid because they have valuable tax exemption privileges to protect from party attack. When a public opinion is created that will make it more profitable to reform than to maintain abuses, the parties will be quick to perceive it. When an alliance with a railroad company no longer contributes to success, it will no longer be sought. Public opinion once aroused, will convert the party caucus into an instrument of reform.[15]

Corbin's advice was prelude to the more concerted assault that followed. Drawing on his analysis, Abbett mounted a public relations campaign to bring pressure on the legislature. The lawmakers were not used to dealing with the pressure a governor could generate. By marshaling public opinion, Abbett showed his determination to make good on his campaign pledge. Public sentiment was overwhelmingly in favor of his bill. By this time, the Republican senators were beginning to feel the heat of an aroused public opinion that the governor had skillfully mobilized in publicizing the issue. Especially annoying to them was Abbett's attempt to generate a public groundswell to sway legislators. They now realized that some sort of tax proposal would have to be enacted.

Confronted with a recalcitrant senate, Abbett kept a watchful eye on the two bills under consideration. He tried hard to pry his bill loose from committee, but to no avail. The Republican senators kept his bill

tightly under wraps in committee, where it died and was quietly buried. The governor held out for his own bill, mainly because it would have raised more revenue. Moreover, if his bill were challenged in the courts, which he fully anticipated, he felt that it would pass judicial scrutiny. As the legislative session drew to a close, the pressure to pass a railroad tax measure grew intense. The equal tax partisans pushed hard for passage of the governor's bill (A-253), while the prorailroad forces would only accept the Joint Committee's bill (A-313). A few die-hards found neither of these bills acceptable. Senator Griggs was worried that Abbett was going to get his bill through the senate and get all the political credit.

A SENATE STRATEGY OF OBSTRUCTIONISM

A deliberate strategy of obstruction was under way. In late March, the senate wanted to appoint another commission to study the railroad tax problem. Incensed by the politics of evasion, Hudson's Senator William Brinkerhoff felt that his colleagues had misjudged public opinion. He saw them trying to thwart the public will. When Brinkerhoff realized that Abbett's bill could not be pried loose from committee, he added an amendment to the Joint Committee's bill (A-313) that required railroad property to be taxed at the prevailing local rate. His amendment, however, was unacceptable to the railroad lobby. The debate intensified. Brinkerhoff made an impassioned speech in which he asserted that the current tax system had almost bankrupted Jersey City and warned his fellow senators that there would be a major public uproar, if they did not pass some kind of tax relief measure. "If justice is not awarded to the people on this question," he shouted, "you will see the greatest Boston Tea Party ever given, equaling in some respects the recent burning of the public buildings in Cincinnati."[16] But that warning went unheeded and the Republican senate refused to budge. The dispute made both sides unhappy and frustrated. The executive and legislative branches faced political gridlock.

Once Abbett realized that his bill was dead, he decided to support the compromise proposal. Rather than see the equal tax cause go down to defeat, he threw his support behind the Joint Committee's bill. After all, it contained the most important feature of his legislative initiative, namely, the franchise tax. With this provision intact, Abbett pushed for the passage of A-313. "Whenever the Governor found a Democratic Senator wavering in the support of the bill in its most stringent shape," Sackett observed, "he subjected him to the pressure that kept him in line for it."[17] With some arm-twisting, Abbett persuaded Republican Senator Ezra Miller of Bergen County to vote with the ten senators who favored keeping the franchise tax in the bill. Republican Senator John J. Gardner

of Atlantic County, a tool of the railroads, desperately tried to defeat this provision, but he was unable to do so.

When Abbett suspected the lawmakers of further delay in hopes of adjourning without taking any action, he threatened to refuse to sign appropriations unless the statute was enacted. He also sent a special message cajoling them to remain in session until they had completed their work. "The interests of the state," he declared, "should be paramount to any consideration of personal convenience, and I trust that no attempt will be made to adjourn either House until definite action is taken in reference to Assembly bill 313."[18] Only grudgingly and under intense pressure did the railroad interests in the senate finally relent. Abbett struck a deal whereby he granted them representation on the newly created State Board of Assessors in return for their support of A-313. The strategy worked. It broke the legislative deadlock. This bill was passed and signed by the governor on April 10, 1884. The first phase of the battle had been won, but the fight was far from finished.[19]

THE SBA APPOINTMENT CONTROVERSY

Hardly had the ink dried on Governor Abbett's signature to the new railroad tax law when he became embroiled in a controversy over his appointments to the State Board of Assessors (SBA). He realized that implementation of the law depended largely on the personnel who sat on the SBA. Its main function was to ascertain the value of railroad and canal property for purposes of taxation and to sit as a review board to hear appeals on its assessments. Such appeals could be brought by any of the companies involved or by the attorney general or any member of the board. Petitions on behalf of the state involved complaints of underassessment or of omitted property. Resisting the SBA from its inception, the Jersey Central Railroad did not want any state agency inspecting its records.

Selection of nominees to fill the four positions on the SBA was a delicate balancing act for the governor. He identified four who met a set of explicit criteria: knowledge about real estate and property assessment, familiarity with the cost of railroad construction and equipment, and government experience. The statute required that the SBA be comprised of two Democrats and two Republicans who were to serve staggered terms. While bargaining to get the legislation passed, Abbett had already cut a deal to appoint two Republicans who were amenable to the railroad interests in the senate. In return, they agreed to confirm his Democratic appointees.

Taking all these factors into consideration, Abbett carefully selected his appointees. At a press conference on April 16, he announced their

names along with their staggered terms. Those chosen were Edward
Bettle of Camden for one year; Abraham M. Reynolds of Newark for
two years; William H. Jackson of Passaic for three years; and Allan
McDermott of Jersey City for four years.[20] Given the political sensitivity
of these appointments, they caused trouble for the governor. Much of the
controversy centered on his trusted lieutenant Allan McDermott. The
governor wanted him on the SBA to offset Bettle who was identified as
a staunch railroad man.

Both Bettle and Jackson were Republicans. Bettle had served as a
state senator from Camden County from 1867 to 1872. He was a seasoned politician and had some experience in valuing railroad property. A
small businessman, William Jackson sat on the city council in Passaic and
was closely identified with the Erie Railroad. Reynolds was a Democrat,
a Newark banker, and the current commissioner of railroad taxation in
New Jersey. Governor Ludlow had appointed Reynolds as commissioner
in 1881, but that position was now abolished by the new law. For his
part, McDermott had served as corporation attorney for Jersey City,
chairman of its Board of Finance, and Hudson County assemblyman. He
was thoroughly familiar with the problems of railroad valuation.

Between them these four nominees met the statutory criteria:
including the bipartisan balance, necessary expertise, and practical wisdom of politics. Three of them brought experience in taxation to bear on
their work, though from different perspectives—small business, banking,
and city government—and the fourth was a former member of the senate
club. Even a geographical spread was evident; four separate counties
located in the northern and southern parts of the state were represented.
All but Reynolds were lawyers, and all had some practical experience in
real estate.

Both Bettle and Reynolds were quickly confirmed by the senate.
The first sign of trouble was opposition to William Jackson, whose name
had been submitted by Robert Stockton of the Erie Railroad. Jackson was
unacceptable to Senator John Griggs, who was already taking credit for
authoring the new tax law. Griggs was miffed because the governor had
not consulted him on Jackson's nomination.[21] Since Jackson came from
the same county as Senator Griggs, the latter was able to block his nomination by invoking the privilege of senatorial courtesy. Griggs favored
Thomas D. Hoxsey of Paterson and now pressured the governor to
appoint him to the board.

As the jostling for positions on the SBA intensified, McDermott
was rejected for purely partisan reasons. It was the politics of personal
destruction. McDermott was objectionable because he was closely identified with Abbett. What upset the governor is that he had made a deal with
the Republican senators. As a trade-off for appointing Bettle and Jackson,
they had agreed to accept Reynolds and McDermott. But several

Republican senators now balked and refused to honor the deal. McDermott's close personal relationship with Abbett left the governor vulnerable to charges of cronyism. This perception was based in part on a personal affinity between the two men beginning in 1871, when McDermott first clerked in Abbett's law office, and continued when Abbett hired him as a city attorney for Jersey City. In this capacity, McDermott had fought the railroads in valuation cases. Under the new statutory classification scheme, the problem of valuing "class two" terminal railroad property was largely a Hudson County problem. Nearly one quarter of the railroad property in the state was located there.

With McDermott's nomination under fire, Abbett refused to withdraw it. In his mind, the Republican senators had reneged on a deal. For the most part, the general public was baffled by the intricate political insiders game being played at the State House. So the governor decided to go public and explain what was happening. At a press conference, he defended his four appointees by saying, "Every Republican who came to see me urged Bettle's nomination. I named McDermott, who is an anti-railroad man, as a counterweight to him. I nominated Reynolds because he is familiar with the duties of the office. Since he had been confirmed by the Senate in previous years, I assumed that he would be unobjectionable. Jackson is a man of intelligence and integrity."[22] Abbett's motives may have been mixed but surely were more complex than his critics would acknowledge. The first round of the confirmation fight had ended in a draw—two nominees were approved and two were rejected.

Realistically, Abbett knew that he would have to give way on William Jackson. There was not much he could do about the practice of senatorial courtesy. It was a long-standing rule that was inviolable. Thus, he substituted Alexander Cattell for Jackson. Cattell was the Republican who had replaced Democrat John Stockton in the U.S. Senate when the latter had been expelled for partisan reasons in 1866. By substituting Cattell, the governor had neutralized Senator Griggs, but he did not appoint Thomas Hoxsey as Griggs wanted. Since Cattell was connected with the Pennsylvania Railroad, he was readily confirmed by the senate. It was the resubmission of McDermott's name that sparked a furor.

It also generated a barrage of criticism from the news media. The Republican press had a field day. William Cloke, the editor of the Trenton *State Gazette*, noted acidly, "The Governor's appointments to the board show as plainly as Holy Writ that he has sold out the people."[23] To some commentators, the appointees may have appeared like a sell out because of the political trade-offs involved. Noah Brooks, the editor of the *Newark Daily Advertiser,* was even more caustic, "Abbett proposes to make it a board for the manufacture of Democratic governors, United States Senators, and other offices."[24]

Abbett saw his fight over McDermott as crucial to the implementation of the new law, because McDermott was the one appointee least susceptible to railroad pressure. As chairman of the Jersey City Board of Finance, he was credited with having saved the city from bankruptcy in 1883. Working in conjunction with the Hudson County National Bank and the Second National Bank, he was instrumental in restoring the city's bond rating through his creative financing. As a result, he was highly regarded by its citizens, who referred to him as a "financial Moses." The editor of the *Jersey City Argus* was effusive in its praise of McDermott, "He is conspicuously the right man in the right place at the right time."[25]

No other nominee, in Abbett's view, was better qualified than McDermott. The governor remained firmly committed to him. On April 18, he made another attempt to obtain McDermott's confirmation before the legislature adjourned. Republican Senator James Youngblood of Morris County played a key role as chairman of the Judiciary Committee. The country squire from Morristown took great pleasure in holding up McDermott's nomination. Youngblood could not abide Abbett. They had already crossed swords over the passage of the "Negro Burial" bill (more about that later). Because of his position as chair, Youngblood was able to keep the nomination bottled up in committee. The confirmation fight had generated a contentious atmosphere.

In an attempt to break the sustained stalemate, Lewis Cochran, the Democratic senator from Sussex County, moved to submit a minority report favoring McDermott's confirmation. At this point, negotiations between the two political parties broke down completely. Cochran's motion was ruled out of order by Senate President Benjamin A. Vail, a Republican from Union County. From Vail's perspective, McDermott was an Abbett loyalist. Two days earlier, Vail had denounced McDermott as a "notoriously corrupt individual," who was utterly unfit to hold the position. A subsequent motion to force the nomination out of the Judiciary Committee was likewise defeated by a ruling from the chair. An appeal of this motion was being debated when, Senator Griggs, with watch in hand, suddenly sprang to his feet and moved adjournment. This motion carried by a dubious voice vote, the gavel fell, and the senate adjourned sine die.[26] Abbett had lost the second round.

Without a fully constituted board, Abbett realized that the new railroad tax law would remain inoperative. He countered by invoking the state constitution's little used emergency powers to call the legislature back into session. The governor promptly called a special session of the senate to act on the unfilled post. Such a move was considered "brazen" and ill-advised. Previous governors were reluctant to do so for fear of alienating the senate. Abbett showed no such inhibitions. He pressed hard for his appointee. At the risk of suffering still another rebuff, Abbett resubmitted McDermott's name for a third time.

The ensuing publicity raised the level of public awareness. Charles Corbin started a letter writing campaign, and in his first letter, he warned the senators that the railroads were trying to capture the SBA. They in turn accused Corbin of having sent them conflicting information about McDermott. Corbin responded to this charge by writing another letter that he sent to the *New York Tribune*. In his second letter, he disputed Vail's criticism of McDermott and chided the senators for their erroneous rush to judgment. This letter read in part:

> In the *Tribune* this morning I am represented as having written to one New Jersey State Senator opposing, and to another recommending, the confirmation of Mr. McDermott as State Assessor of Railroads in New Jersey. This is without foundation. To both Senators I wrote urging his confirmation. To senator Vail, who had declared him to be corrupt, I wrote saying that though Mr. McDermott was a politician and given to 'deals, combinations and bargains,' he was not a corrupt man and was a competent man for the office. To Senator Vail and my other Republican friends in the New Jersey State Senate who declare that a man who makes 'deals' must be corrupt, I have to say: Let him who is without this sin among you cast the first stone at McDermott.[27]

Public opinion continued to favor the governor. That pressure grew in intensity as the antimonopoly forces lobbied hard for McDermott. Both Bettle and Cattell were seen as representing the Pennsylvania Railroad. The Jersey Central Railroad complained about being denied representation on the SBA. With the rejection of Jackson, the Erie Railroad complained that it had been cheated out of a representative. This was simply too much for Charles Corbin who declared:

> Where do the people of New Jersey come in? Some very queer ideas seem to have found lodgment in New Jersey politics under railroad government. To say of an Assessor that he takes the office for the express purpose of exercising his judicial powers with favor to a particular company, or with partiality to railroads generally, is to make a graver charge against him than any that has been brought against McDermott.[28]

This interpretation of power, as expressed by Corbin, appeared on newsstands in conservative, not radical, garb.

The special legislative session that met on April 22 found every senator in attendance. Realizing that the governor was prepared to hold them in session until a fully constituted SBA was in place, they kept their deliberations to a minimum. The session lasted two hours. To save face, Republican Senator Abraham V. Schenck of Middlesex County offered a resolution in which he complained about "the chief executive's unreasonable delay in making his appointments" and about his "lack of due regard for the dignity of the Senate."[29] After this face-saving gesture, the confirmation controversy was quickly resolved. McDermott's name was

favorably reported out of committee, and he was confirmed by a vote of fourteen to seven. Abbett had won the third and decisive round.

With the SBA's four members in place, it proceeded to draw up a set of guidelines for determining taxable values. Under the nominal chairmanship of Edward Bettle and the leadership of Allan McDermott, the board valued separately the several items and parcels of property that together comprise a railroad.

However modest its beginnings, the SBA's reputation for professional competence was soon recognized. McDermott won accolades for his work in drawing up the guidelines. A decade later, Republican board member Alexander Cattell acknowledged his contribution: "Much of the success of the early work of this board is due to the intelligent and faithful service of Mr. McDermott, largely supplemented by his legal knowledge, which was invaluable."[30]

THE LEGAL CHALLENGE OF THE 1883 RAILROAD TAX LAW

Because the Jersey Central had been grossly undervalued and underassessed, it was the first railroad to be reassessed by the SBA. When the company declared bankruptcy in 1877, it had been valued by the commissioner of railroad taxation at $17 million. Subsequently, when the line was leased by the Reading Railroad, Francis Lathrop, the court-appointed receiver, had submitted a valuation of its property for rental purposes at $60 million.[31] The SBA now sought to bring these two figures into line with its true market value.

Defiant as ever, Henry Little objected to the SBA's assessment. He claimed that the values placed on the Jersey Central's franchise and other property were "excessive." One of the sticking points was the method of valuing the franchise. Little argued that his company should not be required to pay taxes on land that it had reclaimed by filling in the mud flats of South Cove in Jersey City. The Jersey Central paid taxes through the American Dock and Improvement Company, a subsidiary corporation that held title to its riparian shore-line property. Exhausting its administrative remedies, the Jersey Central appealed its assessment to the SBA and contended that its rental valuation was based upon its coal fields in Pennsylvania, and therefore it should not be included as part of its true market value. The SBA disagreed. Sitting as a review board, it heard the Jersey Central's appeal and rejected its claim.

"Staff" Little was furious. Smarting from the action taken by the SBA, he took his case to court. The question of whether the Jersey Central Railroad had a special contract under its charter that absolved it from paying certain taxes remained cloudy and unsettled. The controlling case was *New Jersey v. Yard* (1877). In that decision, the U.S.

Supreme Court had ruled that the corporate charter, which the state legislature had granted the Morris and Essex Railroad in 1835, constituted an "irrepealable legislative contract." Little was seeking the same kind of legal protection for his railroad. All this occurred while the newly created SBA was struggling to organize itself, establish its identity, and define its role.

The question of the Jersey Central's tax liability soon became unclouded. On June 5, 1884, the New Jersey supreme court handed down its decision in *Little v. Bowers*. Much to everyone's surprise, the court decided that the Jersey Central did not have a special contract similar to the Morris and Essex.[32] This decision did not sit well with Little; again he returned to court. By now, his motives were clear. While ostensibly seeking to set aside and invalidate the SBA's assessment, he also challenged the constitutionality of the 1884 railroad tax law.

A total of thirty-three railroads soon joined in this class action lawsuit. During the course of the litigation that dragged on for the better part of two years, most of the railroads withheld paying their taxes. Of the ninety-four railroads operating in New Jersey, only those under the management of the Erie and the Pennsylvania paid the taxes that were levied against them. These payments, however, were made under protest that meant that the companies were entitled to a refund, if they prevailed in the litigation.

The railroads retained a battery of prominent lawyers to argue their case. They lined up an impressive array of legal talent. Some of the attorneys came from out of state. Appearing for the Jersey Central was a formidable foursome of Robert W. DeForest, Franklin B. Gowen, George Kaercher, and George M. Robeson. They were all high-powered and experienced attorneys. Gowen and Kaercher were Pennsylvania-based lawyers who had successfully prosecuted the Molly Maguires in 1877. Former Governor Joseph Bedle represented the Delaware, Lackawanna and Western. Thomas N. McCarter appeared in behalf of the Lehigh Valley. Former Chancellor Benjamin Williamson, who was adept at cross-examination, represented the Reading. Cortlandt Parker, who had opposed Abbett in the Jersey City home rule case in 1879, was the attorney for the New York and Greenwood Lake Railroad. Even the small Tuckerton rail line, which owned thirty miles of track, retained Henry A. Drake to represent its interests.

To compete against this kind of high-priced legal talent, Governor Abbett appointed Barker Gummere as special counsel to assist Attorney General John Stockton in litigating any claims that might arise against the state. An intellectual heavyweight who could persuade judges with relevant facts and applicable law, Gummere was considered one of the most brilliant attorneys in New Jersey. He practiced like an English barrister, relying on other lawyers to research and prepare the written brief, while he concentrated on the oral arguments. Few lawyers could match him in his

courtroom advocacy.[33] Stockton was also assisted by Allan McDermott and William T. Hoffman. The latter, an eloquent lawyer from Englishtown, had served for seven years as a state judge in Hudson County.

With the battle lines drawn, the attorneys spared no effort in preparing their case. Scores of witnesses, thousands of pages of depositions, and hundreds of documents were introduced into evidence. Neither side had left any details to chance. Since the validity of a state law was being contested, the case was removed to the New Jersey supreme court on writ of certiorari. It received much publicity in the media before its opening on November 4, 1885. Oral arguments were heard before a panel of three judges. Several particular issues were disposed of on the merits. Chief Justice Mercer Beasley presided over the trial. A distinguished jurist, Beasley presented a striking figure with his gaunt face, shaggy eyebrows, sharp chin, and long gray hair draping over the shoulders of his black robe. Manning M. Knapp and William J. Magie were the other two judges who heard the case.[34]

In one of the most tenaciously fought cases in New Jersey history, the litigating railroads attacked the new tax law as special legislation. Since the statute applied only to railroads and their subsidiary canal companies, they argued that it targeted a particular interest group and thus amounted to special legislation. Hammering home that point, they claimed that it was unconstitutional. They also attacked the concept of valuation by statutory classes.

Warming to his task, Joseph Bedle argued that the railroad valuations were discriminatory and violated both the equal protection clause of the Fourteenth Amendment and the uniformity rule in the state constitution. Franklin Gowen contended that the Jersey Central was being taxed unfairly compared with the Pennsylvania Railroad, whose earnings were much greater. He argued that the Pennsylvania was being given "preferential treatment." Thomas McCarter attacked the method of valuing rail property by statutory classes. He maintained that the scheme amounted to an unconstitutional delegation of legislative authority, because the lawmakers had failed to set forth sufficient standards for the SBA in administering the law.[35]

The legal arguments that the railroad attorneys presented to the state supreme court covered "almost every conceivable objection" to the law, but most of their fire was directed at the franchise tax. The railroads considered this provision to be the "unpardonable error" of the 1884 law. Because of mounting criticism, the SBA had published its rule of franchise valuation. Simply put, this rule subtracted the value of tangible property from the market value of the stocks and bonds, and then took sixty percent of the remainder, or what was called "corporate excess." In the event that the value of tangible property exceeded the value of the capital stock and the debt, an alternative rule of franchise value was to regard twenty

percent of gross earnings as this value. Since the state tax rate was one-half percent, this was equivalent to a tax of one-tenth percent on the gross earnings as a measure of the tax on the franchise. Franklin Gowen tried to persuade the judges that earnings were the only factor that should be considered in valuing railroad property. In all, it took the railroad lawyers two weeks to present their arguments.

Arguing the state's position in tandem, Attorney General John Stockton and Special Counsel Barker Gummere spent the next three days in an elaborate rebuttal. Essentially, they argued that the statute in question met the criteria of general legislation as defined in the state constitution. Citing various legal precedents and drawing on state reports, railroad maps, and other pertinent documents, they attempted to prove that the railroads were being taxed lightly. Again and again, Gummere harped on this theme. Noting that while tangible property of the railroads was valued at $50 million, they paid only $1.5 million in taxes. By contrast, Gummere pointed out that rail taxes in Massachusetts were much higher. He presented empirical and quantitative evidence to support his positions. For example, he cited a statement contained in the 1885 Annual Report of the SBA that declared: "But nevertheless the fact remains that the railroad corporations of New Jersey are benefitted to the extent of half a million dollars by being located in a state notably prudent and economical in its public expenditures—thereby keeping the tax rate low."[36]

Counsel for the state argued that the segregation of railroad property and the system of valuation by classes constituted the backbone of the 1884 law. They further argued that the concept of "corporate excess" was a reasonable standard for the SBA to follow in its calculation of franchise value. If anything, they claimed that the franchises were undervalued and ought to be increased. In matching wits with their legal adversaries, both Stockton and Gummere reminded the judges that the Fourteenth Amendment was intended to help the newly freed slave retain his status as a free man. It was not meant to shield business corporations from taxation.

Gilbert Collins was the attorney who argued the case for the local taxing districts of Elizabeth, Hoboken, Jersey City, and Newark. In his view, the one percent ceiling placed on the local tax rate was totally unrealistic. He contended that the expansion of railroad terminal facilities caused the cities to lose, both in ratables and in revenues, from the transfer of property formerly taxable at the full local rate into a category in which it was taxable only at a limited rate. That is, as the railroads acquired more land for terminal use, this land could no longer be taxed at a rate higher than one and one-half percent. On this note, the state and its political subdivisions concluded their arguments.

While the litigation was pending in the courts, Abbett continued to press his attack. In his second annual message delivered in January 1886, he gave this update:

In view of the allegations of the companies that they are unfairly taxed, the Legislature should bear in mind that the act of 1884 makes railroad corporations a favored class, discriminating in favor of them as against individual taxpayers. Both of the railroad tax bills, as originally passed in the Assembly of 1884, provided for equal taxation. The act as passed by the Legislature, however, contained provisions which secured to the railroad companies advantages under which they pay less than fifty-seven percent of the amount they would pay if their property were assessed the same as individual property....The friends of equal taxation, while not satisfied with the advantages given railroad corporations over individual taxpayers, were obliged to accept the act of 1884 with all its clauses favoring the railroad corporations, or do without any legislation on the subject. They deemed it wiser to accept the great advance made by the act of 1884, and wait for another Legislature to give them their full rights. The present Legislature has it in its power to amend the act of 1884 as to subject these corporations to taxation which will impose the same burden upon them as upon individual citizens.[37]

Less than a month later, on February 18, 1886, the New Jersey Supreme Court delivered a stinging blow to the Abbett administration. In handing down its decision *Central Railroad Company v. State Board of Assessors*, a unanimous three man court invalidated the statute as special legislation that they claimed violated the state constitution. Unmoved by the state's argument, they decided in favor of the railroads. Chief Justice Mercer Beasley wrote the lengthy twenty-two page opinion that narrowly interpreted the law. His main rationale for nullifying the statute was that the separate valuation of railroad property by classes contravened the uniformity rule (Article 4, Section 7, Subsection 12) in the New Jersey constitution.[38] A renown judge, Beasley had marshaled the rest of the court behind him. It was hardly an impartial judiciary, however; rumors of a packed court were rife.

There was some element of truth to these rumors. Of the three judges who had heard the case, two could be considered favorably disposed toward the railroads. Prior to his judicial appointment in 1880, Judge William J. Magie of Elizabeth had served as counsel for the Pennsylvania Railroad. Manning M. Knapp of Hackensack was also a former railroad attorney.[39] Yet none of the judges saw a conflict of interest or reclused themselves from the case. As U.S. Supreme Court Justice Samuel F. Miller candidly admitted in 1875, "It is vain to contend with judges, who have been at the bar the advocates for forty years of railroad companies, and all the forms of associated capital, when they are called upon to decide cases where such interests are in contest. All their training, all their feelings are from the start in favor of those who need no such influence."[40]

This was no mere historical footnote. The adverse decision of the Beasley Court inflicted a devastating blow to the Abbett administration.

It wiped out the tax reform, or so it seemed. Attorney General John Stockton expressed disappointment that the judiciary had not provided an alternative solution. Comptroller Edward J. Anderson told the press, "The immediate effect of the decision is to put a stop to all disbursements for the simple reason that there is no money to disburse."[41] Anderson's statement dramatized a dire financial situation. Without rail tax revenue, the prospect of a balanced budget vanished. There were other constraints operating here. State officials were prohibited by law from borrowing except in anticipation of revenue. Moreover, the constitutional debt limitation of $100,000 could not be exceeded without the approval of a public referendum.

In prudent fashion, Abbett explored what steps might be taken to avert the impending fiscal crisis. He realized that the state government was perilously close to incurring debt beyond the constitutional debt limit. The governor wanted to avoid this option, if at all possible. He did not want a public referendum for fear that it might be construed as a vote of no confidence. Anticipating an operating deficit of $250,000, Abbett was prepared to impose stringent economic measures. In a special message to the legislature, delivered on February 23, 1886, he proposed the more limited options of freezing state jobs, curtailing nonessential services, and selling state-owned securities. If additional steps were necessary, he was prepared to take them. For example, he identified a replacement source of revenue:

> I believe that we can require the railroads of the state to pay a license for every car used by them in this state, under an act requiring state licenses to be taken out by every person and corporation engaged in the business of transporting freight or passengers, and these license fees, with the other sources of revenue, will give the state ample means to meet all demands upon its treasury.[42]

Abbett felt stymied, but his fighting spirit never diminished, and he refused to give up. On February 19, he directed Attorney General Stockton to appeal the court's ruling in the Jersey Central case. Since only three judges had heard the case, further judicial review was possible. It was high-stakes politics. Abbett was convinced that the controversy could only be settled by a ruling from the New Jersey Court of Errors and Appeals, the state's highest tribunal. At his behest, Stockton and Gummere filed their appeal with all deliberate speed. The governor wanted the statute fully adjudicated.

Within a month, the judgment was reversed. On March 20, 1886, in an amazing display of judicial alacrity, the state Court of Errors and Appeals overturned the lower court decision and upheld the constitutionality of the 1884 tax law. Of the sixteen judges who sat on this court (six were lay judges), only Justice David A. Depue, whose family wealth was

obtained through railroad investments, voted to sustain his colleagues Beasley, Knapp, and Magie. In upholding the statute, Chancellor Theodore Runyon ruled that it was framed in general terms; it was restricted to no locality; and it operated equally on all of a group of taxable objects that possessed sufficiently clear and distinct characteristics as to constitute a class by themselves.[43]

Contrary to the findings of the lower court, Runyon found that the New Jersey constitution did not forbid the classification of property for taxation when the basis of classification is reasonable in character and capable of general rather than local and limited application. In a separate concurring opinion, former Governor Joel Parker, who sat on the high bench, wrote:

The act in question is not only constitutional, but is founded on a just basis. While it requires of the companies the payment of one-half of one percent for state purposes, it so guards against imposition in the assessment of local taxes that in no case can a company be forced to pay more than the local rate, but may pay much less. If there be any inequality, it is favorable to the companies, and of this they have no legal right to complain. It is the injured party who has the right to move for the correction of errors.[44]

It was a win that sent shockwaves through the State House in Trenton. Overturning Beasley was a rare event. Seldom was this eminent jurist reversed on appeal. With his primary goal fulfilled, Abbett was elated. He sent a special message to the legislature in which he expressed his satisfaction, "Under an economical administration, this will forever obviate the necessity of raising any money from our people by a direct state tax and establishes the policy recommended in my inaugural and annual messages."[45]

THE RECALCITRANT MORRIS AND ESSEX RAILROAD

But the euphoria was short-lived. Despite the ruling of the highest state court, the Morris and Essex Railroad still refused to pay its taxes. Such defiance symbolized the arrogance of corporate power. The company brazenly flaunted its irrepealable contract as a shield for evading the law with impunity. It was almost as if the ideological ghosts of Theodore Randolph and Francis Lathrop had come back to haunt Abbett.

With characteristic persistence, the governor tenaciously pursued the defiant railroad. An astute lawyer, he understood the impregnable legal position of the Morris and Essex. In the words of Charles Corbin, "The Morris and Essex exemption is unfortunately established by a decision of the U.S. Supreme Court, a decision inconsistent with

subsequent decisions of the same court, but still as yet unreversed."[46] Despite this legal barrier, Abbett was determined to extinguish its contract. Suspicious of the way the Morris and Essex had operated in the past, he began checking to see if its previous tax returns were in proper order. He suspected the rail company of tax evasion.

Soon afterward, Abbett uncovered what he had hoped to find. He discovered a $10-million discrepancy between the valuation figures submitted by the Morris and Essex and those compiled by the SBA. He also suspected that the company had undervalued its property for the past three decades. If his suspicions were correct, it meant that the railroad had illegally withheld about $50,000 in taxes each year.[47] Clearly, Abbett had found some irregularities on the part of the company. The governor asked the Morris and Essex for an explanation and urged the legislature to investigate the matter.

THE LAVERTY IMPEACHMENT

At this point, the political situation took an unexpected turn. What went on inside the state prison at Trenton was typically a mystery to the public and elected officials alike until dramatic events drew attention to it, usually when a dangerous inmate escaped or when a scandal broke. Such incidents usually prompted an investigation and sensational media coverage. In early March 1886, the Republican legislators uncovered what they considered to be a major sex scandal. They brought impeachment proceedings against the prison warden, Patrick H. Laverty, for sexual misconduct. Unmistakably identified as a Hudson Democrat and an Abbett loyalist, the fifty-three-year-old Laverty was charged with having sexually abused five female inmates.

In exercising its powerful oversight function, the general assembly formally drew up the articles of impeachment that accused Laverty of having committed adultery with Minnie Schaeffer, a "comely" female inmate, who had since been pardoned and released from prison. He was also charged with having had "carnal knowledge" with four other female prisoners who included Elizabeth Garrabrant, Annie Lenhart, Mary Smith, and a "mulatto" by the name of Eva Steel. All five women had worked as domestic servants in the warden's house that was located on the prison grounds. Both Minnie Schaeffer and Mary Smith had become pregnant while in prison and each subsequently delivered a child. The Republicans further charged the warden with incompetence and dereliction of duty.[48]

An Irish immigrant who had been brought to America by his parents, Patrick Laverty was raised in Saugerties, New York. His father died when he was sixteen. He went to work in the garment industry in New

York City until he landed a job as a stagecoach driver with the Adams Express Company in California. "During his services with the company," says one account, "he carried millions of dollars in treasure, and, although his path was constantly beset by banditti and the worst of cut-throats, he never lost a single dollar."[49] Returning to the East Coast in 1860, Laverty took up residence in Jersey City, where he worked for the Erie Railroad. In 1871, he was elected to the local school board, much to the chagrin of newspaper editor Zebina Pangborn, who detested Irish Catholics. Three years later, Laverty ran on the same Democratic ticket with Leon Abbett and was elected sheriff of Hudson County. After an unsuccessful run for Congress in 1878, he was appointed "prison keeper" by Governor George Ludlow in March 1881. He had held this position for five years.

Sitting as the High Court of Impeachment, the senate tried the case. The whole sordid episode of charge-and-denial had a certain morbid drama. The proceedings were more theatrical than judicial. Lasting a total of 19 days, the trial played to a packed senate gallery. As the scandal unraveled, the prosecuting attorney, Samuel H. Grey, contended that Laverty had enticed the female inmates into granting him sexual favors by promising to obtain pardons for them. Each of the women testified that the warden had repeatedly lured them into performing improper sexual acts.

The accused sat stoically in the courtroom nearby his wife and six grown children. His defense team argued that Laverty suffered from a serious kidney infection and his medication had made him impotent. Correction officers took the stand and testified that female inmates were not permitted upstairs in the warden's house unless they were accompanied by a prison matron. Evidence showed that the warden had been in St. Louis, Missouri, attending a national corrections conference at the time one inmate claimed that she had become pregnant. In an attempt to destroy her credibility, the defense produced a female inmate who testified that she saw her having sexual intercourse with a convict gardener. Both sides relied heavily on circumstantial evidence.

Anyone who watched the trial could have predicted the outcome. The senate voted fourteen to seven to convict Laverty. The senators found him guilty on two of the seven charges, but they barely mustered the two-thirds vote necessary to convict. Near the end of the trial, the Republicans found themselves one vote short, and they persuaded George O. Vanderbilt, the Democratic senator from Mercer County, to join them. With Vanderbilt willing to cross party lines, the fate of Laverty was sealed.

Abbett saw the partisan storm coming, seeking in the timing of the impeachment proceedings some clue to Republican motives. He felt that the attack on Laverty was a political smokescreen. It was a distraction purposely designed to divert public attention from the legislature's stonewalling on the Morris and Essex investigation. Politics was a blood sport played for keeps. On the one hand, Laverty's supporters believed

that he had been purposely set up by the Republicans. On the other hand, his accusers believed that he had been caught doing wrong and was properly convicted. At any rate, Laverty accepted his fate philosophically. In an interview with the *New York Times*, he attributed his conviction to ethnic and religious prejudice.[50] No one could convince him otherwise. The disgraced Laverty was removed as warden and disqualified from ever holding public office again.

After the trial, Laverty's friends believed that he had been unfairly scapegoated. This was especially true of the Irish in Hudson County. Under the particular circumstances, they felt that it would be fitting if Abbett were to offer the vacant post to James Laverty, the warden's oldest son. The governor's office was flooded with letters and telegrams urging him to do so. Even Attorney General John Stockton, ousted from the U.S. Senate by the Republicans in 1866 for partisan reasons, urged the governor to make this appointment. On the evening of April 22, a delegation of local Democrats, who included Hudson's Senator William Brinkerhoff and legal counsel John Linn, paid Abbett a visit at his home in Jersey City. They pleaded with him to offer the job to James Laverty. After they departed, the governor paced his bedroom well into the night pondering what to do.[51]

Abbett was in a quandary. He felt deeply obligated to Patrick Laverty. On the other hand, Abbett could ill-afford to be seen as condoning this sordid scandal. As criticism mounted, he was under pressure to appoint someone who could restore public confidence in the warden's office. Although he shared the belief that the elder Laverty had been scapegoated, he did not let his personal friendship blur his judgment.

Under fire to clean up the mess, Abbett felt that it would be a mistake for him to appoint the warden's son who had no experience in law enforcement or corrections. The governor therefore chose John H. Patterson. A prosperous farmer and a shipper of agricultural produce from Middletown Township, Patterson was the former sheriff of Monmouth County. He came from a well-connected political family going back to Jeffersonian days. His grandfather had been the chief surveyor of the Delaware and Raritan canal. Patterson himself had run unsuccessfully for Congress in 1872. After his defeat, he had been given the job as doorkeeper for the U.S. House of Representatives in Washington.

The selection of Patterson was a wise choice. He served as warden for the next ten years, from 1886 until 1896. During this decade, Patterson gradually restored public confidence in the management of the state prison. As head of corrections, he reformed the prison system and introduced more humane treatment. He also pushed for the creation of a parole board.[52] As a result of Patterson's endeavors, Abbett not only blunted much of the criticism directed at his administration, but he also undermined Henry Little's influence in Monmouth County.

RESUMPTION OF THE BATTLE

Once the mess at the prison was cleaned up, Abbett returned his focus to the railroads. When the legislators reconvened, the governor sent a special message on April 28 in which he chastised them for stonewalling the investigation of the Morris and Essex Railroad. He also accused the Delaware, Lackawanna and Western Railroad, which leased the Morris and Essex line, of using improper influence in trying to quash the investigation.[53] In a highly charged political atmosphere, Abbett revealed that the Morris and Essex had scaled down its property valuations from $13 million to $3 million over the past thirty-two years. During this period, he calculated that the company had cheated the state out of $1.2 million in revenue. In addition, Abbett accused the Delaware, Lackawanna and Western of using New Jersey as a tax haven. The governor disclosed that it was keeping most of its freight cars, passenger coaches, locomotives, and heavy shop equipment in New Jersey as a way of avoiding taxes in Pennsylvania.

The assembly introduced a resolution calling for a joint committee to consider the issues raised by the governor and instructing it to report back at the next session of the legislature in 1887.[54] Spotting these delaying tactics as further stonewalling, Abbett persuaded the Democrats to defeat this resolution. Before they adjourned, the lawmakers passed an act that authorized the SBA to investigate the disputed tax returns and directed the attorney general to file a lawsuit to collect revenue illegally withheld. The SBA conducted its investigation and published its findings. Released publicly toward the end of the first Abbett administration, the report showed that the Morris and Essex had failed to pay proper taxes from 1853 to 1885, and it owed the state $1.2 million in back taxes.[55]

Meanwhile, Abbett's pursuit of the Morris and Essex was temporarily interrupted by the gubernatorial campaign of 1886. The Democrats ran Congressman Robert S. Green of Elizabeth, while the Republicans countered with former Congressman Benjamin F. Howey of Columbia. Howey was a manufacturer of slate and roofing materials. Green was a former judge and prosecutor. Cautious and conservative, he did not want to alienate the railroads. Most Democratic county leaders urged caution. Yet many saw the election as a referendum on Abbett's railroad tax law. The landmark measure remained a political lighting rod for more than two years after its enactment.

To everyone's surprise, the emotionally charged temperance issue dominated the campaign. Spurred on by groups like the Women's Christian Temperance Union, the liquor question became hot and heavy. In the eyes of teetotaling Protestants, especially Methodists and Presbyterians with the emotion stifling stoicism expected of them, drinking was a scourge that posed a dangerous threat to public morality. They

saw it as the root cause of crime, unemployment, vagrancy, and pauperism. No other question did more to inflame religious and ethnic antagonisms. As the gubernatorial campaign progressed, nativism and anti-Catholicism became inextricably intertwined with the temperance issue. Drunkenness and alcohol abuse were associated with foreign immigrants, in general, and Irish Catholics in particular. Even so, Green, whose Presbyterianism was well known, courted the German and Irish vote and gently embraced the liquor interests. With the support of Abbett's party machine, he fared extremely well in the cities.

The result was a Democratic victory on election day, November 2, 1886. Collecting 109,939 votes, Green defeated Howey who received 101,919 votes. Green's win was attributed to the damage inflicted by the third-party candidate, Clinton B. Fiske, who ran on the Prohibition ticket. Advocating total abstinence as his main platform, Fiske polled 19,808 votes. Since Green only beat Howey by 8,020 votes, the Republicans claimed that Fiske's candidacy cost Howey the election. The split in the temperance vote no doubt hurt Howey. In any event, the Democrats recaptured control of the general assembly, while the Republicans retained their hold on the senate.

After the election, Abbett learned of a new development. In late November 1886, the Court of Errors and Appeals, speaking through Justice David A. Depue, ruled that the Morris and Essex's irrepealable contract completely absolved it from paying any taxes under the 1884 law. Moreover, the court ruled that this tax immunity was conferred to its lessee: the Delaware, Lackawanna and Western Railroad.[56] This ruling strengthened the position of both railroads, but the judges placed an important restriction on their tax immunity. They ruled that the rolling stock, equipment, and other property that was not included under the terms of the original lease could be taxed by the state. That ruling gave Abbett added leverage to move against the Morris and Essex.

At a time of political transition from the Abbett to the Green administration, Abbett desperately needed to force the company to surrender its contract. The pressure and maneuvering intensified, which gave the combatants a sense of heightened urgency. Abbett kept the pressure on by threatening further legal action. In his third annual message, delivered in early January 1887, the governor indicated that he was directing Attorney General Stockton to commence litigation to determine the exact nature and extent of the railroad's exemptions. Rumor had it that he was bluffing, but it was no bluff. As Abbett explained:

> There appears to have been an attempt made to create in the public mind the impression that the state is doubtful of the result of the pending investigations, and it has been suggested that some compromise should be effected in the interest of the state. Should an attempt be made during the present session to pass any act which will interfere with the proper

prosecution of the state's claim against the company, it will not be done in the interest of the state. The officials having the matter in charge are satisfied that the claim made by the state is just and can be successfully maintained in the courts.[57]

Abbett made these remarks as his first term came to a close. Before leaving office, however, he delivered one final blow that brought the recalcitrant company to its knees. As a result of his legal research, he discovered that the corporate charter granted to the Morris and Essex in 1835 contained an escape clause that allowed the state not only to condemn its property after fifty years, but also to purchase it at its original cost. The fifty-year time limit had expired in 1885, which meant that the lessee railroad was legally vulnerable. Armed with this information, Abbett was now ready to play his trump card. He drafted a bill that authorized the attorney general to commence condemnation proceedings against the Morris and Essex. This political squeeze play made Samuel Sloan, the president of the parent company, extremely nervous.

Abbett figured that condemnation proceedings were his only recourse. He asked Assemblyman Thomas F. Noonan of Jersey City to introduce his bill (A-208). Alarmed by this maneuver, Samuel Sloan sent former Governor Joseph Bedle to testify against it. Bedle argued that only Jersey City would benefit from this legislation and that the stockholders of his company would suffer "irreparable injury."[58] Both Thomas Cator of the Anti-Monopoly League and Republican Assemblyman William Corbin argued to the contrary. Corbin put the problem into sharper focus:

We have built up the railroads of the state, and now when they have grown to the stature of giants, we find this one ready to throttle us. It is the Delaware, Lackawanna and Western Railroad, a corporation of Pennsylvania, that is today attempting to take advantage of the generosity extended to a feeble home corporation that planned to run a little railroad from Morristown to Newark fifty years ago.[59]

Sensing that an out-of-court settlement might be reached through a combination of carrot and stick, William Corbin attached an amendment to A-208. This amendment was worded so that the confiscation act would be nullified, if the Morris and Essex surrendered its tax exemption contract. Coming as it did near the end of Abbett's first term, the bill was not enacted before time ran out.

On January 18, 1887, Abbett handed over the executive reins of state government to his successor Robert Green. With Abbett no longer at the helm, the railroads sought to enter into negotiations with the state. As a former railroad attorney, Green had no stomach for continuing the fight with the railroads. Rather than insist on the payment of back taxes and the surrender of the Morris and Essex contract, he took the convenient

way out and submitted the matter to arbitration. Green had abandoned leadership on the tax issue and did not press for a settlement. Without any pressure from him, the arbitrators could not agree on the amount of tax arrears that was owed the state. The dispute languished for the next three years and remained unresolved when Green left the governor's office in 1890. He did not have either the political will or the staying power that Abbett possessed.

ENDNOTES

1 *Evening Journal*, September 14, 1883.
2 See "Inaugural Address of Leon Abbett," *New Jersey Legislative Documents* (1884), Document No. 2, p. 3.
3 *Ibid.*, 14.
4 *Ibid.*, 6.
5 *Ibid.*, 4.
6 Sackett, *Modern Battles of Trenton*, 1:230.
7 *Trenton True American*, February 14, 1884.
8 The authority for this is Lincoln Seffens, who was told by George L. Record of Jersey City. See Lincoln Steffens, "New Jersey: A Traitor State," in *McClure's Magazine* 25 (May 1905), 42.
9 See "Report of the Special Joint Committee on Taxation of the Property of Railroad and Other Corporations," (Camden, 1884), 15.
10 *Ibid.*, 4.
11 Testimony presented at the hearing is taken from the *Newark Evening News*, February 12, 1884.
12 *Newark Evening News*, February 12, 1884; Trenton *State Gazette*, March 11, 1884.
13 *Newark Evening News*, March 12, 1884.
14 *Trenton True American*, March 6, 1884.
15 Charles L. Corbin, *Taxation of Railroads in New Jersey* (Jersey City, 1883), 27–28.
16 *Trenton True American*, April 3, 1884.
17 Sackett, *Modern Battles of Trenton*, 1:235–236.
18 *Trenton True American*, April 5, 1884.
19 For a detailed account of the political maneuvering involved in the passage of the Joint Committee's bill, see Lincoln Steffens, "New Jersey: A Traitor State," *McClure's Magazine* 24 (April, 1905), 659.
20 *Trenton True American*, April 17, 1884.
21 *Newark Daily Advertiser*, April 23, 1884.
22 *New York Times*, April 19, 1884.
23 *State Gazette*, April 25, 1884.
24 *Newark Daily Advertiser*, April 23, 1884.
25 *Jersey City Argus*, April 23, 1884.
26 *New York Times*, April 19, 1884.
27 *New York Tribune*, April 23, 1884.
28 Quoted in Sackett, *Modern Battles of Trenton*, 1:241.
29 *New York Times*, April 23, 1884.
30 Quoted in Alexander McLean, *History of Jersey City* (Jersey City, 1895), 215.
31 *Newark Daily Advertiser*, March 1, 1884.
32 See *Little v. Bowers* 46 N.J.L. 3000 (1884).
33 For a detailed account of Barker Gummere's legal career, see Frederick W. Gnichtel, "Courts, Judges and Lawyers," in *A History of Trenton* (Princeton, 1929), vol. 2, 616–617.

34 See Charles W. Parker, "Some Reminiscences of Leading New Jersey Judges and Lawyers of the Later 19th Century," *53 Proceedings of the New Jersey Historical Society*, 229 (1935).

35 The story of the litigation unfolded in a series of articles that appeared in the *New York Times* beginning on November 5, 1885. The following account is taken from this source.

36 "Annual Report of the State Board of Assessors" (1885), 46.

37 New Jersey Legislative Documents (1886), no. 1, p. 6.

38 *Central Railroad Company v. State Board of Assessors* 48 N.J.L. 1 (1886).

39 Charles Robson, *The Biographical Encyclopaedia of New Jersey of the Nineteenth Century* (Philadelphia, Galaxy Publishing, 1877), 33, 505, 551. See also, Hamilton Schuyler, *A History of St. Michael's Church* (Princeton, Princeton University Press, 1926), 200–201.

40 Quoted in Charles Fairman, *Mr. Justice Miller and the Supreme Court 1862–1890* (Cambridge, Harvard University Press, 1939), 374.

41 Quoted in the *New York Times*, February 20, 1886.

42 Special Message of Governor Leon Abbett concerning the decision of the Supreme Court, February 23, 1886.

43 *State Board of Assessors v. Central Railroad Company* 48 N.J.L. 146 (1886).

44 48 N.J.L. 146, 305–306 (1886).

45 Minutes of the General Assembly (1886), 971.

46 *Newark Daily Advertiser*, February 25, 1884.

47 Second Annual Message of Governor Leon Abbett, January 16, 1886.

48 A detailed account of the Laverty impeachment trail can be found in 9 *New Jersey Law Journal* 158 (1886). See also Edward Q. Keasbey, *The Courts and Lawyers of New Jersey* (New York, 1912), 622–624; *Senate Journal* (1886), 905–959.

49 New Jersey Legislative Manual (1885), 194–195.

50 *New York Times*, April 22, 1886.

51 *New York Times*, April 23, 1886.

52 See James Leiby, *Charity and Correction in New Jersey* (New Brunswick, Rutgers University Press, 1967), 141.

53 Special Message of Governor Leon Abbett, April 28, 1886.

54 Minutes of the Votes and Proceedings of the General Assembly (1886), 995–996.

55 "Annual Report of the State Board of Assessors" (Trenton, 1887), 64.

56 *State Board of Assessors v. Morris and Essex Railroad Company* 49 N.J.L. 193 (1886).

57 New Jersey Legislative Documents (1887), No. 1, 10.

58 *Trenton True American*, March 3, 4, 1887.

59 *Trenton True American*, March 8, 1887.

New Jersey's First Urban Governor

Abbett's attention, energy, and determination in his first term were directed almost entirely to subduing the recalcitrant railroads in his long-running battle with them. But he also had to deal in a timely and practical fashion with other pressing public issues. In a time of great fiscal constraint, the problems of the cities were a major concern to him. These were not conventional times; social demographics were changing rapidly as the newest wave of immigrants arrived in New Jersey. A human tide of foreigners kept arriving all the time to seek a new life and employment in its industrial cities. Wrenching changes brought about by intractable poverty, street crime, illiteracy, child labor, and mental illness were accelerating in a rapidly changing state.

As New Jersey shifted from a farm-based economy to a factory-based economy, it was one of the first states confronted with explosive urbanization. In the 1880s and early 1890s, its demographic profile changed dramatically in urban population and density, a profile that had been shifting over the past several decades. Gradually but ever so persistently, New Jersey had become irrevocably an urban state with its burgeoning thirty-three cities. Given his predisposition as a lifelong city dweller, it is hardly surprising that Abbett became one of the first urban governors in America. Confronted with the problems encountered by its growing cities, he was primarily concerned with urban affairs, though he did not neglect the rural agricultural areas and the farm economy.

Surprisingly, Abbett was one of the rare major party politicians who advocated the cause of New Jersey's black citizens. Shortly after his inauguration, he intervened in a racial incident that portrayed the circle of discrimination, degradation, and prejudice to which blacks were subjected. On January 26, 1884, the members of the First Baptist

Church in Hackensack were denied the right to bury their black sexton, Samuel Bass who was the son of a former slave, in an all-white cemetery. The racially mixed congregation had purchased a burial plot from the Hackensack Cemetery Company and received permission to bury him in its graveyard. When the superintendent discovered that the deceased was black, he notified the coroner who advised him not to receive the body without the expressed approval of the cemetery trustees. After a hastily arranged meeting, the trustees revoked their earlier permission, citing a restrictive covenant in the company's charter that allowed them to refuse burial to any "objectionable person." It was blatant racism.

News of the revocation did not reach the mourners until they had gathered at the Baptist church. The funeral was attended by blacks and whites, and at its conclusion, the Reverend R. M. Harrison, who was pastor of the church, informed those present that they would not be able to bury their beloved sexton in the white cemetery. The body of the deceased was taken back to his residence and subsequently buried in the "Negro cemetery," located on the remote outskirts of town. The *Bergen Index* described the area as "a wild, bleak, desolate spot" on Moonachee Road, where cattle grazed.[1]

The next day every major newspaper in the greater New York metropolitan area carried the story. Almost overnight, this racial incident became a cause celebre. Many people felt that the trustees had acted egregiously. Feelings ran high, especially among blacks and sympathetic whites who saw the injustice. Outraged by this turn of events, Reverend Harrison denounced the action taken by the trustees as "bigoted, unchristianlike and contrary to the spirit of our institutions."[2] He told the press that his congregation would make every effort to ascertain whether the civil rights of the deceased had been violated.

GUBERNATORIAL INTERVENTION AND PASSAGE OF THE NEGRO BURIAL BILL

Now the story broke wide open. The news of the incident reached Abbett on January 27. Wasting no time, he immediately intervened in the dispute. The governor's timing stunned even his staunchest supporters. On January 28, in an unusual display of gubernatorial prerogative, he sent a special message to the legislature, which focused public attention on the issue and framed the ensuing debate. While compassion and social justice motivated the governor, his call for corrective action evinced a fair and dispassionate consideration of the issues. The incident deepened his understanding of what it meant to be black in racist America. His eloquent and rational message leapt far ahead of its time:

The right of the cemetery company to make rules and regulations as to interment is limited to making those that are reasonable and lawful. The regulation that refused a Christian burial to the body of a deceased citizen on the ground of color is not, in my judgment, a reasonable regulation, and therefore the church had the right to make the interment. The state should not attempt to control individuals in their private and social relations as long as they do not interfere with the rights of others. But the Legislature should see that the civil and political rights of all men, whether white or black, are protected, and, when infringed or violated, that punishment should follow. It ought not to be tolerated in this state that a corporation whose existence depends upon the legislative will, and whose property is exempt from taxation because of its religious uses, should be permitted to make a distinction between the white man and the black man. The church and the friends of the deceased may have a remedy in the courts, but the necessity of burial is immediate, and the law's delay would render practically useless the assertion of any such legal right. I therefore recommend the passage of a law which shall make such a refusal, based on color, a criminal offense, with such penalty as shall prevent a recurrence of such an act.[3]

Abbett's carefully worded statement was a worthy stimulus to dialogue. It represented a dramatic change in his attitude toward blacks since his earlier Copperhead days. More and more Abbett had come to realize that adapting to a changing society was essential for him to govern effectively. The realization had come hard and late, but the realization had come to him that racism belonged to the past. No longer did he oppose the advancement of African-Americans. In an amazing turnabout, he now became an advocate for civil rights legislation.

In making this decision, Abbett took considerable risk. Although he knew he was leaving himself open to powerful criticism, he felt it was the right thing to do. Trenton vibrated with speculation about his motives. Skeptical politicians claimed that he did so solely to cultivate a new voting constituency. Political ambitions may have made him more accessible to group pressures. Whatever the motivation, few informed observers could quarrel with the key fact that as the only statewide elected official in New Jersey, he represented all its people, both black and white. As such, he demonstrated that he could rise above partisan politics and claim authority to lead in the name of the governor. He felt that it was a reasonable exercise of executive power.

Secure in his convictions, Abbett drafted a bill (A-195) that made it illegal for a private cemetery to refuse burial on the basis of "race, creed, color or previous condition of servitude." The media quickly dubbed it the "Negro Burial" bill. The governor asked Assemblyman Frank O. Cole of Jersey City to introduce his bill. Cole was a Republican and a highly decorated Civil War veteran. Presumably, Abbett's intent was to engender bipartisan support for the measure. This

was not a policy brought forward by overwhelming popular demand. Nor was there a political groundswell that existed in its behalf. It was simply a matter of executive leadership. As Abbett struggled to take the policy initiative, he showed an inclination to pay attention to such unusual events and to make sure that his ideas were understood, and then acted on.

After the Civil War, jurisdiction over the civil rights of the descendants of slaves became the core political controversy between state and federal authorities. Abbett's intervention goaded the legislature into action, but not without stirring controversy and local resistance. Passing legislation to deal with racial problems proved much harder than expected. Some legislators were antagonistic or indifferent; they resented what they perceived as his unwarranted intrusion into a strictly local matter. Others saw him intruding on the legislative process and usurping their prerogative. Still others balked at his lecturing them. They felt that he was using the governorship as a bully pulpit.

Press reaction varied accordingly. Some Republican newspapers indulged in overreaction. The *Newark Daily Advertiser* took Abbett to task for the way in which he delivered his message. Dripping with sarcasm, its editor concluded, "This method of communication, partaking of the nature of a lecture, is somewhat after the style of Governor Benjamin Butler of Massachusetts and further imitation of that illustrious statesman could hardly be recommended."[4] The *New York Times* agreed with this assessment, but it at least acknowledged the political risks involved. "In view of the fact that the Governor is a Democrat, without presumably special interest in the colored race, the document created a decided impression."[5]

Embarrassed by all the adverse publicity, the cemetery trustees felt compelled to defend their position. In a letter released to the press, John S. Wells, the company secretary, offered this explanation:

The colored people of Hackensack have a cemetery of their own, obtained on their own desire, through the assistance of their white friends, some of whom are trustees of the Hackensack Cemetery. They have themselves no desire to bury their friends among the whites, but want all interments they can get for their own ground. The present disturbance is not their doing, but has been fomented by a few mischievous white members of the congregation where the colored man was sexton. I am told that the great majority of respectable people in that congregation entirely disapprove of their action. The trustees of the cemetery, with perhaps one exception, have no personal objection to the burial of a colored man in their territory. They are, however, only trustees for the parties who own lots and have friends buried there, some of whom strongly object. They deemed it their duty to prohibit the burial, as they had a

legal right to do. The trustees are bound to respect the feelings of those whose friends have already been interred in the cemetery, even though they be the outgrowth of prejudice.[6]

This feeble justification of their actions barely masked the racism that lay behind it. To blacks, it was outright discrimination. In the legislative debate that followed, several lawmakers indicated that most of their white constituents were strongly opposed to a racially mixed cemetery. William Stainsby, the Republican senator from Essex County, was astonished to learn that there was not a graveyard in the entire city of Newark, except for the Catholic cemetery, in which blacks were allowed to be buried. The governor could not have asked for better evidence to justify the need for such legislation.

When Abbett attempted to structure his role along these lines, he crossed swords with Republican Senator James Youngblood of Morris County in a clash of egos that soon became public. Consumed in his own sense of self-importance, Youngblood was determined to kill the governor's bill, or at least to gut it. He amended the statute so that it would not apply to religious societies. This amendment would have exempted almost every cemetery in New Jersey. Therefore, Abbett opposed Youngblood's killer amendment. It was this stand that led to a clash between the two men in the privacy of the governor's office.

Behind closed doors, Abbett and Youngblood apparently engaged in a heated argument. Although there is no verbatim record of their conversation, the essence of what they said was revealed through the press. Youngblood was adamantly opposed to the idea of burial on demand. He argued that religious societies should be exempted from the statute. The First Presbyterian Church in Morristown, which he attended, extended burial privileges to those who had friends and relatives already buried there. He further argued that his church would now be legally required to bury anyone whose relatives requested as much. Abbett told the senator that he was mistaken about the intent of his statute. Burial on demand, in his view, was not the issue. Rather, it was that a private cemetery company, which received its charter from the state, should not be allowed to make a distinction on the basis of race for burying someone. Youngblood shot back that it was the governor who was mistaken. As tempers flared, Abbett pounded his fist on the table and informed the senator that he would veto the bill if Youngblood's amendment passed. "The legislature may pass any bill it chooses," he exclaimed, "I will veto any which I choose."[7] These were fighting words.

Such a statement was too much for Youngblood, whose volcanic temper got the best of him. He exploded in anger, abruptly terminated their meeting, and stomped out of the governor's office, slamming the big

mahogany door behind him. Clearly, Youngblood had underestimated the moral imperative behind the legislation. Still smarting from their encounter, he attacked Abbett on the floor of the senate. Youngblood explained his version of their meeting to his senate colleagues:

I had the temerity to speak to Governor Abbett concerning this bill when it came up for second reading in the Senate this evening. I desired his opinion about the bill. Had the governor quietly kicked me out of his office, I could not have more hastily folded the bill and left the chamber. I framed the bill in regard to this cemetery dispute to carry out the views in the governor's special message.

Intensifying their public feud, Youngblood added fuel to the fire by sarcastically remarking:

The governor will learn before the expiration of his three years in office that there are other people in the state besides himself. Personally, I do no care for his impudence. I do not care whether the bill meets the governor's approval or not. I wish to state publicly that I have been insulted by the governor. All senators calling upon him go into the executive chamber at the risk of being insulted.[8]

Naturally, Abbett's version of what had transpired differed significantly from that of Youngblood's. Asked by reporters about their encounter, the governor purposely downplayed it:

I am not aware that I insulted senator Youngblood either by word or action. He brought the bill into me and asked me for my views on it. I told him that the exemption in favor of religious societies did not meet with my approval. We argued about the matter until finally the senator told me that I did not understand it. I responded that I thought I understood it as fully as he did, whereupon he walked out. There was no exchange of words between us of an unfriendly character, and I had no idea that either of us had been insulted by the other until I heard of his complaint in the Senate chamber.[9]

Unruffled by Youngblood's antics, Abbett stood his ground and felt that his position was sound public policy. Despite Youngblood's opposition, the governor used the threat of his veto to get what he wanted. He bargained for the needed Republican votes in the senate that led to passage of his "Negro Burial" bill in its original language. No longer did Abbett remain a stranger to black America. He did all this while he was engaged in his fight with the railroads over taxation. Still miffed by their previous encounter, Youngblood opposed the governor's railroad tax program and later attempted to block his appointment of Allan McDermott to the State Board of Assessors. Both men, accustomed to being the focus of attention, would continually try to take center stage. Their formidable egos would continue to clash.

ENACTMENT OF THE PUBLIC ACCOMMODATIONS LAW

No sooner had the furor over the governor's meeting with Youngblood begun to subside than Abbett found himself embroiled in another troublesome dispute—the elimination of racial discrimination and segregation in public accommodations. In 1883, the U.S. Supreme Court had all but invalidated a strong federal Civil Rights Act that had been passed in 1875. It provided African-Americans with access to public facilities. The Waite Court ruled that Congress did not have the power to pass such a law, claiming that this power was reserved for the states.[10] Justice Joseph Bradley, who came from New Jersey, wrote the majority opinion. It narrowly ruled that Congress could only pass legislation to supercede discriminatory state laws. This judicial ruling clearly shifted the responsibility for antidiscrimination to the states.

Abbett did not duck the challenge presented by the Waite Court. He saw it as an opportunity for New Jersey to make its own policy and recommended passage of a public accommodations bill. The statute was worded so as to prohibit discrimination in public transportation, hotels and restaurants, barber shops, and theatres.[11] The legal remedy for any person aggrieved was to bring a lawsuit in the courts.

The power of the black vote in a highly competitive state like New Jersey pushed politicians into desegregating public facilities. So bitter was the feud between Republican Rush Burgess and Democrat John L. Armitage that they became embroiled in a fist fight on the floor of the general assembly. They were both Essex County assemblymen who represented districts in the city of Newark. The son of a former Confederate officer, Burgess had lived in Virginia before moving to New Jersey in 1878. Adamantly opposed to the public accommodations bill, he taunted the Democrats and accused them of hypocrisy. A lively orator, Burgess gave a partisan speech in which he declared, "No Democrat down deep in his heart favors this bill."[12] He then singled out Governor Abbett as "the biggest hypocrite of them all." When Armitage rose to defend his party leader, Burgess struck him in the face with his fist. A terrible fight ensued. The resulting publicity aroused public opinion and assured passage of the bill. A varnish manufacturer in private life, Armitage previously had introduced legislation calling for the reduction of tolls over the Newark plank road.

A number of northern states passed civil rights laws that in theory guaranteed equal access to public establishments. But the degree to which such laws were enforced was negligible. The opportunities for enforcement were limited, and no one was willing to bring a lawsuit. In this context, the New Jersey law placed both the psychological and the financial burdens on the offended party. There remained serious concerns about the meager enforcement penalties provided, but the law was a major step forward

nonetheless. The passage of such a law would have been unthinkable a few years earlier. Separation of the races, not integration, was the major goal of race policy in America during the 1880s. With the proliferation of Jim Crow laws in the South, it was a high tide of racism in the country.

THE CONVICT LABOR CONTROVERSY

Since organized labor had played such a pivotal role in Abbett's gubernatorial election, the governor was anxious to fulfill his campaign promise about convict labor. Labor leaders like John Hayes and Joseph McDonnell were taking an openly aggressive stance, castigating this practice as "unfair competition for free labor." They saw the possibility of labor reform on a wider scale, but before they could do anything, they first had to organize for political action. Thousands of workingmen, who had not been previously involved in politics, were recruited into the labor movement, expanding the ranks of the state Federation of Labor and the circulation of the labor press.

The issue of contract convict labor had been thoroughly studied by a legislative committee in 1883. Its work resulted in a written report that was used as a departure point for subsequent discussions with the governor. They recommended three policy alternatives: (1) a piece-price system; (2) a public account scheme; or (3) a state-use plan. According to James Leiby:

Under the piece-price system, prison authorities arranged with businessmen to put prisoners to work on goods that the businessmen hoped to sell. The businessmen put up the capital, sometimes supplied instructors, bought the finished product at a set price per piece, and of course marketed it. Under the public account system the prison authorities went into business for themselves, supplying all the factors of production and marketing the product; under the state-use system they sold their products only to institutions of government—a captive but supposedly quite limited market.[13]

After much debate on the subject, a consensus emerged in shaping the policy agenda. Abbett had correctly identified the attributes of the problem and the options for its resolution. He drafted legislation that abolished convict labor in "all prisons, jails, penitentiaries and reformatories." The governor's bill (A-61) was introduced on January 14, 1884, by Democratic Assemblyman William Harrigan of Newark. Harrigan was an Irish immigrant, who was engaged in the mineral water business. In 1883, he had succeeded in getting a bill passed that required all goods manufactured in the state prison to be stamped with the name of that institution on them. Weighing the three alternatives that were available to

him, Abbett decided to do away with the piece-price system and substituted in its place the state-use plan. This innovation satisfied organized labor in that it kept prison-made goods off the open market and greatly limited their sale. It was a "win-win" situation for the governor.

Abbett may have selected prison reform as his first labor bill, because it best suited his plans to build a legislative coalition that would pass succeeding labor bills, and a public coalition that would pressure the legislature for these bills. This coalition consisted of trade unionists, labor reformers, and socialist radicals, including the Knights of Labor, and the New Jersey Labor Congress, which had changed its name in 1883 to the Federation of Organized Trades and Labor Unions of the State of New Jersey. Their most vocal and articulate lobbyist was labor editor Joseph McDonnell, who spearheaded the federation's legislative committee. Committed to radical change in the economic and social order, he was the moving force behind this promising coalition. The working class, increasingly of immigrant origin, was making its voice heard through his newspaper. What emerged was a policy process that mixed outside and inside participation.

Labor as an organized movement was steadily gaining political strength in New Jersey during Abbett's first term. The workforce grew by leaps and bounds. Of the 126 unions that then existed, 98 were organized in the years between 1880 and 1887. Union membership in the Knights of Labor expanded to 40,275 dues-paying members. Trade unions could claim another 18,000 members. Most of these workers resided in the growing industrial cities. The three most urbanized counties of Essex, Hudson, and Passaic accounted for nearly ninety percent of the total union membership.[14] So the pressure built within the Abbett administration, and with notable public support and debate, to improve the working conditions of the urban labor force. The governor's strategy relied on forcing state government to act by applying pressure from constituency groups at the grass-roots level.

THE PRESIDENTIAL ELECTION OF 1884

On June 18, 1884, Princeton College awarded Leon Abbett an honorary doctor of law degree at its commencement ceremonies. He was nominated for this honor by the Reverend Samuel B. Dodd, who headed the Stevens Institute of Technology in Hoboken and served as a Princeton trustee. At the same ceremony, Princeton also honored President Chester Arthur and U.S. Supreme Court Justice John Marshall Harlan.

In July 1884, Governor Abbett attended the National Democratic Convention, held in Chicago. His name was mentioned as a possible presidential contender, because of his success in taxing the railroads and championing the rights of labor. The *New York Times* observed, "Abbett had some hope that he might be struck by presidential lightning."[15] But such lightning never did strike. Initially, Abbett supported Governor Benjamin Butler of Massachusetts for president. A lawyer and business-man, Butler had been a former Union Army general, state legislator, and congressman. He appealed to the deprived urban lower classes in the Bay State, but he was considered too radical to win the nomination. Despised in the South for his harsh rule as military commander of New Orleans during Reconstruction, he was unacceptable to the southern states. Rejected by the Democrats, Butler promptly changed his party affiliation and wound up as the presidential candidate of the Greenback party in 1884.

When Butler failed to catch fire, Abbett threw his support to Congressman Samuel J. Randall of Pennsylvania. Randall, the former Speaker of the House Representatives, was a high tariff protectionist. Labor leaders Terrence Powderly and Samuel Gompers endorsed him. Asked to place Randall's name in nomination, Abbett gave a rousing speech that he concluded by saying, "Randall would sweep New Jersey like a great cyclone. He is a friend of laborers everywhere. The convention can do no better than nominate him."[16] But Randall, like Benjamin Butler, failed to catch fire.

Grover Cleveland, New York's forty-seven-year-old governor, won the 1884 Democratic nomination and then went on to win the presidency. As the former sheriff of Buffalo County and the former mayor of Buffalo, Cleveland had earned a reputation for honesty and integrity. While serving as governor of New York, he was known as "Grover the Good." Tammany's Democratic boss John Kelly disliked him intensely, but Tammany's hostility toward Cleveland won him the support of reformers in both parties. His opponent, James G. Blaine, was an unabashed spoils politician and the most popular Republican of his generation.

When Blaine's name was presented to the Republican convention in Chicago, the effect was electrifying. He won the nomination without much trouble. But liberal Republicans, who were displeased with him, bolted the party. They charged that Blaine "wallowed in spoils like a rhinoceros in an African pool."[17] These dissident Mugwumps held protest meetings in Boston and New York and announced they would support the Democratic nominee if he proved acceptable. This split in the GOP ranks proved harmful to Blaine. Scandal-mongering dominated the campaign, issues were submerged, and voters were asked to choose between Blaine, who was "delinquent in office but blameless in private life," and Cleveland, who was "a model of official integrity, but culpable in his personal relations." It was soon disclosed that Cleveland had fathered a child out of wedlock.

Cleveland did little campaigning, preferring to remain hard at work in the executive chamber in Albany. In the closing days of the cam-

paign, Blaine stumbled badly. For him, October 29 was "black Wednesday." Urged by his managers to make an appearance in New York City, he attended a meeting of several hundred pro-Blaine Protestant clergymen held at the Fifth Avenue Hotel. Delivering a warm welcoming address, the Reverend Samuel D. Burchard, a Presbyterian minister, concluded his remarks by saying, "We are Republicans, and don't propose to leave our party and identify ourselves with the party whose antecedents have been Rum, Romanism and Rebellion." This indiscretion caused a sensation in the press. Irish Catholics were particularly offended by Burchard's inflammatory remark. They considered it both a religious insult and an ethnic slur.

Later that evening, Blaine attended a lavish fund-raising dinner at the fashionable Delmonico's restaurant, where he hobnobbed with millionaires like Jay Gould, John Jacob Astor, and Russell Sage. The next day Joseph Pulitzer's *New York World* ran a front-page headline that read, "The Royal Feast of Belshazzar Blaine and the Money Kings." The story was accompanied with a cartoon depicting the "Plumed Knight" dining in luxury with the rich while a starving poor man and his family begged for crumbs outside the restaurant. With the country still in the throes of a depression, it is hard to say which caused him more harm—Burchard's remarks or the Belshazzar feast.[18]

Although Abbett was not fond of Cleveland or the Bourbon Democrats, he campaigned for him and the entire Democratic ticket. Cleveland won New Jersey on November 4, 1884, carrying the state by a plurality of 4,412 votes. Ticket splitting gave both sides some lower offices. Few Democrats in New Jersey rode into office on Cleveland's coattails. Quite the contrary, the Republicans gained control of both houses of the state legislature—a control they would not relinquish for the remaining two years of Abbett's first term. So the election was a definite setback for the governor. The Republican press interpreted the results as a renunciation of his policies.

Having a Democrat in the White House did not prove beneficial to Abbett. He and Cleveland differed on domestic policy, especially where labor was concerned. In fact, they were completely opposite in ideology and style, and as such they represented hostile wings of the Democratic party. Cleveland used his presidential power to promote big business, civil service reform, and tariff reduction. His low tariff policy was based on the old laissez-faire ideal of buyers and sellers conducting business transactions in an untrammeled market. He found the politics of spoils distasteful. Conservative in his outlook, Cleveland showed no genuine sympathy for workers, even though he tried to pass himself off as a friend of labor. Orestes Cleveland, the mayor of Jersey City, had advised him to include in his letter accepting the presidential nomination a polite reference to trade unions, but "Grover the Good" refused to do

so.[19] All of which indicated that Abbett had not misread the president. Cleveland's attitude toward labor was about as negative as that of Republican Judge Jonathan Dixon.

Labor continued to remain a source of tension within the Democratic party. Abbett distanced himself from Cleveland as quickly and as far as possible. He formed what looked like a promising alliance with New York Governor David B. Hill, who had succeeded Cleveland in Albany. Hill was a spoils politician and much more to Abbett's liking. They shared similar political views and eventually grew dissatisfied with Cleveland's leadership.

Not surprisingly, Cleveland made U.S. Senator John McPherson his political agent and distributor of federal patronage in New Jersey. The president needed McPherson's support for his tariff reduction program. He also confided in men like Henry Little and Orestes Cleveland, both of whom hated Abbett. Clearly, there was no love lost between Abbett and Grover Cleveland. They held each other in mutual contempt. Rebuffed by the White House on the distribution of patronage, Abbett retaliated by successfully blocking Cleveland's nomination of George McClelland as secretary of war.[20] He also opposed the president's economic policy, speaking out against it publicly more than once.

GODFATHER AT A BLACK BAPTISM

A month after the presidential election, Abbett participated in an interracial baptism in Newark. On December 30, 1884, he acted as godfather for a black infant boy. The boy's father, William H. DeKalb, was an ardent Democrat. DeKalb was a barber by trade, but he also worked as a messenger at City Hall. Abbett first met him while he was campaigning for governor in 1883. At that time, he promised to attend the baptism of DeKalb's first child.

The Reverend J. Borvden Massiah of Saint Phillip's Episcopal Church performed the ceremony at the home of the boy's parents at 15 Maiden Lane. After handing a prayer book to Governor Abbett, the clergyman called for the baby. William DeKalb and the godmother, Miss Lizzie Thompson, who was described in the press as "a comely young colored woman," advanced to the center table with the child. Mrs. DeKalb stood beside Miss Thompson, who held the baby in her arms while the clergyman read the service. "What shall this child be named?" asked the Reverend Massiah. "Leon Abbett DeKalb," replied the governor. Also attending the ceremony were several prominent Newark Democrats, including Mayor Joseph E. Haynes, Judge Ludlow McCarter, Sheriff William H. Brown, and city aldermen James F. Connelly and James Smith, Jr.[21]

There was enormous symbolism in this baptismal event. An inter-racial baptism was a rare occurrence in the Gilded Age. Coming at a time when segregation and racism flourished in America, it took courage for Abbett to participate as godfather. He presented himself as a personal friend of a black family. This brought out the idealistic side of his nature and the humane values that he espoused. But it was also good politics.

Abbett's activism in behalf of blacks engendered scathing comments. Noah Brooks, the editor of the Republican *Newark Daily Advertiser*, taunted him by writing, "Like a hen with one chicken, the Democracy is unreasonably proud of its colored convert, and since City Messenger DeKalb first named the youngest scion of his house Leon Abbett DeKalb there has been a constant fluttering all along the Democratic line in anticipation of the christening of the Governor's protege."[22]

Manton Marble, editor of the vastly popular *New York World* and the leading Democratic journalist of his generation, applauded Abbett for his racial tolerance and his work to engender better race relations:

> The marked liberal advance in all directions is especially emphasized when a Democratic Governor of a Democratic state not only stands as sponsor at the baptism of a black baby, but handsomely contributes and confers his own name. For the present the cooperative christening cere-mony is a serene assurance that old party lines, including color lines and clothes lines, are breaking down, and that real democracy is nowadays demonstrating the still closer connections in the various branches of the brotherhood of man—in a way, too, that would have astonished the natives only a few years ago.[23]

FIGHTING FOR THE CAUSE OF LABOR

While Abbett spent much of his time fighting the railroads, he did not neglect the interests of labor. Arbitration to settle grievances between workers and management was legally recognized and a process estab-lished, but it was completely voluntary. Archaic criminal conspiracy laws were repealed. Employers were now required to report the deaths of fac-tory workers who were killed by industrial accidents and by exposure to workplace hazards. Too often these accidental deaths had gone unreport-ed, which made it virtually impossible to determine their cause. Another statute imposed fines on employers who dismissed or fired their employ-ees without first giving them adequate notice.

Most important of all, the staff of the Bureau of Factories and Workshops was enlarged and its enforcement powers were strengthened. Factories were required to install fire escapes, safeguards for open elevator shafts and hoistways, and adequate ventilation and sanitary arrangements.

Some statutes required protective covering for dangerous machinery, belts, and gears. Still other laws limited the employment of children in dangerous occupations and required factories to provide seats and suitable dressing rooms for women. Workers were protected from usury by making it unlawful for any person to assign their wages. Other laws incorporated cooperatives and home building and loan associations. These financial institutions, modeled after the People's Banks in Germany, had begun in southern New Jersey and gradually spread throughout the rest of the state.

Change in the way industrial workers were treated would only come, trade unionists now believed, if labor men assumed regulatory positions within the administration. Abbett heard the cry of organized labor. Moving quickly, he nominated Richard Dowdall, a Newark hatter and an outspoken trade unionist, as chief of the newly created Bureau of Factories and Workshops. But the Republican senate turned him down because in its view Dowdall was seen as "a labor extremist, a demagogue identified with the Irish Land League, and altogether an unfit person."[24]

Brought up short by Dowdall's rejection, the governor then nominated Lawrence T. Fell, a hat manufacturer in Orange. If the conservative senators thought him a "safe choice" because of his background, they were greatly mistaken. Fell turned out to be what we would now call a "public interest lobbyist," campaigning for improved conditions of industrial employment. He took his work seriously and launched a crack-down on filthy, unsanitary, and unsafe factory conditions. What is more, he ordered factory owners to make the necessary modifications to correct these abuses.

At Fell's urging, Abbett beefed up the bureau's enforcement staff with two deputy inspectors. He appointed Joseph McDonnell of Paterson and Goldsmith P. Hall of Millville to fill these positions. McDonnell was the lobbyist for the state Federation of Labor; Hall was secretary of the Knights of Labor. For the first time in the history of the state, New Jersey had genuine factory inspections. The governor also named another union man, Charles H. Simmerman of Bridgeton, as secretary of the Bureau of Labor Statistics. A glassblower by trade, Simmerman was active in the trade union movement. These appointments gave organized labor some representation in the bureaucracy.

Child labor was a serious social problem. The state Bureau of Labor Statistics reported that 5,591 children were employed in the silk industry alone. Child illiteracy was rampant. The state Department of Public Instruction estimated that of the 364,156 school-age children living in New Jersey, approximately 101,571 received no education whatsoever. These statistics were disturbing to Abbett. He obtained legislation that raised the minimum employment age for boys to twelve and for girls, fourteen. Children under eighteen were not allowed to operate dangerous

machinery. As a companion measure, Abbett drafted the Compulsory Education Act of 1885 that made it mandatory for children to attend elementary school. This legislation introduced the truant officer, whose duty it was to made sure that youngsters did not play hooky from school.

In addition to enforcing the factory laws, Fell's bureau also was responsible for enforcing the compulsory school law. The chief inspector wrote in his first report, "Old faces and dwarfed forms are the offspring of the child labor system. In a country where life is so intense as it is in this, where so much is expected in a little time, childhood and youth should be a time of free physical growth."[25] Appalled by the exploitation of children and the dreadful conditions in which they worked, Fell described in his second report the widespread illiteracy among them:

> Nearly all the children examined were naturally bright and intelligent, but neglect, years of work and their general surroundings had left sad faces upon their youthful forms and minds. There is no exaggeration in saying that threefourths of the work-children know absolutely nothing. The greatest ignorance exists on the most commonplace questions. Most of these children have never been inside of a schoolhouse, and the majority have either been at school for too short a period to learn anything or have forgotten the little instruction they received.[26]

Despite continuing opposition from industrialists and scrutiny by the media and legislators, Fell pressed on. What he learned as chief factory inspector made him a public advocate for remedial and protective labor legislation. He and his two deputies were subjected to withering attack, especially when it was disclosed that both Hall and McDonnell were trade unionists. Republican legislators in 1885 and again in 1886 sought to abolish the bureau. This barrage of criticism led to the removal of Hall and McDonnell. Fell praised them by saying, "The manner in which they have acted is sufficient proof that the advocates of labor interests are fitted to fill the highest [public] labor offices."[27] The governor, in conjunction with the pressure exerted by the state Federation of Labor, frustrated Republican efforts to abolish the bureau. Fell, with strong backing from Abbett, continued as bureau chief until 1895 when a hostile Republican Senate finally rejected his reappointment and forced his departure.

By fighting these battles, Abbett had thrust himself in the vanguard of political leadership for labor legislation. He made the workers' cause his cause, although some statutes were poorly written. Industrialists fiercely opposed the enactment of such labor laws. Few passed without bitter legislative battles, and some became law only after crippling amendments had weakened them. Despite the fact that the Republicans controlled both houses in 1885 and 1886, Abbett could still get his labor program approved, mainly because of the coalition that he had put together. Joseph McDonnell and the federation pressured reluctant Republican legislators

to vote for these bills. As promised, the governor appointed labor men to important positions within his administration. Overall, the rise of the labor movement reflected the changing nature of New Jersey politics.

ABBETT'S MANAGEMENT INFLUENCE AND PATRONAGE APPOINTMENTS

On September 1, 1885, Abbett attended a picnic at Saint Joseph's Protectory for wayward boys in Arlington. He gave a short speech in which he stated that it was important for him as governor to observe the work being done at this institution. Careful to point out that the Catholic Protectory received no state funds, he praised its director Father Curran for the job that he was doing. He cited its vocational education program in particular.[28] Appearing on the same platform with the governor were Bishop Winand M. Wigger, Mayor Joseph E. Haynes of Newark, and Mayor Herman L. Timken of Hoboken.

Increased population growth in the cities resulted in the proliferation of poverty, crime, illiteracy, and mental illness. These social problems put considerable strain on the capacity of such existing state institutions as prisons, reformatories, insane asylums, and almshouses. Party politics and patronage also influenced the growth and expansion of these institutions. They were viewed as sources of jobs and contracts that politicians could bestow on the party faithful. New Jersey built several new institutions during the post-Civil War era.

Abbett had no trouble in finding his own personal style as an administrator. He moved aggressively to gain control of a fledgling bureaucracy and to reduce the large deficit that he inherited. As chief executive, Abbett fought hard for the right to appoint and remove administrators. By clearing out the old and bringing in new blood, he could start with a fresh slate. In this administrative shake-up, both Republicans and holdover Randolph Democrats were dismissed. A case in point was his removal of Ellis A. Apgar, the state superintendent of public instruction, who was a renowned professional educator. To Abbett's way of thinking, Apgar was a Republican who had to go and that was all there was to it. He selected Edwin O. Chapman, the former school superintendent of Jersey City, to replace Apgar. While Chapman was familiar with the problems of urban education, he lacked Apgar's brilliance and distinction. Ironically, Chapman had been removed as the local school superintendent by the Republicans in 1871 when they stripped Jersey City of home rule. No doubt Abbett wanted to settle this old political score.

In similar fashion, Abbett removed Republicans Charles Elmer and John Maclean, Jr. from the state Board of Education. Their removal caused a storm of protest voiced by the public education lobby. A

professional academic administrator, Maclean had served as president of Princeton College from 1853 to 1868 and had also played a major role in establishing New Jersey's public school system. Charles Elmer was a lawyer and a long-time trustee of the Normal School in Trenton. Both men were highly regarded, but this made no difference to Abbett. He was a spoils politician practicing spoils politics.

Abbett worked hard to restructure the leadership of the Democratic party in New Jersey. To secure greater control over the party, he displaced old-line Yankee Democrats with new urban ethnics. He used his patronage power to reward his friends and to strengthen his party machine. In March 1885, he appointed former Congressman Miles Ross of New Brunswick to the state Riparian Commission that leased the state's tidelands to the railroads. The money derived from this source of revenue was dedicated to the school fund. Ross, the Democratic county leader in Middlesex, was rumored to be appointed by Abbett solely to advance his own political ambitions. If Abbett was to become the next U.S. senator, he wanted Ross indebted to him. Ross was in the coal business and worked as the chief lobbyist for the Lehigh Valley Railroad. This glaring conflict of interest made his appointment quite objectionable, but such ethical lapses did not seem to bother Abbett.

Republicans, of course, attacked Abbett's appointment of Ross as inappropriate. It also drew the blistering fire of partisan newspaper editors. For example, the *New York Tribune* chortled, "The nomination reduces some of the Governor's recent anti-railroad professions to the verge of absurdity."[29] Abbett blithely ignored this criticism. Most of his appointments were unabashedly partisan, whether they were highly coveted state judgeships and county prosecutors, or small-time patronage like fish and game wardens, and county commissioners of deeds. There was much public mutual recrimination. What made the Republicans so furious is that many of Abbett's appointments contravened the Civil Service Reform Act of 1884 that was designed to establish a professional cadre of public servants. After all, this act was passed by the Democratic assembly and signed by the governor. So Abbett was not blameless.

Suddenly the debate became far more emotional and vituperative than it had previously been. Abbett found himself a target of substantial criticism. Living up to his reputation for fierce partisanship, Republican state Senator John Griggs of Paterson attacked the governor on March 18, 1885, on the floor of the senate for his patronage excesses. His disdain for Abbett was vitriolic. In a scathing diatribe, which the press described as a "wild speech," Griggs accused him of abusing his appointive power and violating the public trust. "The Governor has not merely filled boards with Democrats," Griggs said with the utmost contempt, "but with Abbett Democrats. He has carried his partisanship to the counties and dictated appointments, not to please Democrats, but to

advance his own personal ambitions. The spectacle that he has presented is one to shame the whole people. We say to the present chief executive: 'You have abused the power entrusted to you by the state and it shall no longer be entrusted to you.'[30] It should be noted that Griggs had made an unsuccessful attempt to become senate president in 1885, but he finally succeeded in 1886.

In any event, Griggs had thrown down the gauntlet. The Republicans were especially angry at Abbett because he had totally abandoned the long-standing tradition of making judicial appointments on a nonpartisan basis. Previous governors had followed this practice fairly consistently. The most dramatic example was Governor Joseph Bedle's appointment of Jonathan Dixon to the state supreme court in 1875. Bedle, of course, was a Democrat, while Dixon was a Republican. An independent judiciary was viewed by many as a sacred cow, if not the foundation stone of democracy, in which partisan politics should not intrude. Abbett did not share this viewpoint. He appointed mostly Democratic judges, though he did reappoint Dixon.

Republicans were furious at Abbett not only for his failure to appoint Republican judges, but also for the cavalier way and almost dismissive manner in which he circumvented civil service rules. Their 1886 party platform expressed their displeasure in rather strong terms:

It was promised by the Democratic party that once entrusted with power, the public service should be elevated and improved by strict conformity to the principle of civil service reform. As a matter of fact, the tone and quality of the public service has been lowered by the removal of honest, competent and efficient officials for purely partisan reasons, and the appointment of persons, also for partisan reasons, who were in many cases, incompetent and unfit for the places assigned them.[31]

Coupled with this barrage of criticism was the accusation that Abbett was an autocrat who was determined to control the executive branch of state government. Smarting from what they viewed as the autocratic rule of "Czar Abbett," the Republicans could hardly wait to retaliate. In 1885, as Senator Griggs had predicted, they stripped the governor of most of his statutory appointments. They could do so because the power of appointment was statutory, not constitutional. No longer could Abbett appoint the state treasurer, state comptroller, trustees of state reformatories and mental hospitals, commissioners of pilotage, county commissioners of deeds, police justices for Newark and Jersey City, a state director of railroads and canals, commissioners of the sinking fund, riparian commissioners, and even lowly fish and game wardens.[32] In stripping Abbett of these executive appointments, the Republican legislators usurped this power for themselves. Thus, they named Republicans Edward J. Anderson as state comptroller and John J. Toffey as state

treasurer. When it came to the judiciary, Abbett was divested of his power to appoint district court judges.

This was partisan warfare at its worst. Even the conservative *New York Times*, which professed no great love for Abbett, disapproved of such outlandish partisanship. Its editor rebuked the Republicans for what they had done:

> It is a bad scheme, and particularly bad as it relates to the judiciary. Governor Abbett is the author of certain declarations touching partisan use of the appointing power which are unsound and absurd, but if he applies them in practice he and the party electing him can be held responsible. On the other hand, the Republican contrivance applies precisely the same views and is equally mischievous, while it will be practically impossible to call its authors and those who carry it out to account.[33]

While this was going on, Abbett made no pretensions about his desire to control the bureaucracy through political appointments that reached far down in the ranks of departments and agencies. For his victory over Republican Jonathan Dixon had been too narrow and his campaign too publicly divisive for him not to appoint some men of substance and ideas. As we have already seen, Allan McDermott was put in charge of the State Board of Assessors, Lawrence Fell was named to head the Bureau of Factories and Workshops, and John Patterson was brought in to replace Patrick Laverty as state prison warden. All these men were Abbett Democrats. What the *New York Times* and other media observers failed to note was the critical element of power signified by these personnel assignments.

When the legislature was in session, Abbett worked long hours in drafting bills, handling voluminous correspondence, reading a variety of newspapers, and holding numerous conferences. He usually stayed in Trenton where he rented a room at the old "Government House" on State Street. Until the time of Governor William Pennington (1813-1815), this had been the executive mansion, but it was later sold and turned into a hotel. When the legislature was not in operation, the business of state was slower, and it did not require Abbett's full-time presence at the state capital. Since rail transportation was convenient, he found it easier to commute by train from his home in Jersey City. Meanwhile, he had to attend to his private law practice in New York City.

From all accounts, the governor took his administrative role seriously. According to Sackett, Abbett designated Tuesday as the day on which he could be expected to be in Trenton when the legislature was not in session. He therefore held cabinet meetings on that day. Cabinet members were expected to give a detailed account of what they had done or not done during the past week.[34] Abbett insisted on written reports from all his department heads and bureau chiefs. He visited the various state

institutions to find out for himself what was going on, and he personally inspected the National Guard troops during their summer encampments at Sea Girt. In October 1885, the *Jersey City Tattler* described his daily routine as follows:

A man of the Governor's energy loses no time in idleness. He dispatches a vast quantity of business, private and official, every day. Besides the cares of the state, he has a large and difficult law practice to manage. Just now the cares of state rest lightly on his shoulders; and he spends only one day in the week -Tuesdays -at the state Capital, but even in the hottest of weather he was there. In the winter season, when the Legislature is in session, he confines himself closely to his official duties. His correspondence is large, and he makes it a point to answer every letter sent to him.

FIG. 17
New Jersey State House.

This is a duty of itself that consumes much of his time. But in addition to it, he critically examines every bill sent to him for approval; and it is not an infrequent thing to find him busy at the executive chamber as late as two o'clock in the morning. He makes time for recreation by rising early; and frequently takes a long walk before breakfast.[35]

Not coincidentally, policy control remained securely in the governor's office. More than any of his predecessors, Abbett exercised his veto power to nullify legislation that he found objectionable. Sometimes he used the threat of the veto to get what he wanted as in the case of the "Negro Burial" bill. Sometimes his veto was overridden. A gubernatorial veto could be overridden by a simple majority of each house; it did not require a two-thirds vote. The only time Abbett was "veto-proof" in his first term was in 1884, when the Democrats controlled the general assembly.

THE STATE HOUSE FIRE

When the State House was partially destroyed by fire in the early morning hours of Saturday March 21, 1885, Abbett personally inspected the fire scene. Despite the heroic efforts of the Trenton municipal fire department in battling the blaze, the entire northern portion of the capitol building was completely destroyed. More precisely, the fire wiped out the offices assigned to the secretary of state, the treasurer, the quartermaster-general, the clerk of Chancery, the chief of the Bureau of Labor and Statistics, and the supreme court clerk. Fortunately, the fire fighters managed to save the offices south of the rotunda, which included those of the governor, the comptroller, the adjutant general, the supreme court, the Court of Chancery, the state library, and both legislative chambers. At considerable peril, the adjutant-general, assisted by the firemen and several military veterans, rescued all the New Jersey regimental battle flags that remained from the Civil War. The fire was believed to have started from the embers of a coal stove that was used to heat the office of Quartermaster General Lewis Perrine, but he claimed that it was caused by a defective chimney flue in the Clerk of Chancery's office.[36]

At any rate, Abbett used the fire as a good excuse to persuade the legislature of the need to construct a much larger state office building. In a special message that he delivered to them, he emphasized that the previous structure had been grossly inadequate for conducting the state's business. In his view, it was overcrowded and lacked sufficient office space to accommodate the various executive departments and agencies. He cited as an example the SBA that had been forced to rent space in a private boarding house across the street from the state capitol building.[37]

FIG. 18
New Jersey State House fire, 1885.

Soon thereafter, an architectural competition was conducted to solicit the best design for a replacement building. Advertisements announcing this contest appeared in local newspapers as well as those in New York and Philadelphia. A cash prize of $200 was offered to the prospective winner. Noted architect Lewis H. Broome of Jersey City won the competition. The building contract was awarded to William H. Burton of Trenton.

The governor then persuaded the legislature to appropriate $50,000 for reconstruction. During the debate over this appropriation, a controversy arose as to whether it might be more appropriate to relocate the state capital to another city. Some legislators wanted it moved to Newark, while others favored the city of Elizabeth. The rationale and impetus behind such an idea stemmed from the fact that most of the state's population was concentrated in North Jersey.

Trentonians worried that they might lose the state capital. John Caminade, the Democratic assemblyman from Trenton, argued that it should remain at its present location. He charged that city officials in Elizabeth merely wanted the state to bail them out of bankruptcy. Furthermore, Caminade contended that relocating the state capital would cost New Jersey taxpayers over $2 million. Legislators from Camden and Monmouth counties were opposed to the move, mainly because they felt that Trenton was more centrally located. At the end of the debate, the decision was made to keep the capital where it was. In 1886, Abbett got the legislature to appropriate another $225,000 to reconstruct the

FIG. 19
New Jersey State House fire, 1885.

rotunda and dome and to complete the restoration and landscaping. When the new edifice was completed, the executive offices were furnished with the "finest fire-proof vaults" for the storage of records.[38]

Abbett's biggest disappointment during his first term was his inability to persuade the legislature to call a constitutional convention. He wanted to simplify the slow and cumbersome procedure for amending the state constitution. An amendment had to be approved by two successive legislatures before it could be submitted for public referendum. More than this, the constitution could only be amended once every five years. The governor went on record expressing his frustration with regard to the difficulty of the amending process:

The Constitution of the United States can be amended without any such delay or embarrassment. I know of no reason why the people of New Jersey cannot be trusted with power to act immediately upon the amendment, or why after they have adopted an amendment they should wait five years before they can adopt another. The time now required to change the state constitution has repeatedly defeated needed constitutional reform.[39]

In 1885, Abbett's call for the convention was passed in the assembly. When the bill emerged from committee, he made a deal with Essex Assemblyman David A. Bell for the critical Republican vote needed for passage. Not adverse to dealing across party lines when necessary, Abbett agreed to support Bell's bill to create the state's twenty-second county. The new county of Carteret was to be carved out of the southern part of Essex County. But it never happened.

The forces resisting these bills were the powerful, rural Republican counties that controlled the senate. Rural senators were afraid that Abbett would try to rectify the malapportionment of the upper house. The rules that determined the conduct of state politics were by no means neutral. They allotted certain advantages to some participants, and by the same token they allotted disadvantages to others. The most dramatic example was the "one-senator-per-county" rule. It gave the sparsely populated rural counties greater representation and thus more political power, than the more densely populated urban counties. Achieving fair representation in New Jersey was the last thing Republican senators wanted to do. They defeated the two bills under consideration. A *New York Times* editorial predicted the demise of the constitutional convention:

It is not an easy matter to induce people to give up an unfair advantage in deference to a principle of indisputable soundness. Whatever defense there may be for the equal representation of the states in the United States Senate, there is no ground on which an equal representation of counties regardless of size in a state Legislature can be defended. The counties are not, and cannot properly be, represented as separate political entities.

It is the people of the state that are represented in one or the other branch of the Legislature, and their rights and interests in that representation are equal. And yet in New Jersey, as in Delaware, the counties have equal representation in the Senate, and Cape May, with 20,000 inhabitants, has the same voice and influence as Hudson, with 200,000 and more. Every effort to rectify this palpable inequality has heretofore been defeated by the selfishness of the representatives of the smaller counties, and a proposition now pending for a constitutional convention one purpose of which is to secure representation in proportion to population is likely to be beaten from the same motive. People may believe in equality and fair play as an abstract proposition, but to put the belief in practice they need to start without any advantage to be sacrificed.[40]

It must have been frustrating for Abbett to lose on this important issue, because reapportionment would have made it a great deal easier for him to have legislation for cities enacted. Despite this major obstacle, he secured his reputation as an urban governor. Living in Jersey City, he was more than familiar with the problems that cities faced. Most of the significant changes in America were taking place in these industrial cities.

That is where the action was. Conflict between the old and the new social order was sharpest there. Industrialists, factory workers, and politicians interacted there. Immigrant and working class subcultures were most vital there. As Herbert Guttman points out, "Politics in the industrial city was affected by these subcultures and an awareness of a potential (and, at times, active) working-class political presence. Many industrial city politicians had special ties to working-class and immigrant voters that usually filtered through a political machine but nevertheless affected the style of politics."[41] The interplay of these forces explains in large measure why urban legislation was possible. Understanding the ways in which they complemented and counteracted one another makes late nineteenth-century urban politics more comprehensible.

In this context, Abbett's railroad tax program was designed to provide cities with new revenue. Indeed, the antirailroad phenomenon was much more urban than rural. This coalition exerted most of the pressure for the governor's urban programs. He had bills passed that authorized free public libraries and paid municipal fire departments. City police and fire fighters were afforded civil service protection, and they could no longer be removed for political reasons. Other urban legislation provided for improved municipal bonding procedures for the construction of city water supply networks and the acquisition of reservoir sites.

As an urban-oriented governor, Abbett obtained legislation that restored solvency to the bankrupt cities of Elizabeth and Rahway. In spite of imperfections, the "Encumbered Cities Act of 1884" was essentially a state bail-out, but it stopped short of placing the two cities in state receivership. It was an ingenious solution whereby city officials could

continue to function without creditors taking them to court. When these officials had been previously threatened with writs of mandamus, they resigned to avoid service of the writs. This meant that they could no longer levy local property taxes and pay city expenses. A group of civic leaders attempted to raise money by voluntary subscription, but this scheme failed. These leaders discussed their problem with Abbett. He drafted legislation that gave the governor the power to appoint state commissioners of taxation who could assess local property and levy taxes. They were required to post bonds for the faithful performance of their duties. Since writs of mandamus could only be served on city officials, this arrangement protected them from their creditors.[42]

To guard against other cities and towns going bankrupt, Abbett proposed amending the state constitution to prohibit them from incurring debt beyond a certain percentage of their tax ratables, but this idea was soundly defeated. It would have required a constitutional convention, and the rural Republican counties were not about to reopen the issue of reapportionment. The idea of municipal debt limitation was not adopted in New Jersey until as late as 1938 in the midst of the Great Depression. So Abbett was well ahead of his time on this issue.

FARM SUPPORT AND LEGISLATION

To win approval of his urban legislation, Abbett had to make certain political trade-offs with the agricultural community. The State Board of Agriculture, reorganized in 1884, wanted to change fundamentally the way farmers did business. At the same time, it wanted to cooperate with food dealers to advance the industry's political interests and to develop new marketing strategies. Dairy farmers, for example, complained vociferously about the sale of oleo margarine and other imitation dairy products. They wanted some protection against "bogus butter." In response to their concerns, Abbett backed legislation that required those selling imitation butter to stamp the real name of the product on the receptacle containing it. He also backed a bill that created the position of state dairy commissioner whose responsibility was to promulgate regulations with regard to the fair-labeling and packaging of dairy products.[43] A number of other agricultural reform bills were passed during Abbett's first term, but both parties tried to take credit for them. The Republicans controlled both houses of the legislature during 1885 and 1886.

Considering these political constraints, Abbett's record of performance in his first term was remarkable—a product of his drive and broad vision. That vision encompassed the economic growth of New Jersey along with the general welfare of its people. It also embraced a wide array of social issues, including those of race and class. Indeed, Abbett had achieved

most of what he had set out to accomplish through legislative enactments. In so doing, he proved himself equal to the task of governing a diverse society. More important, perhaps, he discovered the inherent power in the governorship and overcame its institutional shortcomings. But his style and strategy of governing did not endear him to everyone. Most legislators thought that he was intruding on their turf and usurping their prerogatives. Much of the partisan warfare centered on his transgressing the traditions and protocols of the senate. His executive control of the bureaucracy offended Republicans as well as Democrats. As a public manager, he sought administrative authority commensurate with his responsibility.

Abbett was able to adapt his role as governor to fit the changing times. He was restless, inquisitive, curious, and, at times, infuriating. Instead of remaining aloof and insulated from the people, he provided them with greater access to his office. The essence of the gubernatorial role did not escape him. No longer was the executive a captive of the railroads. They had met their match in Abbett, who could not be intimidated or bought off. The fact that he was so intensely despised by the powerful economic elite in New Jersey provided ample evidence that he was doing his job. He used the power of his party machine to counteract the corporate power of the railroads. In the battles that he fought with the legislature, he won more than he lost. Even though he did not always win, he felt that it was important to get his policy positions on the record. Conflict, in his view, was unavoidable in achieving social change.

By contemporary standards, Leon Abbett was a different kind of governor and a different kind of Democrat. Like his Democratic predecessors, he believed that business was the engine of the economy, but he also believed that American capitalism, as it was evolving, needed to be controlled by preventing its excesses and by tempering its injustices. American individualism gave workers, especially those who treasured their independence, a certain degree of freedom, but at the same time it limited their power to control their lives and rendered them dependent on others. Ordinary working people felt that Abbett made a difference in their lives. He took his representative role seriously and served as governor of all the people. No one was more adept at listening to people, at understanding the nuances of an issue, and at finding new ways to move forward. It was the kind of wisdom that can come only from hard fought political experience. In the mid-1880s, Abbett captured the passion of the times and the imagination of the electorate.

ENDNOTES

1 *Bergen Index*, January 29, 1884.
2 *New York Times*, January 26, 1884.

3 Minutes of the New Jersey General Assembly (1884), 140–141. See also the *New York World*, January 29, 1884.

4 *Newark Daily Advertiser*, January 29, 1884.

5 *New York Times*, January 29, 1884.

6 *Newark Daily Advertiser*, January 31, 1884.

7 *Newark Daily Advertiser*, February 5, 1884.

8 *New York Times*, February 5, 1884. See also *Newark Evening News*, February 5, 1884.

9 *Ibid.*

10 See *Civil Rights Cases*, 109 U.S. 3 (1883).

11 New Jersey Laws (1884) Chapter 219, 339.

12 *New York Times*, March 21, 1884.

13 James Leiby, *Charity and Correction in New Jersey* (New Brunswick, Rutgers University Press, 1967), 131.

14 Leo Troy, *Organized Labor in New Jersey* (Princeton, D. Van Nostrand, 1965), 48 49.

15 *New York Times*, February 8, 1892.

16 *New York Sun*, July 11, 1884.

17 Allan Nevins, *Grover Cleveland: A Study in Courage* (New York, Dodd, Meade & Company, 1932), 159.

18 *New York World*, October 30, 1884.

19 Harry Barnard, *Eagle Forgotten: The Life of John Peter Altgeld* (New York, Bobbs-Merrill, 1938), 316.

20 Edwin P. Conklin, "The Last Half Century in New Jersey Politics," in Irving S. Kull (ed.), *New Jersey: A History* (New York, The American Historical Society, 1930), 972.

21 For more details about the baptismal story, see *Newark Evening News*, December 31, 1884; *Newark Daily Advertiser*, December 31, 1884; and *New York World*, December 31, 1884.

22 *Newark Daily Advertiser*, December 31, 1884.

23 *New York World*, January 1, 1885.

24 *Newark Evening News*, January 21, 1884.

25 Quoted in Gutman and Kealey, *Many Pasts*, 144.

26 *Ibid.*, 144.

27 *Ibid.*, 144.

28 *Newark Evening News*, September 1, 1885.

29 *New York Tribune*, March 27, 1885.

30 *New York Tribune*, March 19, 1885.

31 *New Jersey Legislative Manual* (Trenton, T. F. Fitzgerald Publisher, 1887), 243.

32 *New York Times*, March 5, 1885. For a detailed list of the executive appointments that were usurped by the legislature, see *New Jersey Legislative Manual* (Trenton, John L. Murphy Publishing Company, 1889), 145.

33 *Ibid.*

34 Sackett, *Modern Battles of Trenton*, 2:143–144.

35 *Jersey City Tattler*, October 4, 1885.

36 *New York Times*, March 24, 1885.

37 Special Message of March 23, 1885, found in *New Jersey Legislative Documents for 1885*.

38 For a detailed treatment of the State House fire and its restoration, see Zara Cohan, "A Comprehensive History of the State House of New Jersey and Recommendations for its Continuation as a Historic Site" (Unpublished master's thesis, Newark State College, 1969), 109–119.

39 Inaugural message of January 15, 1884, p. 5.

40 *New York Times*, March 6, 1885.

41 Herbert G. Gutman, "Class, Status, and the Gilded-Age Radical: A Reconsideration," in Gutman and Kealey, *Many Pasts*, 135.

42 *New York Times*, March 21, 1884.

43 New Jersey Laws (1884), Chapters 15, 165, and 194; New Jersey Laws (1886), Chapter 84.

9

The Interregnum

The dynamic leadership that Abbett had shown in his first term set the stage for the events that followed. Motivated by a desire to seek higher public office, he was eager to maintain his populist image. Precluded by the state constitution from succeeding himself as governor, he decided to move up the political ladder. Politics was his passion. Firmly committed to the cause of working people, he was not about to abandon the struggle. Indeed, he was intent on capturing the U.S. Senate seat that would be open in early 1887. In an era when senators were elected by their respective state legislatures, Abbett realized that the Democrats would have a majority in joint session. Under these circumstances, his election seemed almost certain. So he left the governor's chair fairly confident that he would soon be on his way to Washington.

Manifest appearances, however, did not always coincide with latent realities. Retribution came, and its name was railroad power. At first glance, the major barrier standing in the way of Abbett advancing to the U.S. Senate was incumbent Republican William J. Sewell. Having held the office since 1881, Sewell had the power of incumbency as well as the support of the powerful Pennsylvania Railroad for whom he was employed. He was not about to relinquish his seat without a fight. Abbett would have to oust him from the position.

William Sewell's journey from an impoverished boyhood in Ireland to the heights of the U.S. Senate was simply astounding. He was born in Castlebar in 1835. It was a garrison town in County Mayo that quartered British troops at the local barracks. The town characterized garrisoned Ireland. When the terrible potato famine struck, William Sewell and his parents were landless or evicted peasants. Faced with the prospect of malnutrition and starvation, they converted to Protestantism in exchange for being fed in the soup lines. Hence, they were nicknamed

"soupers." At age 16, William left Castlebar in 1851 and departed for Chicago where he sold newspapers and then engaged in mercantile pursuits. Nine years later, he moved to New Jersey where he became active in Republican politics in Camden County just before the Civil War.

Impressed with Sewell, Governor Charles Olden made him a captain and assigned him to the 5th Regiment of the New Jersey Volunteers. The regiment was commanded by General Gershom Mott of Lamberton, one of New Jersey's most distinguished officers. In the battle of Chancellorsville, Mott was severely wounded and sent to the rear. As the next highest ranking officer, Sewell assumed command. Rallying the troops around his colors, he led them into battle and galloped to the front line, shouting, "Jerseymen at least will follow me." They defeated the Confederates in that particular skirmish, but Sewell was badly wounded. He displayed similar valor at the battle of Gettysburg, where he was again wounded. Earning the Congressional Medal of Honor for his bravery, he was a genuine military hero.[1] After the war, Sewell worked for the Pennsylvania Railroad and built a powerful Republican machine in Camden County in which he was the county boss.

What was critical, of course, as far as Abbett's prospects were concerned, was the commitment of the Democratic party caucus. He soon won its endorsement. At this point, the election seemed like a foregone conclusion. Although the Republicans outnumbered the Democrats twelve to nine in the Senate, the latter still held the balance of power. The assembly consisted of thirty-two regular Democrats, two Labor Democrats, and twenty-six Republicans. The two Labor Democrats— John Donohue and Robert A. Carroll—had pledged their support to Erastus E. Potter, a school principal from Port Oram, who had run for governor as a labor candidate in 1886. This party alignment gave the regular Democrats a majority of three votes on joint ballot. With forty-one out of eighty-one possible votes seemingly assured in joint meeting, Abbett appeared to have the necessary votes to win.[2]

But a small band of disaffected Democrats adamantly refused to support Abbett. To show their defiance, they bolted the party caucus. No political act was deemed more treacherous than to defy the party caucus. Such defection was regarded as practically treasonous. The person who instigated this move was none other than Henry Stafford Little. The long-running feud between Little and Abbett had now become a highly charged personal vendetta. A major malcontent, Little was seeking revenge.

As it happened, there was a delay in conducting the election because of the inability of the assembly to organize itself. For three weeks, the lower house was unable to elect a speaker. A dispute arose over the seating of Democratic Assemblymen Henry Turley of Camden and Frederick Walters of Trenton, both of whom were Abbett loyalists. As a result of this delay, the first ballot was not taken until February 15. The

Republicans had their own problems to contend with. Assemblyman William H. Corbin of Elizabeth, who had helped Abbett in his fight against the Morris and Essex Railroad, was disenchanted with Sewell whom he saw as a tool of the railroads. He therefore led a revolt within his party and backed Cortlandt Parker. Because of these intraparty rifts, Abbett and Sewell could only obtain thirty-five votes apiece on the first ballot. The dynamics of the joint meeting resulted in a deadlock between the two men. The remaining eleven votes were split among eight other contenders.

Democrat Rufus Blodgett now entered the fray. A native of New Hampshire, Blodgett had worked as a railroad mechanic at the Amoskeag Locomotive Works in Manchester. When moving to New Jersey in 1866, he was hired by Henry Little as superintendent of the New York and Long Branch Railroad that was a subsidiary of the Jersey Central. Tall and virile, with thick mustache and side-whiskers, the unflappable Blodgett had served as assemblyman from Ocean County from 1878 to 1880. He was defeated for the state senate in 1880 by Republican Abraham C. Havens. Four years later, in 1884, Blodgett managed Grover Cleveland's successful presidential campaign in New Jersey. The dour Presbyterian was a teetotaler and belonged both to the fraternal order of the Elks and the Masons. Like his political mentor Henry Little, he was staunchly anti-Abbett and staunchly anti-Catholic.

The ascendancy of Blodgett and the forces behind him had been dealt a serious blow in 1886, when he was defeated for the Democratic gubernatorial nomination. The Abbett faction had supported Robert Green, a corporate lawyer from Elizabeth with a patrician pedigree. Particularly noteworthy is the way in which Abbett had plotted Blodgett's defeat. He put intense pressure on Henry Kelsey, manager of Blodgett's campaign. Abbett warned Kelsey that if he persisted in his efforts, he would lose his job as secretary of state. Heeding the warning, Kelsey bailed out and absented himself from the party convention. Chairing the convention was Allan McDermott, who ruled with an iron fist and ran roughshod over the Blodgett delegates. In the end, Green not only won the Democratic nomination, but also the governorship. This defeat at the hands of the Abbett faction left the Blodgett forces deeply embittered.

It was a triumph for Abbett. His clever maneuvering had produced a governor who was more to his liking. As a result of such party intrigue, Kelsey broke with Henry Little. This break hastened the demise of the State House Ring, but its members were now determined to block Abbett's senatorial aspirations. Perhaps to their wry amusement, they decided to do so with an "uncouth and uneducated railroad man" whom he had previously vanquished. With Blodgett's unexpected entry into the contest, the political calculus changed accordingly.[3] Through several ballots, the Republicans stayed with Sewell who consistently fell a few votes

short of a majority. He finally withdrew in favor of fellow Republican William Phelps. A gentleman Mugwump reformer, Phelps tried hard to persuade the two independent labor Democrats to support him, but they refused.

At this juncture, with the joint session deadlocked between Abbett and Sewell, the six rebellious Democrats, led by Assemblyman William S. Throckmorton of Monmouth County, conspired with the Republicans and persuaded them to support Blodgett. This situation made for strange political bedfellows. The election contest was now between a railroad man and an antirailroad man. In explaining his vote, Assemblyman Robert Carroll of Paterson, one of the two Labor Democrats, declared himself "an antirailroad man, and that he would vote for Leon Abbett."[4] The Republicans felt that if they could not elect either Sewell or Phelps, they would be delighted to defeat Abbett.

Repeated attempts by Abbett to bring his party in line failed. Try as he might, he could not convince the six rebellious Democrats to support him. The anti-Abbett coalition had worked out an elaborate scheme. Republican Assemblyman Peter Ackerman of Ridgewood led the break for Blodgett. When Democratic Assemblyman William Letts of Hoboken attempted to lead a counterbreak for Sewell, Abbett sensed that he had lost the contest and sent word that he preferred "a poor Democrat to a good Republican." He was angry at the Trockmorton defectors, but his anger did not cloud his judgment. Realizing that he could not prevail under these circumstances, he reluctantly concluded that it would be better for him to bow out gracefully. He did so for the good of the party, but it was an extremely bitter pill for him to swallow. Abbett was distraught; he could not believe that his party had deserted him, and his supporters were equally dismayed. The final tally showed Blodgett with forty-three votes and Abbett with thirty-eight. Thus, on March 2, 1887, Rufus Blodgett, amid a stormy scene on the floor of the assembly, was elected to the U.S. Senate. At the very moment that Abbett's star appeared brightest, it was eclipsed by Blodgett.[5]

A special irony lay in the defeat of Abbett at the hands of the palace guard. The railroad interests had their revenge, but they lived to regret it. As Sackett indicates, "It left the resourceful Abbett in the field to battle them, while there was no compensating gain for them in Blodgett's uneventful service in the great building on Capitol Hill."[6] Outwardly stiff and seemingly humorless, Blodgett was weak and ineffectual as a senator: he lacked style, did not mix easily, seemed uncomfortable with others, and had no idea how to deal with the media or speak effectively. While serving in the U.S. Senate from 1887 to 1893, he did not sponsor any important legislation, nor did he make a major speech on the Senate floor. Blodgett was an irascible character, whose brusque and abrasive manner were ill-suited for political life. A family relative described him as "a mean, stingy,

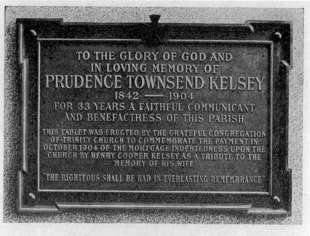

KELSEY MEMORIAL TABLET
Erected by the Congregation

HENRY COOPER KELSEY

FIG. 20
Henry Cooper Kelsey.
From Free Public Library
of Trenton, NJ.

contemptible, and miserly old man with few friends." He had the dubious distinction of being the only U.S. Senator to vote against the Sherman Antitrust Act of 1890. In explaining his political behavior, Russell Decker says, "Blodgett was a railroader—first, last, and always. Railroads had been his entire life. His logic would undoubtedly lead him to conclude that the bill was anti-railroad—and that would have been enough for this hardheaded individualist."[7]

Abbett took his defeat hard. It was an embittered and disconsolate Abbett who left Trenton for the solitude of his home in Jersey City. There secluded from even close friends, he brooded over his political future. Not even his good friend and intimate companion Allan McDermott could console him. Disappointments of this sort continued to test his political fortitude, but Abbett was a resilient party boss who was able to overcome such adversity. He weathered the storm and with the passage of time and change he would make a political comeback. Meanwhile, he worked hard to stay in the public eye and managed to keep alive a personal following in the party.

THE GREEN ADMINISTRATION

With Abbett relegated to the political sidelines, the Morris and Essex Railroad executives lost no time in taking advantage of his absence. They met with Governor Robert Green and proposed submitting the question of tax arrears to arbitration. Attorney General John Stockton recommended acceptance of this proposal to avoid continued litigation and loss of potential revenue. As a former railroad attorney, Green readily agreed to arbitration. Two arbitrators were appointed to resolve the disputed issue of back taxes. Frederick W. Stevens, a distinguished Newark lawyer, was named as the state's arbitrator, while the noted New York railroad lawyer, John F. Dillon, represented the Morris and Essex. The arbitration turned into a long, drawn-out process that lasted for three years.

Green found the popular Leon Abbett a hard act to follow and was a mediocre governor by comparison. A Princeton-educated lawyer, Green brought to the office a commanding presence and the social status of a colonial elite ancestry. A patrician by birth and disposition, he could lay claim to a sterling Yankee background. He was descended from a long line of Presbyterian ministers and a family that had been politically active in New Jersey since the American Revolution. Yet he failed to exploit these advantages. As chief of state, Green was a model of dignity and restraint, a symbol of integrity and social respectability, but he lacked the passion and fire for political life. He was cool and dispassionate, objective and detached, impersonal and logical. The press respected him; the electorate admired him but it did not embrace him the way it had

embraced Leon Abbett. Green lacked both Abbett's zest for politics and his mastery of its subtleties. Although imbued with a strong sense of civic duty, he soon became a captive of the political system and the business interests that dominated it. He was very much a man of his time, who believed in competition and laissez-faire.

Green had spent much of his career as a judge, and this may explain his political behavior to some extent. He had also served one term in Congress. Entering the governor's office at the age of fifty-six, he chose to play his role in a subdued manner, sharing initiative and responsibility with those who could ease his burdens of accountability. In political circles, he was easygoing, soft-spoken, and low-keyed, allowing his wry, often subtle sense of humor to mask his ambition. But he was unable to lead the legislature on the pressing public policy issues of the day. In essence, Green chose to cooperate with party bosses rather than dominate them, and the result was a placid and relatively uneventful term.

COUNSEL FOR THE STATE LIQUOR DEALERS

In the meantime, Abbett, who had returned to his private law practice, was retained as counsel by the State Liquor Dealers Association headed by Republican John Edelstein of Jersey City. It should be remembered that Abbett had defeated Edelstein for the assembly back in 1866. So they knew each other as former political adversaries. The liquor dealers, who had landed in trouble, were anxious to avail themselves of Abbett's legal knowledge and political savvy. Brewers like Robert H. Ballantine and Gottfried Krueger served on the Democratic state committee. Other Democrats of German extraction were prominent in the brewing and distilling industries. Brewers Joseph Schmelz and George W. Weidenmayer were both Democratic assemblymen and contributed generously to Democratic campaign coffers.

The liquor lobby was a powerful special interest group in New Jersey. With some 7,420 saloons operating in the state, it was estimated to be a $15-million enterprise. The tavern business flourished, especially in the industrial cities. Hudson County alone accounted for nearly 2,000 saloons, while Essex County did not lag far behind. Liquor licenses were issued by local excise boards, whose membership was controlled by the local political boss. The distribution of liquor licenses was a valuable political resource.

A stormy controversy over liquor regulation preoccupied much of Green's administration. Temperance zealots made much to do about the state's failure to enforce its liquor law, particularly in Jersey City, where many saloonkeepers openly defied the law and sold intoxicating beverages on Sunday. This laxity in law enforcement outraged Protestant

evangelicals who saw it as demeaning their Christian Sabbath and offending that sense of moralistic propriety so characteristic of small-town New Jersey. A noticeable increase in drunkenness, brawling, and street crime helped turn temperance reform into a coercive movement directed mainly at uncouth Irish and German immigrants. In an extraordinary display of moral outrage, evangelical church groups flocked to Trenton to petition the legislature to stop the flow of "pagan rum." They firmly believed that most of the prevailing social problems could be attributed to the consumption of liquor. Policies toward the poor and urban underclass were premised on an ideology that portrayed social ills as fundamentally individual and moral in origin.

In the late 1880s, the prohibitionists renewed their crusade and sought to obtain more stringent legislation. They put together a coalition of drys that included organized groups like the Women's Christian Temperance Union and the New Jersey Anti-Saloon League. The saloon was also seen as a detriment to honest elections. James McCosh, the president of Princeton and the leading intellectual light of Presbyterianism, spoke out against the evils of demon rum and denounced the corrupting influence that the liquor interests had on the political system. Such rhetoric inflamed smoldering religious tensions. The code words were aimed at the recalcitrant Irish and provided added impetus to nativism. It would be incorrect, however, to interpret the temperance movement in New Jersey solely as a religious crusade. The business community saw the neighborhood pub as the spawning ground for labor agitation and union organizing.[8] Business leaders therefore joined in the crusade to regulate such establishments.

In the elections of 1887, the Prohibition party continued to make substantial gains in what previously had been considered safe Republican districts. The sentiment expressed by New Jersey voters on the liquor issue sent a clear message. Once the Republicans began receiving complaints from their constituents, they scrambled to reverse course. Intense lobbying by the temperance coalition prodded them into passing a stringent liquor control law in 1888. This statute mandated a system of high license fees and provided each county with the option of deciding for itself in a public referendum whether or not to prohibit the sale of alcoholic beverages. The high license feature required localities to charge certain minimum fees for the issuance of liquor licenses. The schedule of fees was based on a sliding scale that ranged from $100 to $500 depending on the population size of the municipality. To make the statute more punitive, the Republicans slapped on a Sunday closing requirement that imposed stiff fines on saloonkeepers who were found violating it. Such violators were charged under the law with operating a "disorderly house."[9]

Disturbed by the implications of this bill, the liquor lobby pressured Governor Robert Green into vetoing it, but the Republicans quick-

ly overrode his veto. Soon afterward, the temperance forces won impressive local option victories in six counties, all located in the rural parts of the state. These included Cumberland, Warren, Salem, Gloucester, Cape May, and Hunterdon, where evangelical Protestants held sway. One by one they all voted to go dry. Stunned by these results, the German and Irish liquor dealers sought to overthrow what they considered a tyrannical puritan blue law.

As attorney for the liquor dealers, Abbett challenged the new law in the courts. He filed two separate lawsuits in which he attacked both the local option and the high license provisions of the statute. In the case of *Paul v. Gloucester County*, he argued that the local option feature was an unconstitutional delegation of legislative power. In the case of *Hart v. Jersey City*, he took the argument even further, contending that the method of establishing license fees on the basis of population size was an improper classification that amounted to special legislation.

Abbett thus presented in capsule a persuasive rationale for the liquor dealers, but his arguments were rejected by the state supreme court. He appealed these decisions to the higher New Jersey Court of Errors and Appeals. Both cases were now joined under the legal citation *Paul v. Gloucester County* (1888). In arguing the appeal, Abbett raised the broader questions of constitutionality and gave the justices the pretext he thought they needed to change their minds, but they again rejected his argument in a close eight to seven decision.[10] Despite this defeat, Abbett brought two more lawsuits. He was able to overturn a dry election in Camden County on a legal technicality that the public referendum had been conducted improperly. In the other lawsuit, he succeeded in having a referendum in Burlington County delayed for more than a year through legal maneuvering.

In the meantime, the Democrats had regained control of the 1889 legislature. Unhappy with the court rulings, the liquor dealers sought outright repeal of the temperance law. But they encountered stiff resistance from evangelical Protestants because it reinforced their moral convictions. Ironically, the high license fees had yielded substantial revenue for the cities and towns. Newark and Jersey City each collected over $200,000. These municipalities did not want to give up such a lucrative source of revenue.

Public opinion remained overwhelming in favor of retaining the "high license-local option" law. In an election year dominated by the subject of liquor control, Abbett sought to contain the almost certain political damage after the local option victories. He therefore advised his clients that it would be unwise to repeal the entire law. Fearful of a backlash in an election year, the Democrats did not want to incite the wrath of voters. Under mounting pressure from church groups, Governor Green stayed out of the fray, leaving other party leaders to resolve the matter.

Negotiating with both sides, Abbett brokered a compromise that retained the high license fees but deleted the local option provision. George Werts, the Democratic state senator from Morris County, sponsored this partial repeal legislation that passed handily.

Although Governor Green sought the support of urban industrial workers, he was out of touch with their problems and did very little to help them. Several labor bills to protect factory workers were introduced, but they failed to become law for want of strong executive leadership. Ideologically, Green conformed to the safe, comfortable conservatism that characterized the Gilded Age. He embraced the business community at the expense of labor. In fact, he signed into law the 1889 statute that legalized the holding company and allowed businesses to incorporate for almost any purpose. With the passage of this bill, the Green administration came to its ineffectual end.

THE DUMP CLEVELAND MOVEMENT

Abbett remained very active in local, state, and national politics during the interregum years of 1887–1890. On the national scene, numerous Democrats were dissatisfied with President Grover Cleveland's conservative leadership, and they wanted to dump him as party leader. Some of this discontent resulted from Cleveland's cozy relationship with big business that was forged at the expense of American labor. Some of the dissatisfaction also resulted from his failure to distribute federal patronage evenhandedly. Among those who desired to wrest control of the Demcratic party from Cleveland and his Bourbon allies was Governor David Hill of New York. By this time, Hill and Abbett had become close political allies. They were both spoils politicians who appealed to similar constituencies. Sackett understood their similarities and their differences. Knowing both personalities, he could see that the two men had much in common.[11] But they did not succeed in their attempt to dump Cleveland.

In 1888, Abbett campaigned actively for Hill when he ran for reelection for governor in New York. With strong support from Tammany Hall, Hill had no trouble winning the governorship that year. Oddly enough, Grover Cleveland, the incumbent president, failed to carry his home state and lost the presidential race to Republican Benjamin Harrison. Ticket splitting and the defection of Tammany Democrats cost Cleveland the election in New York. In the postmortem analysis of the election, Hill was blamed for Cleveland's defeat. Hill's biographer, Herbert Bass, dismisses this analysis as being oversimplified.[12] Irish defections resulted from a factional feud between those who had put Hill in the governor's chair and old-line Bourbon Democrats affiliated with Grover

THE ELECTION FRAUDS IN NEW JERSEY.—THE SENATE COMMITTEE INVESTIGATING THE HUDSON COUNTY BALLOT-BOXES.—DRAWN BY C. BUNNELL.

Cleveland. The Irish urban bosses solidly backed Hill, while they remained cool toward Cleveland.

Despite Abbett's displeasure with Cleveland, the latter carried New Jersey in 1888 by 7,149 votes. He received 151,493 votes in the Garden State compared with 144,344 votes for Benjamin Harrison. Although Cleveland won the popular vote nationwide, he lost the electoral college race. Harrison won the important battleground states that gave him a victory in the electoral college. It was a bitter defeat for Cleveland, but he would reclaim the presidency four years later in 1892.

THE IRISH ASCENDANCY

Throughout most of his career, Abbett continued to help Irish immigrants advance politically. They began to produce their own leaders who increasingly challenged the Yankee hegemony. The Irish were highly efficient in organizing their community. In the mid-1880s, Abbett saw a whole new pattern of political power emerging in Hudson County. By then, the Irish

FIG. 21
State Senate Committee on Elections probing the alleged fraud that elected Leon Abbett as governor in 1889.

were well on their way to becoming the county's most dominant ethnic group. The concentration of political resources in the hands of Yankee Protestants, who controlled the wealth and status of the community, gradually shifted to a more dispersed pattern of ethnic leadership in the neighborhoods. As the history of Jersey City shows, the leadership shifts there in the 1880s fundamentally reflected population shifts as more Irish immigrants arrived. The fact that local Irish politicians could deliver their people with regularity meant that more political power came into their hands. Ethnic control over nominations and patronage steadily increased. In selecting candidates to run for public office, the emphasis shifted from wealth and social standing to ethnic pride and loyalty. The dominance of ethnic appeals and class politics at the local level was due to the relative ease with which politicians could satisfy ethnic aspirations.

Against this backdrop, Robert Davis, sheriff of Hudson County in 1887, provides a classic example of this phenomenon. Other Irish leaders, like Patrick H. Laverty, had been sheriff of Hudson County before, but Davis used the position to far greater political advantage. He personified the new breed of Irish leaders who emerged during the late nineteenth century. These were the professional ward bosses who knew how to acquire and manage the political resources that became available to them. They were mostly second generation Irish-Americans, or "ex-plebes" as Robert Dahl referred to them.[13] Orbiting in this new Democratic constellation were men like Robert Davis, John P. Feeney, Dennis McLaughlin, and Patrick H. O'Neil. Each had attracted a large personal following that he organized into his own neighborhood political club. Known locally as the "Big Four," these men turned the local police and fire departments into adjuncts of their political organization.[14] They were superb organizers.

For the Irish, whose political strength had been diluted through gerrymandering, were still grossly underrepresented. The job discrimination that they encountered in the private sector was pervasive. Is it any wonder then that a disproportionately large number of them sought municipal jobs in the public sector?

More than anything else, Davis was interested in winning elections no matter what it took: to him, the ends justified the means. Under his mischievous leadership, political corruption and patronage flourished in Hudson County. Rampant voting fraud ranged from stuffing ballot boxes to wholesale bribery, intimidation, and herding illiterate immigrants to the polls with premarked ballots. Repeaters and floaters assumed false identities by adopting names taken from old city directories and from graveyard headstones in the local cemeteries. With Bob Davis in charge of local law enforcement, the Irish ward heelers did not have to worry too much about being brought to the bar of justice. They usually withheld election returns until they were sure their party candidate was going to win. In the gubernatorial election of 1880, they held back voting returns

when the outcome looked doubtful for Democrat George Ludlow. They then counted him into office by a razor-thin margin of 651 votes. But the Hudson Democrats were not alone in tampering with voting returns or stealing elections. The Republicans in Atlantic, Essex, and Camden counties were equally adept in stuffing ballot boxes, bribing and intimidating voters, buying votes, and resurrecting the graveyard shift. Neither party held a monopoly on political virtue.

The lack of a secret ballot made voting a visible act that could be easily detected. In casting one's ballot, there was no privacy or enclosed voting booth. Every voter cast his ballot into a large glass box in full view of those working at the polling places. Since the political parties printed their ballots in different colors, it was easy for ward heelers or poll watchers to see how someone had voted and to report those who defected from the party. Employers were known to intimidate their employees by making their jobs depend on how they cast their ballots.

Law-abiding citizens were outraged by the dishonesty and fraudulent voting that took place. The recurring public outcry for honest elections grew louder and more persistent. Their protests led to the creation of the New Jersey Ballot Reform Association in 1889, a pressure group that drew its support from organized labor and reform elements within both major parties. They pressed for the adoption of the Australian ballot as the best way to eliminate voting frauds.[15] The citizens of Massachusetts had adopted such a reform in 1888; it provided for an official ballot printed in advance at public expense and made available at the polls. This ballot listed every candidate running for public office. Moreover, it was the same color for all voters regardless of party affiliation to ensure a greater degree of secrecy and confidentiality in voting.

County bosses like Bob Davis were strongly opposed to ballot reform, because it would force them to clean up their act. Davis' operation of the Hudson Democratic machine provides a good illustration of how political bossism worked in this era. To keep his machine operating smoothly, Davis needed both money and patronage. Money came from the distribution of favors that he could bestow—such as liquor licenses and franchises to operate public utilities. Patronage eminated from all levels of the American federal system. This was the lubricant that kept the Davis machine operating smoothly. Although Davis was locally based, he was involved in city, county, state, and national politics because each level of government provided a source of patronage. If his party or faction lost at one level, then his attachments to the others could provide the means to replenish his county machine. In this way, Davis was able to defy Abbett and the state party organization whenever he felt that it was politically expedient to do so.

To be sure, Davis had allied himself with some powerful Hudson Democrats. He maintained close ties with three men in particular—Jersey

City Mayor Orestes Cleveland, U.S. Senator John McPherson, and businessman Edward F. Young. Young was the financial boss of Jersey City and the real power behind-the-scenes. Davis took his directions from Young, the economic overlord in Hudson County.

In the public sector, Young had served as city treasurer from 1865 to 1870 and subsequently as city comptroller. Although a Democrat, he resided in the fifth legislative district that was a Republican stronghold. Even so, the voters had elected him to the city council and then to the County Board of Chosen Freeholders. In 1880, he cast one of New Jersey's electoral votes for Winfield S. Hancock for president, and in 1888 he was a delegate to the Democratic National Convention that gave Grover Cleveland his second nomination for president. In 1889, the Democratic legislature appointed him state director of railroads in New Jersey for a five-year term. In describing Young, Sackett writes, "His business and political and corporation attachments enabled him to put his hand upon the keyboard of state politics whenever he desired, and to bring a response as often as he touched it."[16]

In a state renowned for its entrenched old-boy network, the foursome of Cleveland, Davis, McPherson, and Young constituted a power elite in Hudson County. The intricate web of their business and political relationships deserves special comment. Before his rise to power, Davis had been employed by McPherson as a meter reader for the Jersey City Gas Company. The political activities of Davis were bankrolled by Young. In return for such largess, Davis selected a slate of candidates who met with Young's approval.

Young also put up the money for Davis to start a hardware and plumbing supply business. Davis sold his merchandise to the city and county governments. When Orestes Cleveland embezzled the Dixon Crucible Company into bankruptcy, it was Young who was appointed as the court receiver. He then became president of the company and turned it into a highly profitable business. The company never prosecuted Cleveland, nor did it disclose the amount of money that he had swindled. There is some evidence to suggest that Young covered up the theft and protected his friend Cleveland.[17] Acting together, Young and Davis engineered Cleveland's political comeback. With Davis' political support and Young's financial backing, Cleveland was reelected mayor of Jersey City in 1886. He retained the office until 1892. McPherson and Young shared the same economic interests and served on several of the same corporate boards.

Abbett had a falling out with Robert Davis. The latter resented the fact that he had not been Abbett's choice to run the Hudson County Democratic machine. Abbett had preferred Dennis McLaughlin, but his preference did not prevail. Although Abbett and Davis frequently found collaboration and mutual accommodation necessary, their relationship

was an uneasy alliance. The Davis machine often operated independently of the state party organization. At times, Davis fought hard to protect its autonomy from outside invasion and interference by the state organization. With some validity, Abbett saw Davis as a local party boss who could not be trusted—either with money or the responsibility of running a state campaign. Moreover, Abbett disliked Edward Young intensely and saw him as a dangerous rival. Factional conflict between the Abbett and Davis groups generally characterized political operations in Hudson County from 1887 to 1893. These two factions were frequently on opposite sides. Thus, the mutual distrust arose in part from the feeling of local party minions that they had to protect their own turf and in part from the thrust of the state organization toward control of deviant or independent local organizations. Even when the factional lines were drawn, however, it was difficult to figure out who was on which side, except for the leadership.

ABBETT CHALLENGES McPHERSON

The political careers of Leon Abbett and U.S. Senator John McPherson sharply collided in 1889. Always unpredictable and secretive, Abbett surprised everyone by trying to unseat McPherson, when his second term expired in March 1889. Every clash of rivals has defining moments in which the parties feel each other out, joust, and then join the battle. It seemed almost inevitable that the personal rivalry between these two Democratic titans would push them into direct confrontation.

To offset McPherson's alliance with the powerful Pennsylvania Railroad, Abbett entered the contest with the support of the equally powerful Baltimore and Ohio Railroad that sought a direct rail connection to New York City. As governor, he had backed the B&O's proposal to build a bridge across the Kill Von Kull to Staten Island. Although the proposal collapsed for lack of consent legislation by New York, Abbett had kept his end of the bargain.[18] At any rate, the McPherson forces were caught napping. Abbett apparently had a majority of votes and could have beaten McPherson, if the balloting had taken place at the scheduled hour. Fortunately for McPherson, the chairman of the party caucus delayed its proceedings long enough for Bob Davis to come to his rescue. Davis pressured nine Hudson legislators into switching their votes for McPherson. This tipped the balance of power, and Abbett graciously withdrew his candidacy. As a result, the senior senator was returned to Washington for an unprecedented third term.

In elaborating on this episode, Sackett suggests that Abbett never really expected to beat McPherson. Rather, he wanted to serve notice and send a signal to the party bosses that he fully intended to seek the U.S. senatorship in 1893 when Rufus Blodgett's term expired.[19] Nevertheless,

the challenge led to bitter feelings between McPherson and Abbett. Yet the damage done was not beyond repair. By September 1889, when the election for governor was underway, matters were smoothed over for the sake of party unity. A reporter for the *New York Times* described the tenuous nature of their relationship as follows:

There has always been a hidden rivalry between Abbett and McPherson, but neither has quite dared to admit it even to himself. They so evenly divide the strength of the Democratic party that neither can achieve results against the opposition of the other. The one who gets the upper hand in each convention has the aid of the other for that occasion in order to keep control of things in the family as it were. They hunt each other like savages through the forests of politics, but when they meet in the open, where a comparison of forces is possible, the one with the weaker backing will shove his tomahawk in the tail pocket of his Prince Albert coat, advance with a gracious smile to the other, extend to him the hand of fellowship, assure him that the army of rival braves had been summoned only as allies, and fall gracefully in behind him.[20]

THE JERSEY CITY POLICE CONTROVERSY

Abbett usually managed to subdue factional differences whenever local Democrats were in trouble. A case in point was the power struggle that took place between Mayor Orestes Cleveland and the Jersey City police board. Under the municipal charter of 1877, it was difficult for the mayor to remove police commissioners. This problem was partially rectified with the adoption of a new charter in April 1889. Although the mayor's removal power was still limited, he could at least appoint those whom he desired. Acting under the provisions of the new charter, Mayor Cleveland appointed three Democrats: John Feeney, Cornelius Benson, and John Kelly. But the holdover Republican police commissioners refused to vacate their positions. They fired police chief Benjamin Murphy and replaced him with Michael Nathan. The Democrats then rescinded Murphy's termination and rehired him. The problem of two police chiefs threw the police department into confusion and chaos.

Mayor Cleveland asked Abbett for his advice and legal counsel. Soon afterward, Abbett filed a lawsuit against the Republican police commissioners who were represented in court by former mayor Gilbert Collins. Collins argued that the new charter was unconstitutional because it amounted to special legislation. Abbett argued to the contrary. Applying the rule laid down in *Van Riper v. Parsons*, the state supreme court agreed with Abbett. The justices entered a summary judgment ousting the Republican police board. Collins then appealed the decision, but

the New Jersey Court of Errors and Appeals upheld the lower court.[21] The Democrats prevailed, thanks mainly to Abbett.

SEEKING A SECOND TERM AS GOVERNOR

After a three-year hiatus in which he was relegated to the political sidelines, Abbett was eligible to run for governor again in 1889, but his renomination was not a sure thing. Businessman Edward Young entertained similar ambitions. Young presented a real threat, because he had the support of both Robert Davis and the powerful Pennsylvania Railroad. On August 5, the *New York Times* commented:

> It is necessary for one to live in New Jersey to appreciate the value of the backing that has been brought to Young. The state is essentially a railroad state. Four of the great trunk lines center there and they have their local spurs stretching into every hamlet in the commonwealth. All along the line the word has been passed that Young is to be favored for Governor, and it has given a quiet but effective boom to a candidacy that otherwise might have exhausted its strength in Hudson County. Abbett's assumed walk-over has become a very precarious struggle.[22]

Young's boom, however, suddenly collapsed when he became ill. An infection caused by an abscessed tooth hospitalized him, and he was forced to withdraw from consideration. On August 16, Hudson County state Senator William Edwards announced Young's withdrawal, and a politically bruising intraparty fight was thereby averted.[23]

With Young incapacitated, Abbett had a clear shot at the gubernatorial nomination. Rumors spread that a deal had been made between the two men, whereby Young would drop out of the race, if Abbett promised to relinguish his opposition to the railroads. But these newspapers stories were based on groundless speculation. On August 19, the *New York Times* squelched the rumors by saying, "There was no deal. Abbett has made no bargain with the railroads. His fight against their interference in state politics will be as hot and aggressive as it can be made."[24]

Counting on his continued popularity, the state Democratic party convention nominated Abbett for governor in 1889. Only after obtaining an agreement from party leaders to raise the governor's salary from $5,000 to $10,000 did he accept the nomination; after a little maneuvering in the party convention, it was delivered to him by acclamation. This was no time for recriminations. Previous conflicts were forgotten or buried for the sake of party unity. Before the convention adjourned, Abbett rewarded Allan McDermott for his dedicated loyalty by naming him state party chairman. These actions tightened Abbett's control of the party organization.

The Republicans had trouble recruiting someone to run against the hardy Democratic wheelhorse. At first, they talked about running Clinton Fisk, who had soared to national prominence in 1888 when he ran for president on the Prohibition party ticket. But Fiske's views on the liquor question were too extreme. They also considered James A. Bradley, a prosperous brush manufacturer from Asbury Park. At the time, Bradley, who was vacationing in the cooler climate of New Hampshire, sent a letter withdrawing his name from consideration.[25] Others nominated at the party convention were Mayor Frank A. McGowan of Trenton and Congressmen George Halsey of Newark, and John Kean of Elizabeth. The Republicans wound up nominating businessman Edward Burd Grubb of Beverly, who proved acceptable to all factions. He was considered safe on the liquor issue.

Although Grubb was a dark-horse candidate, he personified mainstream Republicanism. In addition to being a wealthy iron baron and a large landowner, he was a Protestant dry and a decorated Civil War hero. Moreover, Grubb came from a distinguished Pennsylvania family with a sterling Yankee background. His grandfather had fought in the American Revolution. A year after he had graduated from Burlington College, Grubb volunteered for the Union Army and quickly rose from the rank of sergeant to brigadier general. After the war, he took over the family business and served as president of the Lebanon Valley Furnace Company that processed pig iron mined from the rich Cornwall deposits in Pennsylvania and West Virginia. And Grubb served as commander of the New Jersey chapter of the Grand Army of the Republic. Socially prominent, he traveled in elite circles and belonged to all the right clubs, including the Philadelphia Club, the Reform Club, and the New York Yacht Club. The only elective office he had held was city councilor in his native Burlington.[26]

THE 1889 GUBERNATORIAL RACE

Grubb was a neophyte in state politics, or what is known in the trade as a "blank-slate" candidate. By comparison, Abbett, a former governor with high visibility and name recognition, had a decided advantage. Given the close party competition, all indications pointed to a close race, and Abbett could not afford to take Grubb lightly. For one thing, he knew that the Republican campaign would be well financed. Since Grubb personally contributed $25,000 of his own money to the campaign, he was no doubt picked because of his wealth. "The popularity of certain candidates among the party workers," as John Reynolds points out, "was attributed in no small measure to the size of the financial resources at their disposal."[27] Before the campaign ended, Grubb acknowledged to a friend that party workers had "bled him like leeches." Republican leaders had

earmarked $10,000 in campaign funds for Essex County, but somehow this money mysteriously disappeared without any trace. There were no campaign finance laws to account for the way money was spent.

Few politicians understood the New Jersey electorate better than Abbett. He instinctively knew that it would be foolhardy to take an aggressive stand on the divisive liquor question. The trick was to soft-pedal the issue as much as possible so as not to offend either the non-drinkers or those who liked to imbibe. This is precisely what he did. Both major party candidates tried to sidestep the issue, but it would not go away. George LaMonte, the Prohibition party candidate, saw to that. He trumpeted his independence and gave voters a clear choice for prohibition. Not everyone, however, was keen about the idea of going dry. In addition to its numerous saloons, New Jersey was famous for its home-brewed "applejack whiskey." As one reporter expressed it:

> Democracy and whiskey do not go together in all parts of the state. But there are many Jerseymen who take their applejack apart from their politics, and even an anti-rum crusade will not be sufficiently potent to swing them away from the party of their allegiance.[28]

The 1889 Republican party state platform was filled with platitudes and ambiguities. One plank proclaimed that the GOP stood for "purity, temperance and preservation of the home." Bemoaning the fact that the Democrats had controlled the executive branch of state government for the past twenty-one years, the Republicans promised to restore economy and efficiency in its operations. They attacked Abbett for turning both the Bureau of Labor Statistics and the Bureau of Factories and Workshops into a patronage haven. On the liquor question, the Republican platform was purposely vague. The wording of this plank placed the blame on the Democrats:

> We resent the intrusion of the liquor power as an organized force into the politics of the state. The attitude of the two parties on this question is so clearly marked that no intelligent voter can be deceived by any omission of either, to make a declaration of this subject.[29]

As far as the Democrats were concerned, Abbett entered the race with greater party unity and more newspaper endorsements than he had enjoyed in 1883. County leaders like William Thompson in Camden and James Smith in Essex gave him their full support. Colonel George B. Harvey, editor of the New Jersey edition of the *New York World*, also supported his candidacy. Harvey had moved to Jersey City in 1885 and became one of Abbett's political advisers. Another influential supporter was Henry D. Winton, the owner and publisher of the *Bergen County Democrat*. Urban reformer George L. Record was also in Abbett's camp and actively campaigned for him.

For his part, Abbett fully exploited his dual position as gubernatorial candidate and former governor. His main strategy was to tell voters that he could do more for New Jersey than the inexperienced Grubb. To substantiate this claim, the Democrats distributed a campaign brochure that emphasized Abbett's many accomplishments during his first term.[30] It provided a detailed account of how much new public revenue each of the ninety-eight cities and towns had realized from railroad taxes. It also listed the various labor laws that were enacted. On the cover of the brochure, it asked the voter to pass it along to his neighbor after he had finished reading it.

Outlining the tasks ahead, Abbett promised to help farmers by building more farm-to-market roads, by fighting to reduce discriminatory railroad rates, and by expanding the state agricultural college at Rutgers. His most important campaign pledges included scholarships for agricultural students, no broad-based taxes, and the enactment of ballot reform and anti-Pinkerton legislation. These were promises that appealed to both urban and rural constituents.

Faced by a formidable adversary like Abbett, Grubb's candidacy stood little chance of success unless he could draw a substantial urban vote. Grubb's strategy was to disassociate himself from spoils politics as much as possible, while linking Abbett and his political cronies to spoils and ballot box corruption. At first, Grubb attempted to straddle the liquor issue, but pressure from the temperance coalition and the media forced him into taking a more aggressive stance.

As it turned out, the two overriding campaign issues were liquor control and ballot reform. While Grubb blasted Abbett for his close ties with the liquor interests, other Republicans attacked him for helping to defeat the Kane ballot reform bill in 1889. Assemblyman Daniel M. Kane of New Brunswick had sponsored a bill that called for a ballot similar to the Australian prototype. This bill had been supported by organized labor and the New Jersey Ballot Reform Associaton. Under pressure from the Davis faction to oppose the measure, Abbett had used his influence to help defeat it. So he was vulnerable here.

Seeking to gain the offensive, the Republicans tried to take credit for the enactment of the railroad tax law of 1884. The notion of shared achievement was more than cosmetic. John Griggs, claiming that he was the person most responsible for its passage, told the voters that Abbett had played only a minor role. This misrepresentation infuriated Abbett who countered immediately. Allan McDermott, the state party chairman, delivered a sharp rebuke and chastised Griggs for deceiving the public. He argued that if it had not been for Abbett's aggressive leadership, there never would have been such a law.[31] McDermott's stern rebuke took some of the wind out of Griggs' sails.

Much to everyone's surprise, Abbett shifted his positon on ballot reform and came out in favor of it. In a speech delivered in Newark on

October 10, he declared, "If I am elected governor, I will approve any law that will give a free and secret ballot to the people; and if any man in my party opposes such a law, I will denounce him as false to the principles of democracy."[32] A week later, Abbett raised the stakes and asked the voters to give him a Democratic legislature to enact such legislation. On October 18, he told a Mercer County audience, "No ballot reform measure advocated by a Democratic governor can be successful, if he does not have the support of a legislature that is in friendship and unison with his policy."[33]

Cynics remained skeptical of Abbett, especially since he had helped to defeat the Kane bill. To ballot reform advocates, his actions spoke louder than his words. Some of them had witnessed flagrant ballot fraud in Hudson County. These intervening elites were using the media to speak to one another and to work out their strategies. In political parlance, Abbett was defusing a potential liability by acknowledging it upfront. Once again, he was able to fathom what the people were thinking and feeling.

The liquor issue continued hot and heavy throughout the campaign. George LaMonte, the Prohibition party candidate, took a radical position: he called for "the complete and ultimate destruction of the liquor traffic." LaMonte blasted Abbett for his cozy relationship with the liquor lobby. The Prohibitionists spread the word that the Hudson Democrat would become a "whiskey governor." Even the Protestant clergy got into the act. An energetic campaigner, Presbyterian James McCosh, retired president of Princeton in 1888, came out against Abbett because of his identification with the rum peddlers. "I am a Republican," McCosh declared, "because the Democrats are the saloon party, and I shall vote against Abbett because he belongs to that party and is the champion of the saloon interests."[34]

Attempting to straddle the fence on the liquor issue, Grubb and his Republican allies varied their stances with the audience, depending upon where they spoke. They tried to have it both ways, but the danger of such a strategy lay in being discovered. He told voters in Essex County, where pro-liquor sentiment ran strong, that he was opposed to the high license law. In the meantime, while campaigning in southern New Jersey, where the evangelical Protestant drys maintained a numerical superiority, he came out in favor of local option. Grubb's flip-flop on the liquor issue eventually landed him in trouble. The *New York Times* chastised the Republicans for their duplicitous actions:

> The shifting and evasive attitudes of the Republicans of New Jersey on this question will certainly prove a source of weakness. There is no other question of local and state policy at all comparable with it in popular interest. There are many Republicans in the state who desire to see an energetic policy pursued, and they will be alienated by the failure to maintain the position adopted two years ago in favor of high license and local option. There are many temperance Democrats whose support might

have been won by a vigorous declaration in favor of specific measures of restriction upon liquor, but there will be no inducement for them to break away from their accustomed party attachment.[35]

Speaking before a large audience in Newark, Abbett called Grubb and his party to task for their duplicity. "The Republican party," he said in a mock-serious tone, "is attempting to stand with one foot on local option in South Jersey and the other foot on the protest against high license in Essex County. If they stride much more, they will split."[36] The audience loved it. They howled, clapped, and cheered. Abbett twice accused Grubb of shifting his stand to curry favor with both wet and dry constituencies. He thereby cast doubt on Grubb's credibility. Abbett was playing what he loved to play most, namely, politics. When it came to attracting the votes of Protestant drys, the Republican candidate had to compete with George LaMonte, who captured some 6,853 votes on election day.

The Democrats invited party leaders from out of state to campaign for Abbett. Governor David Hill of New York stumped for him in Newark, Paterson, and Jersey City. Delaware Governor Benjamin T. Biggs campaigned in Camden and the surrounding suburbs. Party unity was the order of the day, but there was some dissension in the ranks. Once again, disaffected Democrats, like Henry Little, Rufus Blodgett, and Thomas Kays, continued to be obstreperous and obstructive. But their discontent was simply a rearguard action.

For that matter, Grubb had more serious problems within Republican ranks. He had offended William Sewell in a patronage dispute. Sewell had backed William R. Williams of Newark for the federal position of internal revenue collector for the northern district of New Jersey. Grubb insisted that the job should go to George H. Large, a former state senator from Hunterdon County. President Benjamin Harrison, who wanted to help Grubb win the election, complied with his wishes. The rift proved costly to Grubb. If he stood any chance of winning, he needed to carry both Camden and Essex counties to offset Abbett's anticipated strength in Hudson. The *New York Times* made an assessment of the political damage:

The disaffection of a man of Sewell's commanding position can make a larger break in Republican enthusiasm than can be repaired by the energetic work of twenty Bedles, Littles, Blodgetts, and Kayses. They all fought Abbett six years ago and made an open campaign against him. But he carried the state in spite of them. On the other hand, the state has never been known to go Republican when Sewell was indifferent concerning the result.[37]

Having no political record to run on, except for his brief stint as a city councilor in Burlington, Grubb tried to capitalize on his military

combat record. The Republicans repeatedly told audiences that while Grubb volunteered and went to the front, Abbett volunteered to stay at home. They depicted the Democratic candidate as a draft dodger. Emphasizing his loyalty to the Union and his military valor, Grubb made a strong pitch for the veterans' vote. He was accompanied on his speaking engagements by Captain Elwood H. Kirkbride, who had served under his command in the 23rd New Jersey regiment. Spellbinder Kirkbride was hired to entertain crowds by telling war stories about Grubb's bravery under Confederate fire at Fredericksburg and Chancellorsville.[38] Waving the "bloody shirt" was one of the most effective ways of campaigning.

In an effort to split the veterans vote, the Democrats countered by telling them what Abbett had done on their behalf during his first term. In a speech given in Trenton, outgoing Governor Robert Green pointedly reminded his audience that Abbett had obtained a property tax exemption for veterans and also obtained funds for a new home for disabled soldiers in Kearney in 1886. In addition, Abbett had arranged for the veterans to obtain "free railroad transportation" to attend the funeral of Ulysses S. Grant in July 1885.[39]

Naturally, the Republicans raked Abbett over the coals. They attacked him for using the governor's office for his own partisan purposes. His judicial appointments came under heavy fire. Not only that, the Republicans hurled all sorts of insults at Abbett. They savaged him in much the same way as they had done in the 1883 gubernatorial campaign, by impugning his integrity and professional ethics. Venting their anger and frustration, they dismissed his rhetoric as typical of his outrageous demagoguery. The use of the word demagogue was standard smear tactics in the Gilded Age. Lincoln Steffens explains why:

> Whenever a man in public life was called a demagogue, there was something good about him, something dangerous to the system. And since the plutocrats could not fasten any crime on him they fell back on the all sufficient charge that he was a demagogue.[40]

For his part, Abbett was adept at handling and deflecting such barbs. He was accustomed to this kind of mudslinging and expected as much. Whimsically, he poked fun at his detractors, "The Republicans say that I am a demagogue. I am a demagogue in the true sense of the word. I am on the side of the people. I appeal to the recollection of every wage earner in New Jersey and ask him whether Leon Abbett has not always been on their side."[41] The audience went wild, laughing, and cheering and calling for more. Abbett proceeded to ridicule Republicans for trying to pass themselves off every three years as friends of labor after attacking labor for two years and six months. Of course, this rhetoric served many purposes and there is no intention here to divest it of meaning in terms of the politics involved. It excited emotions to prevail. It also absorbed

traditional ethnic group antagonisms and reflected cleavages generated by different status and class positions of interest groups.

As the campaign reached its climax, Abbett came out against the use of Pinkerton detectives in labor disputes. This was a hot-button issue as far as the labor movement was concerned. In January 1887, the longshoremen in Hudson County had walked off the job to protest a wage cut imposed on coal shovelers and freight handlers. The effect of the strike was devastating: it shut down the entire port of New York. To counter this move, the shipping companies imported blacks from New York City as strikebreakers. They also hired a host of armed Pinkerton detectives to guard the docks. Such tactics inflamed the Irish stevedores. Violence erupted in Bayonne and Jersey City. As the strike continued, public anger turned against the Pinkertons for their brutality and excessive force in suppressing the strike.[42]

Stoking the fires of class resentment, Abbett denounced the hiring of armed Pinkertons as an unfair labor practice. He promised, if reelected governor, to call for legislation that would prohibit their use in labor disputes. Evidence of this genuine sympathy for the strikers was manifested in the municipal elections that were held in Bayonne and Jersey City in April 1887. City officials who had favored the use of Pinkertons were voted out of office.[43] Abbett's anti-Pinkerton stance galvanized workers in much the same way that convict labor had done in his 1883 campaign.

Grubb all but conceded the labor vote to Abbett and did not try to pass himself off as a friend of the working class. He knew better. The Democrats took him to task for paying low wages to his nonunion employees at the Lebanon Valley Furnace Company. Workingmen in New Jersey disliked Grubb as much as they had disliked Jonathan Dixon in 1883. Therefore, Grubb concentrated on winning the support of Civil War veterans, businessmen, and evangelical Protestants. Not surprisingly, Abbett again won the endorsement of the *Paterson Labor Standard*. Organized labor stood solidly behind him. As one anonymous worker put it, "We love Leon Abbett for the enemies that he has made. They are not in the ranks of labor."[44]

DROPPING A POLITICAL BOMBSHELL

With less than nine days to go before the election, the Grubb campaign was desperately looking for an issue that might sink Abbett. On October 28, Grubb and his managers dropped a political bombshell in the form of a press release sent to the *New York Tribune*. The newspaper ran a bold two-column lead story informing its readership that Leon Abbett and his law partner, Henry Schmitt, had been denied admission to the New York City Bar Association for professional misconduct. According to the story,

they had been rejected for having misrepresented the Erie Railroad Stockyard Company in a contract case in 1870, and for having disclosed privileged information while representing another client in 1886. The story raised an ethical cloud about Abbett's past dealings.

Clearly, the timing of the story was calculated to inflict maximum political damage. Infuriated by these charges, Abbett immediately claimed that the story was untrue. He wrote a lengthy letter of explanation to the *New York Times* that was published the next day. It read in part as follows:

> The statement in the article published in the *New York Tribune* of October 28 that I was excluded from membership of the New York Bar Association and declared by it to be unworthy of membership is false. Neither the committee nor the association acted upon my application, because my name was withdrawn at my request before action.
>
> If the association believed that I was guilty of the conduct stated in the Tribune, it was its duty to prefer charges against me before the General Terms of the Supreme Court. It took no such action. It did nothing. No member offered any resolution on the subject that I ever heard of. The subcommittee, so far as I know, never made any report criticizing my professional conduct or advising any action against myself.[45]

Sensing that he was going to be blackballed, no matter what happened, Abbett withdrew his name before any action could be taken. It was simply a case of his doing it to them before they did it to him. He then went on to explain in his letter:

> My reasons for withdrawal were not founded upon any action taken in the case of my partner, Mr. Schmitt. That statement in the Tribune is false upon its face. Mr. Schmitt's application was not acted upon until after my name had been withdrawn. After I withdrew my name the committee, after hearing all that the enemies of our firm chose to say against us, recommended Mr. Schmitt for membership. He was defeated by the adverse vote, as I am informed, of 17 members, notwithstanding the committee, before whom the charges were made, had unanimously reported in his favor. My name at that time was not before any committee, because it had, with the assent of the association, been withdrawn.
>
> I never have heard of the charges as made in the *Tribune*, and I ask that paper to give the name of anyone who says such charges were made by the Bar Association. I cannot tell what was done in secret there, but I am sure that neither my partner nor myself was charged with having disclosed secrets which had been entrusted to us professionally. If any such charge was made, it was an infamous falsehood, and I call upon any one making it to state what professional secret entrusted to me by a client I ever disclosed. I can then answer it specifically. I can only say to such a general charge that it is a falsehood, and is one made at the end of a political campaign to try to affect the result.[46]

To reassure voters that Grubb and his campaign managers had raised a red herring and bogus issue, Abbett concluded by saying:

My further answer to any statement as to how I am esteemed by the profession in New York is that on the 16th of September, 1889, I was elected a member of the New York State Bar Association by the unanimous vote of its Executive Committee, as appears by its certificate in my possession.[47]

As a campaign issue, the bombshell that the Republicans had purposely planted turned out to be a dud. Since it lacked credibility, it did not have the intended adverse impact. Joseph E. Crowell, the editor of the Republican *Paterson Morning Call,* admitted as much when he wrote:

This is one of the charges against Abbett that was never reproduced in this newspaper for the reason that we did not consider it amounted to anything in a political sense. It makes about as much sense as the Democratic charges against General Grubb, because he belongs to a Philadelphia military company, or because he parts his hair in the middle. There is enough against Abbett politically, from his public record without attacking him personally.[48]

The voters turned out in record number on November 5, 1889. By the end of the day, Abbett won a smashing victory, collecting a total of 138,245 votes compared with 123,992 for Grubb. This was 52.7 percent of the two-party vote. Abbett drew on the same sources of electoral support in roughly the same degree of strength that he had in 1883. He won easily and would have done so even without the election frauds at certain polling places in Jersey City, where the number of votes cast exceeded the number of registered voters. The biggest surprise was that Abbett captured the Republican stronghold of Essex County, where the all-important "wet vote" proved decisive. Grubb's patronage dispute with the local Republican organization over the appointment of an internal revenue collector also hurt him there. Abbett failed to carry Cape May and Mercer counties, which he had done in 1883. But he more than made up for these losses by winning Essex and Morris counties. Abbett once more demonstrated his mastery of New Jersey politics. To top it off, the Democrats won a majority in the state legislature. They took thirty-seven out of a possible sixty seats in the general assembly, while the Republicans barely retained control of the senate that was divided eleven to ten in their favor.

Abbett's victory, however, was marred by serious and substantial voting irregularities in Jersey City. Here the Davis machine delivered Abbett an unprecedented plurality of 13,516. Critics were quick to point out that this figure came close to matching his total victory margin of 14,253. Although Grubb did not challenge the results, the Republican senate soon launched a legislative investigation and found wholesale ballot

irregularities and alleged improprieties. Historian Richard McCormick has summarized the findings of their probe:

> They found, after a check of the registry lists, that there had been around ten thousand false registrations. Scores of voters registered from tugs, canal boats, and cheap hotels. The poll lists contained the names of men who had been dead for fifteen years. Gangs of "repeaters" brought across the Hudson from the Bowery voted as often as ten times in as many election districts.
>
> The election boards were all under the firm control of the city machine. In one district the lone Republican inspector was prevented from entering the poll by sixteen uniformed policemen and a compliant substitute was appointed. In another ward, voters passed through two lines of police and handed their ballots through a door to an election official without entering the polling place or even seeing the ballot deposited in the box. Challengers were so intimidated that they dared not question any voter's qualifications.
>
> There was no way of estimating how many fraudulent ballots were counted. An examination of the contents of the boxes in one-fourth of the districts produced nearly eighteen hundred illicit ballots, most of them of the tissue paper variety. There were wide discrepancies between the number of ballots and the number of names on the poll lists. It was learned that the night before the election Boss "Bob" Davis met with the county Democratic Committee. Davis sat at the head of the room at a table on which there were packages of tissue ballots, of regular ballots and of money. As each committee member's name was called, he came forward and took up his several packages. The tissue ballots were to be folded inside the regular ballots, thereby giving a man a multiple vote. The investigating committee was impressed with the smooth efficiency of the whole vote-stealing operation and concluded that such skill came only from practice.[49]

Reformers like George Record were shocked at the extent of the vote fraud and the flagrant manner in which it had been perpetrated. The local Republicans vowed to put those who had participated in the vote fraud behind bars. Prosecution, however, proved difficult, because the county grand jury was filled with Davis men. Nevertheless, sixty-six Democrats were convicted of ballot fraud and sentenced to eighteen months in state prison. Abbett, of course, kept a safe distance from them and thereby could profess ignorance of the matter. Naturally, the Republicans quickly linked him to the scandal. Said the *Newark Daily Advertiser*:

> Nobody pretends that Abbett sat at the table with Sheriff Davis and the other Hudson County scamps and gave out the money and the joker ballots which the Senate witnesses saw distributed just before the election.

Nobody has proved that he was cognizant of the details of the conspiracy and arranged for its success. But that Abbett—a resident of Jersey City, an active local Democratic politician, and one of the chief beneficiaries of the fraud—did not know what was going on is something hard to believe. A word from him would have stopped the conspiracy. With regard to this crime, the Governor has been discreetly silent.[50]

Obviously embarrassed by the scandal, Abbett sought to have Davis removed as head of the Hudson Democratic machine. Word spread that Davis was about to resign, but such rumors were premature. Orestes Cleveland, John McPherson, and Edward Young all came to his rescue. The only way that Abbett could discipline Davis was to deny him patronage at the state level. For his part, Davis considered Abbett a political ingrate. He felt that he had done more than anyone else to ensure his reelection, and yet the governor excluded him from the party's inner circle.[51]

On December 30, Abbett went on a brief vacation to Norfolk, Virginia, for some much needed rest and relaxation and to recover from a bad case of the Russian flu.[52] Reinvigorated by his stay, he returned home and accepted an invitation to speak at the annual Jackson Day Dinner, held at the Hoffman House restaurant in New York City. This function was a black tie affair, with luminaries from the world of politics, business, religion, academe, and the literary community in attendance.

Resplendent in his formal attire, Abbett told his distinguished audience that political parties made popular democracy possible. Parties were the only political institutions whose interest was to mobilize widespread participation in elections and effectively link that participation to responsible government. "Weaken the political party and you weaken popular democracy."[53] A true populist, Abbett was suspicious of reformers who were about to take much of the excitement out of politics. They wanted fewer parades and more pamphlets instructing the electorate about public issues. Voting, in their view, should be an individual act of informed competence, not an act of group solidarity. All of which ran contrary to Abbett's philosophy. Democrats of his stripe characteristically clung to the principle of party loyalty and believed that public policy should be made by the party in power. He was not about to desert his party for some abstract theories espoused by Republican Mugwumps and "good government" reformers.

ENDNOTES

1 For a biographical sketch of William J. Sewell, see *Biographical Directory of the American Congress 1774–1971* (Washington, D.C., U.S. Government Printing Office, 1971), 1679. See also Gillette, *Jersey Blue*, 171–172.

2 *New Jersey Legislative Manual for 1887* (Trenton, T. F. Fitzgerald Publisher, 1887), 173.

3 For a good analysis of this senatorial election, see Charles S. Tunis, "A Memorable Political Contest," *The Acme Magazine*, vol. l, no. 5, (March 1907), 3–7; vol. 1, no. 6 (April 1907), 31–36. See also, Sackett, *Modern Battles of Trenton*, vol. 1:264–283.

4 Sackett, *Modern Battles of Trenton*, 1:282.

5 *New York Times*, March 3, 1887.

6 Sackett, *Modern Battles of Trenton*, 1:283.

7 Russell Decker, "The Senator Who Voted Against the Sherman Antitrust Act," 77 *Proceedings of the New Jersey Historical Society*, (October 1959) 265–266.

8 Vecoli, *The People of New Jersey*, 154–155.

9 *New Jersey Legislative Manual for 1889*, 171–174.

10 *Paul v. Gloucester County*, 50 N.J.L. 585 (1888).

11 Sackett, *Modern Battles of Trenton*, 1:408–409.

12 Herbert J. Bass, *The Political Career of David Bennett Hill* (Syracuse, Syracuse University Press, 1961), 121–125.

13 Robert Dahl, *Who Governs?* (New Haven, Yale University Press, 1961), 45–51.

14 Sackett, *Modern Battles of Trenton*, 1:307–308.

15 Richard P. McCormick, *The History of Voting in New Jersey* (New Brunswick: Rutgers University Press, 1953), 174–175.

16 A complete biographical account of Edward F. Young is found in Alexander McLean's *History of Jersey City* (Jersey City, 1895), 339–341.

17 Letter from Joseph J. Templeton to Owen Grundy (dated December 27, 1968) suggests the possibility of a cover-up by Edward Young. This letter remains on file at the Jersey City Historical Society. There is also an oil painting of Mayor Orestes Cleveland that hangs in a corridor on the second floor of the Jersey City Public Library. Significantly, the names of Robert Davis and Edward Young are listed on the donor plate.

18 Sackett, *Modern Battles of Trenton*, 1:301.

19 *Ibid.*, 1:303.

20 *New York Times*, June 2, 1890.

21 In re Petition of Mayor Cleveland, 52 N.J.L. 189 (1889). See also, Augustine W. Costello, *History of the Police Department of Jersey City* (Jersey City, 1891), 123–135.

22 *New York Times*, August 5, 1889.

23 *New York Times*, August 16, 1889.

24 *New York Times*, August 19, 1889.

25 *New York Times*, September 8, 1889.

26 There are several good biographical sketches of Edward Burd Grubb. The most complete and historically accurate is the one found in John W. Jordan's *Colonial Families of Philadelphia* (New York, Lewis Publishing Company, 1911), vol. II, 1253–1257. See also E. M. Woodward and John J. Hageman, *History of Burlington and Mercer Counties* (Philadelphia, Everts and Peck, 1883), 165–166.

27 John F. Reynolds, *Testing Democracy*, (Chapel Hill, University of North Carolina Press, 1988), 24.

28 *New York Times*, August 19, 1889.

29 *New Jersey Legislative Manual for 1890*, 159.

30 See campaign brochure entitled, "The Record of Leon Abbett," (Jersey City, 1889).

31 Allan McDermott's letter was published in the *Trenton True American*, October 18, 1889.

32 *Newark Daily Advertiser*, October 11, 1889.

33 *Trenton True American*, October 19, 1889.

34 *Jersey City Evening Journal*, November 4, 1889.

35 *New York Times*, September 18, 1889.

36 *Newark Daily Advertiser*, October 11, 1889.

37 *New York Times*, October 28, 1889.

38 Sackett, *Modern Battles of Trenton*, 1:322.

39 *Newark Daily Advertiser*, October 11, 1889.

40 Lincoln Steffens, *The Autobiography of Lincoln Steffens* (New York, The Literary Guild, 1931), 474.

41 *Newark Daily Advertiser*, October 11, 1889.

42 Vecoli, *The People of New Jersey*, 84.
43 *Jersey City Argus*, April 13, 1887.
44 *Trenton True American*, September 12, 1889.
45 *New York Times*, October 29, 1889.
46 *Ibid.*
47 *Ibid.*
48 *Paterson Morning Call*, October 31, 1889.
49 McCormick, *The History of Voting in New Jersey*, 171–172.
50 *Newark Daily Advertiser*, March 10, 1890.
51 *New York Times*, December 10, 1889.
52 *New York Times*, December 30, 1889.
53 *Newark Daily Advertiser*, January 9, 1890.

Before Abbett began his second administration, George Werts, the Democratic state senator from Morris County, sponsored a bill that increased the governor's salary from $5,000 to $10,000. Outgoing Governor Robert Green hastily signed the measure before leaving office. A provision in the state constitution explicitly prohibited a governor's salary from being either increased or diminished during his tenure. Later on, Abbett appointed Green as vice chancellor to the New Jersey Court of Chancery. Green had purposely kept this judicial position vacant for almost two years, and rumors spread that this was a prearranged deal. But the *New York Times* claimed that the rumored trade-off between Abbett and Green had no foundation in fact: "There was no arrangement made to swap favors. Abbett's diligent attention to the affairs of state make his services worth $10,000 per year. Green is an admirable lawyer and his appointment to the Vice Chancellorship is everywhere commended."[1] If such a deal existed, which is more than likely, the powerbrokers were able to deliver.

SECURING BALLOT REFORM LEGISLATION

On January 21, 1890, Abbett delivered his second inaugural address. He surprised everyone by focusing attention on the recent election-fraud scandal and demanding a ballot reform law. Politely ignoring the fact that the scandal had marred his victory, the governor proclaimed that there was nothing more sacred in government than the ballot box. Declaring himself on the side of the reformers, he said:

> The best sentiment of the country in all the states demands ballot reform
> and honest elections. The safeguards which the law has thrown around

the ballot have been found insufficient to prevent fraud, the intimidation of the voter and the corrupting use of money in elections. The oaths of election officers have not always prevented them from tampering with the ballot-box and receiving and counting fraudulent votes.[2]

The governor proposed a comprehensive program of election reforms, including an official ballot, facilities for secret voting, and limitations on campaign expenditures. In making a political accommodation with his followers in Hudson County, Abbett stopped short of calling for the adoption of the Austrian ballot, and he explicitly advocated the distribution of ballots before election day. Nevertheless, his program that included a statewide voter registration system represented a constructive step forward.

Soon after the legislature convened, a bipartisan joint committee assumed responsibility for drafting a suitable bill. Two months later, this committee reported a bill crafted by Senator George Werts, a Democrat from Morris County, who was already being groomed as Abbett's successor. Reformers considered the bill flawed in that it provided for different colored party ballots that were obtainable several days before the election. The Republicans in the assembly sought to substitute the Kane bill of the preceding session, but they were defeated in a strict party vote. Whereupon they relented, and the Werts bill was passed by a lopsided margin of fifty to one on April 9. At the same time, a similar struggle was taking place in the senate, where the Republican majority was successful in passing the Kane bill. It looked as if the two houses might become deadlocked, but in conference committee the Republican senators agreed to accept the Werts bill on May 21. The pressure was great enough to force the ballot reform bill through, but Abbett incurred the enmity of the big county bosses.

On enactment of this law, the Republican *State Gazette* concluded, "It is not such an ideal measure of reform as we wished for, but it is a very considerable improvement upon the present system."[3] No one was thrilled with the compromise measure. In his seminal work on voting behavior in New Jersey, Richard P. McCormick writes, "Neither the zealous proponents of the Australian system nor the professional politicians were enthusiastic about the new law, but at the same time both groups were able to discern its virtues."[4]

UNFINISHED RAILROAD BUSINESS

Pressed by an agenda of items left over from the Green administration, Abbett asserted leadership with regard to the unfinished business of railroad taxation. The arbitration of the tax arrears of the Morris and Essex

Railroad was still pending. After three years of haggling and intransigence, neither side could agree on the amount of back taxes due the state. Governor Green had allowed the arbitrators to drag their feet without reaching an agreement. Deciding the time was ripe for concerted action, Abbett pressed for a settlement:

> I am still of the opinion expressed by me in 1884 that all special contracts on the subject of taxation should be extinguished. I am prepared at all times to invoke every power of the state to secure such extinguishment, if the corporations will not voluntarily assent thereto.[5]

Only when the governor threatened further legal action did the arbitrators reach an agreement. They agreed that the state should be paid $300,000, while the Morris and Essex received a $65,000 credit for taxes overpaid under the 1884 law. Abbett's strong-arm tactics worked. Under duress, the obstinate railroad backed off. Once the arbitrators agreed on the terms, the company announced the surrender of its tax-exemption contract. In the end, the old-fashioned politics of personal power held sway. By facing down the railroads and imposing his incredible will, Abbett had brought closure to his long-running battle with them. The magnitude of his triumph was in direct proportion to the political clout of his opponents. For he had once again beaten the mighty railroads at their own political game. Nonetheless, the railroad tax issue still generated controversy for at least another fifty years. It would not go away.

THE RACETRACK CONTROVERSY

Although Abbett placed a high premium on party loyalty, he showed that he could operate independently of his party organization. One of his bitterest legislative battles was over his veto of a controversial racetrack bill in 1890. The statute (A-112), strongly backed by urban party leaders, legalized "bookmaking and pool-selling" for a period of fifty-five racing days. It had been introduced by Democratic Assemblyman Leonard Kalisch of Newark. Racing thoroughbreds in New Jersey depended to a large extent on the good will of politicians. To placate them, the racetrack owners distributed patronage jobs and extended free passes to the tracks. Several Democrats moonlighted at the racetracks and a few were even proprietors. Race tracks in Gloucester City, Guttenberg, and Monmouth Park contributed to the local economies.

Camden boss William J. Thompson owned the Gloucester City racetrack, along with a hotel that was famous for serving "planked shad." Commonly known as the "Duke of Gloucester," Thompson established a gambling casino along the Delaware River and ran ferryboats across the

river to attract Philadelphians who could not gamble in their city because of restrictive blue laws. Thompson hired Assembly Speaker Thomas Flynn of Paterson as his race starter. Gambling also flourished in Hudson County, where Dennis McLaughlin ran the infamous Guttenberg racetrack that operated in defiance of the antibookmaking laws. Assemblyman Timothy J. Carroll of Jersey City was a well-known bookmaker. They brazenly defied the law, because the Davis machine protected them from prosecution.

Similar to the railroads, the horse racing interests were well-connected politically. A sleeper for most of the session, the bill in question quietly sailed through the legislature without much opposition. In an election year, Abbett was worried about its potential backlash, especially among hard-shelled Protestants who abhorred gambling and considered it immoral. He sensed that they would be greatly disturbed once they learned about the pending legislation. Therefore, the governor purposely delayed signing the bill. He then turned to the press and let it be known that no one had stepped forward to oppose the legislation. This intentional leak was probably meant as a trial balloon.

As Abbett had anticipated, the news about the passage of the racetrack bill evoked a huge public outcry. A large delegation of Protestant clergy and laymen decended on the governor's office on June 17, 1890. Led by the Reverend Everard Kempshall of the First Presbyterian Church of Elizabeth, who had organized a coalition known as the Anti-Racetrack League, the group presented Abbett with a petition signed by more than 3,000 citizens urging him to veto the bill. To bolster their point of view, they argued that "hundreds of laborers and mechanics, heretofore honest and industrious, now leave their work day after day to gamble on these races."[6] The Anti-Race Track League mobilized public support in opposition to gambling. The Camden Law and Order League joined in the protest and voiced their concerns. So did the Monmouth Baptist Minister's Conference then meeting in Red Bank.

The profusion of moral outrage and indignation continued in Sunday sermons from Protestant church pulpits across the state. Reverend Frederick G. Inglehart of the Central Methodist Church in Newark set the tone when he told his congregation, "The state has already been given to the saloons. Now it is intended to give it to the horse jockeys, blacklegs, and thieves. Louisiana may sell her virtue for $1 million to the Louisiana Lottery Company. New Jersey's legislators are willing to give hers away."[7] Clergy and laymen from all parts of the state voiced their protests. Reverend Arthur H. Lewis of the Seventh Day Baptist Church in Plainfield declared, "All forms of gambling belong to the lower grades of humanity. Betting on animals is the very worst form. If such immorality were legalized, New Jersey's suburban towns would become the reservoir of the scum of the cities."[7]

After hearing two days of protests, Abbett decided not to sign the bill. He simply filed it away with a host of other unsigned bills in the state library. It amounted to a pocket veto. Since this occurred at the end of the session, the legislature had no opportunity to override his veto. Several Democrats were furious at him for vetoing their pet bill, but he had anticipated the political consequences. An overwhelming majority of the public believed that gambling was socially unacceptable. From a practical perspective, Abbett had aroused public opinion and defused the potential backlash with his pocket veto. In the elections of 1890, the Democrats won control of both houses of the legislature. So it was another win-win situation for the governor.

ENTICING BUSINESS CORPORATIONS TO NEW JERSEY

Conditions could not have been more propitious for Abbett in 1890. The governor was riding the crest of his power and popularity in New Jersey. In an age when legislatures were easily controlled by party machines, he began asking it for action on a wider range of issues. The New Jersey economy had never been more robust; unemployment was at a historic low, while consumer confidence was at a record high. Personal income was up, and opportunity abounded. With a prosperous economy and greater industrialization, there was ample tax revenue to pay for capital improvements and to expand the operations of state government.

During the summer of 1890, Abbett made the acquaintance of James B. Dill, a brilliant Wall Street corporate lawyer. Dill also taught courses in business law at the Stevens Institute of Technology in Hoboken. Together the two men conspired to make New Jersey the ideal place in which to obtain a charter for an industrial trust. According to Lincoln Steffens, Dill's proposal was designed "to make New Jersey a mecca for corporations; it was not merely to let business sneak over there for charters now and then, but to open up the state as a wholesale charter factory and advertise the industry in a businesslike way."[8]

By 1891, some 1,626 business corporations had taken advantage of the new laws. Spurred by this success story, Abbett and Dill organized the Corporation Trust Company of Jersey City that was a corporation to organize corporations. Prominent Democrats like Henry Kelsey, Allan McDermott, and Henry S. White were named as directors. Eager to make some easy money that seemed to be everywhere he turned, Abbett bought substantial stock in the company.[9]

As a result of these initiatives, the New Jersey economy prospered with heavy investments in new industrial plants. All of which produced greater tax revenue. Abbett continued to make the Democratic party the

party of economic growth and opportunity. But he made sure that his cooperation with business was not at the expense of labor.

THE CLARK THREAD MILLS STRIKE

Labor leaders pushed hard for the enactment of anti-Pinkerton legislation in 1890, and they were men who could mobilize the working class. Under heavy pressure from labor, Abbett did not disappoint them. Previously, Governor Green had been exceedingly cool to the idea. In fact, Green had offered to send state troops to put down the longshoremen's strike in 1887, but the Jersey City police had spurned his offer.[10] The hiring of armed Pinkertons to crush the strike had left its residual antagonisms. Aware that public opinion was on his side, Abbett used his legislative clout to obtain a law that made it illegal for business corporations to employ nonresident private detectives in labor disputes.

But that was only the start. When genuine crisis occurred, Abbett came up with new ideas for resolving industrial strife. In early December 1890, the spinners at the Clark Thread Mills in Newark and Kearny decided to strike. They were protesting the discharge of forty workers who had simply asked for redress of their grievances. Among those discharged was Frank Hatfield who was respected by his coworkers and considered the best spinner at the mills. Another was Christopher Hughes fired after being employed by the company for more than twenty years. Management had targeted these two workers as trouble-makers.

Worse was to come. The company imposed a lockout, posting notices that the mills would be closed for an indefinite period to replace and repair machinery. The biweekly wages of the women workers were slashed from $15 to $5. Over 3,000 employees were thrown out of work just prior to the Christmas season. The striking workers were poorly educated men, women and children. They complained about the abusive treatment of the general manager, Herbert E. Walmsley, who lived in Orange. Not surprisingly, Walmsley asked for and received police protection during the strike.

The Clark Thread strike lasted for nineteen weeks, beginning on December 9, 1890, and continuing through April 20, 1891—one of the longest and bitterest strikes in New Jersey history. Labor leader Samuel Gompers, a Jewish immigrant whose world was shaped by the cigar-making lofts on New York's Lower East Side, visited the mills and called for a nationwide boycott of Clark thread. When the mill owners imported Canadian laborers to work at substandard wages, the strike got nasty. Worker antagonism toward the well-to-do millowners was almost unbounded. An angry mob stormed the factory gates and surrounded the

FIG. 22
Clark Thread Mills in Newark and Kearney, NJ. Scene of violent labor strike in 1890.

mills refusing to allow anyone to enter. They stoned the scabs and smashed the windows at the Kearny mills. Thomas Corrigan, a company policeman hired through the Fuller Detective Agency in New York, waved his revolver in the face of Christopher Hughes and threatened "to blow his brains out."[11] The local police refused to intervene in the labor dispute, because many of their friends and neighbors were on strike. John J. McPhillips, the sheriff of Hudson County, was summoned to the scene in Kearny, but he refused to cross the picket lines. He personally contributed to the strike fund.

When the local authorities could not control the violence, the company asked Governor Abbett to call out the state militia to restore order. On February 14, he personally toured the mills and talked with the striking workers. He was looking for a way to calm passions on both sides. Uncomfortable with the situation, he was concerned about public safety but wisely decided not to deploy the national guardsmen. "The presence of state troops," said the *New York Times*, "would have fanned the prevailing discontent into open rebellion."[12] Acting under the cover of an emergency, Abbett cleverly defused the volatile situation by deputizing the Jersey City police as state law enforcement officers. Peace was restored.

The governor had learned from prior experience that city police were better trained for such purposes. Unlike military troops, they refrained from using excessive force against civilians. Abbett's ingenious maneuvering not only helped to settle the strike, but it also enabled him to avoid being labeled a "strike breaking governor."

With the crippling strike entering its third month, Abbett sought legislation that would give him the power to recruit state policemen from any municipal police force in New Jersey. The statute also empowered him to take such action even if local officials objected. The debate over the "state police bill" was bitter and acrimonious. On the one hand, Assemblyman Michael Mullone of Jersey City, who sponsored the governor's bill (A-265), claimed that it would do away with "bayonet rule."[13] On the other hand, Assemblyman John R. Hardin of Newark saw the bill as an abridgement of "home rule" and feared that it would put too much power in the hands of the governor. The *Newark Sunday Call* expressed a similar fear, "It would foster the dangerous idea of a paternal government and place in the Governor a power, which in the hands of some men, might be made as hateful as the French Secret Service."[14]

Despite opposition at the local level, Abbett had his bill approved, whereupon he appointed Jersey City Police Commissioner John Parnell Feeney as the first state police chief. The job paid $2,500 a year. Feeney's famed squad of 300 state troopers became an effective law enforcement agency, but it was bitterly resented by those who feared centralized power. The *New York Times* explored the tensions involved:

The localities have heretofore guarded themselves against state interference with their home disputes as jealously as the states stand guard against federal interposition for the settlement of state questions. Before 'Feeney's Three Hundred' were devised the Governor could not take a hand in a local squabble until the sheriff of the county called upon him; the sheriff in turn could not interfere until the town constable had declared himself inadequate to the emergency. But the Governor can now step in whenever he pleases, brush the sheriff and town constable aside as though they were manikins, and do their work for them in his own way.[15]

CONTINUED SUPPORT FOR LABOR

The support of labor was critical for Abbett, if he was to further his ambition for national office. He overhauled the arbitration law of 1886 to make it more effective. This new law created a state Bureau of Arbitration for "the amicable adjustment of grievances and disputes between employees and employers." Abbett then appointed three trade union men to run

this bureau, a mix of old and new faces most of whom he picked: Joseph P. McDonnell of Paterson, Lewis D. Robertson of Frenchtown, and Patrick F. Doyle of Jersey City. John W. Romaine of Paterson served as secretary to the board.

In a second series of labor laws, Abbett added substantially to the impressive record of labor legislation that he had compiled during his first term. The right of trade unions and labor organizations to be incorporated was legally recognized. The work week was reduced from sixty to fifty-five hours. Saturday was made a half-day, and Labor Day was recognized as a legal holiday to give "workers time for recreation and mental advancement." A state Bureau of Labor and Industries was created "as a means of bringing in contact and unison the state and the wage-earners, so as to ascertain their desires and necessities, and make such suggestions as will be for their benefit and advantage."[16] The dreaded "company store" was abolished and workers were entitled to receive their wages in cash, not in store orders. Employers were forbidden to extract pledges from prospective employees not to join a union. This meant that yellow dog contracts were no longer valid. Private labels and trademarks were protected. The mechanics lien law was revised to protect the wages of workers from unscrupulous contractors. More public funds were appropriated for industrial schools and free public libraries and reading rooms. All of which provided for the stability of working-class neighborhoods.

TROUBLE DOWN ON THE FARM

Agriculture throughout the country was experiencing an economic depression in the early 1890s. Debt-ridden farmers in the South and the West were suffering from a shortage of money. As the world market for agriculture expanded in the aftermath of the Civil War, there was a steady decline in the prices of wheat, cotton, and other crops they raised for export. Their farm equipment was expensive and to pay for it farmers borrowed heavily and mortgaged their land at high interest rates. What they needed, they insisted, were higher prices for their produce and more money to pay off their debts. Their discontent culminated in the Populist movement and the agrarian radicalism of Democrat William Jennings Bryan of Nebraska.

New Jersey farmers faced similar problems, but they were not as radical in their demands as their counterparts in the South and the West. Nonetheless, they suffered from high interest rates, poor public roads, discrimination in railroad rates, high local taxation, demonetization of silver, increasing labor costs, and overproduction. There was also a lack of American ships to transport their produce abroad. The value of farmland

in New Jersey had depreciated forty percent during the past fifteen years. Farmers depended to a large extent on the state Agricultural College at Rutgers, along with the Agricultural Experiment Station, for the improvement of farming practices and production through the transfer mechanism of the county agent.

The experience of small growers in Atlantic County, who lost their farms and ended up angry and frustrated, was typical of many. The most dramatic was a sheriff's sale that took place at Egg Harbor City on April 4, 1890. This foreclosure, commenced by the heirs of Stephen Colwell, involved farmlands in Mullica, Galloway, and Hamilton townships. The German farmers were evicted from their mortaged homes. The *New York Times* described what happened:

The sale began at 2 o'clock this afternoon and about two hundred of the holders of the land in question were present...The sale will be continued tomorrow, when parcel No. 46, which contains over two hundred farms owned by thirty thrifty Germans, will be sold. The wives and children of these honest, hard-working farmers gathered around the hotel today, and the scene was one that is seldom witnessed in free America. Over a hundred of these farms have been planted by the recent owners with peach, pear, and other trees. Berries and grapes have also been cultivated extensively. Now all the labor of years has suddenly and legally proved to be for nothing. Among the persons buying these lands are some of the present owners, but they are very few, for most of them are poor. Dr. H. Gehring of New York and William Fink of Baltimore were the buyers. The sale aggregated $80,000. George Lang, one of the evicted farmers, became insane today and burned his buildings and himself to death. Several others are nearly crazy. Great excitement prevails.[17]

The threat to farmers across the state was real. Abbett was aware of their economic woes and promised to work closely with them to solve their problems. For starters, he spoke to the farmers at their annual convention sponsored by the State Board of Agriculture.[18] After his speech, he began putting his words into action. During the legislative session of 1891, he created the State Board of Taxation to deal with the problem of tax equalization. As tax commissioners, he appointed Albert H. Slape, Theodore P. Hopler, and Charles C. Black. All three of whom came from small rural, farming communities. Their work, which led to a substantial increase in property valuation, won the approval of farmers throughout the state.

To further advance the scientific study of agriculture, Abbett got the legislature to provide a $12,000 annuity for sixty-five scholarships at the agricultural school. This endowment no doubt helped Rutgers, but it annoyed its intrastate rival Princeton. An unnamed Princeton trustee accused the Abbett administration of playing favoritism. He wrote a public letter (without his signature) expressing his chagrin:

Rutgers has always received large contributions from the public funds; Princeton never. Both colleges were applicants for the fund appropriated to the state by the national government for the establishment of agricultural colleges. The application of Princeton was refused and that of Rutgers granted. Two or three years ago Rutgers applied for $30,000 to build a chemical laboratory; it was granted; Princeton graduates, then members of the legislature, voting for it. Now comes a demand for $12,000 annually, ostensibly for scholarships in the Agricultural College, for which there is necessity, but really to provide education in advanced science for a select few boys from the several Assembly districts in the state, and to pay Rutgers College that amount of money yearly for doing it, and virtually granting that college an endowment of $250,000 by which to enable her to maintain four additional professorships.[19]

In responding to other farmer demands, Abbett had the legislature appropriate $75,000 for road improvements. Further, he lobbied for federal funds in Washington for public road construction. Three macadam roads in Middlesex County were the first in the United States built under the original federal highway grant-in-aid program.

Since states lacked the power to regulate interstate commerce, there was not much a governor could do about discriminatory railroad rates. This was a responsibility of the federal government. A new federal agency, the Interstate Commerce Commission, had been created in 1887 to ensure uniform railroad rates.

The farmers also sought the creation of a state Weather Bureau Service. Severe thunder storms and intermittent periods of drought had made them vulnerable to extreme fluctuations in weather conditions. With a staff of fifty-four trained meteorological observers, the new agency set up a weather watch and disseminated weekly "weather crop bulletins." Peach growers pushed for a standard of measure to bolster consumer confidence and to assure buyers that they were not being cheated. They obtained legislation that called for a standard-size peach basket with the label "Grown in New Jersey" stamped on it. The state likewise provided a subsidy for the commercial oyster and shellfish industry that was centered at Port Norris and Bivalve in Cumberland County.

MANAGING THE BUREAUCRACY

In budget and management terms, Abbett proved to be a capable and articulate administrator. He cited the long overdue expansion of the state prison as a critical unmet need. Originally built in 1836 to house 706 inmates, it was severely overcrowded, containing more than 1,000 prisoners. To alleviate such overcrowding, Abbett recommended the expansion of prison facilities with the addition of a new wing comprised of sev-

eral new cell-blocks, plus a library and a prison hospital. He also recommended a new family building and interfaith chapel at the Jamesburg Reformatory. The governor also obtained funds to build a home for feeble-minded women in Vineland, as well as a home for disabled Civil War veterans overlooking the Passaic River in Kearny. By way of other capital improvements, Abbett spent $40,000 for a new building at the Normal School in Trenton, $25,000 for improvements at the Industrial School for Girls, and another $25,000 to improve the National Guard camp at Sea Girt.

But these capital improvements were costly, and the tax bill for them was resented. With increased railroad and business taxes, however, Abbett had sufficient money to pay for them. Revenue from these sources had increased from $140,629 in 1885 to $465,452 in 1892. Moreover, he got the legislature to pass a collateral inheritance tax that helped to cushion the blow. Abbett also used the surpluses derived from the sale and leasing of state-owned riparian lands. This money, however, was legally tied up in a special school fund. Under a statute passed in 1871, the riparian funds were dedicated for the support of public schools. Although expressly forbidden to transfer this revenue, the governor considered the dedication of riparian funds as an infringement of his executive power. Other governors, like Joel Parker, had tried to tap this money for capital improvements but without much success. A powerful education lobby denounced Abbett's plans as a scheme to destroy the school fund. As the *New York Times* put it:

The proposition was received with no favor, but Governor Abbett has succeeded in whipping it through both houses, and it has become a law by receiving his signature. The act takes away about $125,000 per year from the principal of the school money, and by the same amount swells the fund at the disposal of wasteful legislators.[20]

Similarly, Abbett abolished the Sinking Fund Commission and integrated its duties with those of the state treasurer. It is interesting to note that a year after Abbett left office, the riparian revenue was dedicated once again to the school fund. Such was the power of the educational lobby against a less forceful governor. In fact, the practice of "earmarking" revenues for special purposes was not eliminated in New Jersey until as late as 1945, when the general fund concept was finally adopted. Much like his efforts to put a cap on municipal indebtedness in his first term, Abbett was well ahead of his time in advocating this fiscal reform.

In 1891, Abbett obtained legislation creating a new department of banking and insurance. He recognized that government regulation of business was necessary for continued economic growth and prosperity. The responsibilities of this new agency included the regulation of 260 financial institutions and insurance companies in New Jersey that ranged

in scope from corporate giants like Prudential Insurance and Mutual Benefit Life in Newark to small town rural banks. One of the agency's first regulations required a standard fire insurance policy. It also cracked down on insurance companies that were fleecing the poor with nickel and dime policies.

Abbett appointed George Harvey as the first commissioner of banking and insurance. At the time, Harvey was a promising journalist and a representative of New York's elite press. Like many of his contemporaries, he regarded newspaper work as preparation for a career as a political broker or kingmaker. It was rumored that Abbett gave Harvey the banking commissioner's job as a sinecure, but he also wanted Harvey's advice to help him improve his relations with an increasingly hostile press.[21] At the time, Abbett was being hammered and unfairly vilified in the media. Newspaper owners typically used their papers for attack journalism and for waging partisan warfare in the Gilded Age. By resorting to yellow journalism, they sold more newspapers and dramatically increased mass circulation. For whatever reason, Harvey departed in 1892 to work in the presidential campaign of Grover Cleveland.

In reshuffling his cabinet, Abbett appointed former U.S. Attorney George S. Duryee of Newark to replace Harvey. Duryee was a protegee of James Smith who was boss of the Essex County Democratic machine. In his relentless drive to become the next U.S. senator from New Jersey, Abbett made several concessions to predatory Democratic politicians along the way. These concessions, which he deemed necessary to appease the rank and file of his party, left the stench of corruption in the air. The governor had ideals and goals to achieve for the public good as he understood it, but he was still determined to go to Washington and serve in the U.S. Senate. And he was willing to use dubious means to placate the men who could deliver the senatorship.

Through powers Abbett acquired over local government, he perpetrated the equivalent of ripper laws in disregard of local desires. He signed a statute that removed Republicans from the local boards of public works in Newark and Camden and replaced them with Democrats. Another statute allowed Abbett to name the fire chiefs and police commissioners for Newark and Jersey City. In 1891, he went along with a notorious gerrymander that ensured the Democrats forty-one of the sixty seats in the general assembly. This scheme was worse than the Republican gerrymander of 1871. The governor played the game of the liquor dealers in getting county liquor license boards to supercede local boards that refused to grant licenses. He also created a State Parole Board that bowed to political pressure. When an infamous embezzler in Hoboken was paroled, the press blamed Abbett for his release from state prison.[22] In another episode, the State Board of Pardons pardoned Hudson County gamblers who had been convicted of violating the antigambling laws.

These abuses of power prompted sensational media coverage and a legislative investigation, but the governor managed to stave off the investigation until well after he had left office.

Leaving himself open to charges of nepotism, Abbett named his oldest son, William Abbett, as judge advocate general in the National Guard. He also made his youngest son, Leon Abbett, Jr., his executive secretary. Not only that, he gave his brother Edwin Abbett a patronage job in the comptroller's office. Republicans, of course, attacked the governor for nepotism and padding the state payroll with members of his own family. Impervious to these attacks, Abbett forced the departure of Republican Edward Anderson as state comptroller and then gave this cabinet post to his close friend William Heppenheimer. It was spoils politics run rampant.

Numerous illustrations of Abbett's willingness to cooperate with county leaders could be cited, but a few will suffice. He began a process that his successors carried on: the appointment of James Smith's cronies to key positions in the state's administrative and judicial systems. To further placate the Essex County boss, Abbett named George R. Gray as state treasurer and Gottfried Krueger as a lay judge on the New Jersey Court of Errors and Appeals. Both men hailed from Newark and were part of Smith's Democratic machine. Gray's appointment was widely interpreted as an oblique jab at Robert Davis, the county boss in Hudson. Davis was miffed because his man, Thomas M. Ferrell, did not get the treasurer's job. Krueger's judgeship no doubt pleased the liquor dealers. Miles Ross, the boss in Middlesex County, was appointed to the newly created state Board of Electrical Subways.

Given his running feud with Robert Davis, Abbett was unable to patch up the differences and bitter feelings that split the Hudson Democratic organization into warring factions. Allan McDermott, a seasoned politician in his own right, tried to unseat Mayor Orestes Cleveland, but he failed. The Davis machine protected Cleveland's mayoralty. While the Abbett faction was able to oust Davis as county sheriff, the resourceful Irish leader got Mayor Cleveland to appoint him as a police justice in Jersey City. Davis then became county collector of taxes, a job bestowed on him by Edward Young, who controlled the county Board of Freeholders. The factional alignment of Cleveland, Davis, McPherson, and Young worked to their mutual advantage. The only way Abbett could discipline Davis was to cut him off from patronage. He distributed state and local patronage through Dennis McLaughlin, who served as county clerk.

Military veterans were another important constituency group that politicians could not afford to ignore. The veterans of the Grand Army of the Republic marched in local parades and were highly respected members of their communities. Historian Bruce Catton writes:

FIG. 23
James Smith, United States Senator.

The Civil War veterans were men set apart. On formal occasions they wore blue uniforms with brass buttons and black campaign hats, by the time I knew them most of them had long gray beards, and whatever they may have been as young men they had an unassuming natural dignity in old age. They were pillars, not so much of the church (although most of them were devout communicants) as of the community; the keepers of its patriotic traditions, the living embodiment, so to speak, of what it most deeply believed about the nation's greatness and high destiny.[23]

Responding to their needs, Abbett pushed through legislation that granted the veterans a $500 local property tax exemption. In 1891, he

persuaded the legislature to appropriate funds to pay for the railroad transportation of the Grand Army of New Jersey, when its local chapters attended the funeral of General William T. Sherman in Washington. Veterans were more than pleased when Abbett appointed his former gubernatorial opponent, Edward Burd Grubb, as a trustee of the state home for disabled soldiers in Kearny. It was a gracious gesture on his part.

With a tighter grip on the Democratic party, Abbett persuaded the legislature to place more administrative authority in his hands. He reorganized and rationalized the state bureaucracy and sought greater managerial control. Among other things, Abbett discharged the trustees of the state mental hospitals at Trenton and Morris Plains and replaced them with a new consolidated board. He then had this new board oversee and inspect the county asylums. Abbett also eliminated the tripartite management of the state prison and gave the warden absolute control and he reorganized the State Board of Education and placed the Normal School and the Deaf-Mute School under its jurisdiction and budgetary control. This was the work of a modern governor.

Most important of all, Abbett won back from the legislature the executive prerogative to appoint and remove administrators. A cadre of distinguished people was actively involved in his second administration. For example, he appointed Dr. Nicholas Murray Butler to head the State Board of Education. A distinguished educator, Butler later became president of Columbia University. Much of the program duplication and overlap that existed within the state administrative system was reduced so that the fiscal and management goals were substantially realized. In part Abbett's victories were facilitated by Democratic party majorities in both houses of the legislature during the last two years of his second term.

Few nineteenth-century governors took advantage of their potential powers both as leaders of public policy and as leaders of their parties. Abbett continued to maximize the potential powers of the office as much as possible, making him a new kind of governor. As historian Edward Conklin explains:

Abbett was an exception. He did things whether in his first term or second. He was the party boss; he used his gubernatorial powers to their limits; he forced, when needs be, the passage of acts of which he approved; often he saw to it that bills passed by the Legislature should not be turned over to him until close to the end of the session so that there was seldom an opportunity given to override his veto.[24]

In fact, Abbett used his veto power more frequently in his second term than he did in his first. With Democrats in control of both houses in 1891 and 1892, the legislature was essentially veto-proof. Abbett often used his veto as a threat to get what he wanted. Sometimes he used it to achieve the public good. In 1892, for example, he vetoed a bill that would have allowed the Newark Passenger Railway Company (street

trolleys) to keep its utility poles that supported its overhead electrical wires in the middle of the street. As the *New York Times* reported, "They are not only unsightly, but constant menaces to the life and limb of the unwary, and public sentiment has severely condemned the City Council for permitting the company to save a little money by placing them there."[25] Abbett insisted that the company remove its poles and suspend its wires to protect pedestrians.

THE OXFORD IRON AND NAIL COMPANY LOCKOUT

Illustrative of Abbett's alignment with labor was the role he played in promoting a mine-safety law. In late January 1892, the governor intervened in a labor dispute at the Oxford Iron and Nail Company in Warren County, where employees were being starved into submission by a lockout imposed in the depths of winter. They worked for the lowest wages under the worst conditions. Oxford was a company town and labor unions were not to be tolerated, nor were employees who dared even to talk such treason. The iron miners and smelters were grossly underpaid and overworked. They had genuine grievances that needed to be resolved. Several of them had been either killed or seriously injured from dynamite explosions, poor ventilation, defective timbering, and cave-ins. The smelters worked thirteen hours a day and were required to make six heats each day. After refusing to comply with the orders of Superintendent Lukens, the smelters were summarily fired and the company was shut down. The Oxford mineowners proved relentlessly hostile to labor's efforts to improve the wages and working conditions of the smelters.

On learning of the lockout, Abbett ordered a legislative investigation. A number of workers were called to testify, but they would not reveal their names for fear of retribution by the company. Coming all the way from Pittsburgh, William Weike, president of the Amalgamated Iron and Steelworkers Union, testified that it was humanly impossible for the smelters to make six heats a day. It took one hour and forty minutes to make one heat. Father Hanley, a Catholic priest from the hardscrabble town of Oxford, testified that Lukens had told him he fired some of the workers simply because they belonged to the Democratic party and because they had voted for state Senator Johnston Cornish who was a Democrat. It was also revealed that Lukens hated Catholics.[26]

As the legislative investigation continued, a terrible explosion occurred in the Harris mine. Theodore Harkey, a miner, was killed, and his coworker Alec Schenkevitski was seriously injured sustaining broken ribs and a badly bruised hand. This accident was one of the twenty-eight accidents that had occurred at the mines since Lukens had become superintendent. The mineowners sent Schenkevitski home without providing

any medical attention. They did not take him to a local hospital or to see a doctor.[27]

The governor sought to put the mineowners on the defensive. Capitalizing on the Oxford investigation, he translated this whole episode into the first law of any significance on mine safety in New Jersey. The bill he filed created the post of commissioner of mines who was given extensive rule-making authority. The commissioner was assigned a staff of inspectors to enforce the regulations that were subsequently promulgated. This law just didn't happen; Abbett made it happen. He further demonstrated his alignment with labor by appointing Robert O'Hara of Phillipsburg, a trade union official, as the first commissioner of mines. The task of implementing the new law fell to him.

When Justice Manning Knapp died on January 26, 1892, Abbett was in a quandary about filling the vacancy on the state supreme court. During his six years in the state senate, George Werts of Morristown had compiled an enviable record, capped by his election as senate president in 1889. He had authored both the ballot reform law and the liquor control law. Fearing that a promising young legislator with political ambitions might spoil his plans to advance to the U.S. Senate, the governor appointed Werts to fill the judicial vacancy in February 1892. Werts' nomination was unanimously confirmed by the state senate.

By putting Werts on the bench, Abbett left the door open for James Smith to run for governor later that year. Such a scenario would give him a clear shot for the senate seat. This led the *Newark Evening News* to conclude, "With Werts out of the gubernatorial contest, Abbett can dispose of Smith as a possible candidate for United States Senator and at the same time employ Smith's forces to boom the Abbett senatorial project."[28] Reinforcing this explanation was a statement made by an anonymous Hudson Democrat:

> Abbett is working his points well. He isn't taking any chances on the U.S. senatorship. With Werts out of the way and Smith the candidate for Governor, Abbett would be almost sure to win the prize that he has long sought.[29]

THE READING COAL COMBINE VETO

Despite his senatorial aspirations, Abbett continued to display his independence in another risky venture. In a cunning stroke, he vetoed the famous "Reading Coal Combine" bill in early April 1892. Its passage had set off a flurry of arm-twisting, threats, and personal pleas involving powerful Democrats. As it turned out, Archibald A. McLeod, president of the Reading Railroad, sought to form a combine to control the production

FIG. 24
Archibald A. McLeod,
President of the Philadel-
phia and Reading Railroad.

and prices of anthracite coal. The plan was financed by William K. Vanderbilt, who represented the New York Central and a half dozen other lines.[30] The statute in question ostensibly authorized certain leasing arrangements, but in fact its real purpose was to increase the price of coal. McLeod saw the lease of the Jersey Central as the linchpin of his plan. To obtain this lease, however, he first had to evade a New Jersey law forbidding the leasing of a domestic company to a "foreign" (out-of-state) corporation. McLeod circumvented this statute by creating a dummy corporation—the Port Reading Railroad—that he then leased to the Jersey

Central. He had previously obtained a lease of the Lehigh Valley line. This put the Reading combine in a most favorable position. The Jersey Central tapped the Mahanoy and Shamokin fields in northeastern Pennsylvania, while the Lehigh Valley extracted its coal from the Wyoming deposits in the Scranton area. Both railroads had access to the New York market by passing through New Jersey.

Democratic county bosses James Smith and Miles Ross, the prime movers of the combine bill, lobbied intensely for its passage. Several legislators were bribed with bundles of cash. The *New York Times* reported that it cost $65,000 to get the bill passed in the assembly, and another $200,000 in the senate.[31] By aligning themselves with the coal combine, Smith and Ross hoped to create a political alliance to match the Republican alliance with the Pennsylvania Railroad. Both men stood to gain financially from the generous stock options offered them. They in turn persuaded party boss James Nelson Pidcock of White House Station to go along with the scheme. A former state senator and congressman, Pidcock was the potentate of Hunterdon County.

Under intense pressure to sign the coal-combine bill, Abbett showed remarkable courage when he decided to veto it on April 5, 1892. He refused to sign it mainly on the grounds that it would hurt consumers by eliminating competition in the coal business. As he argued in his veto message:

The wisdom of insisting upon legislative protection for the consumer, in any bill authorizing a consolidation of the character contemplated, has been deeply impressed upon my mind by the fact that since the passage of this act the market price of coal has been increased to retail dealers, and in addition, the officials of the consolidated companies have stated that there has been no agreement made that would prevent a further advance in the price of coal, and the corporations could not make any such agreement.[32]

This was Abbett at his manipulative best. Some saw him acting in his own self-interest to bolster his populist image. Others believed that he had initially agreed to back the coal combine but then had cold feet and backed out. Critics accused him of double-dealing. Abbett's motives may have been mixed but they surely were more complex than his critics would acknowledge. The governor had become an increasingly "representative" official, one who sought to reflect public desires not only because this seemed the right thing to do, but also because of his expectations of rewards that would follow.

The political fallout from Abbett's veto made Democratic county leaders absolutely furious at him and thus threatened to wreck his senatorial ambitions. They never forgave Abbett for his defection. As the *New York Times* told the story:

They were hopping mad. They charge him with perfidy and treachery and say even worst things about him. Miles Ross, who, if the bill had become law, would have made a small fortune by handling the whole of the coal output of the combine in the New York market, was sick abed with chagrin and disappointment. Former Congressman James Pidcock, whom the managers forced into line against his Pennsylvania interests and preferences, is in a towering rage. James Smith conceals his chagrin under a placid countenance. He is the one man whom the Governor fears and mistrusts.[33]

Ignoring the governor's veto with impunity, the three railroads involved defiantly went ahead with their scheme. When asked if Abbett's refusal to sign the bill would have any effect on the combine, Archibald McLeod replied:

> None whatsoever. We are perfecting our organization and we will not be affected by the action of Governor Abbett. The principal purpose of the bill was to enable dissenting stockholders to have their claims adjudicated. The leases will stand as they have been made, and the leased roads will continue to be operated by the Reading, regardless of the action taken by Governor Abbett.[34]

With the power and prestige of the governorship on the line, Abbett sought to reign in the defiant company. He instructed Attorney General John Stockton to commence litigation immediately. Stockton applied for a restraining order to dissolve the lease, arguing that the tripartite agreement between the Reading, Jersey Central, and Port Reading was illegal. The case was heard by the New Jersey Court of Chancery that granted a temporary injunction ordering the defendant to refrain from operating its railroads in restraint of trade. Chancellor Alexander McGill ruled that the coal combine was illegal, and amounted to "a corporate excess of power" that tended toward monopoly and public injury.[35]

The real counterforce was gubernatorial. When prices did not go down during the next three months, Abbett hauled the railroads back into court and charged that they had deliberately conspired to hike the price of coal in defiance of the court order. Stockton then asked the court to appoint a receiver to enforce its decree and to restrain the Reading from carrying coal in New Jersey until the price had been reduced. Chancellor McGill upheld the attorney general on every point. The Reading Railroad appealed his decision to the Court of Errors and Appeals, but the Jersey Central declined to join in the appeal. On advice from his own railroad attorneys, McLeod finally backed off and dropped the appeal. Only his announcement of the dissolution of the lease prevented McGill from appointing a receiver as the attorney general had requested.

It was Abbett's final triumph. He had defeated McLeod and the Reading coal combine. The observations of Robert H. McCarter, one of the railroad attorneys involved in the litigation, were particularly revealing:

The opinion was filed in midsummer and it upset the combine. All of the counsel being on vacation, an S.O.S. call came to our office for me to come at once to Philadelphia. I found the newly installed President of the combined three roads behind his desk. He had a very large mustachios, but lacked an exhibition of skull and cross-bones. The three General Solicitors of the three railroads stood trembling. I was naturally more or less interested in the case. As soon as the President saw me, he said "Well, so you have permitted us to be licked." I replied that the decision was against him. He inquired if there was an appeal, and to my affirmative reply he asked, "To what Court, and of what does it consist?" I described the Court of Errors and Appeals as it then existed. He cogitated for a few moments, brought his fist down on the desk, and to the horror of the more diplomatic General Solicitors said in low tones, "I tell you what we will do. We will appeal this case to the Court of Appeals and buy every God-damned Judge." There I stood, a young lawyer, brought up to respect and believe in the Judiciary of New Jersey. There were the three General Solicitors hopping around like hens with their heads off, two of them, as well as the new President, entire strangers to me. I indignantly said, "You might as well talk about buying the Angel Gabriel!" I was not thereafter popular with the executive, although his occupancy was short-lived, for the sober second thought of the management, largely inspired by the experienced counsel who had returned from their vacations, determined to accept the decision and to abandon the project. No appeal was taken, so convincing was the opinion of the Chancellor.[36]

And so the Reading coal combine was dissolved. Whatever his motives, Abbett had positioned himself as a guardian of the public interest. The outcome provided further evidence that the railroads were no longer invincible.

THE PRESIDENTIAL AND GUBERNATORIAL ELECTIONS OF 1892

As it happened, both the presidential and the gubernatorial elections were held in 1892. The two offices were chosen simultaneously in New Jersey once every twelve years when the four-year cycle for president and the three-year cycle for governor coincided. Early on, Abbett backed his political ally U.S. Senator David Hill of New York for president. He worked hard in 1891 trying to line up delegates for him. On July 17, Abbett invited Hill to visit New Jersey ostensibly to review the National Guard troops

at their annual encampment in Sea Girt. But in fact Abbett really wanted to test Hill's popularity. Getting a chilly reception, Hill never did catch fire in the Garden State.

Former president Grover Cleveland, who was known for his hard-money views, was the popular man of the hour. Eastern bankers, the rich, and other conservative elites staunchly supported his monetary policy that was based on a firm attachment to the gold standard. Those on the opposite side of the economic spectrum sounded a much different note. Populists clamored for the coinage of free silver. Four months before the 1892 Democratic national convention, the *New York Times* conducted a survey of Democratic delegates from New Jersey that showed the Cleveland forces held a commanding lead.[37] What Abbett no doubt understood, but would not acknowledge, was that he was fighting a losing battle in backing Hill.

Further evidence of this was found in the split among Mercer County Democrats. The Democratic League, whose members were mostly party regulars, favored Hill; whereas the more independent Mercer County Democratic Club was aligned solidly behind Cleveland. In February 1892, George H. Yeaman of Madison organized the New Jersey Cleveland Association that did its best to counteract the drive of the David Hill forces.[38] Yeaman's efforts quickly caught on elsewhere. Independent Democrats for Cleveland and local booster clubs sprang up all over the state. The "Young Democrats" enthusiastically endorsed him.

Most New Jersey Democrats were caught up in the Cleveland boom. The former president now appeared unstoppable. Mainstream

FIG. 25
Leon Abbett and staff in 1891.

Democrats stuck by Cleveland, with encouragement from party notables such as James Smith, George Harvey, John McPherson, Miles Ross, James Pidcock, Edward Young, Henry Little, Rufus Blodgett, George Pfeiffer, James Newell, Samuel Klotz, and George Vanderilt. They all lined up behind the former president. Of these party stalwarts, James Smith was largely responsible for swinging the New Jersey delegation into the Cleveland camp. George Harvey had his friend, William C. Whitney who had been secretary of the navy in Cleveland's first administration, per- suade Smith to jump on the bandwagon. The Newark boss traveled to the Chicago convention aboard a private railroad car supplied by Whitney, replete with wine, cigars, and fine food. A rich Wall Street lawyer, Whitney brokered a truce between the reform-minded Cleveland and Tammany Hall in the 1884 presidential campaign.

U.S. Senator John McPherson also gave Cleveland valuable sup- port that offset Hill's campaign in Hudson County. As one disgruntled Hudson Democrat said, "Our county is strong for Cleveland and if Governor Abbett did not ask for the delegates for himself there would be nothing in the way of making it solid for Cleveland."[39]

There was no way Abbett could hold back the Cleveland tidal wave. Yet, he insisted on going to the national convention uncommitted. Said Abbett, "I'll be damned, if I will go to Chicago with a tag on my head."[40] While he was under tremendous pressure to release the New Jersey delegates, he stubbornly refused to do so. At a critical moment, when he saw that the Cleveland forces would prevail, he released them and asked if he could place Cleveland's name in nomination. Through the intercession of James Smith and George Harvey, the governor's request was granted. Abbett gave a stirring nominating speech that elicited thun- derous cheers. Once again, disagreements and disappointments were papered over for the sake of party unity.

On his return home from Chicago, Abbett fared better in selecting a candidate for governor, though things did not go exactly the way he had planned. For one thing, James Smith refused to throw his hat in the guber- natorial ring. Instead, he was already plotting to become the next U.S. senator, which would put him on a collision course with Abbett. As a lame duck governor, Abbett's power gradually began to wane. Democratic politicians read these signs accordingly. As Sackett astutely observed, "Some of them with keen remembrance of his race track and coal combine vetoes, were even then plotting for his overthrow. Governor Abbett must have suspected their fidelity, but he had made his bed with them, and he was now obliged to sleep with them or with nobody."[41]

By September 1892, the gubernatorial nomination had narrowed to George Werts, Edward Young, or Judge Job Lippincott. Both Young and Lippincott were relatively untried Democrats. Justice Lippincott had gained fame in presiding over the trial of the Hudson ballot-box stuffers.

Since Abbett could not abide Edward Young, he maneuvered to block his nomination by persuading Werts to resign as vice chancellor and enter the contest. As a former senate president, Werts was a popular Trenton insider. But Young had the support of both Robert Davis and U.S. Senator John McPherson. As fate would have it, McPherson was quarantined aboard an ocean liner anchored off of Sandy Hook because of a cholera scare. Federal public health officials refused to allow him to come ashore, which cleared the way for Wert's nomination that he won handily on the first ballot.

The Republicans chose former Congressman John Kean, Jr. of Elizabeth as their candidate for governor. He was a wealthy businessman, engaged in banking, mining, and manufacturing interests. A veteran Republican politician, Kean had won his political spurs in several notable congressional campaigns. He campaigned against the Abbett administration by condemning such abuses as ballot-box stuffing, the sale of political offices, and Democratic favoritism toward the liquor and racetrack interests. These various forms of bribery and corruption presented a sordid picture. All of which meant that the general election would be no walkover.

Like other judges who had run for governor, Werts refused to campaign and sat on the bench. Nonetheless, his campaign was shrewdly managed. Allan McDermott, the state party chairman, devised a winning Democratic strategy. He diverted public attention from Republican charges of corruption by linking the gubernatorial race to the presidential campaign.

For his part, Grover Cleveland thought it was "unseemly" for him to take to the hustings. All fall, he received urgent messages from Democrats in other states asking for his presence or that of his emissaries to swing close contests. McDermott pulled off a major coup by getting the former president to visit Jersey City to campaign for Werts. Cleveland was given a tumultuous reception, replete with martial music, torchlight parades, brass bands, and lengthy processions.

What made the 1892 presidential race even more interesting was the entry of the new Populist party. The Populist candidate for president, James B. Weaver, promised to restore government "to the hands of the plain people." The Populists voiced agrarian and labor demands for antitrust regulation, government ownership of railroad and telegraph companies, a graduated income tax, tougher safeguards for trade unions, and the popular election of senators. They placed special emphasis on inflating the currency by increasing the amount of paper money in circulation and by allowing the free coinage of silver at a sixteen-to-one ratio. Their panaceas for currency expansion, particularly the free silver plank, disturbed fiscal conservatives like Cleveland.

Labor was a front-burner issue in the 1892 presidential campaign. During that summer, 3,800 workers struck the Carnegie steel mill at

Homestead, Pennsylvania. Henry Clay Frick was the organizational genius whom Andrew Carnegie had hired to run his steel mills. The maternal grandson of old Abraham Overholt, the Mennonite whiskey maker, Frick had made his own fortune in the coke business, largely through his dealings with Carnegie who was Pittsburgh's number one coke consumer. He was as much as any figure of his day the high priest of corporate property rights.

Determined to crush the steelworker's union, Frick displayed an arrogance of power that was typical of such business moguls. He proposed a contract slashing wages twenty-two percent. When the union rejected the contract, Frick imposed a lockout, put "scabs" to work, and imported 300 armed Pinkerton detectives to guard the mill. A pitched battle ensued, whereupon Frick ordered the Pinkertons to fire at the workers. He beat the union at Homestead when the governor sent in national guardsmen after the Pinkertons had been routed by the strikers. At the height of the battle, the "coke king" was shot twice in the neck and knifed three times by an anarchist who had no connection with the dispute. Swathed in makeshift bandages, Frick coolly returned to his desk after helping wrestle his assailant to the floor.

Republicans had always insisted that high tariffs meant high wages, but Frick's action—slashing wages while the steel industry was prospering behind tariff walls—contradicted their doctrine. The Democrats made the most of this inconsistency and began citing Homestead in their assaults on protectionism. Many Republicans, including President Harrison, were upset by Frick's behavior. The labor vote, as they feared, went overwhelmingly to Cleveland.

The result was a decisive Democratic victory on election day, November 8, 1892. Cleveland carried New Jersey by 14,965 votes, and the national tide swept Werts into the governorship by 7,625 votes. Victorious presidential candidates usually exceeded the gubernatorial margins. The Democrats had won a majority in both houses of the state legislature. For the first time since the Civil War, they also won a majority in both houses of Congress. It was a clean sweep for them. As America grew more polarized, many people questioned whether the country had paid too steep a price for the industrialization that had so quickly propelled it from an agrarian society to a world economic power.

These dramatic and significant events marked the end of Abbett's second administration. Overall, he had turned in another virtuoso performance. His success rested mainly on his party strength, his sensitivity to his followers, and his uncanny ability to appraise public sentiment and to lead the people of New Jersey in a new direction. Abbett traveled the state and brought aboard men of clashing temperaments to secure different points of view. More than diligence was involved. He relied on his own intuition to determine what was in the public interest or the common

good. For the most part, he was able to sense what the people were thinking and feeling. Although his second term was marred by the corruption of his cronies, nevertheless his positive actions in curbing corporate power far outweighed the negatives. These advances came only after pitched battles with the capitalist powers in America.

As a party leader, Abbett was able to adapt to the shifting winds of political change, and he demonstrated a marvelous sense of timing in shaping the policy agenda. Dealing with an assorted cast of characters and a variety of public problems, he understood when to invoke the prestige of the governorship and when to hold it in reserve, when to move forward and when to pull back. He not only expanded gubernatorial power, but he also improved on the hard lessons he had learned during his first term. Responding to the consolidation of power under his governorship, Joseph L. Naar, editor of the Trenton *True American*, asserted:

> Abbett has redeemed the executive office from the rankling chains of petty annoyance to which a Republican Senate had in the course of years subjected it. He has brought it in touch and cooperation with the administrative officers of the state, and made it what our form of government designed it to be, the power whereby the laws are executed.[42]

Having emerged as the prototype of the modern governor, Abbett established new behavioral guidelines for his successors.

ENDNOTES

1 *New York Times*, May 26, 1890.
2 Inaugural Message, January 21, 1890, p. 14.
3 Trenton *State Gazette*, May 22, 1890.
4 McCormick, *The History of Voting in New Jersey*, 176.
5 Minutes of Votes and Proceedings of the General Assembly for 1890, 678.
6 Minutes of the New Jersey Assembly for 1890 (Trenton, 1890), 974.
7 These quotes are from the *New York Times*, June 17, 1890.
8 Steffens, "New Jersey: A Traitor State," 41.
9 33 *New Jersey Law Journal* (1910), 383.
10 Costello, *History of the Police Department of Jersey City*, 186–187.
11 *Newark Evening News*, January 17, 1891.
12 *New York Times*, May 11, 1891.
13 *New York Times*, February 26, 1891.
14 *Newark Sunday Call*, March 1, 1891.
15 *New York Times*, May 11, 1891.
16 Thomas F. Fitzgerald, *New Jersey Legislative Manual for 1893* (Trenton, 1893), 414.
17 *New York Times*, April 4, 1890.
18 For the full text of Governor Abbett's address, see "Eighteenth Annual Report of the State Board of Agriculture" (Trenton, 1891), 187–193.
19 Quoted in the *New York Times*, March 24, 1890. In this article, the Princeton trustee chose to remain anonymous and did not identify himself.
20 *New York Times*, March 24, 1980.

21 Edward P. Conklin, "The Last Half Century in New Jersey Politics," in Irving S. Kull, (ed.), *New Jersey A History* (New York, The American Historical Society, 1930), vol. 3, 971.
22 *New York Times*, April 27, 1891.
23 Bruce Catton, *Waiting for the Morning Train* (New York, Doubleday & Company, 1972), 189–190.
24 Conklin, *op. cit.*, 970.
25 *New York Times*, April 10, 1892.
26 *Newark Evening News*, February 2, 1892.
27 *Newark Evening News*, March 2, 1892.
28 *Newark Evening News*, February 2, 1892.
29 *Ibid.*
30 For a detailed treatment of the "coal combine" see, Robert J. Casey and W.A. Douglas, *The Lackawanna Story* (New York, McGraw Hill, 1951), 102–103.
31 *New York Times*, April 6, 1892.
32 *Trenton True American*, April 6, 1892.
33 *New York Times*, April 6, 1892.
34 *Ibid.*
35 *Stockton v. Central Railroad Company*, 50 N.J.E. 52 (1892).
36 Robert H. McCarter, *Memories of a Half-Century at the New Jersey Bar* (Camden, 1937), 53–54.
37 *New York Times*, February 22, 1892.
38 *New York Times*, February 10, 1892.
39 *New York Times*, March 10, 1892.
40 *Ibid.*
41 Sackett, *Modern Battles of Trenton*, 1:421.
42 *Trenton True American*, February 22, 1892.

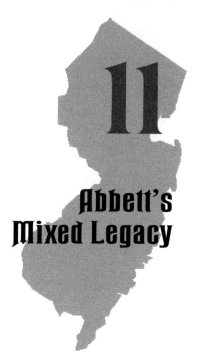

Abbett's
Mixed Legacy

Toward the end of his second term, Leon Abbett had to deal with mounting criticism leveled against him. Long-hounded by journalists, he was routinely demonized in the press. With the rise of mass-circulation newspapers, press barons like Joseph Pulitzer and William Randolph Hearst catered to an expanding reading public and plied their readers with scandals and crusades. This was the heyday of strident tabloids and yellow journalism. Some reporters went so far as to invent stories about Abbett based on groundless speculation and inaccurate information. Whatever the reporters may have lacked in the way of facts, they made up for in imagination. Distortions, wild exaggerations, and outright nonsense were published in just about every major paper in the region. As the Democratic party machine in New Jersey secured complete control of state government, many citizens were frightened by its sheer size, rapacious methods, and inexorable influence. It came to symbolize all the disquieting forces reshaping American politics.

For his part, Abbett had developed a thick skin and appeared unruffled by his critics. He made no attempt to engage them. What they said, real or imagined, apparently did not affect him that much. There was a disconnect between the real world and the slippery, gossipy world of contemporary political journalism. Despite these attacks, Abbett's popularity remained high, especially among his core supporters. No matter how harsh the criticism, they still believed that he could do no wrong.

At fifty-seven years of age, Abbett might have retired gracefully from politics, but his patently unfinished ambitions propelled him to seek national office. He still had his eye on the U.S. Senate prize that had eluded him in 1887. He confided privately to friends that there was no place else for him to go. Nothing would have given him greater pleasure than to oust his old nemesis Rufus Blodgett, who currently occupied the position. When Abbett sought the Democratic nomination for U.S.

senator in January 1893, his opponents accused him of overreaching and grasping for too much power. They saw him as being power hungry and too ambitious.

Because the Democrats controlled the state legislature, Abbett thought that his party's nomination would be his for the asking. He felt a certain sense of entitlement for a job well done and that his party owed him as much. In this context, the signs appeared promising to him. After all, he had the support of the incoming governor George Werts and U.S. Senator John McPherson. In fact, they both endorsed him. Werts' glowing endorsement provided evidence that their interests were clearly aligned. Rumors began circulating that the election was a foregone conclusion. The press initially conveyed the impression that Abbett was an automatic shoo-in who faced no serious opposition. Raising the specter that the election was a fait accompli played nicely into the hands of his opponents. As the election approached, however, there were troubling signs, and to everyone's amazement, it became increasingly doubtful whether Abbett could make a successful run at it. Still, it was a close call.

The feeling among most rank-and-file Democrats was that Abbett deserved to be elected to the Senate. His real strength resided with the base of his party, not with the legislature. He would have much preferred to face the electorate in a popular election, but that was not possible. U.S. senators were still elected by their state legislatures, creating an open season for graft and influence peddling by business interests. Therein lay the paradox of Abbett's predicament: though he was by far the most successful vote-getter in New Jersey, the electorate would not have an opportunity to vote for him. The Seventeenth Amendment, providing for the direct election of senators by the people, would not be adopted until 1913.

Prediction of easy sledding for Abbett was therefore misleading. A daunting combination of factors, some of which were beyond his control, stood in his way. By this time, the governor's star was sinking fast and with it any hopes of capturing the prize. Even Abbett began to recognize that his second administration had run out of steam and he had run out of political capital. Part of his vulnerability was due to his lame duck status that weakened his hold on the party. With his patronage powers depleted and with few favors to bestow on the major players involved, he could no longer depend on this source of power. Nor could he keep his political alliances intact. His working relationship with the powerful county bosses had been severely damaged. Angered by Abbett's earlier vetoes of the racetrack and coal combine legislation, they were smarting for revenge. There was some grumbling about his second administration, but this had been debated in the elections of 1892 without harmful results. The constraints that might normally prevail were now disregarded. All of which revealed the ephemeral nature of the alliances, hostilities, and intrigues that thrived in New Jersey politics.

ABBETT'S LAST HURRAH

As it turned out, the gravest threat to Abbett emanated not from Republicans, but from within his own party. As the governor came to the end of his second term, he was unable to patch up the differences and bitter feelings that split the Democratic party into warring factions. Even long-time Abbett loyalists considered breaking ranks with the outgoing governor.

Sensing the vulnerability of the governor over recent political controversies, James Smith, a conservative Irish Democrat and the boss of Essex County, had the temerity to challenge Abbett. He did so largely on the strength of his success in having swung New Jersey Democrats behind Grover Cleveland in the presidential campaign of 1892. In Smith, whom he credited as the "shrewdest of politicians," Abbett knew he had a formidable rival. Historian Arthur Link described Smith in glowing terms, "He was of the Beau Brummel type, six feet tall, suave, with considerable poise and dignity in his bearing. He had a striking and magnetic personality and was the perfect type of gentleman boss, portly and well-dressed."[1] A cultivated and well-to-do Newark businessman, Smith was a prominent leader in the Irish political community. A second generation Irish-American, he won statewide recognition for the role he played in getting the trustees at the Jamesburg reform school to allow a Catholic priest to provide for the spiritual needs of the troubled youth confined there.

With the Democrats in control of the legislature, the contest was mainly an intramural affair. On learning of Smith's candidacy, Abbett concealed his deep rage with a poker face. Although he tried to sound statesmanlike, his anger leaked out around the edges. Republican newspapers continued their attacks on him. The *New York Times,* a newspaper noted for its virulent hatred of Abbett, referred to him acidly as the "Nimrod of New Jersey spoils hunters." For a time, it seemed as if Abbett might effect a rapprochement with the disgruntled county leaders. But that turned out to be unrealistic. Brooding about his rapidly eroding support, the governor was plainly worried about his prospects and could not conceal his anxieties. Feeling betrayed by Smith, the governor had appointed George R. Gray as state treasurer largely as a concession to Smith. Abbett's anger and desperation were noted in the press. As the *New York Times* reported, "Alarmed and angered by the steadily increasing strength of his formidable rival, James Smith of Newark, the Governor is said to be resorting alternately to promises, threats, and cajolery in his pursuit of votes."[2]

Powerful forces—some obvious, some subtle—exerted tremendous pressure in their attempt to influence the outcome. Much of the politics and press attention focused on Smith who became the central actor in the struggle. As the intrigue unfolded, Edward Young, the economic overlord

of Hudson County, played a critical role in plotting Abbett's demise. He met secretly with Smith and encouraged him to step forward and challenge the governor. To avoid publicity, Young took a carriage to Smith's home after dark, and the coachman waited at the front gate while Young and Smith huddled behind closed doors. Young still resented Abbett for thwarting his own gubernatorial ambitions in 1892. He was now prepared to deliver the Hudson County legislative delegation. If Smith cooperated with Young for retribution, he was amply rewarded.

Notwithstanding Abbett's willingness to meet his party henchmen more than halfway, they turned against him. They were reenacting what must have seemed to him a replay of events in his senatorial bid in 1887. The governor paid a heavy price for his independence. Obviously, his racetrack and coal combine vetoes had cost him dearly. No matter how hard he tried, Abbett could not calm the unsettled old loyalties. The passions and divisions within the Democratic party ran too deep for such reconciliation. Still smarting from the sting of Abbett's vetoes, Miles Ross conspired with William Thompson and James Nelson Pidcock to deny him the senatorship. Ross was able to deliver the votes of Middlesex, Monmouth, and Somerset counties to Smith, while Thompson, the "Duke of Glouster," delivered Camden and several other smaller counties in South Jersey. Pidcock delivered Hunterdon and those counties in the northwestern tier of the state. Smith, of course, controlled Essex County. Over in Hudson County, Edward Young conspired with county boss Robert Davis to line up their votes for Smith. Reform-minded Democrats in Mercer County, who were impressed by Smith for the role that he had played in the recent presidential campaign, followed suit.

With such a powerful array of forces aligned against him, Abbett could no longer hold the party together. So fragile can political power be. What little patronage remained at his disposal produced as much party friction as it did party harmony. Some of Abbett's old political allies deserted him, an unthinkable affront in prior days. Under these circumstances, it was impossible for him to win the party caucus nomination. At a climatic moment, Allan McDermott suggested to Abbett that he withdraw from the contest rather than face certain defeat, but the governor adamantly refused. He could not bear the personal humiliation involved. Worried by how despondent Abbett seemed, McDermott withdrew for him.

Abbett's defeat underscored the decline of his political influence. Smith won the party caucus nomination as well as the election. It was a bone-crushing defeat for Abbett. The scene in the governor's office reportedly was one of profound shock and disappointment. Utterly dismayed and reacting with disbelief, the "Great Commoner" gazed teary-eyed at his colleagues. "And this gentlemen is my reward from the Democracy of New Jersey," he said, with a touch of bitter sarcasm.[3] It

FIG. 26
Edward F.C. Young,
economic overlord of
Hudson County, banker
and business mogul.

was a moment of utter despair for him. Abbett's last hurrah was part lament for a man whose days as a political powerhouse had come to an end and part recognition of the peculiar vulnerability of an outgoing chief executive. Similar to his senatorial defeat in 1887, the lame duck Democratic governor had been cast aside. His political career was over. Abbett was relegated to the sidelines, where he would remain for the rest of his life. Although he was only fifty-seven, he would never hold elected public office again. It was the rejection of the political type who originally led the urban masses.

Abbett's defeat was reminiscent of the one that he had suffered at the hands of the palace guard when they cast him aside in favor of Rufus Blodgett in 1887. Much like Blodgett, James Smith did not go on to distinguish himself in the U.S. Senate, where he served from 1893 until 1899. He was a one-term only senator. His most notable accomplishment was his alliance with Arthur Pue Gorman and other Democrats in defeating President Cleveland's efforts at tariff reform in 1894. A confirmed protectionist and captive of the trusts, Senator Smith used public office for his own personal gain. He turned public service into such a lucrative racket that he amassed a fortune before he died. Later on, in 1910, he and George B. Harvey were the two powerbrokers who persuaded Woodrow Wilson, the president of Princeton, to run for governor on the Democratic ticket. Once elected, however, Wilson promptly broke with Smith and discarded him as a political ally.

Bringing an end to a remarkable political career in New Jersey, Abbett bade farewell to the legislature and retired from active politics. Newspaper reporters wrote stories about the possibility of his running for a third term as governor, but this was idle speculation.[4] Considering the term limit imposed by the state constitution, which prohibited two consecutive terms, he would have had to wait another three years before he could have become eligible to run again. On January 18, 1893, the day after Abbett departed from the governor's office, the *New York Times* weighed in with this condescending critique:

As Governor of New Jersey, Abbett did not strive to secure the support and confidence of the people of the state by faithfully serving their interests in the high station to which they had elevated him. He sought rather to control a party organization for the promotion of selfish ends and to build up a machine upon which he could rely for his own advancement. For this purpose he used his official power in making appointments to office and in recommending and approving legislation. He allied himself with the corrupt elements of his party, and a political ring was formed at Trenton which was associated with a still more corrupt local ring in Hudson County. The changes in the tax laws which were secured mainly by his efforts were intended to increase his official power and to extend it throughout the counties of the state.[5]

In a political world degraded by corrupt bosses and wardheelers, this scathing diatribe was hardly surprising. The media frequently castigated Abbett with such invective.

While the media perception of Abbett may have been accurate to some extent, it is hard to argue that the people of New Jersey did not benefit from his rule. Only the most distorted reading of the history of the period could lead to such a conclusion. What are we to make of such vitriolic criticism? It absorbed traditional ethnic group antagonisms and reflected cleavages generated by different status and class positions of social groups. Beneath the *New York Times'* harsh judgment, however, lay a powerful class bias. Its editorial reflected the attitudes of gentlemen Mugwump reformers and their social peers who were scandalized by the sordid ethics of the new political class. Repulsed by the excesses of political bossism and machine politics, they saw boss rule as an abomination and a scourge on the body politic. For them, Abbett represented all that was wrong with American politics. Small wonder that the railroad oligarchs and their allies in the media rejoiced when they learned of his retirement from politics.

A COMPARISON WITH OTHER GOVERNORS

Conservatives and capitalist powers in America treated Abbett as shabbily as they treated other Gilded Age governors who challenged them. It is therefore useful to compare Abbett with other contemporary governors like John P. Altgeld of Illinois, Benjamin F. Butler of Massachusetts, and David B. Hill of New York. All were maverick governors who defied conventional thinking and were the voices of unrest and change. All were Democrats who came from industrial states and who appealed to industrial workers. All were urban populists who endorsed labor's goals and engaged in class warfare and ethnic politics. Finally, they all sought to wrest control of the Democratic party from Grover Cleveland and his conservative Bourbon allies. While they performed in some significantly similar ways, they also performed in a markedly different manner. That there were differences between them is hardly surprising, but those differences were often complemented by a number of striking similarities. A fuller comparison is instructive.

Among the most tumultuous of struggles in the nation's labor history was the strike in Illinois against the Pullman Palace Car Company in 1894. Pullman workers struck to reverse massive layoffs and wage cuts, triggering a sympathy strike by the American Railway Union under the leadership of socialist Eugene V. Debs. The unyielding George Pullman was unwilling to participate in the effort to settle the dispute through gubernatorial intervention. Governor John Altgeld acted in an

evenhanded fashion and tried to mediate the dispute, but he refused call out the Illinois National Guard as the strike veered toward violence. In a move that served only to polarize the situation, President Cleveland sent federal troops to Chicago, ostensibly to maintain law and order but in fact to keep the trains running. Debs was jailed, and seven strikers were gunned down. As a result, the nationwide strike was broken and the nascent American Railway Union was destroyed. Many observers felt that Cleveland had saved the nation from the forces of socialism and anarchy.

For sympathizing with the strikers and for refusing to crush the strike, Altgeld was denounced by his political enemies as a "communist, a dangerous radical, an anarchist, a fomenter of violence, an alien without a drop of true American blood in his veins."[6] The *Chicago Tribune*, for example, reviled him as "Dastardly Altgelt—a viper and a slimy demagogue." On the other hand, Clarence Darrow, Altgelt's law partner, called him, "The voice for the weak, the maimed, the defenseless, the voiceless, all over America, a soldier in the everlasting struggle of the human race for liberty and justice."[7] Such was the disparity of viewpoints.

Benjamin F. Butler of Massachusetts was tarred with the same kind of criticism. A complex and controversial personality, Butler had started out in Lowell before the Civil War as a Jackson Democrat, an active legislator, and a candidate for governor. He was an apologist for slavery, and in 1860 he attended the Democratic convention in Charleston, South Carolina, where he endorsed Jefferson Davis for president. A year later, Butler became a brigadier general in the Union Army, a member of the Radical Republicans, and one of the most hated men in the South because of the high-handed way in which he conducted the military occupation of New Orleans. After the war, he was elected to Congress as a Republican, where he supported the rights of freedmen and pressed for an eight-hour day. After declining Lincoln's offer of the vice presidency in 1864, he played a key role in the impeachment of President Andrew Johnson.

Butler had unsuccessfully sought the gubernatorial nomination in Massachusetts many times. He was finally elected governor in 1882 on the Democratic ticket and served in that office from 1883 to 1884. While campaigning, he attacked the Harvard Medical School for using the corpses of deceased Irish laborers as cadavers for medical research. In appealing to the Irish, the governor won their support because they saw the cadaver issue as a class grievance. As a state legislator, he had led the fight to obtain compensation for the Ursuline convent fire in 1834. The Irish continued to view Butler as their champion in the face of nativist attacks. Brahmin politicians steeped in Victorian gentility were shocked and offended by what they considered his outlandish behavior. In their view, Butler was a rogue and a scoundrel who transgressed the bounds of social etiquette and good taste. A crossover politician, Butler had no

qualms about switching his party affiliation whenever it suited his purposes. After shifting between the two major parties at different times, he engaged in third-party politics and ran for president in 1884 on the Greenbacker ticket.

Except for party loyalty, where they obviously differed, Abbett and Butler were somewhat alike in style and personality. Both were nonconformists in their political behavior, both were given to old-fashioned rhetorical flourishes and capable of conscious ranting and raving, power hungry, and ready to use their positions to the utmost for their political goals. Each could be outlandish, domineering, good at pretense and deception, ready to publicly denounce someone one minute and privately forget the seeming animosity the next. Both were polarizing figures who took what seemed like shocking positions. Both, in their own unique ways, were superb politicians who sought and won their objectives.

While Abbett was similar in style and strategy to Altgeld and Butler, he was perhaps even closer in philosophy to David Hill of New York. As political actors, they were paired comfortably in ideology and outlook. Both were party machine governors who built strong party organizations; both understood and exploited their positions as popularly elected rulers. Both exercised their gubernatorial powers forcefully and independently, acting as they thought conditions demanded and their conception of the office permitted. Both placed a high premium on party loyalty, and both adroitly used their party machines to expand their executive power. As governors of neighboring states, they not only formed a political alliance within the Democratic party, but they also became good friends. They were often seen sailing together at the New Rochelle Yacht Club.

APPOINTMENT TO THE NEW JERSEY SUPREME COURT

After recovering from the pangs of his senatorial defeat, Abbett began positioning himself for life after politics. He was sardonic, sometimes impatient and gruff, occasionally ebullient, yet always crisp in his thinking. As a consolation prize, he settled for an appointment to the New Jersey supreme court. Governor Werts, who owed Abbett a great deal for his ascendancy in the Democratic party, appointed him to the high bench in 1893. Abbett filled the vacancy created by the death of Justice Edward W. Scudder. A Trenton lawyer and highly respected jurist, Scudder had formerly been a state senator from Mercer County, a staunch war supporter, and a moderate Democrat. Abbett's practical experience as a courtroom lawyer made him a worthy nominee, but his appointment evoked an expected public outcry. Despite this spirited opposition, the Democrats had enough votes in the senate to confirm Abbett on March 7,

1893. Once confirmed, he joined his former Republican adversary Jonathan Dixon on the bench.

Not the least of Abbett's shortcomings was his failure to pick a worthy successor. His anointing of George Werts as the heir apparent has to rank as one of his most egregious blunders. Governor Werts, who was trying to emerge from Abbett's shadow, was content to reside passively in the office. His cautious politics put him out of touch with the electorate. He was hesitant and uncertain where Abbett was firm and commanding. Unsure of his own political instincts, Werts reverted to the old pattern of being submissive to legislative dominance. He was more than willing to follow the dictates of the legislature rather than impose his leadership. Under these circumstances, the tempo of gubernatorial initiative suffered accordingly.

During the 1893 legislative session, the Democrats rushed through a bill legalizing gambling at the racetracks. Hastily enacted, they passed the measure in defiance of public opinion. Governor Werts' initial response was cautious. Near the end of the session, he vetoed the gambling bill, but the so-called "jockey legislature" quickly overrode his veto. Since the override passed with slight of hand and a fast gavel, the Anti-Racetrack League did not have enough time to mobilize support to sustain Werts' veto. Clearly, the Democrats had misread the public and found themselves the target of public anger.

Not all citizens were delighted. Across the state an uproar of righteous indignation arose. The gambling issue raised the hackles of hard-shell Protestants who descended on the State House in Trenton and objected vehemently. To complicate matters, the Catholic church lobbied for state aid for parochial schools. This highly combustible mixture proved disastrous for the Democratic party.

Feeling misled and manipulated, the populace reacted predictably. Levels of distrust and resentment reached startling heights. Although most Democrats tried to distance themselves from the Catholic church, they encountered an angry electorate. They wilted under a ferocious assault by a united front of the media, Protestants, and the antiracetrack coalition. A majority of the electorate believed that greed, corruption, and venality were rampant in the state. In the 1893 election campaign, the Republicans captured control of the legislature. Their success came mainly at the expense of Democratic legislators who had supported the gambling legislation. Only a handful of Democratic incumbents won reelection.

More than patronage and corruption clouded the transition from Abbett to Werts. There was a noticeable dearth of party and policy leadership by Werts. To add to his woes, the depression precipitated by the stock-market crash in June 1893 turned out to be excruciatingly long and painful. Collapse of the economy resulted in grinding and unrelieved misery for the lower classes. During the troubled summer of 1893, both the

Erie and the Northern Pacific railroads failed, followed by many others bloated with debt and riddled with fraud. Massive unemployment across the nation sharpened class tensions. With Grover Cleveland in the White House, the Democrats reeling from the market crash were blamed for this calamity. Werts, of course, received most of the blame in New Jersey. He continued to misread the public. As historian Eugene Tobin observed:

> The governor's failure to provide leadership and his willingness to let the focus of power rest in the legislature, characterized the Werts years. While the public was trying to cope with the most severe industrial depression of this generation, Governor Werts was leaving as his most enduring legacy a budget surplus of almost $1 million.[8]

In the end, it was Werts' misfortune to preside over the dismantling of the Democratic party that had controlled the executive branch almost continuously for three decades.

THE CASE OF STATE V. ROGERS

Sitting on the bench, Abbett could only cast a wary eye and watch these events unfold much to his distress. He remained on the political sidelines and pursued his judicial duties in earnest, but the cloistered life of an appellate judge was a far cry from the excitement of the political arena. Yet, Abbett proved a capable jurist. He was a "lawyer's judge" who brought practical experience to his decision-making on the bench, and he understood the real-life implications of the cases before him. His sound legal knowledge informed his written opinions and contributed to the internal dynamics of the nine justices who sat on the state's high court.

Abbett's judicial career did not last very long, however. It was cut short by his untimely death in 1894. All told, he spent less than two years on the bench. Drawing on his lucid command of the law, he wrote about a dozen formal opinions. These were grounded in legal precedent and a careful review of the law on which the facts were based. His written opinions were too few in number to discern a perceptible judicial philosophy. About all that one can say in this regard is that he valued human rights over property rights, and he showed signs of becoming a dissenter.

The most celebrated case in which Abbett dissented was *State v. Rogers*. This litigation involved a dispute over the seating of the state senate in January 1894. Before the newly elected senators were officially sworn in, the nine holdover Democrats chose their colleague Robert Adrian of New Brunswick as senate president. This move prompted the four holdover Republican senators to walk out. Since the Republicans held a majority of seats in the new senate, they were not about to let the Democrats outmaneuver them. They held their own meeting and elected

Maurice A. Rogers of Camden to the office. As a result, the senate found itself faced with having two presidents, each contending the other had been chosen illegally.

The Democratic minority organized a rump session and refused to certify the eligibility of the newly elected Republican majority. They advised Governor Werts of their decision and asked him to recognize their body as the legitimate senate. Meanwhile, the legislature remained paralyzed by these antics. As Tobin elaborates, "Displaying the same notable absence of courage that had characterized his mishandling of the race-track scandals, Werts acquiesced, following a policy of inactivity and neutrality that allowed the capricious, selfish, and partisan actions of this small group of Democrats to paralyze the state's political process."[9]

In March 1894, the state supreme court, in an eight to one decision, ruled the rump session illegal. It recognized the Republican majority as the duly constituted senate and Maurice Rogers as its duly elected president. Of the nine justices, Abbett was the lone dissenter. Proceeding on the theory that the senate was a continuous body, he concluded that Democrat Robert Adrian had been properly elected senate president since there was a quorum present to conduct public business.[10] The logic of his legal reasoning impressed some lawyers, but others dismissed it as sheer partisanship.

THE DEATH OF WILLIAM ABBETT

As fate would have it, Abbett's last years were filled with a mixture of sadness and joy. Much of it had to do with family. His oldest son William, who expected to follow in his father's footsteps, was well on his way to what seemed like a promising legal and political career. These hopes were cruelly dashed on July 23, 1893, when William suffered a fatal brain aneurysm. He was only thirty years of age at the time of his death, and this tragedy came as a terrible shock to Abbett. Deeply shaken, he grieved inconsolably for he adored William, who was much like his father both in intellect and personality. Filled with unbearable sorrow, the former governor openly wept at his son's funeral. "Political disappointment and physical troubles," Zebina Pangborn wrote in the Jersey City *Evening Journal*, "have already robbed ex-Governor Abbett of much of his vigor. This latest shock was almost too much for the once powerful political leader. He wept like a child and would not be comforted."[11]

Leon Abbett, Jr., the sole surviving son, would pick up his father's mantle and attempt to carry on his political legacy. No one was more daunted by this prospect than the youngest son who felt unsure of himself. He stood in awe of his father whom he regarded with hero worship. Aside from being born into a political family, the son's only experience in

public life was serving as his father's private secretary during his second term. In 1898, he ran successfully for the general assembly from Hudson County, but he could not overcome his own sense of inadequacy. A sad shadow of his father, Leon had too much expectation heaped on him. Three terms as an assemblyman (1899, 1900, and 1901) convinced him that he was temperamentally unsuited to politics—too squeamish for a political career. A New York lawyer of modest ability, he resumed his private law practice and married Lillian Hall. They had three children by their marriage, but they later were divorced.[12]

The one bright spot in the twilight decline of Abbett's life was the wedding of his only daughter who was his special pride and joy. On April 11, 1894, Mary Briggs Abbett, then twenty-four years of age, married Andrew Jackson Post. The wedding was held at Saint Matthew's Episcopal Church, the oldest religious edifice in Jersey City. The bride, who was given away by her father, wore an ivory white satin gown, elaborately trimmed with point lace, and a veil of tulle. The Reverend Montgomery H. Throop performed the wedding ceremony. It was a gala social event and the guest list included many state dignitaries and other prominent people. The reception was held at the home of the bride's father.[13]

LEON ABBETT DIES

Toward the end of his life, Abbett kept busy with his judicial work, but it was a heavy burden for him. The ailing judge, whose own health was precarious, lived long enough to see his fellow Democrat, former Governor Joseph Bedle, pass away. Two months later, Abbett's deteriorating health took a serious turn for the worse. According to newspaper reports, he had not been feeling well for some time and showed signs of fatigue. Having rallied his energies for the fall 1894 court session, he succumbed to exhaustion and melancholy in the weeks that followed. Although he seemed like his old self when he appeared in public, it was increasingly obvious to those closest to him that his vigor and characteristic ebullience had diminished. He was suffering from sugar diabetes and a gastric disorder, his body no longer able to supply the stamina he needed to get through his appointments. After taking a steam bath on Thanksgiving Day, Abbett complained of dizziness and his doctors confined him to bed rest. A week later on his deathbed, he summoned his family. With family members maintaining an overnight vigil at his bedside, he died at his home in Jersey City on December 4, 1894. He was fifty-eight years of age.

Abbett's state funeral was a massive affair. Governor Werts led a large delegation of state officials who attended the services. In a setting of remorse and remembrance, a huge outpouring of friends, relatives, labor and business leaders, and other public dignitaries came to Jersey City to

pay their last respects and to bid a final farewell to Abbett at a public wake. Thousands of mourners came from all parts of New Jersey and queued up along Jersey Avenue to go through the iron gates, up the front walk, and into the big house to view the remains. For three hours the doors were open and a steady procession filed through. Their grief was palpable. The common people wanted to pay homage to the "Great Commoner" who had meant so much to them. He had touched so many people in so many different ways. The Reverend George S. Bennett conducted the funeral services at the Grace Episcopal Church in Jersey City. Ahead of the hearse tramped men of every sort, merchants and professional men, the police, the city fathers, and state officials. After the hearse came the special carriages for the mourners. The funeral cortege followed Abbett's body to New York and across the Brooklyn Bridge to the Greenwood Cemetery. He was buried in the family plot next to his wife and oldest son.[14]

A month later, the New Jersey Bar Association paid a fitting tribute to Abbett for his outstanding public service. The lawyers' group recognized the contributions that he had made both in the political world and the legal world. But they did not try to enlarge him in death beyond what he had been in life. Their formal resolution, published in the *New Jersey Law Journal,* reads as follows:

No man in recent times has more indelibly stamped his personality upon the pages of the state's history. His unusual ability was not confined to one talent; for more than twenty-five years he maintained a commanding position in the arena of law, in the domain of practical statesmanship, and in the judicial department of the state.

He was a lawyer of pronounced ability. His knowledge of legal principles was great; his industry was indefatigable, and his grasp of the salient points of his case was firm and vigorous.

But it was in public life that he won his greatest fame. He was a partisan and a party leader; but his conviction, often expressed, was that no party could retain political power unless it rendered distinct service to the people. His mind naturally grappled with the public questions of his time. He had the qualities of leadership; he knew how to formulate a policy; he was bold and aggressive in promulgating it, and, more important than all, he had the ability to embody his ideas in the statutes of the state. This is practical statesmanship.

These qualities speedily raised him to political eminence in the state, and maintained him there. His great public service was his action while serving his first term as governor, in leading the fight to impose upon the corporations of the state a larger and more just share of the burden of taxation. This achievement fixed his place as one of the great governors of the commonwealth, and gave him his hold upon the people of the state. It is his monument, and it is an enduring one.[15]

EVALUATING ABBETT'S PERFORMANCE

With the spread of populism and the first stirrings of progressivism, a number of American writers and scholars became concerned about the increasing concentration of power in large corporations and the suborning of the political leadership to capitalist interests. These social critics demonstrated that the idealized version of democracy as heralded by politicians, poets, preachers, and editorial writers did not in fact exist. Newspapers and magazines were forced to become interpretive. *McClure's Magazine* soon became America's most impressive periodical. This upstart magazine that Samuel S. McClure started in New York in 1893 gained a position of authority unprecedented in magazine history. Among its talented star attractions were writers like Lincoln Steffens, Ida Tarbell, Ray Stannard Baker, and David Graham Phillips. These American muckrakers attacked the irresponsible trusts and exposed corrupt public officials, the exploitation of immigrant workers, and financial deceit. In April 1905, Steffens wrote "New Jersey: A Traitor State" that appeared in two installments. While Steffens remained even-handed in his analysis, he captured Abbett better than most other Gilded Age commentators. Despite his criticism of Abbett as a flawed politician, Steffens was struck by his strong populist streak, his commitment to the common people, and his indifference to the highborn. He summed up Abbett's career with remarkable frankness and clarity:

> I prefer Leon Abbett defeated, to all the [John] Gardners in Congress, because in his practical, compromising, crooked Jersey way, he did sometimes represent New Jersey and because he is the liveliest Democrat in that state today. For the consequences of his career have lived on; much of both the good and the bad in Jersey can be traced to him, and the effects of his influence have spread all over the United States. Leon Abbett adopted the charter-giving policy of New Jersey. That hurts us, but Abbett didn't care about us. He was for Jersey. That was his great limitation. [16]

Coming from the acerbic pen of Steffens, this was high praise. Both in philosophy and style, Abbett fitted the times, but he was bucking a strong incoming tide of conservatism and sailing against the wind. He left a curiously mixed legacy that included both the good and the bad. On the positive side of the ledger, he attracted industry to New Jersey and thereby stimulated economic growth. He presided over an economic boom that brought the creation of new jobs and a certain degree of social stability. More broadly, he advanced the modest goals of keeping the industrial peace, helping prosperity, and ensuring social justice. He was honored not for prosperity itself but for the uses he made of a growing economy—expanding civil rights, protecting the working poor, providing new revenue for financially hard-pressed cities, and all the other

achievements of those incredibly productive years. In so doing, he walked a political tightrope between radical labor reformers and conservative businessmen. The governor had a clever way of delivering sharp blows against business, but he stood ready to make concessions to cooperative businessmen. In more ways than one, Abbett turned the governorship into an honest broker between capital and labor. He had a clever way of introducing regulation to save New Jersey from social unrest and forestall more extreme measures.

The political genius of Abbett lay in his capacity for party-building and organization. His major source of control was his army of volunteers, many of whom held patronage jobs in state and local governments. He discovered what political scientist Robert Dahl refers to as the "slack in the system." By the term "slack," Dahl means that there is always room for political actors to maneuver and exert influence, because the system tends to leave enough potential power to rectify grievances and social injustices.[17] During the 1880s and 1890s, New Jersey had become a political training ground for a cadre of immigrant Irish and German elected officials, mayors, and city aldermen who first learned about neighborhood politics through their involvement in Abbett's party machine. To the extent that these ethnic groups represented a growing political force, first in urban and then in state politics, they triggered a countervailing response to the economic and political power of business. By taking up this slack, Abbett was able to integrate the Democratic party as none of

FIG. 27
Court House in 1895.

his predecessors had ever done. Nor has any New Jersey governor since had so compliant and coordinated a party organization with which to work. Abbett advocated ideas that drew Democrats together rather than those that pulled them apart. He was viewed by many as a leader who could bring disparate forces together in working toward a common goal. This placed tremendous demands on him—on his understanding of people and goals, on his patience, and on his ability to orchestrate highly discordant elements.

On the negative side, Abbett could not escape responsibility for the excesses of politics and the exploitation of soft money. The prevailing style of political bossism set off a chain of consequence that began in his era. It was in Gilded Age New Jersey that one could observe many of the patterns that have since become familiar in American politics. The public arena became the battleground for successive waves of ethnic struggle—Yankee versus Irish versus German versus Italian most prominently. They produced the cynical politics of spoils and plunder and bosses and machines that stuffed not only ballot boxes, but also the ranks of the civil service with officeholders chosen on the basis of family or patronage.

But it was the Irish who scored the most notable success in urban machine politics. They showed a special aptitude for ward politics and party organizing as well as a penchant for adapting to the changing political environment. As Morton Keller notes, "The clannishness, the barroom bonding, the arts of organization and manipulation that flourished in Ireland under British rule traveled well to the teeming cities of the New World."[18] In Hudson County, a succession of Irish bosses like Robert Davis, Frank Hague, and John Kenny picked up where Abbett essentially left off. They took over the county machine that he had originally built.

The Irish politicians set a pattern that other ethnic groups subsequently followed closely. Robert Davis, John Feeney, Dennis McLaughlin, Patrick O'Neill, and all the rest knew how to make the system pay off for themselves, but no one objected—at least no one who mattered in their personal constituencies. In Boston, Martin Lomasney made a comfortable living out of politics and no one begrudged it for he delivered exactly what he told Lincoln Steffens someone must provide: "I think there's got to be in any ward somebody that any bloke can come to—no matter what he's done—and get help. Help, you understand; none of your law and your justice, but help."[19]

The classic party machine, as many commentators have pointed out, has faded away and almost disappeared as a result of improved social services and the breakup of the ethnic ghetto where the manageable vote resided. Nonetheless, there are still vestiges that remain, especially in the central cities. By the mid-twentieth century, public service had fallen into disrepute. Fed by media accounts of crime, corruption, and the mob, the

citizenry increasingly had come to view public service as a refuge for scoundrels, or at the very least for the untrained and the unmotivated.

Rather than opposing each other on the basis of ethnicity and race, urban ethnic groups, under Abbett's leadership, joined in common opposition to aggressive capitalists who ruthlessly exploited the working poor. Because they themselves felt exploited by profit-hungry capitalists, they became unified in their class feeling and behavior. Yet, Abbett was careful to include the participation of key Democratic constituencies—labor, business, and agriculture. For politicians, winning is a prerequisite for doing what they want to do, and it had been clear for a long time that Abbett's brand of populism was a winning formula. As Paul Peterson observed:

All the talk about cleaning up government and improving the efficiency of public services veiled but thinly the social distance between Yankees and their Protestant allies, on one side, and the mostly Catholic immigrants, on the other. Yet one should not confuse the conflict between political machine and reform movement with open class warfare.[20]

Neither side challenged the control of private property by business interests, and neither side questioned the importance of economic growth for the general welfare of the state.

How does one size up the career of Leon Abbett? That he wanted to do something about the pain and suffering of industrial workers there can be no doubt. To his credit, he took more "stand-up" positions on progressive legislation than any of his predecessors, and he secured in his six years in office the passage of more labor laws than other American governor. Labor leader Joseph McDonnell, who served in his administration, proudly boasted, "No other state in the United States can show greater accomplishments by legislation for the welfare of the wage class during a like period."[21] Not that it was Abbett alone who put industrial workers and their issues on the public agenda. He had help from leaders in a variety of positions, most notably from labor unions and the workers themselves. It was for Abbett a defining mission. It was also, for someone who endured poverty and deprivation growing up in Jacksonian Philadelphia, a very personal mission.

When one identifies the recommendations that appeared in gubernatorial messages and then in legislative enactments, Abbett experienced notable success. Add to the legislative record the policy innovations introduced through executive orders, gubernatorial memoranda, and rules and regulations, and the record is even more impressive. As historians struggle with the Abbett legacy, they will no doubt remember him most for his railroad tax policy and his policies with regard to labor relations. Whatever their verdict on specific policies, they will also remember him as a capable public manager. His cabinet plan matched the best organizational theory of the decade. He reorganized the executive departments and agencies in a

coherent fashion. All of which improved the workings of the administrative system in a managerial sense. No other Democratic leader in New Jersey had so consciously and successfully developed a strategy for involving experts and labor leaders in state government. Many of his appointments were bold and courageous for his era. James Leiby, another distinguished scholar who has analyzed the Abbett years, rounds out the profile as follows:

> Abbett's bold plan was to reorganize the machinery of government somewhat as he had organized the party machinery. He would use the governor's patronage to employ men who were vassals rather than mere allies, and he would reorganize the congeries of boards and commissions so that they would respond to his direction. He had moved in this way during his first term, but now, with more experience and, as it turned out, Democratic majorities in both houses of the legislature, he could better realize his ideas. He changed and fortified old agencies and created new ones.

> In his own mind, probably the most important state functions were assessment, taxation, and municipal government, subjects of which he was master, but his interest extended to banking, insurance, licensing and a state police force. He eliminated the existing boards of managers of the two state insane asylums, set up a single board in their place, and charged it with inspecting the county asylums and accounting for the state subsidies they received. He reorganized the trustees of the school fund and the managers of the State Normal School into a new State Board of Education, put it in charge of the School for the Deaf and Dumb, and increased its powers of supervision over local school districts. Every institution felt his scrutiny and the force of his will.

> Two generations later, it would seem that Abbett's efforts were an interesting attempt to make state government rational and efficient. The organization of the State Board of Education and the subsequent reorganization of the public school districts were recognized even then as desirable. The unification of the asylums was at least reasonable; the official inspection of county asylums was long overdue. There is no evidence that the institutions suffered much in the shakeup.[22]

When one sifts through the several versions of the Abbett record, the weight of the evidence seems to support Leiby's view. Considering the political climate in which he worked and the limitations of the office, Abbett's performance exceeded justifiable expectations. Much of the work that he did to rationalize the state bureaucracy was undone shortly after he left office. The state police force, for example, was dismantled under the retrenchment of the Griggs administration. This agency was reactivated in 1921, but it was then assigned a much different mission. Instead of helping to maintain industrial peace in urban centers where there was much

labor unrest, it took on providing community policing for sparsely populated rural areas where municipalities could not afford to create their own police departments. A true visionary, Abbett recognized the importance of water availability and water quality for urban residents well before the twentieth century. Without water, he knew that a city could not survive. He left a legacy to the cities in northern New Jersey recommending that the power of the state be used to secure a public water supply.[23]

While the scorecard of transforming his ideas into operational programs was impressive in both legislative and executive terms, another criterion for success was even more important. Did Abbett change in any important sense the way in which governors made their decisions? Close observers of gubernatorial politics and power conclude that he did. As Duane Lockard sums up:

Independently of constitutional provisions, a governor is able to achieve leadership if he has personal qualities of leadership and controls other bases of power. Ludlow and others before him had sought equalization of taxes on railroads without avail. Ludlow and others either did not try or tried and failed to assert leadership. But Abbett working under the same constitution made something astoundingly different out of the governor's office—he used it as a tool for vigorous leadership.[24]

A man who spent his entire public and personal life striving to win the governor's office, Abbett broke the machine mold and changed the office in ways that we can now appreciate. He used the governorship to achieve unprecedented political power. Where once it was remote, now it was accessible. Where once the governor was a ceremonial figurehead, now he was the symbol of executive energy. Where once the governor was passive in policymaking, now he was active in governing. Looking gubernatorial was part of his personna. By seizing the initiative and exercising bold leadership, Abbett recast an eighteenth-century institution and redesigned it for the twentieth century. He turned it into an instrument for social change, thereby helping to build a more equitable society.

Whether barnstorming New Jersey seeking to win electoral majorities or prodding the legislature into action, Abbett was a daring, listening, reaching-out governor who made the office more accessible to ordinary people. He was a man of politics and concrete decisions. While he was an avowed partisan, his decisions expressed a consistent set of liberal values. What emerged over time was a governor who consistently protected the weak underdog, while acting in ways that always kept him in touch with the populace. He had his blind spots, most notably in those areas where election fraud was concerned. But he led two exciting administrations with unfailing decency and compassion. He pioneered in the development of urban politics and state government. He was the first modern governor of New Jersey and one of the first in the nation as a whole.

ENDNOTES

1 Arthur Link, *Wilson: The Road to the White House* (Princeton, Princeton University Press, 1947), 140–141.

2 *New York Times*, January 7, 1893.

3 Quoted in the *Philadelphia Public Ledger*, December 5, 1894.

4 *New York Times*, July 3, 1893.

5 *New York Times*, January 18, 1893.

6 Harry Barnard's biography of John P. Altgeld gives an account of his critics: see *Eagle Forgotten* (New York, Bobbs-Merrill Company, 1938).

7 *Ibid.*

8 Eugene M. Tobin, "Biographical Essay on Governor George T. Werts," in Paul A. Stellhorn and Michale J. Birkner (eds.), *The Governors of New Jersey* (Trenton, New Jersey Historical Commission, 1982), 161.

9 *Ibid.*, 160.

10 *State v. Rogers* 56 N.J.L. 480, 632 (1894).

11 *Evening Journal*, July 24, 1893.

12 Letter to the author from Leon Abbett Post, September 28, 1970.

13 *New York Times*, April 12, 1894.

14 See "Last Will and Testimony of Leon Abbett," dated June 25, 1890. This document is found in Docket Book, Number 36, Wills, pp. 612–619. It is on file in the Office of the Surrogate of Hudson County. Interestingly, Abbett directed his heirs to invest the money from his estate in municipal bonds. He attached an important stipulation. They could not invest in any municipality that had defaulted in payment of its bonded debt.

15 18 *New Jersey Law Journal* 30 (1895).

16 Steffens, "New Jersey: A Traitor State," 663.

17 Dahl, *Who Governs?*, 192–199.

18 Morton Keller, *Affairs Of State* (Cambridge, Harvard University Press, 1977), 541.

19 Steffens, *The Autobiography of Lincoln Steffens*, 618.

20 Paul E. Peterson, *City Limits* (Chicago, University of Chicago Press, 1981), 152.

21 Herbert G. Gutman, "Class, Status, and the Gilded-Age Radical: A Reconsideration," in Gutman and Kealey (eds.) *Many Pasts*, 133.

22 Leiby, *Charity and Correction in New Jersey*, 155–156.

23 See Governor Abbett's annual message of January 12, 1892 as found in the New Jersey Legislative Manual (1892), 389–393.

24 Lockard, *The New Jersey Governor*, 88.